BENJAMIN FRANKLIN PUBLISHING, LTD.
900 E. 8th Ave., #300, King of Prussia, PA 19406

LEADER OF LEADERS

A GALLERY OF THE GREATS

"Today's leaders inspiring the leaders of tomorrow."

AN INSPIRATIONAL COMMENTARY

BY

DR. DONALD H. SAUTTER

FOREWORD

This is the most unique Foreword you've ever seen, because it is by a wonderful array of Leaders of Leaders themselves. The first is by the President of the United States of America, who considerately dated his letter on October 30, 1996, when I officially and in writing committed myself to be the Author/Publisher of **LEADER OF LEADERS** on the occasion of the 75th Anniversary of the Main Line Chamber of Commerce at the Valley Forge Military Academy in Wayne, Pennsylvania.

Five days later came another "Foreword" from a local yet national institution, Freedoms' Foundation at Valley Forge.

From a regional standpoint, it was so gratifying to be remembered and inspired by the Mayor of the City of Philadelphia, Edward G. Rendell, on November 12, 1996.

Little did Vice President Al Gore himself realize just how much success as well as answered prayers would come out of last fall's Valley Forge Leadership Prayer Breakfast when he wrote his letter on November 13, 1996.

Although the Author's inspiration for the book is well documented here to be significantly before the Prayer Breakfast last fall on November 13, 1996, he is the first to give much credit to the prayers that were prayed at the Prayer Breakfast for the fruitful outcome of its publication.

Furthermore, equally should credit be given to the Presidents' Summit for America's Future and the Welcome America Week (June 27-July 7, 1997), sponsored by the City of Philadelphia. After all, as the Valley Forge Leadership Prayer Breakfast spurred on the Author/Publisher from the past, the Presidents' Summit and Welcome America Week inspired him on to the future.

Then again, notice another "Double Whammie" in the life and work of your Author and Publisher–the letters from the Vice President, Al Gore and the Mayor of Philadelphia, Edward Rendell, also written within a day of each other. And to be sure these two leaders had absolutely no corroboration.

After all, if Benjamin Franklin is right (and he is) that: "Not even a sparrow falls from the sky without the notice of the Almighty," . . . then how much more does He involve Himself in the affairs of people? Well, that is the theological; now what about the logical? Clearly what would be more logical and even natural and normal for a book called **LEADER**

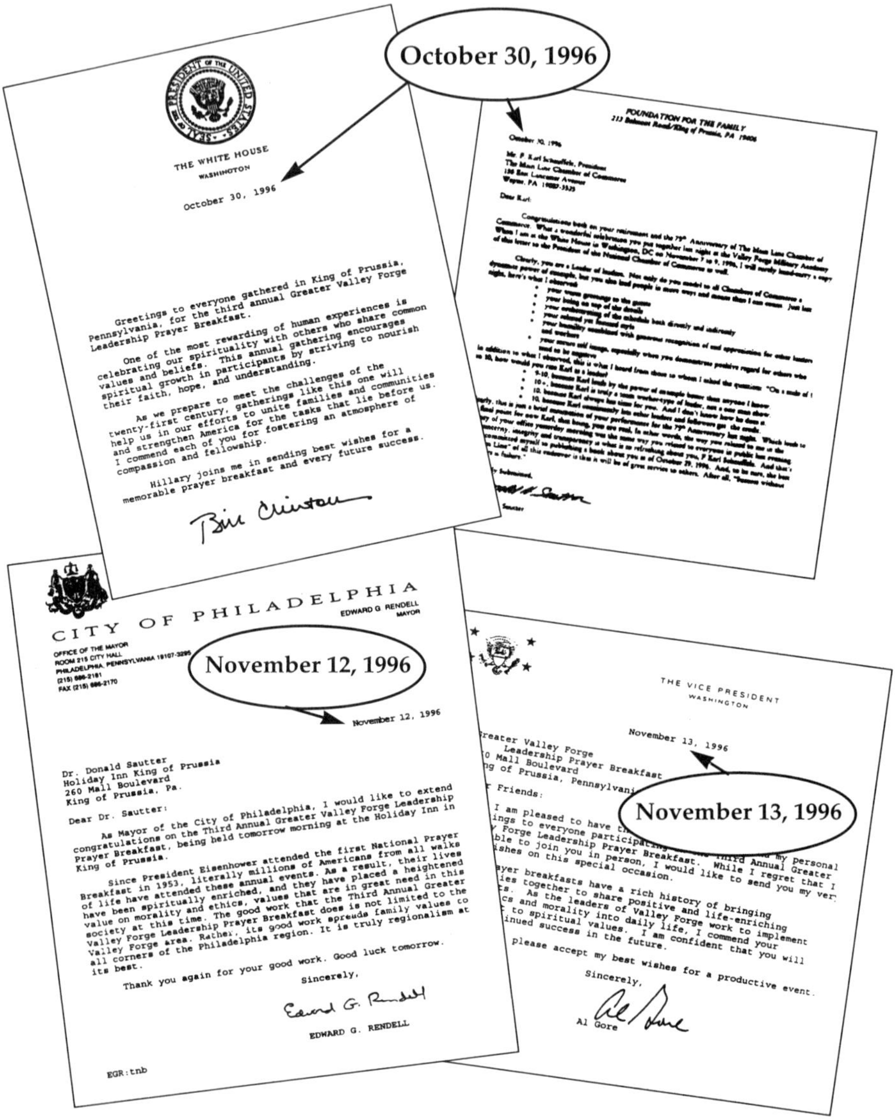

October 30, 1996

THE WHITE HOUSE
WASHINGTON

October 30, 1996

Greetings to everyone gathered in King of Prussia, Pennsylvania, for the third annual Greater Valley Forge Leadership Prayer Breakfast.

One of the most rewarding of human experiences is celebrating our spirituality with others who share common values and beliefs. This annual gathering encourages spiritual growth in participants by striving to nourish their faith, hope, and understanding.

As we prepare to meet the challenges of the twenty-first century, gatherings like this one will help us in our efforts to unite families and communities and strengthen America for the tasks that lie before us. I commend each of you for fostering an atmosphere of compassion and fellowship.

Hillary joins me in sending best wishes for a memorable prayer breakfast and every future success.

Bill Clinton

FOUNDATION FOR THE FAMILY

CITY OF PHILADELPHIA

EDWARD G. RENDELL
MAYOR

OFFICE OF THE MAYOR
ROOM 215 CITY HALL
PHILADELPHIA, PENNSYLVANIA 19107-3295
(215) 686-2181
FAX (215) 686-2170

November 12, 1996

November 12, 1996

Dr. Donald Sautter
Holiday Inn King of Prussia
260 Mall Boulevard
King of Prussia, Pa.

Dear Dr. Sautter:

As Mayor of the City of Philadelphia, I would like to extend congratulations on the Third Annual Greater Valley Forge Leadership Prayer Breakfast, being held tomorrow morning at the Holiday Inn in King of Prussia.

Since President Eisenhower attended the first National Prayer Breakfast in 1953, literally millions of Americans from all walks of life have attended these annual events. As a result, their lives have been spiritually enriched, and they have placed a heightened value on morality and ethics, values that are in great need in this society at this time. The good work that the Third Annual Greater Valley Forge Leadership Prayer Breakfast does is not limited to the Valley Forge area. Rather, its good work spreads family values to all corners of the Philadelphia region. It is truly regionalism at its best.

Thank you again for your good work. Good luck tomorrow.

Sincerely,

Edward G. Rendell

EDWARD G. RENDELL

EGR:tnb

THE VICE PRESIDENT
WASHINGTON

November 13, 1996

November 13, 1996

reater Valley Forge
Leadership Prayer Breakfast
0 Mall Boulevard
ng of Prussia, Pennsylvani

Friends:

I am pleased to have th ings to everyone participat ... Third Annual Greater y Forge Leadership Prayer Breakfast. While I regret that I ble to join you in person, I would like to send you my personal ishes on this special occasion.

yer breakfasts have a rich history of bringing ies together to share positive and life-enriching s. As the leaders of Valley Forge work to implement cs and morality into daily life, I commend your to spiritual values. I am confident that you will inued success in the future.

Please accept my best wishes for a productive event.

Sincerely,

Al Gore

Clearly, no man or woman could get even half the credit for all this timing, timing, timing / location, location, location. Hence, the Author/Publisher ultimately gives the credit and glory to God:

> ***"For God works all things together for good to them who love God and to them who are called according to His purpose."***
>
> *Romans 8:28*

OF LEADERS to be birthed in the preparation for a leadership breakfast? Enough said.

The word "FORE" is a watchword at each golf course and/or country club in the world. And, when it is uttered, the golfers within hearing distance stop, look, and listen. Hopefully, this is what you will do, my dear reader, with this book from the beginning to the end. Now see, this "Foreword" is precisely chosen at the outset to alert you that there is a lot more than a golf ball powerfully driven your way, which may be too close for comfort.

The information experts relate that communication is 55% body language, 35% tone of voice and 10% words. Well then, we shall conform the composition of this book, **LEADER OF LEADERS,** to that standard of quality and quantity control. Hence, in this foreword, we draw your attention to the "body language" in terms of life messages of a body of fifteen leaders of leaders instead of one. Hopefully then, we are already more than halfway successful in communicating our message to you, especially because it is by means of an Inspirational Commentary rather than a paralysis of analysis. As for its "tone of voice," you will find it to be clear, distinct and concise. Some chapters are shorter and some longer, but altogether they give you the awesomely beautiful sound of a symphony. Likewise, you can be sure that the words which make up the chapters of this book are no more than 10% of what could have been written. Clearly, **LEADER OF LEADERS** is the result of 38 years of research both in some of the finest institutions of our nation as well as on the streets of experience.

Yes, since age 18 when I chose the fork in the road to go on to college and graduate school instead of to work in the machine shop, I have consistently and persistently never ceased learning the science and art of leadership. My particular path carved its way through 12 full-time years of double-whammies: 2 Diploma disciplines, 2 Bachelor disciplines, 2 Masters disciplines, 2 Doctoral disciplines culminating on May 17, 1970, my 30th birthday, when Times Mirror Corporation of Los Angeles, California through its Subsidiary, The Southwestern Company of Nashville, Tennessee awarded me an Honorary Doctorate in Business and Sales Management. You see, it was a "Streets Smart" degree for my seven-year track record in the Southwestern Company for building a 500-person sales force during my graduate and post-graduate studies to finance my educational process and support my wife and children without dropping out of school. I simultaneously built a company within a company that was #1 each consecutive year. Of course, I must confess that I never completed my doctoral dissertation in Greek nor went onto my oral examination because I compromised all this by becoming too preoccupied with my business. Furthermore, I rationalized that "Streets Smart" is superior to "Academic Acumen." Hence, the Honorary Doctorate on my birthday took "the wind out of my sails" for the completion of my academic doctorate, so onto my seventh and final sales field I plummeted full speed ahead.

What a stupendous summer on the Western Seaboard it was with hundreds of managers and salespeople under my leadership! And, yes again, we were #1 out of over 7,000 nationwide. And, without a doubt, the pace we set was followed by the rest of the company. We were proud to be earning over six figures of income, which in 1970 was a big income, at least for full-time students. We were also gratified that our Sales Manager Spencer Hays, kept being promoted as we kept progressing: Sales Director; Vice President of Sales; President; Chairman; Executive Chairman of the Board. WOW! We literally lifted our leader to his ultimate. Oh how much fun that was! As Steven Covey would say, "It was a WIN-WIN relationship and a WIN-WIN result."

Then, that September of 1970, I was personally invited to his very first Institute of Successful Church Leadering there at his Garden Grove Community Church near Disneyland. And, what a wonderful transition that was from 12 years of education to the coming 27 years of ministry in Valley Forge, Pennsylvania.

Just like I had "Double-Whammies" in my degrees, so I felt that I had a major "Double-Whammie" of academic smarts on the one hand, and street smarts on the other as I began my ministry on September 25, 1970, as Founding Pastor of Christ Church of Valley Forge. And just one week later, we had 22 people in our first service on October 4, 1970 in the George Washington Motor Lodge at the Valley Forge Interchange of the Pennsylvania Turnpike.

In those precious 7-2/3 years of ministry we experienced thousands of changed lives as our church grew from scores to hundreds. Many times our attendances were over a thousand, but what was most important was how their lives were transformed from weak to strong; from foolish to wise; from sick to healthy; from insignificant to significant.

But there was one problem . . . the logistics and demographics of our greater Valley Forge/Main Line/Philadelphia Region indicated that the non-churched families were increasing in the population explosion faster than the church families. I thought that our emphasis on an interdenominational church would overcome that problem, but it did not. Then, I coined the word "All Denominational" and/or "Pan Denominational," but it did not help. Finally, I really coined a word that I felt would work without fail: "SUPERLICALIFRAGILISTICESPI-ALODOCIOUSJUDEOCATHEOBAPTILUTHEDOXIPEN-TAMETHOPALIANPRESBYGATIONALIST CHURCH." But, guess what: it also did not work!

Therefore, feeling called to the families of the non-churched community, I established Foundation for the Family as a 501(C)3 Non-Profit Organization for Religious Purposes Only in 1978, of which after 18 wonderful years, I am still Executive Chairman. The joy of it all is that we fruitfully touched the lives of non-churched families by means of counseling, literature, seminars, conferences and conventions. And now we were impacting lives and families by tens of thousands.

What a privilege it was during those wonderful years to serve our local Upper Merion Township, even to the extent of becoming Proprietor of the Upper Merion Swim Club for 2 years. How exciting it was to become the Publisher and Owner of the first Main Line Magazine. This led to serving the Mayors of Philadelphia for three consecutive administrations by being Executive Chairman of Family Day Philadelphia, 1982 when over 10,000 attended a three-day Family Life Seminar, featuring Tim and Bev Lahaye. This caught the notice of then President, Ronald Reagan. The next thing I knew, I was appointed Executive Chairman of National Family Week, 1984, celebrated at Valley Forge, "The Birthplace of the Nation." This led to serving three consecutive administrations of Presidents, which brings us right up to the present. Was this a coincidence or was it Providence? Indubitably, it was Providence because the alternative is an insult to God!

The thrill of all the above is too much to contain. And yet, it is not the whole story. We could proceed also to reproduce the letters from Pennsylvania State Senator Tighlman representing the Main Line; US Congressman Jon D. Fox of Montgomery County; Russell Schultz, Executive Vice President of Freedom's Foundation; Senate Chaplain Ogilvie and four US Senators as well, but I believe that the point is sufficiently made in this Foreword.

All of these local, regional, state and national leaders stand together in the spirit of the age-old Proverb of Solomon, King of Israel, as recorded in the Bible: "In a multitude of counselors is wisdom."

Having then established the credibility of the book to deserve your trust, let us crystallize the need for **LEADER OF LEADERS.** Why another book on leadership? Why not "walk the talk" of the ones already in print? Here is why: to help fulfill the prophecy of Isaiah the Prophet recorded over 2700 years ago: "AND A LITTLE CHILD SHALL LEAD THEM." Yes, for the most part, these words have remained dormant all these years since the prophecy. But without a doubt, there has been an unmistakable groundswell of awakening to the real meaning and ultimate fulfillment of these powerful prophetic words.

Clearly, God has inspired numerous "stirrings" to this prophecy all over the world in this recent year or so. But, the most significant realization of it all is right here and now happening in the creative sequel to the Presidents' Summit for America's Future!!! Is it not phenomenal??? And, is it not awesome that you and I have the high, holy and honorable privilege and pleasure to be servants of it all!?!? Thus, **LEADER OF LEADERS** is our guidebook for encouraging our youth to lead us into the future. Stupendous!

Now see, my dear readers, **LEADER OF LEADERS** is synergy. It is the "little child leader" leading the adult leader, who also is undergirding with supportiveness, the mission of the child-leader. (Submission in its purest meaning. More to come.) HOW DO YOU DO THAT? Read the book and find out. And, as you do, you shall behold a SYMPHONY OF SYNERGY as overwhelmingly beautiful and glorious as "The Messiah" in Handel. You shall interpret incredible reality of synergy through all your six senses, not just your eyes. And the symphonic orchestra from which this "Symphony of Synergy" comes is made up of a "Maestro" /or Master Mentor, F. Karl Schauffele whose 1st position of honor in Chapter One of the book speaks for itself.

Then there is the select group of special soloists, also synergizing into a quintuplet: Lita Higgins, Executive Associate/Management; Charlene Lewis, Executive Associate/Administration; Noreen Mallory, Executive Associate/Publicity and Stanley Simpkins, Executive Associate/Marketing; Dr. Donald H. Sautter, Executive Chairman/Author. This "Master Mind Group" as the great Winston Churchill called it, are the synergistic leadership core of **LEADER OF LEADERS**, who channel all their time, talent and energy through the Coordinators of the 22 leadership sectors: political, big business, small business, legal, medical, banking, real estate, development, judicial, municipal, club, organizational, religious, educational, associations, women's, parental, juvenile, sports, recreational, minority and rehabilitational.

By the way, once again we have a "coincidence." As there were

22 people at the premier service of Christ Church of Valley Forge on October 4, 1970, so there are 22 leadership sectors at the **LEADER OF LEADERS** PREMIER CELEBRATION on October 14, 1997. Some would say – so what? And in reply I say – since I was faithful with the small 22, I have the confidence to be faithful with the big 22. And the Biblical precedent for such confidence is David, before he became king of Israel: "God gave me a lion, God gave me a bear, and God shall give me this giant Philistine, Goliath." And God did. And God will do it again, because "God delights in the prosperity of His servants."

That is why through the channels of these 22 leadership sectors shall come delegations by the hundreds of profit and non-profit corporations, hundreds of students from the 22 clusters of the Philadelphia School District and from the 23 high schools of the Suburban 1 League. Furthermore, as there shall be synergy between the city and the suburbs, so there shall be synergy between high schools and colleges/universities. Likewise, there shall be synergy between the rich and the poor, between the white and the black, between the adults and the children, between the city and the county, between the country and the cosmos. Now, how is that for a pizzazz presentation?

But, all of this would be in vain without a binding contract of commitment to the completion of THE PHILADELPHIA MODEL: 2000 by 2000. Hence, we take that "Leap of Faith"; we laugh at the "risks"; we dismiss our fear of failure. "Fight the good fight of faith" as we "press toward the mark" and "let our light shine" one step at a time, one life at a time until we come into AD 2000

- when there shall be 2000 more Mentors
- when there shall be 2000 more Associates
- when there shall be 2000 more jobs
- when there shall be 2000 more companies
- when there shall be 2000 more scholarships

But, you ask – Is this not overdoing it? No, it is not enough, because by the year 2002 THE PHILADELPHIA MODEL shall be reproduced at least in one major city of each of the 50 states. And because 165 Foreign Embassys shall be represented at our **LEADER OF LEADERS** PREMIER CELEBRATION on October 14, 1997, there just is no telling how far-reaching other nations of the world shall be penetrated and permeated with the wonderful reality of synergy in terms as articulated by **LEADER OF LEADERS**.

Therefore, dear reader, "Come on in – the water is fine." Be refreshed by the inspirational commentaries of the **LEADER OF LEADERS** in the 15 chapters of this book. And you will never be the same.

However, I caution you, this book is not "Reader friendly." That is what New York Publicist, Lynn Goldberg, told me after she finished the manuscript in August, 1997. You see, serving as a volunteer in the Presidential Summit for America's Future, led by General Colin Powell, "Letting out all of the stops", as is my serving style, I have had the privilege of being in Colin Powell's office. Furthermore, I was deeply touched that I was referred to General Powell's very own Publicist, Ivan Held, Senior Publicist at Random House. And, when he felt unable to be my publicist, since I chose to publish my own book, having been involved in the publishing world since 1963, he referred me to his former boss, Lynn Goldberg.

But, she urged me to make **LEADER OF LEADERS** "Reader Friendly." And I said that I could not, because from its inception at the leadership prayer breakfast it was designed and destined to be "LEADER FRIENDLY." Therefore, if you are a leader and desire to grow and become a **LEADER OF LEADERS**; if you are a **LEADER OF LEADERS**, but need to synergize into a statesman; if you are not a leader, but want to become a leader; if you are a child and want to fulfill the prophecy of Isaiah; if you are a parent and want to inspire your child to become and grow up to be a leader; if you are a failure and want to be a success; then, **LEADER OF LEADERS is for you.**

INTRODUCTION

The Declaration of Independence as communicated in and through the Constitution of the United States of America promises us "Life, Liberty and the PURSUIT OF HAPPINESS." Now, wait a minute. Did you notice the PURSUIT OF HAPPINESS? You see, although there are simple laws of our nation that insure our lives and freedom, they cannot protect or even guarantee our happiness. So what does this mean? It simply means: "If it is going to be, it is up to me," as the title of Dr. Robert Schuller's latest book says. Is that not well put? As a matter of fact, even though I would not get a dime for this upcoming endorsement and, furthermore, even though I may risk influencing you onto a tragedy, I still must enthusiastically urge you—go to the bookstore at your earliest convenience and get yourself a copy of this runaway best seller. You will be so glad you did. Clearly, even if you did nothing more with the book but lay it down somewhere in view, so you could see the title a few times a day as you passed by it, you would be doing yourself a great favor. Do you see what I mean? Here it comes again: "IF IT IS GOING TO BE, IT IS UP TO ME."

Why is that? It is because that is how God made us. Yes, I know, at first this seems unfair, because all of your life, thus far, you have been looking for happiness to come to you through someone else, whether it be a family member, friend, mentor, minister, or even a spouse. This was your honest-to-God expectation. Well, do not feel bad because just about everyone ever born has had the same unrealistic expectations.

So what do we do about it? You and I make a commitment with ourselves and God to "get back to the basics," and forward to the fundamentals about "Where did I come from?" and "Where am I going?" OK? Ok! Do not these questions sound familiar? Have we not heard these questions so many times over our lives? Yes, I have. But, my dear reader and friend, I have found the answers to these questions and I'm sure you can too.

Now what would be more fitting and proper than for us to utilize the opportunity of this introduction to do just that—to get a handle on ourselves? After all, if you and I accomplish this, we will be free, able and willing to draw the most from the 15 Leaders of Leaders, our *"Gallery of the Greats"* in the chapters before us. Furthermore, according to *Webster's New World Dictionary*, "Introduction" means "anything brought into use" and "introducing or being introduced"—Huh? That said nothing! Let us go on the second meaning, "anything brought into use, knowledge or fashion". That is better. So let us proceed to more. "The preliminary section of a book or speech." OK. A preliminary guide to text. I like that. "An opening section of music." My wife would especially appreciate that -- see chapter three -- "Disposition: The Power of Attitude." The formal presentation of one person to another." WOW!!! That last one clinched it, for that is precisely what I as Author of my own book deliberately choose to do in this "Introduction". . .literally!

Remember that definition earlier expressed: "Anything brought into use. . .(L/B) fashion?" Well, it is my intention in this Introduction to sit at your feet and bring to our new friendship "in appropriate FASHION" for *your* mission and purpose in life to help you to help yourself, so that you can help others who in turn will help others. (By the way *that* is the heart and soul meaning of what LEADER OF LEADERS is all about.) So, can you feel it? We are already getting our act together! Is that not exciting? Yes!! As real friends, you and I look out for one another's best interests. And, because of that priority, I as Author exert the ONGOING INITIATIVE to help you to crystallize *your* vision of *your* mission. That is another way of saying that I am helping (note that I am *only* helping, for primarily and ultimately you must do it for yourself) you to figure out "where you came from" and "where you are going." You see, this deals with your mission in life. However, in the real and literal spirit of submission I take the initiative to volunteer to put myself "UNDER" the questions, issues and answers of your "MISSION" and make myself vulnerable, transparent and accountable to you as your servant, whereby I am supportive of your mission in life.

Ah, but you say "Why? Why would you do that for me? Who, or what am I to you?" And my spontaneous answer to you is "You are my neighbor." That is enough of an answer, is it not? No? OK. Let me proceed to explain it, because as I do, you shall quickly begin to catch hold of a glimpse at least of *your* mission in life. You see, God created you and me in such a "FASHION" which will never wear out for us to "Love our neighbor as ourself." That is why it is the SECOND GREATEST COMMANDMENT AND FINAL COMMANDMENT, THE FIRST OF

WHICH IS TO LOVE GOD WITH ALL OUR HEART, MIND, BODY, SOUL AND SPIRIT. . .because upon these two commandments all of the commandments of Moses and the prophets are established. Are you beginning to feel a little more stable and secure? If not, stop here, dogear this page and go back to the beginning of this Introduction and reread it. And after you get back to this part, if you still do not feel a *little* more stable and secure at least, repeat this exercise, and repeat this exercise and repeat, and repeat and repeat it all until you get it. Why? Because that is *exactly* how I got it. And, because I am loving you as I love myself, I am encouraging you to do likewise. Console yourself also that if you do not go this way, my dear reader, there is no where else to go! Have you not already up to this point in your life spun enough wheels on the wrong roads of life to be convinced?

Cornelius Van Til, my Mentor and Head Professor of Philosophy and Apologetics in my Masters Degree at Westminster Theological Seminary described the human being who does not practice this commandment like this: "A PERSON OF MUD IN A POOL OF MUD CLIMBING OUT ON A LADDER OF MUD ONTO A GROUND OF MUD." It is rather graphic, is it not? But is it not also familiar and painfully descriptive of you and me without our being on the solid road of loving our neighbor? Now, in contrast to the person of mud, let us take a look at the Good Samaritan. He was a "second class" citizen to the Jew in the first century. He was a halfbreed—half Jew and half Gentile, a human mongrel. And, for that matter, he was much more despised by the Jew than the Gentile on which the Jew also looked down. Yet, the Good Samaritan on his road of life helped heal a man on his way to the next place to which he was going. He stopped, looked and listened to the hurting person in his pathway. And, he loved the person, his "neighbor" as himself. So, he helped him to get other help, so he could be healed. And, he "paid the price" for the healing process of his neighbor. He "put his money where his mouth is." He did, in fact and reality, "WALK HIS TALK."

What a striking contrast this beautiful image of a human being is to the two religious leaders who "passed by on the other side" because they did not want to get involved; "they were too busy;" "they did not have the time;" "they did not have the energy;" "they did not have the money." Are you getting INTRODUCED to the true fashion, from and/or style of your journey in life? Or, to put it another way, WHAT DOES YOUR RELIGION DO FOR YOU? If your religion or philosophy or psychology has made you a self-centered, preoccupied, uninvolved, uncaring, uncompassionate, unfeeling and insensitive person in relation to the needs of others who are hurting whom you encounter on your journey of life, then your religion is meaningless, purposeless and has made you helpless to others and ultimately yourself.

On the other hand, if you want to be genuinely REAL as a human being caring for others as you were created to be and do this as your mission, because it is the beautiful exemplification of the image of God in and through you, get acquainted with the real you as your Creator made and FASHIONED you to be. Get to it. . .that is, focus on your real value. You see, you are so precious to God that He loves you as His very super special creation—more than anything else in the whole world. There is no gold, silver or precious stone in all the world more valuable, no matter what its quality and/or quantity that comes close to your value to God.

It seems too good to be true, does it not? But it is. Why? Because you are created in the image of God. That means you are God's "neighbor." Therefore, ergo, it must necessarily follow that you agree that God also must "practice what He preaches" by loving you as His neighbor, *just like* the Good Samaritan loved his "stranger/neighbor". After all, God is no less a being than the Good Samaritan would be, is He? Of course not. Clearly, the Good Samaritan is a human illustration of God's divine love.

I do not know about you, but this makes more sense to me than anything else in the world. This principle, truth, reality, call it what you want, but nevertheless it has become my OVERCOMER LAW which is so awesomely powerful and even practical that it enables me to "get my act together," "manage my moods," "blend with my friend," "get with it" and ultimately "go with the flow" into the rest of my future, both for time and eternity. Love. Without it, you and I are empty shells. Loving your neighbor as yourself—this is proof that you have learned to accept God's love for you and respond with your love to God. Yes, this will work!!! You see, to succeed in anything (or even *everything but* love) is not only foolish, stupid and futile, it is insanity. Why? Because without love you and I are nothing. But why again? Because anything and everything in the world under God's heaven and above Satan's hell does not last!!! But "Now abides faith, hope and love, and the greatest of these is love." That is why. And I have experienced for myself and proven already to many others IT IS MORE THAN JUST WORDS.

Ah, but you are still not convinced are you? I understand, my dear reader, for there was a time in my life that I was not convinced either.

Hence, let me love you as myself by sharing this with you, hoping that it will really and truly help you to help yourself, so that you too, having experienced the real thing, shall be able to help others too. But, before I proceed, let me clarify something. I am not RAMBLING, NOR PROLONGING THE LENGTH OF THIS INTRODUCTION. Rather, I am serving you at your very feet as our Lord Jesus Messiah stooped and washed his disciples' feet *(John 13).* Indubidably, you are not going *anywhere* if we do not clean up your feet—symbolic of going in the right direction and on the right path in life; and clear the "Hair, mud and filth of Terra Firma" *(as Socrates, the Greek Philosopher put it)* in front of you on your path of life. So, as the Good Samaritan, exert the ongoing initiative to do "whatever it takes," to do (in this Introduction) "whatever needs to be done to get the job done." By the way, these familiar expressions are the *"Standards of Excellence"* by which A-1 professionals apply their great expertise and achieve their stupendous wealth. Thus, because you are so valuable and precious, let me treat you with this first class professionalism. After all, because you are the best, you deserve the best.

Now I am ready to confide in you. And why not? "A stranger is simply a friend whom you have not met yet." Then again, at least a few of our more special friends are newer friends rather than older friends; more reliable friends who meet our needs better rather than older friends, who prefer not to be so involved. But I do take the initiative to get involved because that is how I get connected sufficiently to be the necessary help others need me to be. I do not forget how others became so involved with me so that they could adequately help me. They did not set "appropriate boundaries" on my deeply seated infirmities. They did not "tap me on the shoulder" when I needed them to help me "straighten my face". They unconditionally committed themselves to "hang out with me until I was healthy, wholesome and strong enough to "go home and do likewise" for others.

Hence, with the above as the covenant that binds us, let me open up and lay my heart bare to you by sharing with me the worst experience of my entire lifetime—an almost unbearable, unending experience. But having communicated that to you, then I will also "INTRODUCE" to you the greatest discovery of all my life.

It was during my birthday month of May, 1989 that I was involved in an almost fatal auto accident. A 20 year-old young man who was high on drugs sped through a stop sign as though it were a green light from my left into the intersection of a major highway on which I was driving at 50 miles per hour, minding my own business. SMASH!!! The head-on collision of my automobile into the passenger side of his car drove his car halfway through the intersection into the next block. Ironically, the driver at fault didn't get hurt at all, but I was made unconscious. And when the paramedics resuscitated me, I was diagnosed as suffering from a closed head injury. You see, that auto accident *literally* drove me out of my mind. The frightful symptoms that persisted for years and years to come were loss of long-term and short-term memory; loss of cognitive thoughts; loss of focus; loss of attention span; loss of concentration. In other words, I was not only "driven out of my mind", but also "I lost my *mind*". Therefore, it was nowhere to be found. It was neither "in" or "out", "up" or "down." It just was not. What used to be humorous expressions now very accurately described my mental condition.

Although I was subjected to a month at Lankenau Hospital in the psychiatric ward with the finest of psychiatrists, psychologists, brain surgeons, neurologists and even physiologists, nothing seemed to help. No matter how much scrutiny, therapy or scores of drugs in "guinea pig" experimentations, nothing helped. Clearly, "All the king's horses and all the king's men could not put Humpty Dumpty Don back together again."

You talk about mood swings! You should have been my neighbor then. By the time you became 50% introduced to me I was already a different identity. And, by the time you got to know *that* me, I was another me. It was during this era of my life that I at last learned the difference between the neurotic, psychotic and psychiatrist. You see the neurotic is one who builds castles in the sky. The psychotic lives in them. But the psychiatrist collects the rent. True story. More than once I have asked this question of psychiatrists. A few of the best answer, "There is no difference between all three. Ha! But what does that say about the psychiatrist? Buyer beware!!!

Without a doubt, I have been there, and I mean everywhere. I have been neurotic. I have been psychotic. And yes, I must confess that I was so mentally ill I was a "psychiatrist," fooling more than I dare to tell even other psychiatrists!!! Again, if I were able to fool them, what does that say about them??? Forget about me!!! Oh, now that we are acquainted you do not want to forget about me. OK, then let me share with you an allegory to help describe how I was!

Once upon a time Mr. and Mrs. Skunk began to train their young twin skunks, In and Out, to venture out of their cozy cottage and fend for themselves. So, after Mom and Dad Skunk discussed how it would be done, Dad Skunk went off to work. Shortly after, Mom Skunk told In to go out and play. And In stayed in because In was afraid. Next Mom Skunk told Out to go out and Out would not go out. So Out stayed in with In and nobody went out. After a while Mom Skunk became firm and ordered In out. So In went out and In stayed out. It was not long before Out realized how much fun out was because of all the fun In had out. And all of a sudden Out went out. But to the surprise of Out, In was no longer out because In went far out. Obviously, one thing led to another, so Out went in to tell Mom Skunk that In was far out. Then Mom Skunk and Out went out and also far out to find In. Unfortunately, by the time Mom Skunk and Out got far out, In had gone way out. Stress and more stress and even much more stress took over at which time Dad Skunk had arrived home from work to enjoy his wife's well prepared home-cooked full-course dinner, but when Dad Skunk went in he found no one in. Worst of all, he saw no dinner ready. Angry as can be, Dad Skunk went out to find Mom Skunk, In and Out; but no one but he was out. As a matter of fact, none but the three were in or out. They were either far out or way out. So, all this blew the mind of Dad Skunk. And because it never occurred to him to go far out or way out let alone back in, since there was no dinner ready to consume, it "blew him away."

However, while Dad Skunk was blown away, In decided to go from way out back to far out where he got back together with Mom Skunk and Out. By then, they were so glad to get back together with each other far out that they could wait to get back to where Dad Skunk was. Distressfully, however, by the time they found Dad Skunk, they all could tell that he was not only out but "blown in his mind." His mind had "blown away" all because he did not get "his way" and "his stomach full." But then a miracle happened because in an instant, he went forward to his new mind. (Note: He never went "back".) And even though he was still out, he was "with it," especially with his family. And now that he had his wonderful new mind, he thought of others as well as himself, especially his wife and children. And, now that he was thinking right, he started feeling right, and with his thoughtfulness and kindness, he escorted Mom Skunk and In and Out "out" to dinner to celebrate that they wonderfully got it all together!!!

Is it not wonderful that Dad Skunk learned two morals through this awesome experience: (1) he learned that the real way to go in life is not only for his own self-centered interests; (2) he learned that the only way and the only wholesome and lasting way to live is to serve others, looking out for their best interests, while trusting them to love him the same way.

By all means, do not minimize the truth of these two morals just because they were articulated to you through an allegory. After all, some of the most profound truths that God Himself gave us were through not only allegories but also parables, synecdoces ,analogies and illustrations. So, "Go for the gold!" Sift through these two priceless principles out of this Introduction and wisely apply them to the rest of your life. Remember that without love, you and I are nothing. With love, we can do anything. And, if even Satan gets in your way, he will have a "rundown" feeling. Remember also that when you have the power and energy of love working for you and through you to others, you automatically have the "Overcomer Law" working for you even to the extent of steamrolling over Murphy's Law. Believe it. You will be adequate for anything in your way for your highest good, your neighbor's highest interests and God's highest glory. Now, that is what I call a person who has his/her act together!

Of course, on your way to all this, watch out for tangents, no matter how good they look. Let me give you one striking example but please do not take this personally, especially if you are Irish because what I am about to point out to you is *"An Old Irish Blessing"*, which means well, but is not kosher to put it frankly.

May the road rise up to meet you

(Sorry, but that will never happen in a million years for two reasons: (1) roads do not rise except in calamities like earthquakes and you have been in enough calamities already! (2) because you are responsible to get on the right road, not the road to meet you. And you will, reader, because you will feel your way to the path of love and "Go with the flow.")

May the wind be always at your back

(Sorry again, for that is not real. Sometimes, it is good for you to have the wind blow in your face, because you will learn and grow better by the trials of life. Furthermore, along with loving your neighbor, you will encounter winds of difficulty as part of the turf, because loving your neighbor as yourself includes sharing his/her burdens and lightening his/her loads. But your love shall be greater and make you stronger to overcome it. Then again, you shall become so secure, stable and strong that you will actually rejoice in suffering, knowing that it is like the refining process or purifying the precious golden character of your life.

You get the idea, don't you? I could go through the rest of the greeting, but I believe that I have made enough comments to summarize it all like this:

With love abiding in you and flowing through you to God and your neighbors, you alone stand as a majority against whatever enemies or obstacles come your way. We could take this a step further and also say that you could actually invite challenges and testings to come; take risks that previously you would never consider; love and pray for those who despitefully hurt you.

And so that you may really believe and buy into all this practically as well as spiritually, let me share my doctoral expertise in the Greek language and culture, from which this awesome reality is descended. Please do not take this for granted in the slightest for three reasons:

(1) because it is the best of the best results of my therapy in the past eight (8) years of rehabilitation;

(2) because it cost my Keystone HMO health insurance company over $500,000;

(3) because you will not find anywhere what you are now about to receive. All I ask is that, having received so freely, by all means, freely give to others who in turn will give to others. . .for the best interest of all concerned.

Synergy is a compound word from the most awesome, accurate, transparent and resourceful language in all the world—the Greek. Hence syn + ergy equals "working like" or "working together", but with multiple results. So, 2+2=not 4, but 5, 6, 8, etc. Synergy has a symphonic effect whereby the unity and harmony of its constituency has an almost supernaturally productive and geometrically reproductive outcome. It is absolutely glorious. But the common misnomer about its real meaning is twofold: (1) the great majority of our world does not really understand even though they give lip service to it and also bluff about it to save face; (2) those who do know something about it because of a seminar they attended or a management book they have read, never have it occur to them that synergy must first happen *internally* within themselves before it can be partaken of *externally* with others. This explains why the thrill, flair and multiplied results of synergy do not really happen however much the "synergists" synergize their respective projects.

Clearly, we revisit it with the proper notion of individual responsibility the relevant words of Schuller: "If it is going to be, it is up to me." To be sure, synergy is not substitute for or shortcut around individual integrity or responsibility. Concerning the cultivation of this reality of synergy, there are no shortcuts. The core meaning and essence of integrity implies that, in addition to honesty and ethics, integrity also means wholesome and having it all together. And, synergy on the inside of us makes that happen. Again, God created us that way. Therefore, let us not take anything for granted. Let us go to the first chapter of the first book of the Bible, Genesis 1:26, where God says: "Let US make man and woman in OUR own image." US? OUR? Yes, because God is a Trinity, involving the Father, Son and Holy Spirit. Hence, since they are one essence but three persons, they are divine synergy. Think of it! God is synergy. For that matter, He is perfect synergy, bringing everything into being according to His perfect will. But when it comes to the human being, God created us after His own image. Having the human being like the divine being also is synergy.

Clearly, we are "awesomely and wonderfully made", exclaims King David of Israel (Psalms 39). That is why I personally believe (with all due respect to my neighbor's belief, whatever that may be) that I would greatly dishonor, disrespect, insult and offend God for referring to the origin of the human being as the evolution from a monkey. No, the human being is created synergy, not evolved monkey. Perhaps, one of the reapings of our sowings in evolution is our idiocy in synergy. In such, we dishonor and degrade ourselves. And, if so, God help us.

Nevertheless, let us hasten to conclude this Introduction and hopefully make ourselves fit to proceed to know by experience as well as theory the glory of synergy. If no one else in the whole wide world attains its reality, so what! You and I shall, for it is in our own best interests. And, because it is, I shall introduce you to synergy. Yes, I can even introduce you to the simplicity of synergy. But, only you can and must embrace it, digest it, interrelate it and then, in turn, apply it in yourself for yourself, by yourself, self-sufficiently whereby you finally are happy, healthy and wholistic for your highest good and for God's highest glory. Then, and only then, are you ready, able and willing to help your neighbor help himself to help his/her neighbor.

But, you ask - how am I a "synergy"??? Good question. Because you were created in the image of God, you are God's image bearer, have a three dimensional being of cognition, emotion and volition. And, to be sure, this three dimensional destination sets you apart uniquely from all the rest of God's creations, even the monkey! Perish the thought!

It logically follows, therefore, that:

- the cognition which thinks
- the emotion which feels, and
- the volition which decides need to unify, harmonize and bet-

ter yet, synergize.

And, to the degree that the human being does all this well, to that degree he/she is in harmony with God's plan. And to be sure, it is also true that to that degree that one does not synergize with himself/herself to that degree he/she regresses to unreality. Clearly, herein we find the varying distinctions of mental illness, emotional illness and lack of willpower. It surely makes sense to me. Does it not to you too? That is why one Jewish psychiatrist logically and consistently declares: "There is no such thing as mental illness; there are just varying degrees of human responsibility." Wow!

So if you are a leader, but really aspire to become a leader of leaders, if you are a follower and desire to become a leader, remember this secret and apply it to your pursuit, especially as you learn what's in this book. And please, realize it is not a book to be speed-read. Rather it is to be read provocatively, repeatedly, and reflectively as you read, mark, study, and memorize and inwardly digest its many secrets of leadership.

Furthermore, beware of the pitfalls along the way as you feel yourself getting good at it: money, power, and ego will do you in every time. What is so ironic about these devastating deterrents is that in many places all over the world as well as the Main Line, they are such commonplace "Status Symbols." But as you'll see in your CELEBRATION: KARL, LEADER OF LEADERS section next, Karl from the start to the finish never let these attractions become his distractions. And so must you if you really want to be a leader of leaders.

The same caution must equally, if not more so, be made about the two greatest curses ever perpetrated on society and which have been crammed down our throats! And so that we will not "digest" them ever again, let's spell them out right here and now:

- The curse of the lie: "There is a generation gap impossible to overcome, so we need to accept this fact and live with it the best we can." WRONG! This is a cop-out not only for leaders but also for men and women of integrity. You cannot drill a man out of the corps regardless of his age. You cannot dichotomize the Church of Christ. You cannot segregate the age levels of a family. Younger people desperately need older people and older people seriously need younger people who are going to carry on the next generation. That is why in the fall of this year following the premier of this book, we shall honor the youth, the "Future Leaders of America and the World" by awarding them one million dollars in scholarships over a two year period with a commitment from the respective colleges and universities that they fund the scholarships for their third and fourth years of study. And that's why the young are honored on the same evening with the mature leaders, both present and past.

- The second curse is the fallacy of retirement. Retirement is not a Biblical concept, but rather a cultural concept. For instance, you may retire or be forced to retire from your company, and you may not have an option. But you never retire from your commitment to your community; from your devotion to God and your church or synagogue.

Yet in so many cases, the only thing society knows to do with the elderly is to put them out to pasture and encourage them to enjoy their hobbies and pasttime activities. God forbid! Have you noticed how many men there are over fifty who are reaching for the bench, who are sliding for home? At the very time when they should be "cashing in on their wisdom and experience," they are "throwing in the towel!" It is no wonder that the statistics of how many men die shortly after retirement are so alarming! The explanation is obvious–They No Longer Have A Vision, Mission, Passion. . .and as a result, we are losing an incredible leadership pool.

So dear reader, even if you have accomplished great feats of leadership for your entire career, this book is for you because you need to "revisit yourself," "take inventory" and then "reinvest for the best" dimension of your life–from now to the finish line, so that you "Blaze out into glory!" Or if you are still currently working at your career, clearly you really need refinement of your leadership skills. Take honest inventory of those areas of the fifteen principles of leadership in which you do not excel. Admit that you, like the rest of us, have not arrived. Genuinely cultivate the attitude, "I have so much to learn." Then let's become a LEADER OF LEADERS.

Last, but not least, to the young person whose career, vocation and/or profession is still before you, do not settle for the mediocre. Go for the best. Give it all you've got as Socrates advised the young man. Or better yet, let us all at every age level, sex, color, creed, culture and country be challenged. . .inspired. . .motivated. . .activated, by the word of God through the "Wisest man who ever lived," Solomon, the King of Israel in Proverbs 2:1-4:

". . .Turn your ear ot wisdom. . .
Apply your heart to understanding. . .
Look for it as for silver. . .
Search fot it as for hidden treasure!"

Now you have it, reader/neighbor. Do not let it slip away! Hold onto it for dear life itself, because it is. After all, what good is knowledge if you do not apply it? As the Book of Proverbs in the Bible says: "Without wisdom a person is a fool." But do not stop at wisdom either, for there is one more step. Hence, with the wisdom of Solomon, go *beyond* the gold, not *for* the gold. And, go for an understanding heart. According to 1 Kings 3, that is precisely what Solomon himself asked of God, when God in a dream appeared to Solomon to grant him whatever in the whole world he wanted. (Come on now, reader/neighbor, honestly, what would you ask for right here and now, if God gave you the same opportunity? Hmmm???) Solomon requested of God, "Give your servant an understanding heart so he may lead your people well." Does that sound familiar? Servant? Understanding? Understanding heart? Lead? And, is not understanding the basis for submission? It really fits together, doesn't it?

Well then, Solomon with his cognition of thinking, emotion of feelings and volition of decisions harmonized it all together with an understanding heart toward God (spirit), mediation, within himself (soul) and synergized with people experienced in the reality of synergy. No wonder he was the wisest human being of the earth in his day. And that is why those of us who want to be wise should emulate the wise. But, keep going from the Old Testament of Solomon to the New Testament, for as another Jew, John the Baptist prophesied as the Forerunner to the Messiah, "Behold, a greater than Solomon is here!!" The *LORD JESUS MESSIAH*. And it is He to Whom I ultimately point you in Chapter 10 as The Leader of Leaders, as the Prophet Isaiah called Him, Lord of Lords and King of Kings.

But, so that you may not turn away because you do not believe as I believe, I point you to 14 other Leaders of Leaders too. And I implore and encourage you to exert some ongoing initiative too. Then, after all is said and done, you and I can keep on being good neighbors and special friends, who respectfully and free may agree to disagree as we major on the major and minor on the minor. Clearly, we can and will finally experience the reality of synergy which is gloriously wonderful enough to include our unique identities and diversities.

Hence, as author and reader, let us mentor one another as we make friends with all of the other Leaders of Leaders in this Gallery of the Greats.

By: Dr. Donald H. Sautter

Dr. Donald H. Sautter

Sunday, August 24, 1997

(The same day of the reopening of the Arch of Triumph at Valley Forge)

In Honor of Our Two Statesman/ Presidents

Dear Reader:

Just in case you feel that too much space has been devoted to Chapter Ten on "Demonstration: The Power of Life Messages", simply revisit the two greatest Presidents and Statesmen of our nation's history as you see highlighted below and then proceed to rediscover your roots of heritage from the same source Washington and Lincoln had: i.e., the Judeo-Christian tradition.

In this fast-food/fast disposable age and culture of ours, such a "research" shall be refreshing for you.

IN HONOR OF THE PRESIDENTS OF OUR NATION
On Presidents Day, 2/17/97

Here in King of Prussia, Pennsylvania on Presidents Day, the largest mall of the nation is booming with Presidents Day sales. "Next Door" in Valley Forge, the birthplace of America, so few patriots like me are there to celebrate what Presidents Day is all about. So I felt prompted in my spirit to do some research on the Hallmark Presidents, who both are a legend for their pure, profound and persistent faith in God, and who therefore stand heads and shoulders above so many, to inspire our President, Mr. William Clinton, and local leaders as well to follow in their steps. Therefore, please note, digest and apply for your highest good and the nation's highest honor the following:

WASHINGTON AT HIS INAUGURATION

Taking the oath of office as first President of the United States on April 30, 1778, Washington spontaneously added this four-word prayer of his own: *"So help me God,"* an invocation still used in official oaths by those taking public office in courts and other legal proceedings.

WASHINGTON IN HIS DAILY ROUTINE

"It would be peculiarly improper to omit in this first official act, my fervent supplication to that Almighty Being who rules over the universe - who presides in the council of nations - and whose beneficial aids can supply every human defect."

WASHINGTON IN THE FACE OF WAR & CONFLICT

"Let us therefore rely on the goodness of the cause and the aid of the Supreme Being, in whose hands victory is, to animate and encourage us to great and noble actions."

IN ORDERING CONGRESS TO SUPPLY CHAPLAINS TO EACH REGIMENT IN THE FIELD OF BATTLE

"The blessings and protection of heaven are at all times necessary, but especially so in times of public danger."

LINCOLN

He coined one of his most memorable phrases when he declared Americans *"an almost chosen people"* whose rise *"held out a great promise to all."* He hoped to be a *"humble instrument in the hands of the Almighty."*

LINCOLN'S STATEMENT ON AMERICAN SLAVERY

"Offensive against God," and the scars of *"this terrible war"* demanded compassion: *"With malice toward none; with charity for all,"* North and South must *"bind up the nation's wounds. . .and to do all which may achieve and cherish a just and lasting peace among ourselves and with all nations."*

LINCOLN. . .WHEN ALL ELSE FAILED

"When everyone seemed panic-stricken. . .I went to my room. . .and got on my knees before Almighty God and prayed. . .soon a sweet comfort crept into my soul that God Almighty had taken the whole business into His own hands."

Henceforth, Mr. President and leaders everywhere, may God grant you the passion to love and trust your life, your family and your nation to God, who is called: *"Wonderful, Counselor, Mighty God, Everlasting Father, and Prince of Peace."* and equipped by his absolute, supernatural power may you: *"Expect great things from God, attempt great things for God, and thereby achieve great things with God."*

Happy Presidents' Day, Mr. President and Mr. Leader!!! God Bless you superabundantly!!!

Respectfully Submitted

Dr. Donald H. Sautter

Dr. Donald H. Sautter
Author, **LEADER OF LEADERS**

DEDICATION

This book is dedicated to Helen Leflar, the Mother of the Author/Publisher. It is no accident or coincidence that Mom died at 1:45 a.m., May 2, 1997, the preliminary deadline for the manuscript of this book to go to the production plant. The incredible timing is certain. What is uncertain is the reason why. Does the "Author and Finisher of Time" have a special meaning in this? I believe so. You see, until Mom's death, I had two or three options for this dedication section. And I was going to consult with my Associate Publisher when I committed the manuscript to production. And then with his input, I was going to make a final decision, go into a quiet room and finish writing these pages. But it was decided for me, was it not? You may call it destiny, but I prefer to call it God.

The Sunday morning before the funeral, I felt deeply compelled to write my WELCOME message to our Memorial Service guests for two reasons: (1) it provided me with a "crutch" to read from just in case I became too emotional; (2) because I felt the desire to let each and every guest have it as a special gift, since it has precious Motherly advice and Godly counsel that could really apply to all, even though it was primarily intended for me.

That is why my Mother and I have a "DOUBLE WHAMMY BLESSING" for you. (1) My literary portrait of her in light of the acrostic formed by the word "LEADER"; (2) her literal and final message to me during the last week of her life in light of the word "WELCOME."

Clearly, her life message is immortal because its source is divine and its timing could not have been more providential–the very day of the publisher's deadline for this book. Indubitably, all of these factors working together for good reminds us of Romans 8:28 *"For we know that God works all things together for the good of those who love God and who are called according to His purpose."* Likewise, the very Life Message of my beloved Mother also reminds me of the precious words of our Lord Jesus Christ: *"The Kingdom of God is like a mustard seed, which must first die, and then after it is planted in good soil, it comes forth in a 30%, 60% and 100% fashion."*

Therefore, my good reader by all means anticipate, without any concern of unrealistic expectations, that the "Seed" of my Mother's twofold Life Message shall be multiplied abundantly in and through your life and leadership of others.

Now, let us turn first to my Mom's Life Message.

Love:

How perfectly does this acrostic start to describe my Mother. Above all, Mom was first and foremost a person of love. Having never gone past sixth grade in her education, she surely made up for it with compassion. It was her primary driving force of life and work to start a home for us in Ardsley, Pennsylvania when she was sixteen, and it was her sustaining power that kept our family together when Dad left when I was at the age of eight.

Example:

Not being an eloquent person with words, Mom let her works speak for themselves. Whether it be working from 7:00 a.m. until 7:00 p.m. at the dry cleaners and then coming home to keep house, or whether it entailed guiding us to church on Sunday, Mom's example was dependable.

Attitude:

Perhaps the reason I prize my wife so highly in the chapter on Disposition is because I prized attitude so highly in my Mother. As we're going to see, "Disposition is the power of attitude." And Mom surely had lots of it. That is why I agree with Dr. Chuck Swindoll that the older I get, the more I tend to value attitude higher than any other asset I have.

Dedication:

One of the last things my Mother said to the Oncology Specialist, Dr. Warshal, was that for 67 years she lived and raised her family at 600 Edge Hill Road. That's dedication, especially these days when people change jobs and homes so frequently. Even though there were unstable things in our family life, this certainly was not one of them. Mom was dedicated. Interesting as it seems, she was so dedicated that she often expressed her desire to go to be with the Lord from that house. And, to be sure, she did. So peacefully during her nighttime sleep, she breathed her last breaths and went to heaven. That is dedication, par excellence.

ENTHUSIASM:

Mother was one Polack who was unashamed of being Polish! So secure was she about her passionate heritage that she could and would laugh with everyone at the ethnic jokes she heard. Mom was quite confident that her enthusiasm for life as expressed by her bubbly personality gave her a great edge on life. And without a doubt, Mom knew that the passion of the Polish was rooted in her origin in God.

REPRODUCTION:

Helen Leflar did not feel constrained to reproduce herself in her four children: Eve, Frank, Don and Sharon. Most important was the fact that she reproduced her wonderful character, qualities in her children, grandchildren and great grandchildren. And, isn't that what leadership as well as the Creation Mandate is all about? "Be fruitful and multiply and replenish the earth." Once again, the timing is so perfect because just this past week the PRESIDENTS' SUMMIT FOR AMERICA'S FUTURE has just completed its stay in Philadelphia. And its final message was an appeal of reproduction–it was a "Call to Action" for us to go and do likewise.

Last, but not least, is my Mother's literal and final life message to me during her last week on earth. It ironically is a word of "WELCOME."

WELCOME

This memorial service in honor of Helen Leflar is one of celebration. From the start we celebrate her homegoing to Heaven. We therefore praise the Lord and rejoice with one another that she has no more sickness, pain and tears. Isn't that wonderful?

SO LET US CELEBRATE BECAUSE OF HER COMPLETION

Notice I did not say conclusion, but rather completion. Just because Mom's or Nana's spirit is no longer in her body, does not mean that she's done, finished or over. No. Let's instead celebrate that she is now complete with her glorified body in heaven forever. There is no doubt that Mom/Nana knew for sure where she was going right to and beyond her last breath.

SO LET US CELEBRATE BECAUSE OF HER CONSOLATION

You see, I prayed fervently for her miraculous healing, and I really felt that I met all God's terms. After all, is He not in the miracle business? And since millions of miracles are happening everyday, can't I grab my share? So why not? It made me angry that God did not answer my prayer. But then my cousin, John Pfuhl, during a long distance call on Saturday, reminded me, "God's plans are not always my plans." Well put, isn't it? His words of consolation reminded me also of Jesus' words in the Garden of Gethsemane, "Not my will but thine be done." That's a wonderful consolation, isn't it? Then again it's like: "Do your best and commit the rest."

SO LET US CELEBRATE BECAUSE OF HER CRYSTALLIZATION

In the last week before Mom passed away, she clearly got across to me a very important wish. Just before she, Sharon, Frank and I went to the shore for our last family time together, she asked me to promise her that I would not take issue with my sister or brother, but just be nice. At first it didn't really impress me what she was trying to accomplish. But now I know.

Mom was not just trying to avoid a tense situation. Mom was giving me Motherly advice and Godly counsel. Mom was guiding me to focus my energies on love which suffers LLLOOONNNGGG and is kind, rather than on criticizing, arguing or complaining which has been the Sautter tradition. WHAT A FAREWELL MESSAGE! Mom had also planned to get me the latest book by Dr. Robert Schuller that she saw featured on HOUR OF POWER, called "IF IT'S GOING TO BE IT'S UP TO ME." But she became too ill to do so. So another precious family member is doing it for her. Why? Because it is an elaboration of her Farewell Message. What a consolation! So as my expression of appreciation for Helen Leflar, I close with her favorite life message:

"YOU HAVE TO SAY YOU ARE
WHAT YOU WISH YOU WERE
IF YOU EVER HOPE TO BECOME
WHAT YOU REALLY WANT TO BE."

by Donald H. Sautter

ACKNOWLEDGEMENTS

The book, LEADER OF LEADERS, has quite an interesting story behind it, for it was birthed during Sautter's promotion of the Valley Forge Leadership Prayer Breakfast last fall of 1996. Having obtained official endorsements and proclamations from President Clinton, Vice President Al Gore, Senate Chaplain Lloyd Ogilvie, Pennsylvania State Senator Richard Tilghman, Philadelphia Mayor Edward Rendell, Montgomery County Chairman Mario Mele, Upper Merion Township Manager Ronald Wagenman, and Chairman of the Board of Supervisors Ralph Vole, Sautter was significantly instrumental in getting a "MOVEMENT" going and not just a one-time event. Thus, the book **LEADER OF LEADERS** and the sequel, **LEADER OF LEADERS PREMIER CELEBRATION**, coming on Tuesday, October 14, 1997, at the Freedoms' Foundation on Valley Forge Road, Route 23, Valley Forge, Pennsylvania.

Actually, the springboard for this coming event was the Valley Forge Prayer Breakfast on November 13, 1996. Dr. Sautter was asked by John W. Boyer, Jr., Retired Chairman of the Board and CEO for Philadelphia Suburban Water Company, who is using his retirement years following his passion to do special ministries for the Kingdom of God on the Main Line, especially as expressed through the Main Line Christian Ministries Organization, of which he is a board member. Boyer asked Sautter to be his Assistant Coordinator because of Sautter's expertise and past track record of working with secular leaders during his past 33 years of publishing magazines, books, and even the Gospel. Their problem was that in the First Annual Valley Forge Prayer Breakfast they had 300 in attendance, and in their Second Annual, 400, but almost all were religious and/or church leaders. And because Boyer and the rest of the Citizens Committee wanted many secular leaders also to come, they engaged Sautter, who gladly accepted the challenge.

Result? The records indicate that over 400 RSVPs of some secular leaders were the outcome, making it a grand aggregate of almost 900 in attendance at the King of Prussia Holiday Inn Atrium Room. At 6:45 a.m., Wednesday morning, November 13, 1996, the room was prepared with 75 tables of 8 chairs each (600 seating capacity), but it was not enough! So they added two more chairs per table (150 more seats). But by 6:55 a.m., there were still not enough seats for the long line of leaders waiting patiently to get in. So they again added two more chairs per table (again 150 more totaling 900 seats). Finally, when Boyer gave the greeting, he mentioned that there was just an empty seat here and there. Wow!

Such a smashing success got the notice of F. Karl Schauffele, the retiring President of The Main Line Chamber of Commerce. Once a year, the Chamber sponsors an Inspiration Breakfast, but its attendance is in the 200s at the Valley Forge Military Academy. So Sautter got the attention of Schauffele whose "Main Line Turf" was overwhelmingly responding. But Schauffele got Sautter's attention, too, although Sautter had known Schauffele since the early 70s when Schauffele was the Head of the Planning Commission for Lower Merion Township. Still, Sautter was a close friend of Robert Geerdes, Manager of Upper Merion Township, and it was not until this fall that Schauffele really got close. Yes, Schauffele had previously respected Sautter, especially for his being Owner and Publisher of the first Main Line Magazine, but the strong trust wasn't a reality until this fall of 1996. One thing led to another, and on October 30, 1997, at the 75th anniversary of The Main Line Chamber of Commerce, Sautter officially committed in writing and publicly that he would publish a book called **LEADER OF LEADERS** to honor F. Karl Schauffele as a Leader of Leaders.

At first, Sautter intended it to be a book all about Schauffele, but after months of Schauffele's insistent encouragement to include others (as is the wonderful Schauffele style), and also because of the professional advice of his Contributing Editors who also helped in interviews with Schauffele, by unanimous consensus it was decided to let others enter the book. The first two were at Schauffele's recommendation: 1) Tony Campolo and 2) Arthur DeMoss. Unfortunately, Arthur DeMoss' widow and children vetoed the idea of our having the ARTHUR DeMOSS STUDENT SCHOLARSHIP FUND in honor of him at our Premier, whose request we respected as an Executive Committee. In the place of DeMoss, Sautter honored Millie Dienert, whose consistent exemplification of *Mission: The Power of Words,* was equally, if not more, appropriate. Sautter also has included David Wardell, Ph.D., Co-Founder of Promise Keepers, a million-man movement; Ray Coleman, Executive Secretary of the Suburban One League; Roman Kupecky, Pastor of Abrams Community Chapel, King of Prussia; Jon D. Fox, U.S. Congressman; Judith Ann Sautter, his dear wife as a wonderful Caregiver; Jerry Heffel, President, Southwestern Great American Publishing Company; Dave Stoddard, National Director, CBMC,

"Living Proof"; Tony Campolo, Ph.D., Missionary Statesman, Modern Day Prophet; the Lord Jesus Christ, what love is and does; Lon Weber, Ph.D., Senior Vice President for Education, Freedoms Foundation at Valley Forge; James Dobson, Ph.D.., Focus on the Family; and Edward Rendell, the Mayor of Philadelphia.

The Editor for the very recent PRESIDENTS' SUMMIT FOR AMERICA'S FUTURE headquarters in Philadelphia, the City of Brotherly Love, is now another Contributing Editor of LEADER OF LEADERS by Author/Publisher Dr. Donald H. Sautter in King of Prussia. James Rollins, Esquire, of Washington, shall orchestrate the progressive stages of the 350-page, 15-chapter "Inspirational Commentary" with Contributing Editors. The first half of the LEADER OF LEADERS manuscript went to typesetting, layout, and design on May 7, 1997 and the second half on May 15 with final check & balance and graphic arts/camera-ready production spearheaded by Carl Lotz on Friday, August 23, 1997. Then on Friday, August 29, 1997, it goes to press; –all under the Associate Publisher's quality control over the total production process until Monday evening, October 14, 1997, when the book is premiered in **LEADER OF LEADERS PREMIER CELEBRATION** at the Freedoms' Foundation Convention Center before a full house of thousands of leaders. Mr. Kerry Freeman, Publisher and Editor-in-Chief of Chilton Book Publishing Company and owner of LKF Associates, is the Associate Publisher/Editor-in-Chief/Production Manager for LEADER OF LEADERS.

The book covers every vital aspect of leadership, from Celebration to Vision, Disposition, Selection, Mission, Association, Passion, Impartation, Inclusion, Demonstration, Delegation, Revision, Supervision, Reproduction and, finally, Conclusion. By design, it is intended to enrich the lives of followers who want to become leaders, but also leaders who want to become Leaders of Leaders. Furthermore, the hundreds of rich insights about leadership can be derived from three dimensions of this book: 1) Principally, as the reader studies the titles of the chapters themselves; 2) Biographically, as the reader does a character study in each chapter which illustrates the given principle; 3) Procedurally, as the reader diligently wants to "fill in the gaps" of his own leadership style with the missing "ingredients" of some of the GUIDELINES, METHODS, SYSTEMS, AND/OR FORMULAS he has not yet mastered.

Clearly, the Valley Forge Leadership Prayer Breakfast, the book, **LEADER OF LEADERS**, and **LEADER OF LEADERS PREMIER CELEBRATION** are, in essence, ONE. You see, the prayers that were prayed by the spiritual and secular leaders at the Prayer Breakfast became answered prayers. After all, why pray if you don't want answers?! For instance, there were prayers:

- for honoring regional and national leaders
- for the betterment of leaders
- for the guidance and blessing of God upon our nation
- for more righteous leaders

And, to be sure, the book and the Premier are the logical, natural and also spiritual progression and fulfillment of those prayers!!! To have any other explanation would be ingratitude and unthankfulness, not to mention taking God for granted.

But lest we take any human leader for granted, please note the following WHO's WHO that have given either their RSVP, support, cooperation, and/or unreserved testimonials to our "unique enterprise" of all the above:

I. EXECUTIVE ENDORSEMENTS

President William Clinton
Vice President Al Gore
U.S. Senate Chaplain Lloyd Ogilvie
U.S. Congressman Jon Fox, Master of Ceremonies - Leader of Leaders Premier Celebration
U.S. Senator John Ashcroft
U.S. Senator Carl Levin
Russell Schulz, Executive Vice President, Freedoms' Foundation at Valley Forge
Lon Weber, Ph.D., Senior Vice President for Education, Freedoms' Foundation at Valley Forge
Honorable Lita Indzel Cohen, Pennsylvania State Representative, 148th District
Pennsylvania State Representative William R. Adolph, Jr., 155th District
Pennsylvania State Representative Connie Williams
Pennsylvania State Senator Richard A. Tilghman
Grant from an anonymous foundation
Fred Semback, Vice President of Pennsylvania Chamber of Business and Industry
Mayor of Philadelphia, Edward Rendell

Judith Williams, Assistant Superintendent, Philadelphia School District
The Honorable Paul Mattas, Chairman of the Delaware County Commissioners
Payson Burt, Executive Vice President, Montgomery County Chamber of Commerce
Karen R. Martynick, Chairperson, Chester County Commissioners
Clark Shuster, Executive Vice President, Lower Bucks County Chamber of Pennsylvania
Jack Holefelder, President, DELCO, Chamber of Commerce
F. Karl Schauffele, President Emeritus, Main Line Chamber of Commerce
Richard Force, Wynnewood Valley Civic Association
Kay Gordon, Director, Ardmore 2000
Sue Cooper, President, Narberth Business Association
Richard Fuchs, President, Bryn Mawr Business Association
Dr. John F. DeFlaminis, Superintendent, Radnor School District
Stephen D'Orio, President, Wayne Business and Professional Association
Robert D'Amicantonio, Vice President, Wayne Business and Professional Association
Matt DiDomenico, Sr., President, Berwyn-Devon Business and Professional Association
Robert DiSomone, President, Paoli Business and Professional Association
Charles "Chip" Roach, Jr., Manager/Partner, Roach Wheeler, Devon
Abigail Silvers, Lower Merion Unit, American Cancer Society
Suzanne Young, Director, United Way of Southeastern Pennsylvania
Ralph Volpe, Chairman of the Board of Supervisors, Upper Merion Township; Executive Host, Leader of Leaders Premier Celebration
Ray Coleman, Executive Secretary, Suburban One League; Executive Chairman, Scholarship Committee, Leader of Leaders Premier Celebration

II. EXECUTIVE COMMITTEE

Ray Coleman, Executive Secretary, Suburban 1 League
Chuck Coles, V.P. Development, Salvation Army
Charlie Glass, Mid-Atlantic Director CBMC
Wilson Goode, former Mayor of Philadelphia
Helen Leflar, Treasurer, Foundation for the Family

Sharon Sandy, Secretary, Foundation for the Family
Don Sautter, Executive Coordinator
Judy Sautter, Administrative Assistant
Lon Weber, Senior V.P. for Education, Freedoms Foundation

III. EXECUTIVE TASK FORCE
Louis Alfieri, Telemarketing Consultant
John Bach, Principal, Upper Merion High School, School Model Facilitator
Phyllis Boggs, Telemarketing Consultant
John Byrd, Human Resources Specialist
Tony Campolo, Ph.D., Guest Speaker for celebration
Linda Culbertson, Commonwealth of Pennsylvania
Lynn DiDominicis, Coordinator of Woman's Groups
Sydney Eltringham, Ph.D., ED., Contributing Editor
George Falconeiro, CPA, Accounting and Auditing Firm
Peter Forster, Special Student Scholarships
Jon Fox, US Congressman - Master of Ceremonies/Guest Speaker
Kerry Freeman, Associate Publisher/Production Manager
Joseph Ginyard, Wise Choice Transition House for Unwed Mothers
Paul Hendricks, Focus on the Family
James Holton, Ph.D., Medical Sector Consultant
Charlie "Tremendous" Jones, Special Inspiration Speaker
Rudy Lucente, Special Music Consultant
Daniel Moore, The Southwestern Company/Youth Employment
Robert Murphy, Seminar Facilitator
Lloyd John Olgilvie, US Senate Chaplain/Intercessor
James Rollins, Esq., Editor-in-Chief, Leader of Leaders
Russell Schulz, Executive V.P. Freedoms Foundation/Celebrity Consultant
David Wardell, Ph.D., Promise Keepers Guest Speaker
Linn Washington, Contributing Editor
Curt Weldon, US Congressman, Keynote Speaker
Lisa Welsh, Special Student Scholarship

IV. EXECUTIVE STEERING COMMITTEE
Carlos Acosta, Philadelphia Empowerment Zone
John Byrd, Human Resources Consultant
Calvin Cary, Inner City Specialist
Ray Coleman, Student Scholarships Committee
Chuck Coles, Youth Sponsorships

Louis Cortez, Top 20 Hispanic Leader, USA
Joseph Ginyard, Wise Choice-support system for unwed mothers
Charlie Glass, Mid-Atlantic Area Director for CBMC
Wilson Goode and/or Son - former Mayor of Philadelphia
Dr. Stuart Lord, Executive Director, President's Summit/ Consultant
Jim Marra, Ph.D., Professor in Journalism, Temple University
Mary Ella Marra, Publicity Specialist
Manny Ortos, Inner City Ministry, Professor at Westminster Seminary
Donald H. Sautter, Executive Chairman
David Sorin, Special Event Consultant
Skip Voluntad, Delegate PSAF, Mayor's Commission for Asian Affairs
Lon Weber, We The People Student Scholarship Committee
Brian Wright, Special Event Consultant

V. EXECUTIVE CONTRIBUTING EDITORS

Kerry Freeman, Editor-in-Chief
Kathryn Deane, Synergistic Editor
Lita Higgins, Integration Editor
James Rollins, Esq., National Editor
Sharon Sandy, Stylistic Editor
Judith A. Sautter, Finetuning Editor
Edward Zinser, Ph.D., Coherence Editor

VI. EXECUTIVE ASSOCIATES

Lita Higgins, Executive Associate/Management
Charlene Lewis, Executive Associate/Administration
Noreen Mallory, Executive Associate/Publicity
Stanley Simpkins, Exeuctive Associate/Marketing
Donald H. Sautter, Executive Chairman/Author

ABOUT THE FRONT COVER

It is clearly in the Providence of God that the unveiling capstone and dedication ceremonies commemorating the preservation of the National Memorial ARCH at the Valley Forge National Park, Valley Forge, Pennsylvania was celebrated on August 24, 1997, the very day I as Author/Publisher of **LEADER OF LEADERS** put to writing this inscription.

It is the Arch of Triumph at the Valley Forge National Park, dedicated to the Leader of Leaders of our nation, George Washington and his Continental Army. Hence inscribed on the Arch are these words:

The Arch of Triumph
in Valley Forge
Erected by authority of the Act of Congress, June 25, 1910
Dedicated to the officers and private soldiers of the
Continental Army 12/19/1777 to 6/19/1778

"They shall hunger no more nor thirst any more. (Rev. 17:16)
And here in this place of sacrifice in this valley of humiliation in this valley of the shadow of that death out of which the life of America rose regenerated and free let us believe with an abiding faith that to them union will seem dear and liberty as sweet and progress as glorious as they were to our fathers and to you and me and that the institutions which have made us happy preserved by the virtue of our children shall bless the remotest generation of the time to come."

Sept. 8, 1991 Henry Armitt Brown

The reason for its selection for LEADER OF LEADERS is fourfold:

#1 because it symbolizes the awesome reality of **LEADER OF LEADERS** who have paid the price to make our nation a secure, free and happy place to live

#2 because it stands at "The Birthplace of the Nation" where our first President and Commander-in-Chief gave birth to the nation by means of the birthpangs of the Revolutionary War

#3 because of our **LEADER OF LEADERS PREMIER CELEBRA-**

TION where we renew our dedication in volunteer service to support the 5 purposes of the Presidents' Summit for America's Future
#4 because it is the sacred ground to which God called the Author/Publisher 27 years ago to fulfill a lifetime of service to God first, family second, and country third

Rich in God's Loving Kindness

Dr. Donald H. Sautter
Author/Publisher
Chairman of the Board, Foundation for the Family
Executive Chairman, **LEADER OF LEADERS PREMIER CELEBRATION**

Table of Contents

There isn't a leader in the whole world who possesses all fifteen (15) principles of leadership as highlighted below in the chapter headings for this book. Hence, may each and every reader approach his/her reading of LEADER OF LEADERS with humility of mind and hunger of heart to learn, grow and excel.

You will see that each of the fifteen leaders of leaders featured in his or her own respective chapter is there for a very special purpose – BECAUSE THAT PARTICULAR PRINCIPLE MOST DOMINANTLY CHARACTERIZES HIS/HER LEADERSHIP STYLE. Yes, this GALLERY OF THE GREATS has a good number of the fifteen (15) principles well applied in their lives and work, but the one in which they're highlighted is their forte. So, even if you are a leader of other leaders, with an open mind you can learn something new and more to enrich your leadership style. Or, if you are a leader who desires and aspires to be a leader of other leaders as well as of followers, you can benefit so much from this book. Last but not least, if you are a follower and aspire to become a leader, then pay the price and memorize, meditate, inwardly digest and outwardly apply it!!! After all, whoever you are . . .

"YOU HAVE TO SAY YOU ARE
WHAT YOU WISH YOU WERE
IF YOU EVER HOPE TO BECOME
WHAT YOU REALLY WANT TO BE."

"BECAUSE ITS FOUNDATION IS ON THE ROCK"

CELEBRATION 1

THE POWER OF EXAMPLE

FEATURING

F. KARL SCHAUFFELE
PRESIDENT EMERITUS
THE MAIN LINE CHAMBER OF COMMERCE

"Nothing will make us so charitable and tender
to the faults of others as by
self-examination thoroughly to know our own."

-- Fenelon

Throughout life we witness and share a variety of celebrations ; weddings, anniversaries, graduations and more. Yet, in the midst of all these celebrations, few of us celebrate life. We think only to celebrate events that happen because we are passing through various stages of life. Instead, I propose to you that every day should be a celebration of life—from the time we awake in the morning until we retire for the evening. Unfortunately, while we tend to daily responsibilities, we often forget to enjoy the life we are living; we don't recognize life as a celebration. For those who do, however, this celebration can become a principle of leadership—because of its power of example.

Come along to a most unique celebration of life. Party with me as we share the example of Karl, a leader of leaders. Picture us at a beautiful breakfast table in the Radnor Hotel's dining room, January 3, 1997. Though it is Karl's 69th birthday, but we didn't plan it that way. An assortment of distinguished key leaders of the Main Line Chamber of Commerce are here to share tidbits of the life of F. Karl Schauffele, who was their president for 15 years and retired a few days before. Each has taken time from his or her busy schedule to gather around this festive table for only one reason—Karl, a leader of leaders by example. They've agreed to be a focal group to synergize and enhance the content of a book about Karl. But without realizing it, we're immediately and magically involved in a deeply felt celebration of Karl's life. Listen to the conversation flow to our left clockwise around the table.

"I learned a lot from him when he was head of the Lower Merion Planning Commission," begins Chip Roach long before our food arrives. "He is the most organized leader I know." Pausing with his coffee cup raised, this partner for Roach Wheeler/Better Homes and Gardens Real Estate on the Main Line reflects warmly, "Karl knows a million people, yet he makes you feel like you are the only one in the world when you are with him."

With the flow of memories begun, Felice Barsky, who owns Hollander Communications in Karl's hometown of Wynnewood, smiles and recalls, "Karl never has shared his 'magic of leadership,' so perhaps I can now learn it." She adds affectionately, "I appreciate his passion. Karl opened lots of doors for me."

Andy Wilson, entrepreneur and real estate professional, picks up the conversation as he notes with awe, "Karl runs a 36-hour day in 24 hours. I admire how he knows everyone on the Main Line. Karl has a great energy level, yet he always has time for me." Next is Art Megraw, former Chamber Chairman and a retired executive from a lifetime of service with the internationally known Chilton Publishing Company, who chimes in to say, "Karl has always been enjoyable to work with." Completing the circle is Beverly Dotter, who Karl calls a "dynamo." Dotter, director of communications for Sun Company in Philadelphia, succinctly notes, "I agree with all of the above. Trying to capture Karl is very interesting to me."

All of the above is Karl's power of example from one end of the Main Line to the other. He is a person who rises above the mudhole of mediocrity, but steers clear of the dead-end street of perfection. Of himself, Karl says, "I have always been a public servant," and that example is the motivation for this book. Remember, there was a time when this vision of himself was first an idea in his mind. That idea grew into a conscious reality, and was noticed because of Karl's power of example — an awesome and encouraging example for each of us. Because through his example we can learn to shed our pessimism and defensiveness. We can catch that vision of ourselves in the power of Karl's example. We can celebrate life. We can move out to get an education, learn a trade, take a vacation, get a life. When one asks F. Karl Schauffele, "What is your favorite quotation from leaders you admire?" He answers: "Seventy-five percent of a matter is just showing up." It sounds so simple, not very profound or inspirational — or does it? Ponder it for a while and the magnitude of its meaning emerges in a multifarious fashion. Karl's choice of quotations is by another leader, Daniel J. Haley, president of Finnaren & Haley, Inc., a Conshohocken, Pennsylvania paint manufacturer. Over the years of growing up in this Philadelphia suburb, Haley observed that if his employees would show up for work, they were well over half way and as much as 75 percent on their way to a successful job. Haley's daughter, Regie, clarified that, "not so much in our business, but we've seen in so many other businesses that people just don't even show up. . .for whatever reason or excuse. Hence, what my father means by this quote is that so many people don't show up in life itself, whether it's about a job, hobby, sport, and most important about their dream."

In short, this succinctly summarizes Karl's leadership style. From his initial power of example to the ultimate reproduction of Karl's leadership style in the lives of future leaders, this is what makes Karl tick. Let us picture in our mind's eye F. Karl Schauffele "showing up" for something, for instance, work. What does that take? First it takes Karl getting up at 4:30 a.m. After his preparatory priorities at home, Karl is at his Chamber office by 7 a.m. Since no one meets with him at this hour, why is Karl there so early? Well, by traveling so early he misses the congested traffic. More importantly he has the psychological edge ;

"The early bird gets the worm." He also has time for further preparation for his next meeting. To do this, he reads four newspapers regularly, two books a week and does weekly research in the library from which he reviews his copious and appropriate notes for related meetings. And, he has time to line up work for the rest of the staff and volunteers. Karl is the first to admit it is no secret that a relaxed, comfortable working environment requires planning. Planning requires time. Since a typical day is full of interruptions and the "urgent," Karl shows up before all this to guarantee the "urgent" will not interrupt that day's priorities. When "Mr./Ms. Urgent/Demanding" shows up, Karl says he empathizes with them and makes necessary notes on his "next-to-do list," and tells them this: "I am not comfortable about jumping into that at this moment, but I assure you we will attend to it ASAP." He once told Helen Cooper, staff writer for the Suburban, "The person who holds this job can not be married because of its 24-hour demands." She said, "He lived The Main Line Chamber of Commerce; he was its catalyst and genial problem-solver."

Now to further break down the principle of demonstration, let's consider the awesome, taken-for-granted reality of body language, for one's mere presence implies a vested interest. The individual who shows up knows that talk is cheap. He knows that others value his presence, which indicates support to others whether he says a word or not; furthermore, he knows that the purpose of showing up is for work, not for words alone.

A real leader is the first to dive in and take on a task. He knows what must be done and he just does it with a matter-of-fact approach. He does not complain about the task at hand or about those working with him. By demonstrating that he values each and every facet of a project, he is willing to take on the lowliest of tasks, while his team learns by his example and no preaching is necessary on his part. He knows that actions speak much louder than words.

How does a leader of leaders who exercises the power of example so well, know when to delegate to others? The example of the Lord Jesus Christ comes to mind. He said to his disciples, "Follow me and I will make you fishers of men." Have you ever thought about what happened after this? Jesus did it all. Whether the task was preaching, teaching, counseling, healing, traveling, or working miracles, Jesus did it all as his disciples watched and learned by observing his example. Although initially they did not always fully understand, these very examples were the greatest lessons they ever received from the Master.

During this era, classes always seemed to be in session, even in the most informal of settings. The Master's leadership was demonstrated at the lowest level of society—in the streets where He served the ordinary people of his time. In my opinion, His power of example as a public servant elevated Him to great heights. By simply living and doing, He demonstrated to all who were able to understand that he who is greatest among them shall be servant of all.

On the contrary, a "wannabe" leader is likely to rule like a dictator, demanding total obedience from his team. In addition, he is likely to be controlling and manipulative and thus creates distrust amongst the team members, rather than instilling faith and trust. This disillusioned individual wants to be a leader because he desires power and self-gratification. He is the kind of person who wants everyone to lick his boots to fuel his own ego. The bottom line is that he truly cares about nothing but himself. He shouts loudly, demands much and gives little. He is nothing more than a glory seeker and we have all seen him in action at one time or another. He is a poor substitute for a leader. Worst of all, he fails to understand how he is undermining himself and a project when the team feels demoralized.

In contradiction to this scenario, don't we all produce our best work when we are in a safe, comfortable, supportive environment? The leader of leaders innately knows how to create such an atmosphere and he realizes that doing so is critical to the outcome of any project. Happy and content team members gladly contribute and are even willing to go the extra mile, while those who are frightened, worried or overburdened become resentful. Yet, at the same, this leader of leaders knows how to encourage individuals to step out of their comfort zone to take on new assignments or venture into unknown areas.

A true leader demonstrates his ability to organize and prioritize to all around him. He finetunes and hones these abilities until they become second nature. He knows everyone is counting on his ability to lead the others on a smooth path, and is therefore wise enough to expect and plan in advance for the inevitable bumps along the way. He leaves nothing to chance and plans for every possible event, twist or turn in the path. In his wisdom, he knows that he can handle any situation that might arise because he is alert and well-prepared.

He approaches things straightforwardly, knowing instinctively how to establish the order of things. He has no hidden agenda nor intent. A leader of leaders cares about each member of his team as an individual; he cares about the outcome of any project and strives for superiority. He actively participates in working toward any goal, never thinking himself too important or grand to take an active role. He demonstrates the principles of honesty and integrity as he exhibits the old fashioned work ethic to everyone, yet he considers himself to be above no one.

Above all, a leader of leaders demonstrates strength of character. His word is as good as gold and he always delivers on time. He does not turn away from adversity, problems or even that which is seemingly impossible. Yet at the same time he maintains a balance and is not easily distracted from his vision of the end result. He is more than a visionary who sees only the end result, for the leader of leaders knows how to get from point A to that elusive point B. He knows what steps to take and what precautions must be considered to ultimately achieve results.

In spite of personal problems, the real leader stays on track, further demonstrating his strength of character. Nothing and no one gets in his way, yet the wise leader rides roughshod over no one. He can be counted on to get the job done, but hurting none along the way. Regardless of what others say, a leader of leader pays no mind to those who voice their opinions about why this or that cannot be done. He is strong in his sense of self, knowing he can do even that which may appear to be the impossible to others.

A leader of leaders plays many roles as he demonstrates all aspects of leadership. He runs interference for those on his team and protects them as a father protects his brood of children. By example, he gains the respect of others and endears himself to those on his team. Deftly he enables each team member to stand on his own feet. The true leader, like a good parent, prepares those under him to come into the acknowledgment and validation of their own strengths. He binds no one to him, realizing that his strengths are within and as such, those strengths are not dependent upon the actions of any individual, nor can his strengths be diminished in any way by others. He knows that he is what he is. He knows his strengths and because he is willing to face his weaknesses, they too become his strengths.

Last but not least, the wise leader of leaders demonstrates humility. He is unassuming and totally unpretentious. He is at ease with himself, others and the world around him. He is free from pride, without arrogance, and tends to be reserved and unassuming at all times. The true leader of leaders is gracious, obliging, agreeable, tolerant, polite and respectful. These commendable character traits are the measure of a true leader of leaders.

I think Jesus' gesture of humbly washing the feet of His disciples drives home the fundamental truth that if you want to be great in God's kingdom, you must be willing to serve as a lowly servant to all. In taking on such a role, Jesus willingly played the part of a common servant of the day — that of one who sat at the entrance of a home and washed the feet of weary traveling guests as a gesture of welcome and hospitality.

This glimpse into Jesus' demonstration of leadership reminds me of a memorable experience of my own. I had the privilege some years ago of visiting a beloved friend and pastor who was residing in the northern hills of the Jamaican countryside. It was the time of a joyous occasion ; the celebration of his 50 years of pastoral ministry. I found our conversational times to be especially meaningful as he willingly shared his years of service with me. Finally I had to ask, "What is the number one secret of your 50 years of pastoral success? What has made thousands of people, even those from the lowest classes of society, love and cherish you so much?"

I will never forget his sure, yet succinct response, "He who wants to help greatly the needs of people must be willing to stoop in order to serve and to teach (lead)." To this day, when I recall his words, I think, WOW!! What a commentary on true greatness! This humble man's words still personify the pure, unadulterated traits of true leadership to me. This man communicated his true leadership qualities to the people around him in his everyday actions and deeds. He realized that words are nothing unless they are strengthened by action.

I think it is clear that effective communication boils down to about 55 percent body language, 35 percent tone of voice and 10 percent words. The power of example and other valuable life messages are always in style, for every millennium. Many things come and go in life, but the impact of the power of example never diminishes.

In light of the foregoing, it seems to me that it is time to return to the basic fundamentals of leadership training. A great deal of leadership training today takes place in the classroom, office and seminar conference rooms, but the real and lasting lessons about leadership are to be garnered by simply observing the facets of leadership in action. I recall that in his day, Vince Lombardi spearheaded a return to the basics of football, thus by staying true to his leadership role, he produced a consistent world championship team. Virtual life will never replace real life!

Have you ever observed a young mother or father watching their baby learn how to walk? Beginning with the struggle to become balanced on his feet, the child slowly, clumsily puts out one foot with hesitation, as he glances at the parents for encouragement. The parents smile, clap their hands and hold out their arms, encouraging the baby to take just one more step. Even when the baby loses his balance and collapses in a heap, they lavish words of praise upon him. They gather him into their arms and cover his chubby face with kisses, all the while telling him what a good job he has done. When he is set back down on the floor, he is eager to give it another try because he loves the attention, praise and adoration his parents so freely bestow upon him.

In much the same way, a wise leader knows that when those on his team are taking on tasks that are new and unfamiliar, one feels uncertain, and unclear about what to do, or even how to take that first step. Knowing the beginner is eager to please, the wise leader offers encouragement, helpful suggestions and support to enable the novice to keep going. When fault is to be found or errors must be pointed out, the wise leader knows how to sandwich the correction in between words of praise so as not to discourage.

A leader of leaders knows that when he creates an atmosphere of synergy and family, everyone on the team will work together for the betterment of the whole because everyone has a stake in the outcome. Thus, a good and wise leader knows how to get people to work together, while giving their best at the same time, not because they are required to do the job, but because they want to do the job to the best of their ability. This leader of leaders knows how to make people care about each other, the project and the outcome.

One can learn much from what a leader of leaders demonstrates quietly, in his day-to-day life, if one would take the time to observe what is before him. If we have the eyes to see and the ears to hear, much can be learned from the leader of leaders. A true role model demonstrates who and what he is because leadership is not worn as a cloak that shrouds or encloses him, nor is it worn as a badge of pride. The true leader lives up to his own high standards and principles every minute of every day.

Non-verbal demonstrations of leadership are powerful messages indeed, for those who wish to develop leadership attributes. One must simply take the time to observe the demonstrations of a true leader for instruction.

Let us journey back a few months to October 30, 1996, the celebration of the 75th Anniversary of the Main Line Chamber of Commerce, and capture more lasting impressions of Karl. We are at the Valley Forge Military Academy's stunning Mellon Hall, which is packed with 240 VIP's. This celebration is striking in that leaders from all over Pennsylvania's Southeastern region are here to join in the festivities. A major part of the evening's program is a videotaped presentation that shows the faces of many well-known Main Liners who have been part of making the Main Line what it is today. When the face of Karl appears on the screen, there is a significant interruption in the program as those assembled seize the chance to recognize and to honor Karl. Anyone hearing the testimonials given by delegation leaders from the five-county region, including state and national officials, could not help but be overwhelmed by this show of warmth and enthusiasm for F. Karl Schauffele.

"I first met Karl putting up barricades in 1978 for the Labor Day Celebration. He was a genuine good neighbor," offers Richard Force of the Wynnewood Valley Civic Association. "I didn't know who he was as far as his importance, because he was one of those who got his hands dirty." This reminds Force of his piano teacher who once told him, "If you want pretty flowers, you have to dig in the dirt," and he relates that to Karl. "Nothing is beneath him to get the job done. When I was president of the Association, you went to him to get things done. He just generally knows everything and everybody, knowledge which he freely shared." After a moment, Force muses, "Karl reflected a very genuine interest in the community." Sam Pilotti, owner of Metric Realty, agrees and adds, "Karl is the kind of person you can communicate with at any level. . .a very pleasing person with whom to work. He exemplified what the area really needed ; community service." When Karl first started on the Main Line Chamber of Commerce Board of Directors, Linda LeBoutillier was there. "Karl was as elegant a freshman (on the Board) as he was a senior," she remembers. LeBoutillier, co-owner of Waterloo Gardens, calls Karl "a great guy," adding, "His profound friendship is evident."

"To publish a book about Karl Schauffele as a leader or leaders is wonderful," enthusiastically rejoins Hal Real, Chairman of the Committee of the Year 2000 for the Main Line Chamber of Commerce.

We learn more from Paul G. Mattus of Economic Development for Delaware County. "During his two decades of service on behalf of the business community, Karl has provided sound counsel to enhance job creation and opportunities to flourish throughout Delaware County." Mattus lauds his "tremendous management skills" and calls Karl "always a true gentleman who provided an outstanding example for young men and women who are seeking to make their way in the world of commerce." Mattus points to Karl's "natural friendliness which always created an ambience of dignity and respect wherever he traveled going about his daily tasks on behalf of the Main Line Chamber of Commerce. His courteous and professional touch will be missed." From Delco Chamber of Commerce President Jack Holefelder we hear, "Karl was one of the few leaders in the region that I could always count on for guidance. . .always willing to be of assistance to his colleagues around the state." Karl's "words of wisdom and encouragement" helped Payson W. Burt, Executive Vice President of the Montgomery County Chamber of Commerce. He is "a mentor" to Clark Shuster, Vice President of the Lower Bucks County Chamber of Commerce. Clark added, "Karl has been really well-respected. . .always willing to share himself with others." Karen L. Martynick, Chairperson, Chester County Commissioners, says: "Southeastern Pennsylvania is often called the 'economic engine' of the state. Thanks to Karl, the Main Line has played a key role in strengthening the economy of our region and our Commonwealth.

"The work of Karl Schauffele as a public servant is regionalism at its best," says Philadelphia's Mayor Edward G. Rendell. This is echoed by Fred Sembach, Vice President of the Pennsylvania Chamber of Business and Industry. "When you think of local Chambers, Karl always comes to mind. He is an excellent example of a Chamber professional, and I mean professional. It is on legislative matters that I have the most contact with him. He is a natural in the legislature; he knows how to frame an issue, how to get the points through in a manner you always remember." Sembach summarized, "There is no better ally when you are pushing an issue; no better friend when you are having a problem; and there is not a better gentlemen when you are in the midst of political wars."

As a tried and true rule of thumb, history has reminded us over and over again that man does not learn from history. In addition to the historic accounts themselves that validate this, there are also the four "Ms" of the historical cycle. So let's review them as we prepare to relate them to our theme.

The first "M" is (generic) "Man." Whether you call it "chance," "history," "providence" or "God," the point is that some powerful force raises up a man or woman as a new leader of a cause. Usually this person is characterized by a great deal of charisma, conviction, and commitment. So phenomenal is his contagious influence that it spreads to the people around him. Before long, the "person" is now leading a "movement," and the movement accelerates in momentum. Because of the dynamics of its mission it permeates through the culture, color and creeds of the human society and spreads beyond its geographical proximity. Sooner or later other leaders and speakers of influence who want to join this "movement" and follow this "Man" analyze the specific ingredients of it all and thereby formulate "METHODS" that because of the transferable techniques, the masses can now get involved. Obviously, no two movements of the masses run their course as the same course through the corridors of history, but this we know—there comes a point that the "Man," the "Movement" and the "Methods" run their gamut. And the gravity of it all demands a "Monument." You see, somewhere along the way, the original message of the "Man" was lost. Hence, to regroup their thoughts and crystallize their perspective, the masses build a "Monument" in memory of it all.

Now, a good example of this is John Calvin, the Founder of the Presbyterian Church that is so preeminent on the Main Line in the western suburbs of Philadelphia, Pennsylvania. Obviously, whole sets of books have been written on his life and work as a "Monument" and tribute to him. Yes, and literal statues were made of him as well in Geneva, Switzerland where he established his model of commerce as well as Christianity. That's right! John Calvin was the "Father," Founder and First President of the original Chamber of Commerce. Now let us briefly glance at his movement that so impacted history. Calvin was a contemporary of Martin Luther, the Father of Reformation in the 1500s. Although Calvin in many ways agreed with Luther, especially about eternal life being on the basis of faith alone in the redeeming merits of our Lord Jesus Christ, Calvin had a distinctive way to live and work it all out. It became known as the "Calvinistic ethic." The model of his lifestyle in community and commerce became so great in Geneva, Switzerland, that its prosperity and popularity cut across denominational, cultural, political and racial lines to the point that the "Calvinistic ethic" became more broadly known as the "Protestant ethic," thus going with the flow of the overall Reformation movement throughout Europe. And as we all well know, it was just a matter of time that it evolved into the free enterprise system after it swiftly spread across the ocean to America, the "land of the free and the home of the brave." Of course, somewhere along the way, the realities of greed, avarice, and exploitation crept into the picture—so much so that today an average person on the Main Line would never know that free enterprise stemmed from John Calvin! The Swiss banks in Geneva are an ever-living memorial to him and reminder to me.

Yet, on the other hand, there is a very special person who does understand it only too well. His name is F. Karl Schauffele. For the past 15 years he has been the president of The Main Line Chamber of Commerce in Wayne, Pennsylvania. Rather than proceed to relate to you at this point the standard facts of: (1) his family background; (2) his business record; (3) his avocational pursuits, let us first prioritize our focus on Karl Schauffele's values. From a child, Karl has emulated the kind of person that you would expect from ***The City of Brotherly Love.*** This quotation is, (as many in this book are) from the Greek words:

Philos Adelphos, literally, "love for brother" or "love of brother," ergo Philadelphia is "The City of Brotherly Love."

Karl always has been the calibre of a man who "brings to the party" values like the dignity of the human being, the equality of people, the priority of integrity, the freedom of enterprise, the wisdom of thrift and the joy of giving. In a sentence, that sums up the life of F. Karl Schauffele. He is one of the best "unconscious competents" that I know. Later, we shall expound on all this, but let me now just say that even Karl needs this book on ***Leader of Leaders*** to understand consciously who and what he is unconsciously. As his author/publisher, let me tell you—you, too, are in for the experience of your life as you become conscious of the competence of Karl. But you say, "I don't know of him or about him." I say in return, "If you did, I as author/publisher wouldn't have a job!" Even to the members of the Main Line Chamber of Commerce Karl reveals as little of the essence of his competence as an iceberg reveals its tip; therefore, I'm open for business night and day.

Whether you are already a great leader, average leader, mediocre leader or a future leader, this book is for you. Of course, you will quickly discover that it is not the typical biography, self-help book or manual on leadership. In essence, it is the life message of Karl and fourteen other Leaders of Leaders, to you and me. Throughout my research process and interview appointments in 1996 and 1997, I said to Karl at least a dozen times with deep gratitude and much respect for him, "I hope that what I'm learning from you for my book by any and all means rubs off on and sticks to me!" My dear reader and friend, you will find in Karl one of the best friends you'll ever have in your whole life. "What," you say, "a friend in books?" Absolutely. I first became acquainted with this wonderful reality when I had the distinct privilege and responsibility of working for the late Dr. Donald Grey Barnhouse, Sr., as his landscape gardener and lifeguard at his gentlemen's farm in Doylestown, Pennsylvania during the summer and fall of 1959. His daughter-in-law, Kathy, married to his son, Donald, Jr., used to share with me over and over in that refreshing country atmosphere about her "many friends in books." She made them so "real" to me that I would not have been surprised if one of them walked out of the barn as we dialogued.

Therefore, there isn't the slightest doubt in my mind and heart, my friend, that you will experience that with Karl for three reasons: (1) because of Kathy Barnhouse's lasting influence; (2) because of my own cultivation of friendships in books for the past 38 years (Remember: ***"practice makes perfect"***); (3) because Karl is such a good friend that the pages of this book could not prevent his friendship with you, if he were virtually the first friend anyone found in a book!!! If you are still skeptical after all this, you will see. Sooner or later you will unfold your arms and hold onto ***Leader of Leaders*** for dear life, because it really is. If it isn't, nothing is.

By the way, with reference to Karl's favorite quotation, have you asked yourself why I quoted the daughter of Daniel J. Haley? It is because of a very practical reason—she was readily available when I needed the meaning behind the quotation, since she was capably running the business while her father was traveling. That makes quite a statement all of its own. Secondly, her explanation carries with it all the more impact because she represents the next generation of her dad's business. To realize that she has such a profound belief in such a statement of reality that is just as good as, if not greater than her father's beliefs, is to appreciate leadership at its finest. After all ***"success without successors is failure"***.

Throughout life we witness and share a variety of celebrations ; weddings, anniversaries, graduations and more. Yet, in the midst of all these celebrations, few of us celebrate life. We think only to celebrate events that happen because we are passing through various stages of life. Instead, I propose to you that every day should be a celebration of life—from the time we awake in the morning until we retire for the evening. Unfortunately, while we tend to daily responsibilities, we often forget to enjoy the life we are living; we don't recognize life as a celebration. For those who do, however, this celebration can become a principle of leadership—because of its power of example.

You see, above and beyond the conscious reasons for Karl's favorite quotation are the unconscious ones. Before we go into a detailed analysis of Karl in light of all this, let us first of all crystallize our thinking about the power of example in each and every one of us. By this I mean that when it comes to the example that we portray in life whether good or bad, there are four levels of consciousness:

Unconscious Incompetence: This is that unfortunate reality in which the person is not aware of how bad he/she is. Very sad!

Conscious Incompetence: This is a more hopeful condition because at least now he/she is aware of how bad it is, and perhaps will want to improve the situation — that is, knowing and understanding the problem is over 50 percent of the solution. Very encouraging!

Conscious Competence: This is what some people, at least initially, would deem as the ultimate, because he/she is good or competent at what he/she is and does, and is also aware or conscious of why and/or how. Very good! But we are not there yet.

Unconscious Competence: This is it! This is the lifestyle and leadership style in which we all really want to be. Why? Because it is so competent that it is learned behavior to the point of habit. Think of it. Wouldn't you love to live around the home, community and church/synagogue so beautifully and yet so habitually that you could pull it all off without even thinking about it? Wouldn't you love to succeed at business or at leadership in whatever venture as easily as you drive your car? Now you have the picture or better yet the vision. Unconscious competence. Daniel Haley is there. His daughter, Regie, is also there. Fortunately for us, we can utilize the lifemessage (Biography) of F. Karl Schauffele for the wonderful mission and purpose of us all getting there. After all, do not forget, "75 percent of the matter is just showing up." The very fact that you are readers of this book proves that you are 75 percent there too!

Indubitably, the power of example is working for and/or against us all the time as it does for Karl. The only difference is that Karl has paid the price to work through the grids of these four levels of competence throughout his 69 years of life thus far and most of us have not. It is not that we did not have to or rebelled against it. We just did not understand. So when others would point out faults of ours that they could see but that we could not see, we instinctively did what the rest of creation does ; defend ourselves. Yet somehow, some way along life's path since January 3, 1928, when he was born, Karl discovered a better way that also became instinctive (unconscious), but very positively powerful, and put him on the offensive instead of defensive.

We see in Karl the image of a person who rises above the mudhole of mediocrity, but who also steers clear of the deadend street of perfectionism. Karl says: "I have always been a public servant." But there was a day that this vision of himself was, first of all, an idea in his mind. That idea grew into a "conscious" reality. The first anyone else noticed was in the power of example in Karl. This is awesome and encouraging for each and every one of us. This encourages us to shed some of our pessimism and our defensiveness. Let us catch that vision of ourselves in the power of Karl's example. Let us get a life. . .get an education. . . get a trade. . .get a vocation and while we are at it let us get an avocation too.

It is good to know that Karl believes he has been a public servant for all of his life. That is the reason why this book exists. At least three times Karl turned me down about my writing this biography about him.

His stated reason was "I really feel uncomfortable about publicity." I could not have approached him at a worse time. He was going through his intense transition of retiring from 15 years as president of The Main Line Chamber of Commerce in the western suburbs of Philadelphia, Pennsylvania. Consequently, because of his phenomenal track record, he was virtually barraged by publicity in all the local newspapers and three times in the full-color *Main Line Today* Magazine. For weeks he appeared in full-color on the front page of *Main Line Times, Suburban Wayne Times, Main Line Life, 202 Corridor,* and the *Philadelphia Inquirer.* Never in the history of Philadelphia metropolitan area, or for that matter in the entire state of Pennsylvania has a president of a chamber of commerce or anyone else ever received even half the recognition.

On top of all this, Karl was honored at the 75th Anniversary of The Main Line Chamber of Commerce on Tuesday evening, October 30, 1996, at the world famous Valley Forge Military Academy in Wayne, Pennsylvania. In the successive weeks that followed, he found himself embarrassed because of the love, respect and special VIP programs at which Karl was "roasted" in more ways than one. Just to cite one example, one of the finest educators of the greater Valley Forge/Main Line/Philadelphia area, but also our nation, Dr. John DeFlaminis, Superintendent of the Radnor School District, had such a devotion for Karl that he actually spent the time and effort to write a poem about Karl and read it publicly at the People's Light & Theatre Company for a VIP gathering on Tuesday evening, February 4, 1996. Since this is the affair from which yours truly was exempted, I am grateful that Karl himself was kind enough to share a copy of that poem for all of us to enjoy.

By now you can probably identify with Karl that all this recognition was almost too much. It is a good thing that my mother taught me, "Don't start a job unless you can finish it," because I would have given up on the book at this point. Karl proceeded to decline my offer for another good reason — because he was super focused on securing the new president of The Main Line Chamber of Commerce that was so dear to him. After all, what could be more important than his replacement? For Karl, this involved not only an intensive and extensive interview process, but also a prodigious transition.

However miraculous as it seemed, the one single thought that got Karl's attention and which led to Karl's decision to let me do his biography was "Success without successors is failure." This is a quotation from Robert Schuller, Founding Pastor of the world renowned Crystal Cathedral in Garden Grove, California, that I learned under his teaching in September 1970 at a seminar he led called "Successful Church Leadership Institute." It is a good one and surely came in handy. You see, I saw Karl purely and sincerely committed to this very truth: ***"Success without successors is failure,"*** in reference to his immediate successor. So I simply and instinctively related to Karl that there are many other "successors" waiting for him in leadership land. That unless he commits himself and his time and focus to my interview and research process, they will never be able to benefit from the endless resources of his leadership. Thank God, that is when Leader of Leaders was born. So, on October 30, 1996, I presented to Karl my official letter of commitment (this was serendipitously the same day that President William Clinton sent me his letter of encouragement and challenge to make the Valley Forge Prayer Breakfast of which I was Assistant Coordinator and the book, Leader of Leaders, an ongoing movement, not an event) to publishing and authoring this chapter on him, which would serve both as a unique biography and also manual on leadership. This is why I refer to the book as an **"Inspirational Commentary"**. Because of the wonderful environment of teamwork that Karl had cultivated over 15 years in The Main Line Chamber of Commerce, Karl was assured that I would interface by interview and research process, not only with the business sector but also educational sector. For instance, Dr. John DeFlaminis, Superintendent of one of the finest school districts in our nation, and Dr. David Hornbeck, Superintendent of the Philadelphia School District, will have significant input into the development of this book, so that it will be a required textbook on leadership in the classroom as well has have a popular appeal to the business leader in the marketplace.

Why stop there? Since this book was born in the midst of my promotion for the Valley Forge Leadership Prayer Breakfast, this book should also be appealing to the entire 12 core sectors of leadership that I targeted for the prayer breakfast. Mr. John W. Boyer, Jr. former Chairman/CEO of the Philadelphia Suburban Water Company in Byrn Mawr, Pennsylvania, was coordinator of the Valley Forge Leadership Prayer Breakfast for its third annual happening. Although it successfully had 300 attendance in 1994, and 400 attendance in 1995, John was not satisfied, because more than 95 percent of the attendees were active church members of the community. And the vision of the Citizen's Committee of the Valley Forge Leadership Prayer Breakfast was to include the secular leaders of the community.

Therefore, I was appointed to the task of securing such leaders. It took almost a quarter of the year of 1996, but it happened. I felt my way to the other 11 sectors of leaders that were involved in National Family Week, 1984 when President Ronald Reagan appointed me as Executive Chairman to organize a celebration at Valley Forge, the birthplace of the nation. Hence, as President Ronald Reagan made his proclamation for National Family Week at Valley Forge in 1984, so President William Clinton made his proclamation for Valley Forge Leadership Prayer Breakfast in 1996. With that sense of national priority, I approached the educational, business, political, patriotic, medical, legal, civic, organizational, club, vocational and recreational leaders of the greater Valley Forge/Main Line Area. It was absolutely thrilling to see leaders from every last one of these sectors commit to attend. As the word of mouth continued to spread, we wound up having official endorsements and proclamations from every level of politics: from the Township Manager and Chairman of the Board of Supervisors of Upper Merion Township (in which the Valley Forge Leadership Prayer Breakfast was held ; at the Atrium of the Holiday Inn, King of Prussia); from the Chairman of Montgomery County and the Chairperson of Chester County, which both border Valley Forge National Park; from our Pennsylvania State Senator; representing the Main Line; from the Mayor of Philadelphia, Pennsylvania; from Senate Chaplain Lloyd Ogilvie; from several other U.S. Senators; and Vice President Al Gore and from the President and the First Lady.

The result—an overflowing house! The 75 tables of eight chairs each were "revised" to 75 tables with 10 chairs each. As the crowd kept on coming in at 7 a.m. on October 13, 1996, they *again* "rearranged" the seating to 12 chairs per table! The coziness I did not mind. In fact it was exciting! But I had to whisper a prayer of confession for violating the fire code!!! After all was said and done, not every seat was taken of the 900 "creatively" available. That is why when Coordinator John W. Boyer, Jr. greeted everyone, he said that we had a few empty seats here and there, as the audience chuckled. But all this to say that this wonderful attendance of almost 500 secular leaders plus the 400 religious leaders is not the only result. The result is better leadership throughout our nation in every sector. Yes, because the prayers for God's guidance of our nation, blessings on our nation and for the present and future leaders of our nation. . .***GREATER LEADERSHIP SHALL BE!!!***

Just as surely as George Washington is the Father of our nation, Valley Forge gave birth to our nation because the birthpangs of the Revolutionary War were first experienced there, so we dedicate his immortal prayer at the birth and beginnings of this book:

"I now make it my earnest prayer, that God would have the United States in His Holy protection;
that He would incline the hearts of the citizens to cultivate a spirit
of subordination and obedience to government;
to entertain a brotherly affection and love for one another;
for their fellow citizens of the United States at large, and
particularly for their brethren who have served in the field; and finally,
that He would most graciously be pleased to dispose us all
to do justice, to love mercy, and to demean ourselves with that
charity, humility and pacific temper of mind,
which were the characteristics of the Divine Author of our blessed religion,
and without an humble imitation of whose example in these things,
we can never hope to be a happy nation."

And following the power of example of our first President, the visionary leaders of the third annual Valley Forge Leadership Prayer Breakfast, sponsored by The Main Line Christian Ministries, Inc. "Go with the Flow," from Washington to Valley Forge to the Main Line and from the Main Line to the nation. WOW!! Is there some destiny to all this?

You say, "Why say all this? How does this all relate to Karl and The Main Line Chamber of Commerce?" Very simply: this caught Karl's attention! Although he himself is not a regular church goer (But he is a long-standing member in the Episcopalian Church — Holy Apostle PE Church), he was still quite impressed with the groundswell of the Main Line to the Valley Forge Leadership Prayer Breakfast; for he himself hosted an inspirational breakfast at Valley Forge Military Academy annually. Only he said that their average attendance was in the 200's and ours was quadruple, so he naturally became interested. One thing led to another, and the relationship between us that started back in the early 1970's really seasoned and matured. Of course, this only explains "where we are coming from." The bigger related and relevant reason for all this is where it is all "headed to" i.e., you can be sure we shall retrace this super track record and revisit all these spheres of influence when we premier this book all the way from the Main Line to the Capital of the nation! That is how it relates! It is our pathway to this book as a national "best seller."

It is because of this unique relationship of a quarter of a century that we can look into the next century, and for that matter the next millennium, and visualize what will be. Believe it or not, I wrote the initial draft of the epilogue to this book before this section. You might think this is presumptuous. Not really, for we should all know where we are going before we get going. Do we drive a car before having a destination, even if it is only the local store? Do we build a skyscraper before we know the end from its beginning? It is best to target our market instead of approach it in a "shotgun" method? Therefore, should I not know where this book is headed before I write it?

This conveniently brings us to our next step in the logical progression of Karl's thinking. So our next consideration is why is this Karl's favorite quotation? In short, it is because it succinctly summarizes Karl's leadership style. From his initial power of example to the ultimate reproduction of Karl's leadership style in the lives of future leaders, this is what makes Karl tick. Yes, it is another way of saying Robert Schuller's words: "Success without successors is failure." Hence, we shall break this all down and analyze it by way of overview now, and then in the successive, unfolding insights by going into more detail.

What a stress reliever — not just for Karl but for his team! What a safeguard also for the successful completion of the plan already in progress when the interruption came. Preparation. Prioritization. What else does "showing up" mean to Karl? Projection—Karl understands what real communication is. The experts tell us often that communication is 55 percent body language, 35 to 40 percent tone of voice, and 6 to 10 percent words. No wonder "talk is cheap!" Unfortunately, most of us live and act as though it were the reverse. But not Karl! As unconscious a competent he is, it is not in this. Karl is well aware of the value of just "showing up" and being there. That is why there is a sign of relief when Karl walks into a Board of Directors meeting and takes his chair. Because someone else quite capable is the chairman of the meeting and because there are a good number of directors quite competent as well, Karl may go a long time without saying a word. But, do not think for a moment that he is not communicating during the entire time of that board meeting. Do not forget, communication is 55 percent body language. So by a certain expression of his face, Karl greatly communicates. By the shifting of his body posture to a certain position, Karl makes a statement. Likewise, tone of voice is 35 to 40 percent communication. With his baritone resonance, can he ever make a "MMMM" sound just as he wanted! Matt Di Domenico, Sr. described him this way: "He is the facilitator, the one who gets us together to figure out ways to enhance business along the Main Line corridor. He had the foresight to recognize the need and then try to do something about it. It takes initiative, but in a low-key fashion. People have respect for his ability and knowledge. He does not come at you with both barrels—he is much more persuasive and persistent. By his actions, he gets the appropriate reaction out of you."

However, let us not conclude that all of this 90 percent plus of communication is to send a message. Karl naturally and sincerely does this also to receive a message. And is Karl ever good at doing that! To be sure, even at the age of 69, Karl continues to be a good learner. What an example! When I interviewed him about his five *pro bono* years from 1976-1981 and asked him, "What did you enjoy the most as your number one passion (What you really loved to do)?" He answered, "It was all the wonderful things I learned." What? Here he is, retired for the first time after 25 years serving Lower Merion Township, and he says the greatest thing he experienced is learning? That is Karl, but maybe that is why he has so much to share with us—from the power of example in learning.

Clearly, if we are talking, we are not learning. Sometimes even when we are listening, we are not learning. "To listen well is to listen with comprehension," says Bishop Milton Grannum, Founding Pastor of New Covenant Church of Philadelphia. Let us admit, a lot of us may sit quietly while the other person is talking, but that does not mean we are listening. We could be thinking what we are going to say next. Some of us think so much when the other person is talking that we are not even aware that we have interrupted the other person in the middle of a sentence, because without realizing it we evolved from "thinking in silence" to "thinking aloud!" (That's right— "Unconscious Incompetence.") Hence, when the other person criticizes us for being discourteous or rude, we become upset, not caring that we already upset the other person by our rude interruption.

No, Karl would not refer to this as good communication. That is why "just showing up" to Karl means good manners in dress and disposition along with courtesy of personality is all a part of it. Karl is one of the finest gentleman I have ever met. He has an unusual blend of the traditional and the contemporary. That is why the more stately ladies of the Main Line and the modern feminists feel comfortable around Karl. In fact, one of them was a member of his Board of Directors in 1996. Pennsylvania Representative Lita Indzel Cohen reflects on her first meeting with Karl: "In 1973, I met Karl when I was appointed to the planning commission—the first woman appointed to any such commission. He has the quality, especially with new people, that he never makes you feel dumb even though you may be asking what some would consider a stupid question."

It is not easy for any person to "have his/her act together" on a consistent basis. Karl does because he believes that you do not show up without fine-tuning. So another reason why he "shows up" early, long before the mutually scheduled appointment is to do "fine-tuning." This is another way of saying "always be prepared," as the Boy Scouts taught us. It is interesting that the spouse of my typist is the head mechanic of a fine golf club, located in Lower Merion where Karl was the head of the planning commission in his later part of the 25 years in Lower Merion. His head mechanic absolutely plans for a two-week, fourteen hour-per-day period of time of fine tuning all equipment *after* all equipment is already reassembled and before opening day so it can cut the grass evenly on the greens one sixteenth of an inch high. Just as fine-tuned equipment is the norm for this golf course, finetuned leadership is what Karl shows up with at his appointments. Logically then, one could understand why Karl is at least 75 percent of the way, for most people do not require of themselves such finetuning. So, make a note here that this will definitely give you an edge if you do.

Probably, Karl's discipline in "finetuning" stems back to his conviction that everyone should have a trade. For him it was draftsman, a fine trade that he learned at Murrell Dobbins Vocational School System. What is interesting about his vocational development is that he progressed into his work experience with Piasecki Helicopter as a draftsman in 1945. To be sure, he is quite proud of his accomplishment just in being a "part of the programs", Karl says of that character building experience.

Now observe the smooth progression of his career. He spent the next year of 1946 at the American Chemical Paint Company employed as draftsman/surveyor. Then from 1947 to 1950 he worked at Keasby and Mattison as draftsman/estimator. In 1951, he began his 25-year stint with Lower Merion Township as cartographer (draftsman of maps). He also moonlighted as a cartographer with Franklin Survey Company for twenty years from 1950 to 1978. At this point, it would do the reader well to review the Schauffele Schematic:

1945 ; Draftsman
1946 ; Draftsman/Surveyor
1947-1950 ; Draftsman/Estimator
1951-1978 ; Cartographer (Draftsman of Maps)

Of course, the power of example speaks for itself. Karl who was unquestionably destined to be not only a great leader, but also a leader of leaders, spent 30 years of his life as a performer, as a producer, as a follower in a trade as draftsman. It is no wonder that he says, "Everyone should have a trade!" It would do us well here to make a popular play on words with the familiar advice of parents for their child: "You should have a trade to fall back on." That is one way to look at it. Yes, it does give one an option, an alternative. If one is not careful, it also could hold one back from progressing forward to the next dimension. Such an attitude tends to prevent what could have been a phenomenal future to an advanced pursuit of vocational progression.

Without a doubt, this is exactly what Karl experienced. His trade as a drafter practically became the foundation of his ultimate calling as a public servant. That is why Karl can honestly say (although his official beginning as a leader was not until 1963, when he was appointed to Director of Planning for the Township of Lower Merion Planning Commission): "I have always been a public servant." It is so simple, yet so profound. It is absolutely awesome! The power of example energized Karl from follower to leader, from leader to leaders, from draftsman on paper to draftsman of commerce and legislation. Karl reminds us of that age old Proverb of Solomon, the wisest man in the world of the Old Testament: "A man's gift makes room for him and stands him before kings." What that says in our modern day colloquialism is that "A person's talent will elevate him/her to high spheres of leadership, if that person masters it."

To put it another way, the German language has two words for talent or gift: (1) *gabe;* (2) *aufgabe.* The first, *gabe,* refers to talent or gift itself; whereas the second, *aufgabe,* means "A talent or gift 'worked out.'" It is cultivated talent. It is well-practiced talent. It is finetuned talent. One could almost say that Karl's career as a public servant was "played out" or "worked out" like a symphony.

We could raise the question as to when did Karl first come to the realization that he was a leader? Frankly, I personally and professionally do not believe that Karl himself knows the answer to that question. At best, he might guess at it, but he is too sincere and too full of integrity to be dogmatic. In fact the genuine reality of all this is that he was unconsciously competent as a leader before he was consciously competent as a leader. Hence, how does one measure that? Does it really matter?

What does matter is that Karl was content with his competence whether unconscious or conscious. Karl was not one to "force it" or "make it happen." He would be content to "plan the work" until it was time to "work the plan," and then ultimately lead others to do likewise! That is why his gentle cautions to me even recently in the form of the words "don't force it" means so much to me. Unquestionably, Karl's power of example is permeated with a generous, lavish giving to others of all the time and space they need. The fundamental reason why Karl does not need to resort to high pressure tactics and manipulative measures to "get ahead" is because he is content to let the power of his good example pave his way. Even if it means pausing for a while or even experiencing a setback, that is OK, because Karl's foundational background and experience as a draftsman equips him with a greater perspective of the overall design and/or master plan that requires a specific timing that a driven professional would not anticipate or appreciate.

We all have heard of the expression "Prosperity is being at the right place at the right time." All right, now relate that to two other factors: (1) Karl's favorite quotation: "Showing up is seventy-five percent of a matter," (2) Karl's power of example. Now what do we have? All in all, we see that showing up at a location is 75 percent of the matter and the other 25 percent is doing what Karl does when he gets there, "he blooms where he's planted" until the sufficient time of seasoning runs its course from unconscious competence (success, prosperity) to conscious competence, success and/or prosperity. We would do well to clarify a very vital insight ; namely, that even the timing cannot be accurately defined for our success either, for we too would have to admit honestly that it happened before we were conscious that it happened. But as to how soon before we do not know and are not supposed to know.

This is a good antidote for us in an age of our high-pressured, stress-induced and materialistically motivated business world. The status symbols of ego, power and money disillusion many good people into the reality of a nightmare instead of the fulfillment of their dream. Clearly, the genuine reward for our hard work is not always found in these supposed symbols. Karl is living proof that the greatest reward is in one's satisfaction of a job well done. That we have served others well is a wonderful reward. So real is this and was this to Karl as far back as the Bicentennial Year, 1976, when he retired for the first time, that he committed himself to continue working as a public servant, but only on a *pro bono* basis.

We also see how the vision of Karl's leadership style was magnified not only by the power of his example but also by his sense of mission. You see it is his overall vision of himself as a real public servant that frees him up to make his statement of mission to the ones he serves. Ed Rendell, the Mayor of the city of Philadelphia said, "The work of Karl

Schauffele as a public servant is regionalism at its best." Because he has the best interests of those he serves in his heart, they allow him to experience his passion: doing what he really loves to do — being a public servant. Because this pursuit has endless potential, the next dimension of inclusion happens. Others gravitate to his leadership as flecks of steel to a magnet. Then something almost miraculous falls into place; precision; people working together, doing their best to produce a quality product or service. Then again, another almost supernatural reality; multiplication because of the force of synergism wherein one + nine equals 20 or 30! Then we arrive at the zenith of leadership ; reproduction, by which Karl translates his realities into the lives of others, thus realizing Karl, ***Leader of Leaders.***

Speaking of your freedom of voice, now let us focus it on the type of other leaders you follow. . .and, may I add, the type of fellow leaders with which you want to associate. What shall be your criteria of selection? "By What Standard," as Rushdooney so powerfully asked, "do you live and lead?"

There is quite a classic story about one of the most heroic leaders of all times in the nation of Israel. And it is about a leader who is not too well known like Abraham, Isaac, and Jacob. In fact I firmly believe that this lesser known leader of leaders had even greater leadership style than those who were more well known. This reminds me of a check and balance statement that one of my lawyers, Saul Solomon, Esq. made. Saul posed this question to me: "Are you sure F. Karl Schauffele is the well renowned leader you think he is? I too was raised on the Main Line, but I never heard of him." Good question!

And my answer is twofold: (1) out of the thousands who have heard of him, there is not one who does not hold him in high esteem; (2) therefore, it is my job as author/publisher to make him known to millions more as *Karl, Leader of Leaders.* After all, if too many knew him, I would be out of a job! There would not be a need, or better yet, demand for me as an author and publisher. In addition, the fact that even among those who know him there is a great need to know him much better. I said it before, but since repetition is the greatest law of learning, I will say it again; even those who worked the closest to Karl as chairpersons, executive committee members and/or as the Board of Directors have frequently referred to Karl as having a "mystery" and/or "magic" to his leadership style. That is why, frankly, some serve with me on the Focal Group on this book, as their means and measures to get to know Karl better.

We could end this exposition right here, but it just seems fitting and proper to enlarge its frame of reference beyond the Reformation era and the free enterprise system to the whole gamut of the Judeo-Christian tradition. Hence, let us see how this book is solidly based on the rock bottom foundation of the *Bible*, especially Genesis "The Book of Beginnings." It reveals to us in the very first line: "In the beginning God. . ." It relates how God created man in His image and likeness. Yes, the human being is God's ultimate dream fulfilled in all creation.

Relax! We are not getting religious here. Not at all! As a matter of fact we're getting more "real", not religious. If I were to take a national survey, I am convinced that it would validate that millions of Americans have problems with religion because so much of it is not real. Our purpose is not to get into religion any more than we will politics. Both have their proper place in spite of their problems, but not in this book. However, we will draw upon the rich resources of our Judeo-Christian tradition, for we want to discover and more fully appreciate our roots of heritage.

Now that we have established this understanding and also set the tone for the book, let's focus on the image of God in the human being. There is no one or no thing in all of the rest of God's creation like it. As providence would have it, Karl's priority value; the dignity of the human being, is figuratively founded upon the awesome reality of the image of God in the human being. Unfortunately, because of God giving man and woman the freedom of choice, they (Adam and Eve) as our federal head, opted to misuse it, and as a result, catapulted the entire human race into Murphy's law: I mean the problem of evil. Since then, down through the corridors of time, we have seen the four ***"MS"*** of historic cycles as explained above and repeated here for necessary emphasis: ***(1) MAN; (2) MOVEMENT; (3) METHOD; (4) MONUMENT.***

Indubitably, and consistently without exception, every person or persons whom God raised up to help the human race (By the way, do you know what "horse sense" is? It is that above reliable intelligence not to bet on the human race!) was a man and/or woman of vision. You see, just as violating the law of gravity causes us to fall down, perhaps even fatally, so also violating the law of vision causes us to fall short of the glory of God and the dignity of man. "Where there is no vision, the people perish." (Proverbs 29:18). By the way, the word "vision" here also can be translated from the Hebrew as "Revelation" like it is in the *New International Version* of the *Bible*. It serves as a good reminder, check and balance as well as quality control to keep man in his proper place. By this I mean that vision could mean that man is the originator of vision. But in light of the precise and literal meaning of the word, that's an invalid conclusion. By the very nature of the case and also the creation, God is the author and vision of its revelatory character. Only man in his arrogance and egotism would boast and claim that something as wonderful as vision came from man himself. Furthermore, who would ever want to follow a leader like that, who was so filled with conceit?

Look where it got Adam and Eve when they followed Satan, the Serpent's presumptuous temptation to partake of the forbidden fruit. As a result of their conceited, prideful act of disobedience, they fell into that unfortunate reality that whatever could go wrong will go wrong. My only question is how did Murphy get credit for this? Is Satan's last name Murphy? By the way, while we are at it, what did they all say back there when God came by and held them accountable? When God asked Adam, he said: "It wasn't my fault, God. Ask the woman you made for me." Then, when God approached Eve, she said, "Not me, God. It was the serpent." But when God approached the serpent *he did not have a leg to stand on!*

All this and then some say that a man or woman of vision is wonderfully raised up by God to help the people to get back on track and get things going right for a change, in spite of Murphy's Law.

The last third of the book of Genesis portrays the life of Joseph, son of Jacob and descendant of Abraham, the patriarch of the Jews. What a man of vision Joseph was! Although it would be great to remember Joseph as a person of vision, the fact of the matter is that he had several at least. Unlike Karl, Joseph was much too proud about the way he communicated his vision to others, even his own brothers. So they became so envious and upset with him, they eventually "sold him out" to slavery. Because Joseph's heart was right, God overruled all this and worked it out for good. So Joseph eventually reappeared as a very responsible steward of Potiphar's house in Egypt. Once again Joseph's unwillingness to commit adultery with Potiphar's wife, who kept seducing him, cost him and he was sentenced to the dungeon. Even though he was moral, was he too "holier-than-thou" that it upset her unnecessarily? It's hard to tell.

Ah, but you say, "Some great visionaries themselves have perished with vision." Yes, but if they did, they died as martyrs for a great cause. What a way to go! After all, we all got to go sometime, someway. So why not "Blaze out into glory with a great cause!!!" For that matter, let us take a closer look at one like that.

"I have a dream!," Martin Luther King, Jr. said. Remember those imperishable and immortal words, echoing through our century? Yes, his vision cost him his life, but wasn't it worth it? That one vision brought into being civil rights in action, properly so called. Oh what dignity, equality, opportunity and prosperity this has generated for the minority groups of our nation! Yes, it was worth it. The Lord Jesus Christ said, "No greater love has a man than this that he lay down his life for his friends." To be sure, Martin Luther King, Jr. did just that. On top of it, he is better off in heaven where he is now. So don't feel sorry for him. You and I are still in this world, dominated by Murphy's Law. Don't feel sorry for yourself either. Misery loves company, but that is only because misery doesn't get company, for no one likes the company of misery. So if you are going to have a "pity party," you are going to do it solo.

Wouldn't you really rather have the challenges that accompany a wonderful vision? Aren't you glad that Karl is here and now for you? Since he is all the more a public servant through this chapter, take full advantage of him, especially before he gets too busy, standing before kings and presidents. It's just a matter of time. Karl's vision of regional accomplishments, with his former premier organization of 53 Chambers of Commerce into the Southeastern Pennsylvania Region Executives has already brought him before the state Capital and the nation's Capital with a lot of clout. He also got the distinct notice of the United States Chamber of Commerce about it.

Presently, I am involved with the White House to give the "top gun" Leader of our nation first choice concerning the premier of the book *Leader of Leaders,* especially as you see how the book so providentially and naturally relates to the President's Summit for America's Future with General Colin Powell as Chairman of the Board. (See Chapter XV - Conclusion: The Power of Commitment). And, in the proper priority, we will revisit the Governor, Senators and Congressmen of our Commonwealth of Pennsylvania. Certainly, we will maximize our already well established rapport with the Mayor of Philadelphia, as well as the chairpersons of Montgomery, Chester, Delaware, Bucks, Berks and Lancaster Counties for openers. Of course, on the way to all this, we will saturate Leader of Leaders from one end of the Main Line to the other.

Sooner or later we will reproduce this model of target marketing to the rest of the mid-atlantic states, eastern seaboard states, western seaboard states and from both ends to the middle of the nation. Then we will springboard to Europe, Asia, Africa and finish up in South America. Therefore, the sooner you get to Karl the better, that's if it is meaningful for you to have a personal audience with him.

You probably think I'm kidding, don't you? Well, that's only because you haven't experienced as of yet all of Karl's personal touch. Believe it or not, as long as he is able, he will be a mentor to you as Thomas Edison was to him. That's why he still, at age 69, gets all turned on at Thomas Edison's challenge to his students: "Stand on my shoulders and go higher!" Those phenomenal words should inspire any leader and future leader. Future leaders? Some say the leaders are born not made. I don't believe that for a moment. What is born is not the leader, it is the vision. Now what the individual does with his/her vision determines whether he/she is a leader. You see, the Latin original for leader is "one who guides out of." There simply is no way for a leader to lead "out of" without the vision of "where to go." So the vision is born and the leader is made by acting on that vision. Hence, go for it with all the gusto you can muster.

You still hesitate and wonder—is leadership for me.? Then see yourself as Karl sees those around him. Karl sees people as they are in the fulfillment of their potential. So Karl tends to use the projects they are working on to build people rather than use people as tools to build projects. What is incredibly amazing about this observation about Karl is that he virtually is the antithesis of the professional whom he admires most ; Frank Lloyd Wright, the greatest architect of our century. Just last week I returned to Karl the five best books on Frank Lloyd Wright, which I, too, devoured during the month of January 1997. Oh the grandeur of his construction! To be sure, the one that consternated me the most was Beth Shalom Synagogue in Elkins Park, Pennsylvania — only five minutes from my hometown of Ardsley, Pennsylvania. He and his "assistant architect," the Senior Rabbi, envisioned the sanctuary to be constructed so that too appeared and felt like the congregation was in the "hands of God." From the sky looking down on this superb structure of art, you would have a bird's eye view of the star of David. WOW!!!

We could go on and on with one glorious illustration after another, but our purpose is to introduce *Leader of Leaders.* Therefore, let it suffice to say that one even greater than Frank Lloyd Wright is here. Yes, you finally got it ; *Karl, Leader of Leaders!!!* And why not? You tell me who or what is greater; the one who uses people to build projects or the one who uses projects to build people? There you have it. Now, having relished this "celebration" in the power of Karl's example, let's go on!!! Projects?. . .People?. . .Public Service? Does all of this sound familiar? Yes! It reminds us of the celebration here in the city of Philadelphia not even a month before Memorial Day, May 26, 1997. Yes! People by the thousands and tens-of-thousands celebrated public service voluntarily or volunteer service publicly by working at all kinds of projects to revitalize the "City of Brotherly Love" both materially and spiritually. Perhaps it was new to some, but not to others. Then there are those leaders of leaders who have been "forerunners" of public/volunteer service (like John the Baptist was a forerunner of Christ) for over a half a century, who would rather do volunteer service than eat or sleep.

Well, all I can say is that I personally have planned another celebration in Karl Schauffele's honor but on a regional basis, not just a Main Line basis, of which he has already enjoyed more than enough. In one interview, Karl related to me that the largest audience he ever spoke before was a group of 1,000 at the Church of the Savior in Wayne, Pennsylvania. Well, you can be sure that the audience waiting for him at Freedom's Foundation at Valley Forge will be much greater than that. Because it is meant to be a regional celebration in light of his decades of efforts to synergize the city and the suburbs, thousands of leaders from 22 distinct leadership sectors of Southeastern Pennsylvania shall come together in celebration. Our master of ceremonies shall be F. Karl Schauffele because he is the leader of leaders who inspired this book. One of our distinguished keynote speakers is Bob Richards, two-time Olympian winner of pole vaulting and #3 inspirational speaker in the nation. Because Karl's generosity all his life has been noted by his charitable contribution, then shall be the F. Karl Schauffele Student Scholarship Fund, from which tens of thousands of dollars shall be given in his honor that evening to encourage future leaders of America.

For more detail, you can refer to the Acknowledgements section at the beginning of this book. Suffice it for now to say that you have it! Now having relished all this celebration in the power of Karl's example, let me close for now by sharing with you one of my most favorite plaques that reminds me of Karl:

That Man Is A Success
who has lived well,
laughed often and loved much;
who has gained the respect of intelligent men
and the love of children:
who leaves the world better than he found it,
whether by an improved poppy,
a perfect poem or a rescued soul;
who never lacked appreciation of earth's beauty
or failed to express it;
who looked for the best in others
and gave the best he had.

Just the other night on ABC-TV there was a movie about two lawyers. The younger one said to the older one, "you have fought many, many battles in court over your career and won the great majority of them." The older retired lawyer said, "Yes, but I've done some good too, haven't I?" Well, as for Karl Schauffele, we all unequivocally say that he has done much good.

A BIOGRAPHICAL SKETCH OF F. KARL SCHAUFFELE

This is a unique resume and summary; it is unlike anything that you have ever seen. From the beginning, you can tell it has to be the fine piece of an exceptionally adept draftsman. It is also one of the finest profiles of volunteerism, beautifully exemplified by a man whose heart blazed this path long before volunteerism became fashionable.

BIRTH DATE:

January 3, 1928

Philadelphia, Pennsylvania

MARITAL STATUS

Divorced, No children

EDUCATION

Philadelphia Public School System
Murrell Dobbins Vocational School
Standard Evening High School
Drexel Institute of Technology (Planning Course)
Massachusetts Institute of Technology (Planning Course 1962)
Georgia Institute of Planners Course
Fels Institute of Local and State Government (University of Pennsylvania)
Completed In-service courses - Public Administration, 1955
Public Service Institute of Pennsylvania Planning Courses, 1955-1971
Temple University, 1976-1978
University of Delaware - Institute of Organizational Management, 1981, 1982
University of Notre Dame - Institute for Organizational Management, 1982

MILITARY

U.S. Army and U.S. Army Air Corps, March 1946-September 1947, Active Duty; 1947-1950 Reserve Duty
U.S. Air Force, August 1950 - August 1951, Active Duty

"Just a cursory glance instantly reveals that his heart and soul have always been in pro bono public service."

PROFESSIONAL & CIVIC AFFILIATIONS & OFFICES:

National Association of Housing and Redevelopment Officials (NAHRO), Delaware Valley Chapter
Member 1965 to present,
Vice President 1974 - 1977
President 1977 - 1979 Middle Atlantic Regional Council
MARC-NAHRO Board of Directors 1977-1979
American Society for Public Administration
ASPA Philadelphia Regional Chapter
Member 1951-1982, Secretary- Treasurer 1973/74, Council Member 1974-1980

Delaware Valley Regional Planning Commission
DVRPC Member - Citizens Committee on Land Use, Housing & Open Space
Vice Chairman 1978
Member - Land Use Technical Advisory Committee 1977
Member - Council of Citizens Committee 1978
Chairman - Council of Citizens Committee 1982-1982
Chairman - Citizens Advisory Committee 1982-1994
(Renamed Regional Citizens Committee)

U.S. Dept. of Treasury - Savings Bond Division
Chairman - Montgomery, Chester, Delaware counties 1988 to present
American Planning Association, Eastern Pennsylvania Chapter
APA Program Co-Chairman 1979, 1981

Philadelphia Electric Company
PECO Customer Council - Main Line Division 1982 to 1988

Delaware Valley Torch Club
Member 1967-1982
Council 1969-1982
2nd Vice President 1973-1974
1st Vice President 1974-1975
President 1975-1976
1st Vice President 1981-1982

American Cancer Society

- Board of Directors, Lower Merion Unit - 1977 to present
- Vice President, Lower Merion Unit 1979 - 1981, President 1981-1983
- Residential Campaign Chairman 1978-1980 - (Lower Merion)
- Member - Residential Campaign Committee 1980 - (Philadelphia/Montgomery County Division
- Chairman - Residential Campaign Committee 1981-1982 - (Philadelphia/Montgomery County)
- Board of Directors - (Philadelphia/Montgomery County Division) 1982-1987; 1989-1993
- Honorary Life Member - 1993 to present
- National Subcommittee on Residential - 1983-1987
- Chairman Field Services Committee - (Philadelphia Division 1983-1987)
- Chairman Legislative Committee - (Philadelphia Division 1989-1993)
- Executive Committee - (Philadelphia Division 1983-1987; 1989-1993)
- Chairman Awards Committee - 1992-1993
- Chairman Reorganization Committee - 1994-1995

Metropolitan Policy Club

- Co-Founder - 1977
- President - 1978-1981

Wynnewood Valley Civic Association

- Member - 1961 to present
- Membership Chairman - 1963-1973
- Vice President - 1976-1977
- President - 1977-1978
- Board of Directors - 1978 to present

Federation of Lower Merion Civic Association

- Delegate - 1976 to 1982
- Vice President - 1979 to 1980
- Chairman - Recreation and Parks Advisory Committee 1979-1980
- President - 1980-1982

Advisory Board - 1982 to present

In Plant Printing Management Association
Co-Founder - 1971
President - 1975-1976

United Way of Southeastern Pennsylvania
Speakers Bureau - 1975 to 1988
Section Chairman - Suburban Business District 1976
Chairman - Municipalities Campaign 1976
Board of Trustees - 1984 to 1989
Chairman - Montgomery County Campaign 1984
Member - United Way's Public Policy Cabinet 1991

Leukemia Society of America
Board of Trustees, Eastern Pennsylvania - 1988-1991
Member Advisory Board - 1991-1992

Community Health Affiliates
Board Member - 1966-1989
Vice President - 1970-1978
President - 1978-1979
Foundation Board Member - —— to 1989
Director Emeritus - 1989 to present

Southeastern Pennsylvania Home Health Care Association
Chairman - 1977-1979
Administrator - 1979-1980
Board of Directors - 1981-1983

Episcopal Diocesan Convention - Delegate 1976

Holy Apostles PE Church
Chairman Self Study Committee 1980
Chairman Capital Improvement Program Committee 1980-1988
Member - Vestry 1983-1988

Wynnewood Election District - Majority Inspector 1979 to present

American Red Cross - Southeastern Pennsylvania Chapter
Reorganization Committee - 1982
Nominating Committee - 1989 to present

Greater Valley Forge Transportation Management Association
Board Member - 1992 to present

Ardmore Rotary
Member - 1983 to present
Board of Directors - 1988 to 1993
District 7450 Vocational Service Committee - 1991 to 1995
Chairman - 1993-1995

Boy Scouts of America Valley Forge Council
Robert Morris Awards Program Committee - 1992 to present

The Lower Merion Society for Detection and Prosecution of Horse Thieves and Recovery of Stolen Horses - 1981 to present

Delaware Valley Citizens League - Board of Directors 1982

Regional Task Force on Efficient Transportation
(RIDE TO) Member - 1983-1981
Vice Chairman - 1981-1989

Hugh O'Brien Youth Foundation
Advisory Board, Eastern PA - 1987 to 1992
Member - Corporate Board of Directors - 1992-1993
Advisor to Board —— - to present

Pennsylvania Public Health Association (Region One)
Member 1978-1986
Council 1980-1986
Vice President 1984-1986

Southeastern Pennsylvania Health Systems Agency
Member Montgomery County Sub Area Council 1978-1979
Member Long Term Care Planning Committee 1980

Coalition of Advocates for the Rights of the Infirm Elderly
Member Home Care Committee 1978-1980

Strategic Planning Task Force 1992 to present - Lower Merion School District

Ardmore Business District Authority - Member 1994 to present

Radnor School District Education Foundation - 1994 to present

Pennsylvania Chamber of Commerce Executives
Member 1981 to present
Board of Directors 1983-1987, 1991-1994
Chairman - Membership 1993-1994

Southeastern PA Chamber Executives Group
Founder 1981
Member 1981-present

Montgomery County Federation of Chambers 1993-present

Community Advisory Council
Bryn Mawr/Lankenau Hospitals
Member 1995-present

Development Committee, Saunder's House - 1997

Lower Merion Township - Personnel Review Board
Member 1992-present
ElderNet
Community Advisory Council - 1994-present

OTHER MEMBERSHIPS

Philadelphia Committee on City Policy
American Society of Planning Officials

VISITING LECTURER AT:

Fels Institute of Local and State Government (University of Pennsylvania)
Villanova University
Temple University
Haverford College
Lower Merion and Haverford School Districts - High School Classes
Main Line Adult Night School
Other Professional and Civic Organizations

WORK EXPERIENCE

Piasecki Helicopter - Draftsman 1945
American Chemical Paint Company - Draftsman/Surveyor 1946
Keasby and Mattison Draftsman/Estimator 1947-1950
Franklin Survey Company Cartographer 1958-1978 (moonlighting)
Township of Lower Merion, September 1951-January 1976
    Cartographer
    Planning Aide
    Director of Planning 1963-1976
    Comprehensive planning, zoning, subdivision, land use controls, real estate records, liaison with citizen groups, capital improvement programming
    Planning Consultant 1977-1979
Southeastern Pennsylvania Home Health Care Association - Administrator 1979-1980
Main Line Chamber of Commerce, President 1981 to present

RECOGNITIONS

Main Line Chamber of Commerce
    Community Service Award 1973
    Recognition for Service to the Main Line 1976
    Recognition for 1,000 members, 1989
Tau Alpha Pi National Honor Society -Temple University, 1972
The Chapel of the Four Chaplains
    Legion of Honor - 1978
Montgomery County Planning Commission
    Citizens Advisory Committee (CITAC) Service Citation
American Cancer Society
    Volunteer Service Award. 1979
    Division Volunteer Achievement Award, 1982
    Division Distinguished Service Award, 1986
Wynnewood Valley Civic Association
    Resident of the Year, 1982
Community Health Affiliates
    Advancement of Home Care Award, 1989
Pennsylvania Chamber of Commerce Executives
    Keystone Award - 1995
Founders' Bank - Quality of Life Award - 1995
American Flag from U.S. Capitol - January 1997
County of Delaware Certificate - Official Recognition - March 1992
U.S. Department of the Treasury - Award for Patriotic Service - 1995

Pennsylvania Senate Citation - Senator Robert Thompson - June 1996
Berwyn-Devon Business & Professional Assn., - Outstanding Achievement Award - June 1996
Pennsylvania House of Representatives - Rep. Colleen A. Sheehan - July 1996
Pennsylvania Senate Citation - Senator Richard A. Tilghman - November 1996
U.S. Small Business Administration - Certificate of Appreciation - December 1996
Pennsylvania House of Representatives - Rep. Robert Flick - January 1997
Southeastern Penna. Chamber of Commerce Executives Lifetime Achievement - January 1997
Township of Haverford Proclamation - January 1997
Township of Lower Merion - For Civic Influence - January 1997
Valley Forge Military Academy & College - Retirement Recognition - January 1997
Paoli Business & Professional Assn. - January 1997
City Council, City of Philadelphia - Citation - March 1997
Wayne Lions Club - The Main Line Award - May 1997
Rotary District 7450 - Vocational Service Award - Spring 1997
Leader of Leaders Award for Volunteer Public Service - 1997

To sum up: Long before volunteerism became fashionable, especially in the Presidents' Summit for America's future, F. Karl Schauffele set the pace for us, didn't he? Therefore, let us benefit from the power of his example.

2 VISION

THE POWER OF GOALS

FEATURING

DR. DONALD H. SAUTTER
AUTHOR/PUBLISHER, LEADER OF LEADERS

"A vision without a task is a dream;
A task without a vision is drudgery;
A vision and a task is the hope of the world."

-- Anonymous

"Leading an organization to constructive change begins by setting a direction— developing a vision of the future (often the distant future) along with strategies for producing the changes needed to achieve that vision"

John P. Kotter, Ph.D., Harvard Business Review, 1990. "What Leaders Really Do"

Many self-help books, both theoretical and practical, talk about "having vision." What exactly is it? How do we get it? Can it be learned or is it something with which we are born?

Let us define and describe "vision." According to Webster's New World Dictionary:

> ***"It is the act or power of seeing; something supposedly seen by other than normal sight, as in a dream or trance; the experience of having seen something in this way; a mental image; the ability to perceive something not actually visible, as through mental acuteness; force or power of imagination."***

The ability to visualize is merely the ability to see in our minds what we want to accomplish or be. Somehow, envisioning what we want, helps us take the necessary steps to attain what we want. Visualizing organizes our abilities to bring the vision to fruition. In order to mobilize all our abilities, we must draw a clear picture in our minds of the end result of our visions.

Having vision is closely related to setting goals. Goals serve us by giving meaning to selected actions. When our actions have meaningful results, we are motivated to perform them.

For instance, if my goal is to become a musician and I know I have the talent, I would envision myself playing on the stage before a large audience. The mental image of my stage performance is a potent motivator, but no one would know why. I would then practice day and night, seek out significant contacts in the music industry to further promote myself, and learn all that I could about securing stage appearances. The closer I would come to realizing my vision, the more meaning my actions would have.

Vision works the same way for everyone. It magically reinforces our belief that we can achieve, limited only by our desires, aspirations and level of commitment.

Many people will tell you this concept is misleading: "I can't become a major league baseball player just by fantasizing about it," says Jake, the high school senior. Yes, that is true, fantasies are very different from visions. A fantasy is an exercise in fun that allows us to taste what it might be like to be rich, famous or well loved. That budding baseball player must dedicate much of his waking life to practicing, working out, perfecting skills and committing himself to a baseball career. Unless he is committed to taking care of responsibilities attendant to making his vision a reality, the vision will remain unfulfilled.

Vision helps us to make the commitment to things we really want in our lives. If we really do not want it or want it for the wrong reasons, the vision, by itself, will not be powerful enough to carry itself into realization. Even if we eventually fail at our vision, it will have helped us in some way. Perhaps it helped us learn discipline; in the case of the budding baseball player, daily practice and exercise helped keep his body in shape and taught him the value of persistence.

Having vision allows one to see beyond present circumstances to a better end result. Having vision is quite similar to having a dream. In a booklet I wrote 23 years ago entitled, *The Master Plan at Work* in the Business World, I told the story of Jesus Christ and his vision for the master plan. An excerpt from this booklet follows:

> ***"[The beginning of The Master Plan] was very unobtrusive, as Jesus called just a handful of men to follow Him. It was on this small group that Jesus concentrated His life's work. One should not think for a minute that Jesus completely neglected the many for the purpose of His ministry to the few. The vision of the multitude was always before Him. The New Testament frequently cites His numerous ministries to the masses. Jesus was wise enough to see that the multitudes would need more personal care than He alone could give. His real hope of ministry lay in training a small group who could later lead the multitudes to God."***

In addition to this spiritual influence was that of my mother, who would remind me periodically that following one's vision can be lonely. Vision becomes our constant companion. Can you imagine what loneliness exists without the vision? A rehabilitated, jailed criminal with vision is "more free" than the average person without vision. The Bible states: "Without vision the people will perish." Visions start out as ideas. The well-conceived idea blossoms into a clear vision and becomes a goal towards which we move by adopting clear objectives that propel us to our end.

On the other hand, a hazy, uncertain idea will produce a vision but without definition, a vision that most likely will die naturally. What kinds of ideas come to your mind? How clear are your visions and mental goals for the future? You must get those ideas in focus before they ever materialize into tangible form. Then the fun begins!

The process of turning our good ideas into the final tangible result is wonderfully appealing.

In his book, *Maximum Achievement* (Simon & Schuster), Brian Tracy writes about what he calls, the "law of subconscious activity. According to Tracy, this law states that any idea or thought that you accept as true in your conscious mind will be accepted without question by your subconscious mind. Your subconscious will immediately begin working to bring it into reality. When you begin to believe that something is possible for you, your subconscious mind begins broadcasting mental energies and you begin to attract people and circumstances in harmony with your new dominant thoughts.

IDEAS INTO VISIONS INTO GOALS

Most people today spend more time planning a two week vacation than planning their lives by setting goals. It has been said that achieving goals is not a problem ; Setting goals is the problem and most people do not do it. They leave their lives to chance ; and usually end up broke by the time they reach retirement. So how do we come up with clearly defined goals that ultimately become our visions? Here are some steps to take from Hilton Johnson, the sales coach.

Make a list of your values - - What is really important to you? Your family? Your religion? Your vocation? Your leisure time? Your hobbies? Decide what your most important values in life are and then make sure that the goals you set are designed to include and enhance them.

Begin with the end in mind - - Tom Watson, the founder of IBM, was once asked to what he attributed the phenomenal success of IBM and he said it was three things. First, he created a very clear conception of what he wanted his company to look like when completed. He then asked himself how this company would be operated on a daily basis. Then, in the very beginning of building his company, he began to act that way.

Project yourself into the future - - The late great Earl Nightingale created a whole new industry (self improvement) after a 20-year study on what made people successful. The bottom-line result of his research was simply, ***"We become what we think about."*** Whatever thoughts dominate our minds most of the time is what we become. That is why goal setting is so critical in achieving success because it keeps us focused on what is really important to us. He then said that the easiest way to reach our goal is to pretend as if we have already achieved it. That is, begin to walk, talk and act as though we are already experiencing the success we seek. Then, those things will come to us naturally through the power of the subconscious mind.

Write down 10 things you want this year - - By making a list of the things that are important to you, you begin to create images in your mind. It has been said that your mind will actually create chaos, if necessary, to make images become a reality. Because of this, the list of 10 things will probably result in your achieving at least eight of them within the year.

Create your story board - - Get a piece of poster board and attach it to a wall in your office or home where you will see it often. As you go through magazines, brochures and other visual material, cut out pictures of things you want and glue them to your story board. In other words, make yourself a collage of the goals that excite you ; knowing full well that as you look at them every day, they will soon be yours.

Identify the three most important things - - Select three things that you want to achieve before you die. Then work backwards listing three things you want in the next 20 years, 10 years, five years, this year, this month, this week and finally, the three most important things you want to accomplish today.

Ask yourself good questions - - As you think about your goals, instead of "wishing" for them to come true, ask yourself how and what can you do to make them come true. The subconscious mind will respond to your questions far greater than just making statements or making wishes.

Focus on one project at a time - - One of the biggest mistakes people make in setting goals is trying to focus their attention on too many things at one time. We should recognize that there is tremendous power in giving laser beam focused attention to just one idea, one project or one objective at a time.

Write out an "Ideal Scenario." - - Pretend that you are a newspaper reporter who has just finished an interview about the outstanding success that you have achieved from your vision, and the article is now in the newspaper. How would it read? What would be the headline? Write the article yourself, projecting yourself into the future as though it had already happened. Describe the activities of your daily routine now that you are very successful. Don't forget the headline! (Example: "John Doe Wins Top Salesperson Award of the Decade.")

Pray and meditate - - As you get into bed each evening, think about your goal before you drop off to sleep. Get a very clear colorful image in your mind of yourself doing the things you will be doing after you have reached your major goal. (Remember to include your values.) Then begin to ask for these things through meditation and prayer.

This brings up the whole issue of goal setting as well as focusing on a vision and why most people avoid it. Just about every person in the entire nation, at one time or another, has made some attempt at setting goals. Whether it was a New Year's resolution, an educational or vocational goal and a marriage vow for better or for worse that still ended in failure, we have all tried it. As a result, about 90 percent of us avoid them thereafter. Obviously, none of us like the feeling of failure so we tend to play it safe and protect ourselves from future pain. Others of us choose not to work hard, but go through such positive stress to fulfill our vision, carry out our dream and accomplish the goal. We are all basically lazy, but some of us really do not want to pay the price to overcome our inertia of laziness. Even though God himself never intended for us to become submerged in the slimy swamp of a status quo existence, that is what the greater number of us has chosen to do. What an awful way to exercise our freedom of choice in the land of opportunity! We do it more than not!

- **Today's success scientists report the following statistics:**
- **90 percent do not make goals**
- **Of the 10 percent who do, only 2 to 3 percent write them down**
- **Of the 2 to 3 percent, less than 1 percent commit those goals to memory and revisit them at least once or twice a day**

A vision is the culmination of an idea or attaching sight to the idea. Bringing a vision to culmination takes time. It requires patience and commitment. It requires unending passion. Given these requirements, the process of choosing those ideas to turn into goals and turning those goals into visions must be a thoughtful, well-planned process. Powerful visions can lead others, guide organizations and even organize entire nations. If we captivate ourselves with noble dreams and infect people with our enthusiasm for those noble dreams, only good can occur for all.

Leaders constantly study their vision in progress. Parts of the vision may change or be abandoned altogether. New opportunities, passage of time and other outside influences may alter the vision. This constant refining allows the vision to evolve and grow.

Bill Gothard, Institute of Basic Youth Conflicts, teaches Four Stages of Vision:

1. **Birth of Vision**
2. **Death of Vision**
3. **Rebirth of Vision**
4. **Fulfillment of Vision**

Gothard believes that many visions die near birth and this is normal. Vision may die as a result of destructive criticism (allowing another person's attitude to affect our own) or over-expectation, because it is ahead of its time or because it was not powerful enough to force us to take the steps necessary to see it through. Our vision may be reborn as we find ourselves back at the drawing board to refocus and finetune it. We must preserve the priority of people over projects and not forget that we are one of those people. The second commandment tells us to love our neighbors as we would ourselves, but we seem to neglect the second half: loving ourselves.

A good friend of mine told me that he believes in the power of expectations. "What do you mean, I asked him? If you expect the worst, that's what you'll get. Expect the best and that's what you'll get too." As leaders, teachers, spouses or friends, we can influence others by having positive expectations about them. As leaders, we can greatly influence outcomes, by having positive expectations about those outcomes, as well.

Quite often our visions lead us to unknown places, people and events. This may cause us to abandon our vision because we fear the unknown. Change and difference can be daunting if our attitude is one of fear. If our attitude is one of expecting the best and seeing the unknown as a chance for opportunity, the fear melts and vision may be reborn.

I believe vision is the primary motivation for leaders. From Martin Luther King's, "I Have a Dream," to Mother Theresa's unrelenting vision of making the poor more comfortable, we can see that visions can be powerful motivators. Try not to delay setting goals and forming visions as you await some future event. I have known many persons who have said, "I'll do such and such when I retire" or "When I move to a better location, I'll do that." Putting artificial barriers in front of our wants may mean we do not really want these things, because visions have the power to overcome all boundaries.

VISIONARY TIPS

1. **Have a vision.**
2. **Translate the vision into a goal.**
3. **Write it down.**
4. **Commit it to memory and revisit it every day.**
5. **Share your vision with those that you love and trust.**
6. **Make sure your vision meets the test of universal values.**

Not all of us have access to unlimited financing, state of the art computer equipment, a sympathetic ear or helpful mentor-useful tools that alleviate the burdens of our journeys. We all have access to the most powerful tool of all - - our own minds.

Those of us who have a burning desire, a firm commitment to our goals and clearly defined visions are those who come out on top. We will have a plethora of ideas throughout our lives. Some we will take and mold into goals and visions. Some we will abandon. All are valuable keys showing us who and what we are and what we can ultimately become.

To be sure, we should establish ***minimum, medium and maximum*** goals for ourselves. The problem with goal-setting is that people will often set a maximum goal, and once it is achieved, they let go and never try again. If we create different levels of goals for ourselves, we will continually move in some predetermined direction, even after we have achieved one maximum goal. Because there are smaller, less difficult goals to achieve, we will be continually focused until we are ready to undertake the next maximum goal.

One of the practical benefits in going through a doctoral residence in Greek is the appreciation for, and of the relevancy of, its grammatical and syntactical guidelines to everyday life. For instance, in Greek you have what is known as the four conditional classes in this prioritized order:

- **1st Class Condition: The Condition of Certainty**
- **2nd Class Condition: The Condition of Probability**
- **3rd Class Condition: The Condition of Possibility**
- **4th Class Condition: The Condition of Impossibility**

What is interesting is that the average person, and many times even the average leader, gravitates to the first class condition because it is human nature to want the security of certainty that is ready-made. Of course, we don't want to pay the price for it, so we wind up settling for so much less in life. It never occurs to us that there is a process that we may need to go through—from that which is not to that which is—from impossibility to certainty—from dreams to reality.

Believe it or not, the process begins at the "bottom line" of the Greek priority order, the fourth class condition: the condition of impossibility. This is where the leader of leaders actually feels comfortable because of his desire to dream of what could be and then to focus his vision. Now, so that you can communicate clearly and simply, let us use four positive words that help me to describe the nuances of the process:

The Nesting Phase: The experts in the field of psychology and human resources tell us that the average brain has ten-thousand ideas going through it daily, but that 90 percent are negative. So the above-average person or leader takes the initiative to concentrate on the 10 percent positive by crystallizing those thoughts into a vision. This leads to the next phase.

The Testing Phase: This is where we apply the fourfold test of key questions: (1) Is the vision creative; (2) Is the vision constructive;(3) Is the vision in tune with the age old success formula: "Find a need and fill it; find a hurt and heal it"; (4) Is the vision glorifying to God? If and only if the vision passes all four tests, we are ready to move forward, but no longer alone. Until now, it may have been a lonely path since solitude and such disciplines are not a popular activity or pastime. When you and I are convinced that it will not only meet the needs of others but also glorify God, then something happens on the inside of us. It is called enthusiasm. This too is a compound word that comes from the Greek, which is thus: en = in; thus = God. Hence, enthusiasm is the human reality of being in God. Clearly, it is man in synergy with God. And, since Hebrews 13 describes God as a consuming fire, you figuratively get "turned on,""get fired up" or "become consumed" by God. No one or nothing can stop a person like this. He/she is like a human dynamo. We become, as it were, set ablaze by divine unction. The world looks at it and describes it as "energy", and that is true too, but it is more than that. We know, for it is also the "crowning glow" that guides us through the remainder of the process.

The Investing Phase: This is the phase of commitment. It is the fork in the road that we choose by our free will with the full realization that we will "pay the price" at whatever the cost. Most people refer to this as the point of risk or the "leap of faith." I can understand that especially about people who do not know the wonderful reality involved in the disciplines of the first two phases. However, if we have truly done our homework in the cultivation of the vision, we in fact know its certainty long before the average person. And it is no great risk for us to invest our capital, collateral and even that of those who trust us. You see, what others call "risk," we call the "rent" that we pay to live from unreality to reality.

The Arresting Phase: What is not so pleasant about visions is that they are so delicate and even fragile that they may die, not just once but twice, thrice, even up to four, five, or yes, six times before they are resurrected into that which is suitable and acceptable for its ultimate fulfillment. So the question becomes: what does one do in this process of the birth, death and rebirth of the vision? I simply say revision. Later in the book there's a whole chapter on *Revision—The Power of Revisiting*, I will not belabor the point here except to say that the wisest, healthiest and most wholesome thing to do after the vision dies is to go back to the nesting and testing phases and literally revisit the crucial questions involved. Remember, paramount leadership, which sets us a breed apart from the rest of the pack, is the ability to ask the right questions.

Now as a bonus point, I will add a fifth phase—THE CRESTING PHASE. This is the fulfillment of the vision in the time-space matrix acceptable to the most materialistic observer. It is when you reach the top of the mountain. Lest you think that you then have arrived, be aware that this is also the point of a new plateau, a vantage point from which you are able to see the challenge of even greater mountain peaks to climb.

Just one last caution—beware of the "paralysis of analysis." Clearly, the right questions must be creative, constructive and positive questions, not negative, destructive and critical ones. As in a "Brainstorming session" nothing negative is allowed; so it is in the resurrections and rebirth of the vision.

In the Holy Land, God created the Brook of Jabbock as encouragement for life's journey. The brook sits in the midst of a vast wilderness that is thought to be devoid of water. Miraculously, it is there, surrounded by a lush patch of greenery, and birds flying above. Likewise as you and I move through the wilderness sectors of our lives, we too live by the life-giving currents of our vision as they positively impact the environment through which we travel for the wholesomeness of those around us.

No obstacle, no challenge, no person, no place, no thing, can alter our vision. Our vision forms the river of our destiny. If a huge rock appears, the river goes around it and flows more strongly. Fill the river with scum and it slogs along. Generously fill the river with crystal water and it sparkles and dances down stream in the merry waltz of life. Our rivers make their own path. Even a mountain cannot stop them. They wend their way beneath the mass of rock and dirt. Eventually they reappear on the other side.

As we all know, in a different realm of nature, the butterfly begins its existence, not flying free, but rather as a small, crawling caterpillar. One day this caterpillar crawls into its cocoon and seemingly dies. Then in the fullness of time it appears in a "new" image. In order to escape totally from its cocoon, it must go through a painful struggle to free itself. No one can help the butterfly during this stage, otherwise the butterfly will emerge with a dry, drab, dull color. It is the positive stress of struggle for freedom of flight that causes all the muscles of the butterfly to burst with blood, thus causing the brilliance of its colors!

Likewise, the same is true of you, our dear friend. We are quite confident that you will make your own appropriate applications to and from your vision! You will then see your former life draw to a close and witness your "new" life become colorful and free as well as fulfilling.

By now we can see that there is much more to vision than the theoretical, abstract projection of our ideas. It requires a concentration of our entire being—of intellect, emotions and volition. It includes written goals coupled with consistent ethics and morals. It spans the whole spectrum of reality from our inspiring dreams, on the one hand, to the focused follow-through on the other, and everything else between. In short, it virtually involves the best that we have to offer. For then and only then do we really experience the indescribable joy of it all.

Remember. . .

"If you don't know where you're going, you might end up somewhere else."

Casey Stengle

But, on the other hand: "What you see shall be."

DISPOSITION

THE POWER OF ATTITUDE

FEATURING

JUDITH ANN SAUTTER
EXECUTIVE FINETUNING EDITOR
LEADER OF LEADERS

"Of all earthly music that which reaches
farthest into heaven
is the beating of a truly loving heart."

-- Henry Ward Beecher

According to *Webster's New World Dictionary*, the words "Disposition" and "Attitude" describe ways of acting, feeling or thinking; one's disposition. Note—feeling or thinking; one's "disposition." Disposition is an inclination or tendency; temperament i.e., one's customary frame of mind. They all interrelate, don't they? That's why we'll refer to it all here as: **DISPOSITION: The Power Of Attitude.**

You see, disposition is so deeply rooted in the leader that it is practically the very "nature" or "temperament" of the person; whereas attitude has more altitude above such depths of the nature of the human being. Disposition is in the fathomless depths of the unconscious competent; whereas attitude is in the realm of the conscious competent. That is why it is almost impossible to change the nature of the person, although it is possible to change the attitude of the person. Furthermore, our only hope is that through sufficient, positive change of attitude, we can change the nature or disposition of the leader at his/her very core of being.

> ***"The longer I live, the more I realize the impact of attitude on life. Attitude, to me, is more important than facts. It is more important than the past, education, money, circumstances, failure, successes, or what other people think, say or do. It is more important than appearances, giftedness or skill.***
>
> ***It can make or break a company, a church, and a home. The remarkable thing is that we have a daily choice regarding the type of attitude we will embrace for that day. We cannot change our past...***
>
> ***We cannot change the fact that people will act in a certain way. We cannot change the inevitable.***
>
> ***The only thing we can do is play on the one thing we have and that is our attitude...***
>
> ***I am convinced that life is 10 percent what happens to me and 90 percent how I react to it.***
>
> ***And so it is with you...we are in charge of our attitudes."***

WOW!!! Does that not say it all? If you knew Chuck Swindoll as well as I do based on a 26-year long relationship and most intimately as his author/publisher, you would think he is the originator of that awesome quotation. Good guess, because it virtually describes him as well as any person I know. So that would be a well-deserved compliment and tribute to Karl, but, no he is not the author. Clearly, millions of people might hasten to say that it is by Norman Vincent Peale. After all, is this not what the power of positive thinking is all about? If Norman Vincent Peale were still alive I am sure he would have felt honored for the ascription, but he is not the correct author. Well then, it must be from Robert Schuller, the founding pastor of the Crystal Cathedral, world-renowned television preacher on the "Hour of Power" every Sunday morning, and best-selling author of 26 books, emphasizing "possibility thinking." Excellent guess, but Robert Schuller is not the author.

Then, is the source anonymous? Well, practically, the author is less prominent in the secular world than those figures mentioned above. You see, he was a school mate of mine from graduate school, but he was also more. We were both attending Dallas Theological Seminary in Dallas, Texas; he was pursuing his Master's Degree in Theology while I was doing my doctoral residence in Greek with a minor in Hebrew. What is ironic is that he appeared to me to be insecure because of his humble attitude, speech impediment and joking nature that I perceived to be a cover up for his insecurity. That was a wrong conclusion on my part, which I will explain in a minute. On the other hand, I appeared to be secure because of I was receiving an "A" average in my courses, and because I was a "good talker" which resulted in my being the number one salesman out of 7,000 nationwide for the Southwestern Publishing Company of Nashville, Tennessee for three consecutive years. As a result, I was able to afford the only brand new luxury car in the seminary parking lot. . .that is, until my wife became so embarrassed that she persuaded me to "tone down" a lot and to trade it for a used Volvo!

Chuck Swindoll, who is the author of the above quotation, was not only my classmate but also my mentor in many ways. Yes, he was a couple years older and was therefore sooner to graduate. But he was also upper-classman in his attitude. And his track record through the years is living proof. Besides several successful pastorates, the last of which included thousands of members in California, Chuck is also nationally known to millions of Christians who listen regularly to his daily radio broadcast across America, not to mention his many best-selling books! Finally after receiving a number of honorary doctorates, he is currently the president of Dallas Theological Seminary.

There is another reason why my reference to Dr. Chuck Swindoll is in order. It is because of the truth. "In the presence of two or three witnesses, let every fact be established." This Biblical quotation from the Laws of Moses is the very legal basis of our court system, especially in terms of the trial by jury system. That's why just one or two eye-witnesses in a trial can make or break a case, and wise is the lawyer who will utilize the witnesses effectively. Likewise, it is a very convincing reality for the reader to have "two or three eyewitnesses."

The secular world basically distinguishes two kinds of attitudes, negative and positive or pessimistic and optimistic. Robert Schuller has popularized the terms "impossibility thinking" and "possibility thinking," but basically they all boil down to the kind of attitude that tends to see the dark side of life and the bright side of life. What makes the difference is one's beliefs. Clearly, from childhood into adulthood, each of us has formed certain beliefs that govern our behavior and a lot of this is unconscious. So deeply rooted are these beliefs that when confronted with certain decisions we tend to act without thinking. To the superficial bystander, this might appear to be presumptuous. This is not necessarily so, because our beliefs are something so powerful and strong that we follow the strength of their current.

On the other hand, it is a healthy experience to revisit one's beliefs, and by beliefs I mean not only your religious beliefs or philosophical beliefs, but also your beliefs about the social, vocational, educational, physical and even recreational aspects of your life. Unquestionably, a leader, and especially a leader of leaders in order to be a wholesome one, must go through this reevaluation exercise.

So what we will do is make an acrostic out of the word "belief" and have it stand for the six basic ingredients of any type of belief we might have, for instance: Boldness, Excellence, etceteras.

Now let's discuss each one of these ingredients step by step. To begin, **B stands for Boldness**. Psychologists and psychiatrists tell us that in the face of fright, the average human being reacts with either fight or flight. Fright or fear is the "rude interruption" of our calm existence. Fight or flight are our defense mechanisms to help us cope with the fright. The wholesome personality does not do either. Instead, he/she stands in the face of the fear or fright with a boldness or courage of heart. After all, the fright can result from a number of influential reasons: 1) our own imagination, 2) outside manipulation, 3) satanic opposition. And one thing is for sure: if you or I do not express courage or boldness to take a stand and face it for what it is, we will never know. That is why fight or flight is not the solution or answer.

Now let's examine one's own imagination. This is not to be confused with one's beliefs. If not properly checked and balanced, imagination may become one's beliefs, and then they would not be wholesome beliefs, would they? Such would be found in the more uncivilized parts of our world, and even of our culture. Nor do we mean the creative aspect of our imagination, which is a God-given gift for us to explore and discover new realms of reality. What we are referring to is that vain and wild imagination that our fears and fright cause us to let get out of control. Consequently, our imagination runs away with itself, and we wind up believing what is simply not real. It is unreality.

The professionals have terms for this when one's condition becomes acute: 1) neurotic, 2) psychotic, 3) psychiatrist. Do you know the difference? The neurotic is one whose imagination builds "castles in the sky," 2) the psychotic "lives in those castles," and 3) the psychiatrist collects the rent! There is a lot of truth to that! And that is why we must be bold enough to take a stand and face what is real and unreal. Since we tend to play tricks on ourselves, this is necessary.

Once we have satisfactorily dealt with this issue, we should explore the possibility of outside manipulation by another. After all, no one likes to be controlled by someone else. Yet, it happens all the time. But rather than delve too deeply, I refer you to Chapter Six: The Power of Relationships, in which this is thoroughly discussed, especially in terms of guidelines and boundary lines.

The third and final area should not be minimized. Some may feel as if they are "witch hunters" if they suspect satanic or demonic interference. Well, this may be true if you disregard the first two areas and impulsively choose this one. But if you deal with the other two areas (imagination and outside manipulation) in proper balance, you are on stable ground to investigate this satanic interference as well. Remember, the "Devil is a shrewd, calculating, deceiving, lying, manipulating and counterfeiting evil spirit. So he will do whatever he can to outsmart you, even make you believe that he or his demons do not exist. To be sure, if you do not believe in the devil, Satan or his evil spirits, then they could be in a strategic position to work against you, couldn't they? So be vigilant. Be sober. Be prudent.

Perhaps in our civilized society you will not have to worry about gross forms of demonic possession as may be manifested in the form of horrible symptoms in the body or even speaking uncontrollably in weird languages. But have you ever considered the more sophisticated forms of possession in terms of addiction? Do you really think that all addiction in the United States is humanly induced? If it were, it would be headlines. And then what about the counterfeits of the true, the good and the beautiful. If Satan appears to Eve in her innermost state of perfection as a beautiful counterfeit of a being of life, and described her, couldn't he not pull that off with you, too? So be on guard. Take a stand of boldness and know your enemy. Sometimes there is nothing else that you can do, but be bold and take a stand. So remember, you do not always have to run forward and fight, nor are you required to run backward in flight. With boldness, take your stand, having done all to stand. Without doubt, this is the very bedrock foundation of your belief system.

E stands for Excellence. Oh, what a beautiful word, for it means a beautiful reality for us in which we may be fulfilled. God did not create us in His image to be destined to exist in the mud hole of mediocrity or failure. Nor is God a curt taskmaster who demands of us the unrealistic expectations of perfectionism. In between these two awful extremes is a happy medium called excellence. It is doing our best with which we have, nothing more and nothing less. It is doing our job well whereby at the end of our lives we will hear "Well done my good and faithful servant," from the lips of our Lord and Savior. Therefore, a sound belief system does not burden one with too much, nor does it cop out with too little. Since it takes its firm stand on this foundation of boldness, He establishes excellence as His standard of performance.

L stands for Liability. It is a good balance for excellence because those of us who do excel, especially as leaders and even leaders of leaders, need to be on guard about egotism, pride, arrogance and other forms of "holier-than-thou" attitudes. Clearly, each of us has liabilities for we are our own worst enemy. As Martin Luther; the founder of the Reformation, put it, "My greatest enemy is not the religious zealot in the church that regards me as a heretic, it is not some dangerous criminal, it is not an evil spirit, not even the devil himself. Rather, my greatest enemy is my own deceitful heart," Then he quoted a Bible verse, Jeremiah 17:9, "The heart is deceitful above all things and desperately wicked. Who can know it?" And if we were honest, we would admit that this is true of all of us. Hence, we are much closer to reality, truth and honesty itself if we realize that our primary liability in life is ourselves. Thus, we are far better off giving the benefit of the doubt to others and being suspicious of ourselves. At least, we will avoid paranoia this way. And we might also experience a happier family and have more friends.

I stands for Insistence. Notice that I did not say intelligence, but rather insistence. This is another word for drive or willpower. Is it not true that most of the greatest achievements and discoveries of all time are the result of dogged drive, determination and willpower? Calvin Coolidge put it this way, "Nothing in the world can take the place of persistence (drive). Intelligence will not, for the world is full of educated derelicts."

Intelligence without the spirit of the little choo-choo is worthless. Remember the bedtime story that our parents read to us? Remember how the little choo-choo got up the mountain when others failed? And do you remember why? It is because from the beginning he said to himself, "I think I can, I think I can, I think I can." And when he finally did it, he said, "I thought I could, I thought I could, I thought I could." That's drive. That's insistence.

Furthermore, insistence is the key to the "second wind" of the runner on the track. Without the human dynamic of insistence, a runner will never experience the joy of discovering his hidden inner resources. But how do you cultivate such drive? First, be sure you are bold enough to take a stand in the face of reality. Then set your sights on excellence, nothing more and nothing less. Take into account that you are your own liability and by then your insistence will be at its proper level. That is why IQ should stand for "insistence quotient" rather than intelligence quotient.

So true is this that if I had to choose between intelligence and insistence, I would unhesitatingly choose insistence. It is a good thing that I do not have to choose. So can you imagine how great things can be with both/and instead of either/or?

E stands for Endurance. It is a good thing that there are two "E's" in the word belief, because the first "E" of Excellence could never he achieved without the second "E" of endurance. Jesus cut right to the chase and said, "He who endures to the end shall be saved." Anyone can look good for a while. But then he or she is like the spot that splashes up out of the frying pan ; it is there only for a brief moment. Such performances in the motion picture industry are called "Hollywood fadeouts." Very sad. They are here today and gone tomorrow.

But the leader who has endurance is a person for all seasons. There was a great motion picture film called "A Man for All Seasons," that conveyed the same message. It portrayed the life of Sir Thomas More, a leader in the Church of England during the 16th century who would not compromise his morals and ethics, no matter what "season" of trials and tests he encountered.

F stands for Fight. But its rightful position in this word, taken in context with the other five words of this acrostic gives the word "fight" a totally different meaning. Here, it is not a defense tactic, but rather an offensive one. Here, it is not a coping skill, but rather it is a quality of the "overcomer." To be sure, it is a fight to the finish, for the Apostle Paul said at the very end of his life, "I have fought the good fight and have kept the faith."

"The longer I live the more I realize the impact of attitude on life."

BELIEF. With the above resourceful ingredients, an individual, especially a leader of leaders, should be totally capable of doing whatever he or she believes. So go for it, and remember, "all things are possible to him or her who believes."

As for myself, I have had to consciously cultivate these six ingredients over the years on my own, because I was not raised in a home of wholesome belief. When fright came on the scene, fight was usually the reason. When fight was not adequate, then we resorted to flight. Hence, one of my common experiences was "let me alone," but we took flight to our course of isolation and even reclusivity.

But that is why I thank God for His being my Heavenly Father and making me a part of His spiritual family, and so compensate for what I lacked as I grew up. I am also very appreciative for my wife who had that exceptional privilege of being raised in a positive, wholesome, Christian home, for she was fortunate to grow up with that wonderful disposition of a positive mental attitude.

In light of all this, I am so grateful to be married to Judy for 32 years, because she has such a wonderful disposition. What a blessing it is to live with such a beautiful human being day and night who consistently sees the bright side of life, who is positive, upbeat, happy, kind, patient, supportive and gracious. Right to the core of her character Judy is noble, and as such her worth is far more than rubies. I have the fullest confidence in her and have no doubts or regrets. Judy brings me good, not harm, all the days of our lives.

Her calling in life is ministry of music. I used to say music period, but I now realize that it is a ministry of music, because when she touches her fingers to the keyboard for a thousand people to hear every Sunday morning at church, or whether she gently teaches one pupil at a time in our home or at school, she is ministering. . .serving others with her God-given talent. Not just her talent as a musician, but also with her temperament that can only be described as being wonderful in disposition. She uniquely and delightfully plays such appealing sounds to the ears and the spirit. *(See illustration)*

Judy is a self-starter. She is always hospitable to our many guests, as well as faithful in preparing my meals. During these past four years, she has expended a great deal of her energy caring for her mother who has Alzheimer's, as well as being supportive of her dad, who is the primary caretaker of her mother, yet she still continues to persevere. Obviously, she could not do it all without a wholesome, positive mental attitude.

Judy also seems to know how and when to approach me about our

To give you a clear idea and finetuned feeling of her passion for music and God, ponder the essence of the plaque of inspiration that hangs on the family room wall.

finances. In spite of the fact that she has no formal business background, she seems to have some very special insightful knowledge for me when I need to make a financial decision. Sometimes we agree. Other times we do not agree, but I always respect her point of view.

In addition to being a very beneficial and profitable partner in the grace of life to me, she also opens her arms to the less fortunate. Whether they may be people who need clothes, food, education or a whole new lifestyle, Judy is willing and able to help. Yet, at the same time she does not become unbalanced. She does not go from one extreme to the other. Hence, when inclement weather sets in, when tough times hit, Judy seems ready for the occasion. As a result, she does not neglect the needs of those closest to her. Yes, balanced priorities reinforced by the power of her positive attitude maintain her equilibrium as she fulfills all her roles as wife, mother, daughter, pianist, teacher and friend.

She understands, very well, the reality that communication is 55 percent body language. That is why she ensures that she and our children are dressed properly. Judy does not try to "keep up" with the Joneses nor does she go to the opposite extreme and not care at all. She lies in the happy medium, she takes good care of our children and herself. She also gives me reminders when I need them. Throughout our marriage, there has never been a day that Judy was not appropriately dressed. Because the style of her clothing is a reflection of her winsome disposition, Judy, as the old saying goes, "wears it well."

No wonder I have the privilege of working together with many other leaders and leaders of leaders on township, county, city, region, state, national and even international levels, because Judy is not only a great asset, but is also wonderful partner in the grace of life.

What also amazes me is that Judy has a special knack for investments. She refers to this strength of hers as intuition. I must say that whatever Judy wears in material clothing does not compare to her spiritual cloth of strength and dignity, the latter is of far greater value. These qualities helped her through my eight-year disability period, precipitated by an almost fatal closed head injury in May of 1989 which I am now close to full recovery.

So as we ponder the future which includes aging parents who may soon die, (my own 83- year-old Mother, Helen, recently passed away as a result of stomach and bowel cancer during the final stages of this book) or the uncertainties of the economy, Judy greets the future with a good disposition and a positive mental attitude.

These are the reasons why I chose to honor, value and praise my wife so early in the book. "Charm is deceptive, and beauty is fleeting, but a woman who honors the Lord is to be praised. Give her the reward she has earned, and let her works bring her praise at the city gate." (Proverbs 31: 30, 31) And is it not interesting that Judith means "praised one".

Frankly, it took the writing of this book to have me realize that Judy is a greater leader than I, because she helped me along as a friend who sticks closer than a brother for 34 years without "lording over me," without "competing for control," without "playing games." She did it so humbly and so unassumingly that only she and God noticed! Which means that not even I appreciated her, let alone even noticed her as much as I should have. Clearly, it takes a quite wonderful person to keep on keeping on when people offer no word of thanks as they should. In fact, it takes a person with a good disposition and a persevering spirit. So for all the times I did not express appreciation, as well as for the times I did, I now officially go on the record and say it all here with the express intention of continuing to express my appreciation every day for the rest of my life.

You know, Charlie Glass's definition of leadership is so special, and it fits here so appropriately: "Leadership is the sensitive process of helping the other person to make one more step of progress toward his/her goal." WOW! That is my wife Judy! And I thought I was her leader!

SELECTION 4

THE POWER OF PRIORITIES

FEATURING

JERRY HEFFEL

PRESIDENT, THE SOUTHWESTERN COMPANY

"This above all:
to thine own self
be true."

-- William Shakespeare

"Failure is one of the uglies of life. We deny it, run away from it, or upon being overtaken, fall into permanent paralyzing fear.

Probably because of our reluctance to face it, not much is written about the anatomy of failure...

Wave our visionary banner proclaiming "Victory," refusing often even to admit that the path to ultimate victory may include intermediate bloody noses."

Dr. Howard G. Hendricks

Just as Jesus carefully selected a handful of men to help him personally minister to the masses, the wise leader must carefully select persons to help him carry his vision to fruition.

The wise leader's real hope lies in training a small group who will carry the leader's message forward, thus furthering the leader's mission. This process of selection–choosing the fellow workers (leaders) willing to learn and exhibit as much enthusiasm about the leader's vision as he does–is the next step in becoming a leader of leaders. It is significant to recognize that no one can fulfill the maximum potential of a vision without being able to effectively implement the power of priorities.

Before proceeding further, it is important to view the process of selection and the power of priorities from a basic level.

A leader's priority must always be his family, whether it be blood relatives, neighbors, co-workers or his most trusted partners. This basic priority is essential because projects are never more important than people. Another way of looking at the power of making our family a priority in our life is realizing that success without satisfaction offers little reward. We cannot experience satisfaction without being surrounded by people about whom we care.

A leader's first priority should be to establish a happy family. Family fulfillment enriches those within the family unit and can flow beyond the family. A reservoir of resources becomes a significant asset within the family and to others. Very often, our truest critics are our family members, if we are humble enough to accept their correction. When former President Ronald Reagan issued his Presidential Proclamation for National Family Week in 1984, he declared "the family is the basic unit of society." This maxim is a necessity for an effective leader. It is out of the reservoir of family resources that we are able to be a significant asset to our colleagues, fellow leaders and our followers.

The power of example is a core message of this book. Without exhibiting the power of example, the leader is an empty shell. Without the walk of example, the talk of a leader is cheap.

This is why our rich Judeo-Christian tradition has always had very high standards for leadership qualification in synagogues and churches. Both the Old Testament and the New Testament of the Holy Bible clearly defined qualifications for leadership. According to the Bible, (I Timothy 3:1-7) to qualify for a leadership position in a synagogue or church, one must:

- Be above reproach
- Be the husband of one wife
- Be temperate
- Be self-controlled
- Be respectable
- Be hospitable
- Be able to teach
- Be not given to much wine
- Be gentle
- Be not quarrelsome
- Be not a lover of money
- Manage his own family well
- Have a good reputation with outsiders

These qualifications are equally relevant for leaders in secular spheres beyond the confines of church and synagogue.

We must remain mindful about another aspect of qualification. The ministers and those who lead in the church are also called servants. Being a good minister is synonymous with being a good servant. Extending this into secular spheres, the heart of a leader, the ultimate meaning of being a leader, is being a good servant. This concept of a leader being a servant is embodied in the titles bestowed on holders of top governmental posts in certain nations, like minister (servant) of finance, minister (servant) of agriculture and minister (servant) of education.

With the priority of family in place and due recognition to the power of example in implementing the qualifications of leadership, we can turn to selection.

Selection involves choosing, as other leaders for our team, those we care about to share our vision. Having faithful people around us, who will make our vision a part of their vision, is vital to the leadership process. We place a great deal of trust in those people who in essence become a part of our extended family. We get to know them intimately, so when we delegate duties to them, we have confidence that those duties are something they will find enjoying and satisfying. Therefore, we accomplish two things: we make progress in attaining our vision and we help others to attain fulfillment.

Jerry Heffel, president of The Southwestern Company, is a leader adept in the art of selection. The Southwestern Company is a book publishing firm with a century-plus legacy of employing college students as salespersons. Since its inception in 1868, The Southwestern Company has prided itself on its leadership training program for college students. This program stresses leadership, service, and taking the road less traveled.

"Although the financial rewards of the program can be considerable, students gain more important benefits in the independence and self-confidence which come from setting their own goals and determining their own success," said Heffel, noting that one goal of his firm is to help students realistically prepare for their lives and careers.

"We're the first to admit that selling books is hard work. We don't apologize for that fact. For the young person who is willing to discipline himself or herself, working in the Southwestern program will not only make a difference to their summer, but to the rest of their lives," said Heffel, who paid his way through both college and graduate school by working as a student book salesman with Southwestern.

"Experience has shown us that people who can dedicate themselves to learning the lessons this program has to teach are the same kind of people who do well in their future careers, whatever and wherever those careers happen to be," Heffel continued. "And that's the kind of person we are looking for!"

Selection encompasses choosing whom we want to be in our family. Those choices may remain with us for a very long time–even a lifetime, so the process must be a thoughtful one. Selection also means abandoning some options in favor of others, because wise leaders realize there are limits and boundaries to their power. Wise leaders understand they cannot accomplish it all by themselves.

A wise leader is always alert to people he can help, like Jesus helped Blind Bartimaeus. According to the Gospel of St. Luke, Jesus was traveling through the town of Jericho when he heard a man cry out from the middle of a crowd. "Help me, help me," the man repeatedly cried out, though many in the crowd tried to silence him. Finally, Jesus heard the man and said, "Someone is calling my name. What do you want?" Blind Bartimaeus replied, "I want to see!" Consequently, Jesus healed him.

The moral of this story is that we must keep on calling for help until we get the attention of the leader. Keep on calling for help until: (1) you get above and beyond the crowd, thereby not letting the curious and/or callous keep you down; (2) you get the attention of your sought after leader, and (3) you get the leader to stop what he is doing and focus on your need.

"What do you want?" is what every true and great leader and public servant asks. The subject of selection is of more importance in the story of this encounter between Jesus and Blind Bartimaeus than healing physical blindness. It involves healing our spiritual blindness.

One of the first steps in getting our leadership act together is getting a vision of whom and what we are to become. Remember, "What you see is what you'll be." That is why the famous blind leader, Helen Keller, had a very insightful response when she was asked, "What is the greatest tragedy of all?" Many might expect Keller to have listed being sightless or some other physical handicap. But Keller answered: "It is to be able to see but not to have vision." Vision is seeing with our spiritual eyes. Vision is using with imagination the brain God gave us. Vision is utilizing our creative powers as human beings, created in the image of God; for as God is Creator, He wills for us to be creative after His image and likeness.

The selection of others to help us attain our vision is vital in attaining fruition of that vision. All great leaders know that a job can never be done by one leader, even if he labors day and night.

When Jesus' 12 disciples were arguing about who among them would be greater in the Kingdom of God, Jesus responded: "He who is greater among you shall be servant of all." A simple way to prioritize anything ; our schedules, duties and obligations ; is to examine each task and to ask ourselves if it relates to our vision or enhances our mission. If our vision is similar to other great leader's, then serving others will be our highest priority. In making other's our highest priority, we elevate ourselves.

Another perspective for examining selection is realizing that it is simply a choice from a menu of options. Throughout our lives we have the free will to select from numerous alternatives. We can make no wrong choices by staying close to our vision.

Leaders strengthen their selection through how they interact with others. Martin Buber, the renowned existentialist thinker, taught that in the totality of life, we deal with people in one of three ways:

1. The I-I Relationship: This is the way of the self-centered, egotistical, arrogant and thoughtless person who is interested only in "Me, Myself and I."

2. The I-It Relationship: This is the way of manipulation, abuse and exploitation. It is the using of people to achieve the projects we want, instead of utilizing the projects to build people. This method is used by manipulative people who usually value the project over the people.

3. The I-Thou Relationship: This ultimate method of relating to others results in everyone being a winner. This method focuses on how we can enhance and do good for each other. This method is the relational means by which you and I (Thou & I) "encounter" one another for each other's highest good and God's highest glory.

F. Karl Schauffele, the former president of the Main Line Chamber of Commerce, exemplifies the I-Thou relationship.

Selection also means abandoning some options in favor of others, because wise leaders realize there are limits and boundaries to their power. Wise leaders understand they cannot accomplish it all by themselves.

There is no better way to illustrate this reality in Karl than in "the passing of the torch" from Karl's presidency to his successor's presidency at The Main Line Chamber of Commerce. It was masterfully orchestrated over a period of months in terms of appropriate announcements, in-depth interviews and smooth transition between Karl and his successor, Robert Pucci. Pucci began working full-time in the weeks prior to Karl Schauffele's official retirement on December 31, 1996. Because of Karl Schauffele's incredible expertise and commitment, he continues to come into the Chamber's office two or three days a week as chairman of the Chamber's Legislative Committee, serving the new Chamber president, Robert Pucci. Now that's class and the kind of leadership model to emulate.

This story doesn't end there. Robert Pucci says, "Hopefully, the passing of the torch was made less painful because it was passed to someone in whom Karl had great confidence and respect. Perhaps Karl had taken the Chamber as far as he reasonably could, and the time was right for a change, but not so big a change that Karl's disciples will feel uncomfortable. This means I don't have to run the Chamber the same way that Karl did ; but that significant growth is still probable and likely."

When asked what would it take to make that "significant growth" occur, Pucci confidently answered, "Hit the ground running! Build on the foundation Karl built. Take the Chamber to a new level of prominence and strength and have the Chamber improve in both inward and outward ways. These will be obvious to the Main Line community. I would also like to help orchestrate overall stronger business districts throughout the Main Line region."

One project Pucci is working on is the Chamber's Year 2000 Plan. This Plan involves the Chamber regionalizing, enhancing its legislative advocacy at all levels of government from local to federal, becoming a catalyst in advancing the technology of business and expanding services to better meet the needs of the Chamber's members. This succession at The Main Line Chamber of Commerce is an example of the I-Thou relationship in action with a win-win result for all concerned.

Another important aspect in this focus on the selection of Karl Schauffele's successor is the priority of Robert Pucci's family, even over the Chamber. Despite all of the people Pucci knows, the persons most important and valuable in his life are: his wife, mother, son, daughter, brother, best friend, Chamber staff and Chamber Chairman of the Board, Bill O'Connor. What is instructive about those persons most valuable in Pucci's life is that Pucci's character emulates that of the Old Testament/New Testament qualifications for an overseer or leader of a synagogue or church. As noted earlier in this chapter, these qualifications largely emphasize marital and parental values as foundational for community leadership.

Robert Pucci brings to The Main Line Chamber of Commerce a new dimension, different from that of his predecessor. In this succession, we see complementation of their I-Thou relationship. This succession exemplifies a statement by Thomas Edison, who once said: "Stand on my shoulders and go higher."

Any discussion of selection must consider the influence of money. To adequately examine this critical influence, examine the original model of our U.S. government tax structure.

It was Huey P. Long, former U.S. senator and former governor of Louisiana (the most backward state in the Union), who was responsible for much of the current tax structure. Long proposed to provide for the people an economic structure, a model to the nation for the tax structures. Long's proposal was designed to redistribute wealth from a few for the poor to share. It was based on the Year of Jubilee, which made Israel the most prosperous nation in the world.

The key value of the Year of Jubilee was its principle ; tax makes money serve the people, not people the tax." This Year of Jubilee was so well received by the people that it became known as "the acceptable year of the Lord." This is why the dating system for our calendars say "in the year of our Lord."

Politicians encourage us just to keep the Ten Commandments and the Sermon on the Mount. Well, in the Sermon on the Mount preached by Jesus, he told us not to get all up tight about money and certainly not to put money first. Remember, the word selection doesn't just mean choice. It means preferred choice. And money is not it.

We have examined the high standards for a leader established in the Old and New Testaments. We have also reflected on the relationship of a wholesome family life to a successful role in leadership. Let's turn now to examine the crowd ; the masses of humanity out of which leaders come.

Just as there are the four cycles of history (man, movement, methods and monument) there are three types of people in a typical crowd. These three types are:

Curious Posers - These are people who are not going anywhere in life but they do like to know what's up and what's coming down. Curious Posers have no vision, mission or purpose. At best they're just curious:

Critical Opposers - These are the destructive, devil's advocates.

They don't offer constructive criticism to help but they do get satisfaction out of tearing down the leader and achiever. Usually, the motive of Critical Opposers is jealousy; they use criticism to bring the leader down to their level since they can't get up to the leader's level.

Callous Losers - These are the by-standers who were disqualified in life, perhaps by themselves or others, from being in a significant role of leadership. Rather than becoming better, callous losers become bitter through experience. Through their bitterness, they have become blinded to their fresh starts in life, and thereby regard their potential stepping stones as stumbling blocks. Callous losers see the dark side instead of the bright side ; they are tuned into the negative and not the positive.

Blind Bartimaeus did what he could to get above the crowd, thereby not letting the curious, critical and the callous keep him down. A leader of leaders stays alert for persons he can help such as the Blind Bartimaeus's in this life. Leaders of leaders are alert for other leaders and followers who desire and aspire to make the fullest use of their potential. Make no mistake, those aspiring to make fullest use of their potential are hard to detect, let alone select from the crowd. As Karl Schauffele says, "Sooner or later, the cream rises to the top and I then know."

Karl Schauffele does not have a personal list of "do's and don'ts" for his criteria of selection, neither does Schauffele play favorites. He is not political and therefore does not play games with egos or power plays or pulls at the power of the purse. The bottom line for Schauffele is serving, especially those who in turn will serve others. Being committed to being a public servant all his adult life, Schauffele realizes that the job will never get done by one leader even if that leader labors round the clock. Thus, Schauffele does not make serving an end in itself.

When the Lord Jesus Christ taught his bickering 12 disciples a key lesson about genuine greatness by saying, "He who is greatest among you shall be servant of all," the disciples were obviously at a very immature level of leadership. The disciples, arguing about who among them would be greater in the Kingdom of God, were bent on the interest of self and not upon the interest of others. They were egotistical and arrogant because their goal was to exalt themselves and not exalt others.

Instead of the win-win I-Thou attitude advocated by existentialist Martin Buber, the disciples were mired in the I-I attitude, therefore indicating their relationship with others was one of abuse, manipulation and exploitation, no wonder they were all losing control and becoming angry toward one another! Imagine, the 12 Apostles of the Christian Church fighting for their supposed rights instead of being sensitive to the needs of other persons. Jesus, being the master communicator, did not correct his disciples with words at first. He must have known that body language is more than 55 percent of communication, because he equipped himself with a towel and knelt down to wash the disciple's feet. Adding this act to his tone of voice when telling them about serving all made an impact.

Jesus utilized his vision to help guide his disciples to further growth. Jesus walking the walk and talking the talk–leading by example ; inspired his disciples at a crucial junction. This inspiration enabled them to continue Jesus' mission.

The leader of leaders must select his small group, train and nurture them, to carry on his mission and his vision.

Mission 5

The Power of Words

Featuring

Mildred Dienert
Woman of God

"Speech is a mirror
of the soul:
as a man speaks, so is he."
-- Publius Syrus

Mission is the articulation of our vision or putting our vision into words. When put into words, it becomes our mission statement. As a concrete statement it may be transmitted to others including selected leaders who then pass it to the followers. Mission becomes a potent force when put into words.

We may develop and own more than one mission in our lives. It may be our mission to develop a loving, healthy, family or excel at our jobs. A mission can broadly, yet specifically, cover the spectrum of our entire lives (e.g., My mission in life is to help the sick and infirm in the poor areas of Appalachia) or refer to a particular time-limiting project (e.g., My mission is to complete this project for my employer in the time allotted.).

Our personal and professional mission statements may change from year to year. They need not be set in stone. Missions are merely tools to remind us of our current purpose and keep us on the path that leads to fulfillment of that purpose. Mission usually becomes the cause for which we do something. It becomes the driving force that guides us in the right direction to realize our goals.

Achieving our personal mission depends on the roles and goals we select for ourselves and then on how effectively we carry them out. The act of writing a personal mission statement is a significant part of beginning a personal leadership system.

Many leaders find the concept of having a mission appealing and helpful because it sets guidelines. It defines what we believe, what we value and what we want to make of our lives, our organizations or our projects. By referring to it and internalizing its meaning, we make choices that serve our selected values and reject those issues and items that oppose our selected values.

It is in this quest of one's mission that I resumed fellowship with Mildred Dienert, at 4 p.m., Tuesday, May 20, 1997 ; she prefers to be called Millie. The purpose of our meeting was for me to obtain her counsel concerning different aspects of the Leader of Leaders Premier Celebration. Although we already had a number of women involved in certain ways, I felt the deep instinctive need to call upon her, as well, for help.

For those of you not familiar with Millie, let me begin her introduction in a more plebeian manner. She is the widow of Fred Dienert, owner of Walter Bennett Communications, which represents the Billy Graham ministry and a host of others. In light of this, I felt that Millie would have some fine strategy to suggest that would really offer some sophisticated tools to enhance the Premier. Well, she really did, but not the sort of thing I was expecting.

Instead she so graciously, yet so provocatively, asked me one key question: "Don, do you have a lot of mini prayer meetings going?" Huh? Prayer meetings? A lot of mini prayer meetings? I have to confess that I hadn't even thought of it, although I myself am committed to daily prayer. Then she proceeded to explain that the real secret to Billy Graham's wonderful ministry is not the high-tech promotional tools of Walter Bennett Communications, although they have their place. The real power is in the thousands of mini prayer meetings going on all over the targeted area of the crusade.

As she so beautifully shared this, I thought of President George Bush's "Thousand Points of Light" being exemplified by these radiant mini prayer meetings. Then I related that to the title of this chapter, "MISSION: The Power of Words." The connection that I came to is that mission for Millie Dienert is first, the power of her words to God in prayer. This is only half of it, because she went right on to emphasize, as Billy Graham does, "the Bible says." In this we see that mission is the power of God's Word to Millie. And that's why Millie says in her own words: "For all our technological advances, man has changed very little since the Bible was written, and the mistakes they were making thousands of years ago are the same errors we are making now. The Bible addresses those errors, and points to the solution."

Millie Dienert is a woman on the "GO" for God. She received Religious Heritage of American's Churchwoman of the Year Award in 1990 because of her "significant contributions to the religious life of our country." She has been called the Christian world's first lady of prayer because she has assembled a worldwide prayer chain of more than a million people in 94 countries to pray for some of the greatest evangelistic efforts of our time. She has been dubbed "the Dot Lady" because she has flooded the globe with hundreds of thousands of small dots that her intercessors affix to such things as wristwatches and refrigerator doors as a reminder to pray. She also answers to "the Flying Grandmother," a title she has earned as a result of speaking engagements around the country and world.

The mother of three children, she began teaching small Bible classes in her suburban Philadelphia home almost four decades ago. She came to her teaching gifts naturally as the daughter of the late Reverend Theodore H. Elsner, a gospel radio pioneer and a founding father of National Religious Broadcasters. As her children grew older, she was invited by the Billy Graham Evangelistic Association to visit cities, where the evangelist would hold crusades, to encourage prayer support for his forthcoming meetings. In the mid-1950's, she visited England, crisscrossing the country, urging families to open their homes for neighborhood prayer meetings on behalf of Dr. Graham's 1954 London Crusade. Nine-thousand British homes were opened for prayer, and Millie's worldwide ministry as a Christian speaker began.

In the nearly four decades since then, Millie Dienert has covered the United States, most of Canada, and much of the world, speaking to women's groups at banquets, retreats, Bible studies and conferences. She brings her listeners words of encouragement and inspiration as she tells them how to apply the timeless truths of the Bible to situations that confront them daily. The Bible is quite simply her guidebook for living, as relevant and dependable today, she says, as when its words were first written. "What makes such an old book so relevant and dependable today?" I asked. "The power of its words," she replied. "The power of God's word is truth that transcends time, so its source and content can be trusted in all times and for all time."

Being an internationally-known speaker is just one of her many activities. Millie also has urged the world to pray for such 20th century evangelistic efforts as the Lausanne Congress on World Evangelization in 1974; the 1983 and 1986 conferences for traveling evangelists held in the Netherlands; and Billy Graham's multi-nation television outreach called "Mission '89."

Prayer and Scripture-soaked life are things she knows firsthand. Millie acknowledges that she is alive today after injuries from a serious automobile accident as a young woman through the intercession of her family and friends.

As for the Bible, it is quite simply her guidebook for living,

> ***"as relevant and dependable today, she says, as when its words were first written."***

Now for those of you readers who are tempted to jump to conclusions about Millie's being evangelistic, please familiarize yourself with her profile:

Educational Background:

University of Pennsylvania English Major
Philadelphia College of Bible Graduate

Activities: Community Bible Class Teacher
Lay speaker at conferences, retreats
International consultant Christian Women's Club of America
Member President's Council
Philadelphia College of Bible

	Religious Heritage of America's "Churchwoman of the Year," 1990
Family:	Widow after 54 years of marriage to Fred Dienert, advertising executive Children: Ted, Darlene, Marilyn Grandchildren: Nine

With this dynamic background, Millie's mission is the personalization of prayer and the Word of God. Millie went on to say that leaders are in a position to wield the power of their words like swords to wound or dressings to heal and effective leaders are marked by their choice of "arsenal." Swords she says, divide, destroy and deceive, but blessings bind, build and beam with rays of light that penetrate truth to promote healing. As for her, she will emulate the leadership style of Jesus Christ and use the power of her words to "speak the truth in love."

Our mission is our purpose. It is necessary to ask ourselves, "What do I really want to do with my life?" In order to formulate a mission, we must be totally honest. We must determine what is most important to us and make it central in our life.

To some of us, this question has never been posed. We may be living the life we learned from our parents or until now our schooling, jobs and family have pretty much determined the nature and structure of our lives. Take the time to discover where you want to go, where you need to go!

> *"I have no idea where I will go on this journey, but I know I must take it."*
>
> Martin Luther King, Jr.

This brings us full circle to Blue Bell, Pennsylvania, where we met for a "spot of tea" in the Whitpain Diner. It's only because I was willing to accept the two priorities of prayer and the Word of God, that Millie Dienert is willing to be on our Executive Committee, and to be featured in a chapter of this book.

A leader of leaders like Millie makes you keep thinking long after they leave your presence. And the more I thought, the more questions like these arose:

- **Who else do I know that is personally responsible for getting more than 1,000,000 prayer meetings going all around the world as a catalyst of a "Thousand Points of Light"?**
- **Is it because Millie is humble enough to pray so much, that God has so remarkably prospered her?**
- **Do I need any more convincing that the problems of evil and the conditions of the world have, in fact, not been improved by**

modern technology?

• If Vince Lombardi, one of the best football coaches who ever lived, proved that "getting back to basics" was the winning policy for his team, then shouldn't I all the more get back to the basics in leadership by prioritizing prayer and the Word of God?

• In light of the inspirational words of Paul Riley, general manager of Gene's Book Store at the Plaza in King of Prussia, Pennsylvania, "Remember your purpose," hasn't Millie proven that her mission is tried, true and tested?

• Why should I try to improve upon it? Why try to reinvent the wheel?

• Haven't I learned by now that my plans, my ways, and my goals are not always what's best for me, others, or God?

• Why not have the support system of prayer and the Word of God in my life?

I have no doubt that all these questions will be fully answered as I endeavor to cooperate with Millie Dienert, and let her be a leader to me, as a leader. Although I do not see how everything will work out, between this Memorial Day, May 26, 1997, and the Leaders of Leaders Premier Celebration day on June 30, 1997, this I do know ; It will go a lot better with Millie's leadership than without.

Mission is the articulation of our vision or putting our vision into words. When put into words, it becomes our mission statement. As a concrete statement it may be transmitted to others including selected leaders who then pass it to the followers. Mission becomes a potent force when put into words.

I'm actually inspired enough at this very moment to "rough-draft" a vision statement about the promotion of all this. Before I proceed, remember that I said "rough-draft," for the time of the deadline is just about here. Hence, I only have time for one draft and one edit; so here goes.

I see in Millie Dienert a woman of God, as well as leader of leaders, who will absolutely stay 100 percent focused on prayer as the supernatural and miraculous power source for the Premier. As such, when she is confronted with major problems, she won't complain or get negative. Rather, she'll pray and get others to pray.

In some things I actually visualize that things will get even worse after prayer. But, this will not discourage Millie or others that she positively influences. So I see them ask, seek, and knock with persistent prayer. In the due course of it all, I see the progress of their praying being compatible with the poem:

"When your Prayer is not Right,
God said No;
When you are not Right,
God says Grow;
When your Timing is not Right,
God says Slow;
When Everything is now Right,
God says Go!!!"

Through all the grit and grind over the next 35 days, I visualize that there will even be times that I'll feel totally victimized and expressly overwhelmed ; as I feel the sensation of losing grip at the end of the proverbial rope. When there seems to be no way out, no favorable circumstances, and no positive coincidences, I see that God's answers to prayers will provide us wisdom, solution and abundant success.

Ah, but you say that you have prayed and failed. So have I, but that's because I didn't pay the price of "praying through" the four dimensions of the power like Millie Dienert does. Furthermore, I have to confess that I have also probably and egotistically tried to win and succeed in many other ways and failed even worse! Dear reader, are you willing to humbly admit the same? Haven't we all missed the mark?

• fallen short of the mark?

• stepped over the mark and/or gotten all twisted up trying to find the mark?

• and had enough with Murphy's Law?

It's taken me 56 years, but I finally figured out what Satan's last name is. It's Murphy! How do I know? Because the very first time and place that things went wrong that could go wrong was in the Garden of Eden when Satan got Eve and Adam to fall from perfection. Ever since, Murphy's Law that states: "Whatever can go wrong will go wrong" has existed. Therefore, Satan's last name is "Murphy."

Don't take me seriously about the last name of Satan, but please accept the real point of all this ; that if you and I want the power of words to strengthen our mission in life, then we need something more than the average to overcome Murphy's Law or the problem of evil ; call it what you will. Rather than just self-talk to verbalize my mission and prayers, I'll rely also on prayer. Rather than depend on my word only, I'll depend on the Word of God that does not fail.

Surely, all of us have heard the saying "Talk is cheap." Why is this so true? Primarily, it's because people's talk has nothing to do with a genuine mission and purpose. Even for the small percentage of people who do have a mission, most of them forget, if not practically forget it in the everyday responsibilities and duties. Hence, they are interrupted, distracted and detoured by what is urgent rather than priority as dictated by their mission.

Yet, whatever you do, become a leader who has a clearly defined mission that is so genuine that you will be sure from now on to remember your mission by reviewing it several times per day, consequently having it guide your priorities, places, and even hourly schedule. Clearly, take very seriously the classic saying: "Time is the stuff out of which life is made." Then secure your meaningful mission to it, and you will find that, on the one hand, you'll stop wasting time and on the other hand, you'll also stop hastening time with negative stress.

Formulating a mission statement helps us identify those goals in life that are most significant to us. Placing our goals into words provides a written and verbal guide to refer to when we need help prioritizing a busy day or selecting from a numerous list of options.

• **How can we formulate the right words to guide us on our personal path to happiness and success?**

• **Practice writing several mission statements relating to our current goals and lifestyles.**

• **Study what we have written. Does it match our wants? Will it fulfill our needs? Does it concern the welfare of others as well as ourselves?**

• **Think carefully about our current goals and select those which are the most significant to us and directly relate to our mission.**

6 Association

The Power of Relationships

Featuring

Charles Glass
Mid-Atlantic Director,
Christian Businessmen's Committee

"People are lonely
because they build walls
instead of bridges."

-- Joseph Fort Newton

The outstanding career of Charlie Glass spans leadership posts in the military, private industry and missionary work with the Christian Business Men's Committee of USA (CBMC). One element that stands out about Glass, an element that has helped him achieve and excel in those various occupational venues, is his great ability to get along with people.

Born in Iowa and raised in Minnesota, Charlie Glass spent nearly two decades in the Navy where he earned many awards and commendations for development of training programs, administration and career counseling. He trained personnel in the field of helicopter search and rescue and anti-submarine warfare in helicopters and patrol aircraft. Retiring from the Navy in 1980, Glass designed computer training programs for the Unisys corporation.

A resident of Warminster, Pennsylvania, Glass is the Mid-Atlantic area director for CBMC, serving full-time ministering to business and professional men and their spouses. Glass had conducted numerous CBMC ministry workshops at conferences and retreats throughout the U.S., Canada and Bermuda.

Nurturing relationships is a part of the principles Glass has developed on the topic of leadership. One principle Glass holds dear is always "being honest and vulnerable in relationships and expecting the best from others." Additionally, Glass considers it important to always "encourage, direct and allow others to bloom where they are planted."

Nurturing relationships was a key tactic of Spencer Hays, Executive Chairman of the Board for Southwestern Publishing Company. Hays would motivate his budding executives by telling them: "There are two kinds of people in this world: those who find ways and those who find excuses. It takes no brains and courage to find excuses. Anyone can do that and unfortunately most people do. Be one of those to find ways and you'll be among the successful few." It is all too easy to allow relationships to die for lack of time, inclination or whatever other excuse we manufacture. It is the leader of leaders who finds ways to nurture and develop relationships because he knows how vital they are to everyone concerned.

Sustaining healthy relationships parallels another of Charlie Glass' principles: Problems don't exist–only challenges do. The dynamics of relationship is a central focus of the CBMC's ministry. CBMC stresses that the lives of its believers should reflect Christ in such a way that persons around the believers, at home and at work, are brought closer to Christ as a result of the believers "relationship" with those persons.

By studying the life of the Lord, we learn that he used the principle of association with his disciples. The essence of Jesus' teaching program was simply having his disciples near him and thus they learned by association with him. As Jesus' ministry grew into its third year, He gave an increased amount of time to the 12 disciples. Almost every act performed by Jesus was done in the presence of a disciple. Jesus knew He was shaping their character by being with them and allowing them to observe His words and actions firsthand. Unfortunately, in our highly impersonal society, we have lost sight of this invaluable principle learning through association. . .the essence in the power of relationships. I didn't learn the power of this principle myself until I discovered it in the Scriptures.

During my second year as manager with Southwestern Publishing Company, I spent time with the sales crew under my tutelage throughout the school year. I took time for leisurely discussions, sharing good and bad experiences with the student sales crew. I tried to inspire them to apply to their college studies the concepts that had made me successful in selling. I found myself interested in them as people rather than merely sales representatives. I didn't just tell them how to sell. I showed them. We went together door to door, two by two. I met with my men weekly in team meetings, spoke with them by telephone throughout the week and when necessary conducted personal visits. As a result of this association, my sales team was number one that year and I was the top salesperson for two years in a row.

Good relationships with coworkers, peers, friends and family form the spokes of the wheel from which we build our careers, families and leisure pursuits. Cultivating good relationships with coworkers, peers, family and others produces synergism and cooperation that enhances our lives in many ways. Our own associations may be composed of a handful or a house full–depending on our respective capacity for love, coupled with how much time and care we are able to offer others. There is no set formula - - the emphasis is on the organism and not the organization. A leader gives his very life to his constituency through the leaders he has selected (selection) to carry forth his vision.

"Everything rises and falls with leadership," Charlie Glass notes. "You cannot lead anyone further than you have been in Christ." When we prize relationships with other people, our cups runneth over in many other areas of our lives. It is therefore prudent for leaders to understand the necessary ingredients for good relationships.

A beginning point in understanding these ingredients for good relationships is having some insight of boundary lines. Ironically, good boundary lines result in freedom, not bondage. Whether the boundaries be the Ten Commandments, the Sermon on the Mount, ethical codes and/or company policies, these lines (also known as guidelines) are necessary for "our little corner of the world" just as much as for the world in general. Boundary lines help you get your heart right with proper motives and thus your lips and behavior will be in harmony.

Curiously, we are inclined to say "yes" in order to be close to people. But, the truth of the matter is that by having good, wholesome boundaries and saying "no", we become close to and intimate with people. With wholesome boundaries, we become more connected with and attached to people, because it frees up the permission to say "yes" without being abused. Having no freedom to say "no" is like hiding behind a mask because we don't have boundaries. Without a proper understanding of the guidelines that make up the comfort zones of others, we cannot possibly avoid manipulating people on our sincere way to motivate others.

One essential guideline making up the comfort zone is that "have to" one. Sure, people might be led to do something that they "have to" for a while but that won't last. A leader who tries to motivate by having people do by "have to" in essence really is a manipulator of fear and guilt. People just are not comfortable with that approach and eventually won't put up with it.

Recognizing the dynamics of boundary lines/guidelines is important for a leader. With this understanding, we can proceed with what I feel are some of the necessary ingredients for developing and sustaining good relationships.

MUTUAL RESPECT

A good example of what respect looks like is accepting our friend's boundaries even though we may not understand them. I had a friend in college who refused to get on an airplane for a vacation we had planned together. He insisted I take the plane and he would take the train and we would meet at our destination later. I didn't understand his fear, but accepted it. Having no particular attachment to the plane ride, I traveled across country with my friend on the train.

Mutual respect doesn't permit any element of control to permeate the relationship, whether the manipulation be through guilt, fear or criticism. Mutual respect means saying "no" to friends when saying "yes" violates our own ethics and values. Finally, mutual respect means honoring other's choices even if we disagree with those choices or beliefs.

Reassure yourself that as you respect the boundary lines/guidelines of others, you become more self reliant and realistic. Others will admire you for your example so much more. Automatically, they will be drawn to you and then become willing for you to depend on them to help you. This is because they now trust that you won't violate their comfort-zone. Their confidence will be that you will treat them as they want to be treated. The commitment of mutual respect gives each person the space to choose, to be separate; to balance out the freedom of interaction between his intellect, emotions and will; the full opportunity to fulfill.

Just think of what wholesomeness there is in your relationship with others when they experience no guilt or fear from you when they say "no" to you. Who said we have to hear "yes" all of the time anyway?

COMMITMENT

Building powerful relationships takes genuine commitment that involves our thoughts, time and feelings. Commitment also means we neither fight nor flee when trouble hits the relationship. Relationships do not thrive unless genuine commitment is present. Just as neglected plants wither and die, so do neglected relationships. Charlie Glass points out that "In every adversity, there lies the seed of a greater benefit, an opportunity to excel."

Commitment means avoiding isolation. Isolation is often utilized as a defense mechanism but we don't get better in a vacuum. There is no compatibility and accountability in isolation. We are healed by the synergy of relationships.

LOYALTY

Creating powerful associations requires loyalty ; from always speaking good of our friends to always being there for them when needed. If we utter malicious statements, we cannot call ourselves a friend. If we turn our backs on people in times of need, we cannot call ourselves a friend. Loyalty extends to interceding for a friend when necessary plus having the courage for a friend when called for and sacrificing for a friend in times of need. Stop criticizing or condemning other people, realizing that your fear of their boundaries reflects back on you.

An aspect of loyalty is forgiveness. We will never have grace until we own our wrong. I can't really be forgiven until I realize how wrong I am.

Without a doubt, the sickest people in all the world are self-centered people with no sense of loyalty to others. These people should be avoided like the plague.

ATTENTION

Attention is the essence of all good relationships. It involves tuning our eyes, ears and senses to the person we are with. This is not an easy thing to learn, for as humans, we all appear more interested in self than in others. Yet through careful attention, as our interest in other people grows, so does our contentment with life.

Paying heed to the needs, concerns and issues important to all of our friends, including our spouses, enables us to build powerful associations that touch our lives in many ways. On one hand, this careful attention to the detail of other's lives demonstrates our love of others. This demonstration makes other people feel worthy and important. In turn, our friends learn to care about us and others as well. In a way it's as if we've created a river of caring that flows from one to the next, never ending and ever enriching.

GIVING

We must give without thought of gain because friendship is not based on what each can do for the other but on how we may enrich each other through sharing. As we give to others, so we shall reap the riches of shared memories, communal experiences and common ideals.

Giving to our friends most usually involves our time–one of our most precious commodities. An attitude that we share instead of sacrifice is paramount in creating good friendships and this attitude then influences the friend. Like a snow ball rolling down the side of a hill, giving and sharing gains strength and is passed from one hand to another.

ENCOURAGEMENT

Building powerful associations requires encouraging others to be the best they can be. True friends find joy in the well-being and success of others. Good leaders know that urging others to do their best is good for that person and good for the community or organization as well. Encouragement, for Charlie Glass, means always being willing to take the initiative to help "a person move one step closer in the process of their pursuit of Godly maturity."

Powerful friendships have neither space for nor understanding of jealousy, so feeling joy on behalf of our friend's good fortune is as easy as being joyous over our own good luck.

SUPPORT

Constructing powerful relationships involves giving our support and assistance when called upon and offering it at times when needed but not called upon.

Support may be in the form of our ear–a vehicle for friends to "get it out" without need or request for advice or assistance. A careful and thoughtful listener may be all our friend needs. We should be alert to those times when our friends need a "listen-to-me" moment. Support may materialize in the form of consoling friends during times of grief or offering a hand when a friend is physically overwhelmed.

Support is also manifest by recognizing and cultivating the talents of our associates.

CONSISTENCY & FAITHFULNESS

In order to enable good relationships to thrive, we must offer dependable support to our friends consistently. Our faithfulness also extends to remembrance after death as a way of keeping that person alive in our hearts and minds.

"Encouragement, for Charlie Glass, means always being willing to take the initiative to help "a person move one step closer in the process of their pursuit of Godly maturity."

SETTING BOUNDARIES

I prefaced this examination of the necessary ingredients for developing and sustaining good relationships with a brief discussion of boundaries/guidelines because good relationships have boundaries, as do all things in life.

Accepting friends as they are is one way of allowing people to be who and what they are. This gives them permission to believe in things contrary to our thinking without fear of ridicule.

Setting boundaries means we make no judgment about who they are, what they do or how they think unless they hurt others. Setting boundaries allows a person to be the owner of his own problems.

We, as friends, may offer advice if asked or help if necessary, but we must be aware that we are not responsible for our friends happiness. Thus, setting boundaries protects our individuality as well as that of our friends.

Guidelines for each relationship in our lives will be as different as the people in the relationship. What works for one will be poison to another. The leader who understands and accepts other's differences is the one who draws others to him, giving him more power and resources than the person who fights differences.

To fully appreciate the concept of boundaries, it is necessary to explore a few of the myths associated with boundaries.

One myth is that if I set boundaries, I am being selfish. This is untrue. Boundaries define freedom and make self-control possible. Boundaries enforce good relationships with God and others. It is in relationship that I am liberated from isolation and self-hate. Boundaries are stewardship and not selfishness.

Another misconception about boundaries is that they are a sign of disobedience. The reality is sometimes we say "no" to others because we say "yes" to God.

Establishing limits does not mean you are going to lose love. Setting limits in fact connects you to others. People with limits have more love than anyone in the world. People with limits attract healthy people. They repel "users and takers" and they are better able to discern good and evil.

Setting boundaries will not hurt others because boundaries are not an offensive weapon. Boundaries are not a sign of anger. Boundaries are proactive, not reactive. People with boundaries are not angry. They are calm and at peace because their boundaries protect them. Setting boundaries is not isolating yourself from others who have done much for you. Love is always a free gift. Remember, when you respond to love in guilty compliance, you are not really loving. There is no fear or guilt in love. One of the most important things to realize about boundaries is that while they are permanent, they are not set in concrete. Boundaries can be subject to change. Boundaries can be negotiated and renegotiated.

Clearly, as you embrace as well as welcome the boundaries/guidelines of others, you will learn to love more and be loved more. Without this give and take, you have nothing. Or to put it another way, when the other person is free not to care for you, then they want to do so. Paradoxical isn't it? Yes, but that's life.

While many leaders seem to be born with natural people skills, that flair to go with the flow, it is a fact that many leaders and those followers who want to be leaders do not have natural people skills. It is important for the leader of leaders to constantly polish personality skills. This requires revisiting the ingredients for good relationships, constantly improving character development, always enhancing the cultivation of personality and consistently refining communicative skills.

Wise is the leader who revisits and refines!

What ultimately occurs when we nurture and develop close ties with a variety of people is the formation of a personal support network. This network is a necessary ingredient for personal happiness that cannot be substituted. This lifetime asset–close relationships–is one of the leader's most potent weapons in meeting goals, overcoming obstacles and produces a life worth living. A component of relationships is becoming interdependent, which is the happy medium between the two extremes of independence and over dependence.

We must all realize that focusing on the organism instead of the organization gains more for both as well as reaping bountiful rewards for ourselves as well. The gains then multiply as we share more of ourselves with others until synergy is established in the form of people harmoniously working together producing startling results. As illustrated in the Old Testament, one champion slays 1,000 but two champions slay 10,000.

7
PASSION

THE POWER OF ENTHUSIASM

FEATURING

ANTHONY D. CAMPOLO, PH.D.
MISSIONARY STATESMAN, CAMPOLO MINISTRIES

"Faith is the daring of the soul
to go farther
than it can see."

-- William Newton Clarke

No one can deny the tremendous power of being caught up in a wave of enthusiasm. We see it in winning sports teams, the players of a well-received stage drama or in the simple fun and pleasurable antics of children at play.

What makes passion and enthusiasm so magical is how easily it spreads its influence for the good of others. A good leader is passionate about every facet of his work from the smallest detail to the largest agenda. He realizes that caring deeply about all aspects of his mission is vital in bringing forth a fruitful and beneficial outcome.

A leader's passion is often translated and transferred to his constituents as they visualize his dreams and embrace the leader's goals as their own. The combined enthusiasm of the team then spreads outward like a great ocean that seeps into the masses drop by drop. Enthusiasm motivates and inspires. It is a leader's natural conviction that what he is doing or attempting possesses seeds of greatness that benefit all people. This enthusiasm is born from vision, not money, power or material possessions. And without it, nothing great can be accomplished.

Passion is internalized power that radiates to others around us. Enthusiasm generated for causes and good rather than self-serving ends will always be shared and passed on from generation to generation in our ever vigilant striving to make this a better world. It is the leader's responsibility to pass the torch of enthusiasm to each of his followers to ensure its longevity and keep its flame vibrant. In so doing, he also ensures the chances of passing the passion for the goal to others along the way and thereby builds up his power base of constituents and followers. People who work from a base of passion do so with joy and fervor. Difficult tasks become less so. Suddenly, mundane work seems pleasurable. Team effort creates new relationships with a common goal.

When I first asked Tony Campolo to accept my nomination of him as a leader of leaders, I also gave him a choice between several leadership sectors for which I thought he was qualified. I was surprised when he chose the religious sector, because it made perfect sense that Tony would choose the regional sector. As a person who works and lives in prosperity in St. David's, Pennsylvania on the Main Line, he exemplifies a true leader of leaders because of his work in bridging the gap between his community and the inner city and has served the lives of thousands. He even became a member of an African-American church in Philadelphia, Pennsylvania and serves on their board so that he might better "tune in to their needs." He even counseled me to "go thou and do likewise," if I was at all serious about really impacting my time, talent, and money in the city, not just the suburbs. I personally followed

Tony's example and for almost a year now, I have been involved in two churches: one in the suburbs, and one in the inner city, New Covenant Church of Philadelphia. I have already discovered the wisdom and benefit of his advice. So I ask again, why would he not want to be honored for regionalism?

We could also raise the question about missions, or international leadership. Certainly, Tony has excelled in the phenomenal work he has done in Haiti. Some of the more than 20 books he has written have been translated into foreign languages. Immediately after he committed himself to accept this nomination and to attend our Leader Of Leaders Premier Celebration, Tony left the country and went around the world to speak in Hong Kong!

I will always remember the surprise I felt upon receiving the thoughtful postcard he sent me, recognizing that, while I was still going through rehabilitation while on disability, I was also taking on the challenges of the Valley Forge Leadership Prayer Breakfast, Promise Keepers and Harvest Crusade. Here is what he wrote:

> ***"The words of William Carey are important as you undertake the Harvest Crusade***
>
> ***'Attempt great things for God. Expect great things from God.'"***

TONY CAMPOLO

Those who are at least familiar with Tony know that he is a passionate visionary who is not a stickler for detail! For instance, it was not the missionary statesman William Carey of India, but rather Hudson Taylor of China. Secondly, he reversed the lines of the poem! Of course, these distinctions are inconsequential because I know that in sharing them with me they come from Tony's heart. His passion touches my heart! And that's what counts. My only question is–how did Tony Campolo ever get a Ph.D. with such recollection powers? Someone has answered, "Tony's degree is a Doctorate in Passionate Heart." That would explain it.

What brought Anthony Campolo to the leadership role he now plays throughout the world? He is many things to many people: minister, teacher, visionary, prophet, speaker, lecturer, sociologist, politician, evangelist, author, television personality, humorist, husband, father and friend. His passion is to make this world a better place in which to live by having each and every person believe in what God has in store for them in the future. Their dreams and vision of what they might become, nurtured by the Holy Spirit, will impact their lives more than anything else that they have endured. Apparently, it is his own clear vision of his life's work that has thrust him into what has become this leadership role.

In his book, *Wake Up America! Answering God's Radical Call While Living in the Real World,* Tony Campolo issues a prophetic call for committed Christians to wake up and minister to those who have been excluded from the American dream. He echoes the call of Jesus Christ with convincing authority, a message that comes straight from the Word and from his own heart. In our prosperous nation, a land of opportunity and plenty, we tend to sidestep the tough issues of poverty, hunger and fear that are daily realities for some. He presents a new vision, a new purpose for the lives of many sincere, committed Christians who feel an emptiness, a yearning that material well-being has been unable to satisfy. He offers a call to action for "middle range" Christians–believers who live in the "real world" of careers, family commitments and credit card bills, yet feel the need to experience something of the radically transformed lifestyle that Jesus promises. He challenges Christians to involve themselves in grassroots ministries that work for change in America. His is a clear and inspired voice of a modern prophet bringing Christ's message to the crowded wilderness of our cities' streets, a voice that unequivocally asserts that a life of conviction and service is synonymous with a Biblically based life of faith, a life driven by compassion, idealism and justice.

John Perkins who is the president of John M. Perkins Foundation of Pasadena, California, stated, "I believe that *Wake Up America!* could become one of the most important books of our time." Lloyd John Ogilvie who is pastor of the First Presbyterian Church of Hollywood, said "A penetrating diagnosis of the sickness of the soul of our culture and an urgent call for an authentic spiritual awakening that leads to obedient discipleship. This book is solidly Biblical and a bracing analysis of what it means to run with the Master on a two-legged gospel of personal commitment and compassionate mission."

Author Philip Yancey observed, "Tony Campolo is too funny to fit the usual stereotype of prophet. But he certainly says prophetic things that the church needs to listen to. And in this book he takes the further, more difficult step of pointing to examples of people who are doing it right." Author J. I. Packer stated, "Here Tony Campolo, activist extraordinaire and visionary motivator, opens his mind and heart on aspects of the spiritual renewal that America needs. Perceiving that true revival has feet, he maps out paths of neighbor-love along which quickened Christians should be walking today. One need not agree with all his opinions to find profound instruction and challenge in these pages."

Ruth A. Tucker who is visiting professor at Trinity Evangelical Divinity School, notes, "A powerful, prophetic message for America in the 1990s. A must-read for all followers of Jesus."

In his book, Tony Campolo asserts that we need a prophet in America today. "We need more than a sociological critique explaining what is wrong with us and how we got this way. We need a prophet who will weep for America, who sill stir us to a memory of what we were meant to be, who will reach into our collective consciousness, and who will draw out of it the sorrowful memory of the real American dream." He illustrates that a prophet will also have to teach us to weep, that weeping will break the numbness of our hearts and minds and teach us how to feel again, and will break the mesmerizing spell of the deadly present and show us how to be passionate again.

> ***"If the message of the prophet is needed anywhere, it is needed on the campuses of this nation. There are students at just about every college and university who concur with the diagnosis that apathy rules as the predominant psychic condition of the academic community. The kind of rallies and riots that marked the sixties are gone and forgotten. What was once an emotionally upset and angry student population has settled down. And while there have been a few petitions against apartheid in South Africa and some isolated forums on environmental issues, there have been few signs of the revolutionary fervor that was so evident among students during the Johnson and Nixon years....But there are rumblings. In the midst of this pervading collegiate apathy, something new seems to be struggling to live."***
>
> Tony Campolo, *Wake Up America!*

He further explains that a greater task of the prophet will be to nurture, nourish and evoke a vision of an alternative to the dominant system and generate hope for something that lies beyond the present order to energize us, motivate us to act and give us courage. The prophet will project a new dynamism for change that dispels apathy and generates passion.

In a conversation with some young people, they reflected on the times in which we live and were asked by Tony to suggest what such a prophet might be like if God should raise one up today–which voice out of the historical past would America most need to hear today. Among those mentioned was Mahatma Gandhi, who profoundly altered the course of history for India and England. His call for nonviolent opposition to tyranny, his compassionate plea for people to recognize their common sacred humanity and his hope for a world in which spiritual sensitivity to all living creatures might prevail all amounted to a message for our time.

> ***"A national news network does a special on the changing behavior of college students during spring break. Whereas in former years they all seemed to flock to such resort areas as Palm Springs, California, or Ft. Lauderdale, Florida, there is a rising tendency for some of them to spend this time in community service. Working among the poor in Appalachia or on Native American reservations in Arizona, a new breed of students is demonstrating that it gets its gratification out of helping and giving."***
>
> Tony Campolo, *Wake Up America!*

The young people also agreed that St. Francis of Assisi could be a prophet for our time. Tony observed that if St. Francis were here today, he would not so much condemn us for our consumer-oriented materialism as he would weep over our failure to see where life and love can be most fully experienced and actualized–among the poor. St. Francis was, above all else, committed to the poor. He found in them a real presence of Christ and was convinced that as he embraced the poor, he embraced the Lord Himself. St. Francis' commitment to peace was also attractive to these young people who have become cynical about wars and the economic interests behind them and skeptical of the related political slogans. With St. Francis, peace was not just an absence of war created by a balance of power. Instead, it was an attitude toward those who would define themselves as enemies. His only goal was to tell them about Jesus and help them to realize that in Jesus they could all be brothers and sisters.

"Feeling is the interpretation of reality through the senses. Emotioin is strong feeling. PASSION is extremely strong feeling."

A third suggestion as prophet was Martin Luther King, whose voice called us away from the deadness of our consumer-oriented way of life and challenged us to an idealism of an America that is "not yet." He almost made us believe that we had a higher calling and a more noble destiny than we were living. We resonated to his words as he set forth his prophetic vision, and they are repeated here, because it represents so strongly the beliefs, ideals, and passion of Tony Campolo:

"I say to you today, my friends, that in spite of the difficulties and frustrations of the moment, I still have a dream. It is a dream deeply rooted in the

American dream.
I have a dream that one day this nation will rise up and live out the true meaning of its creed: 'We hold these truths to be self-evident; that all men are created equal.'
I have a dream that one day on the red hills of Georgia the sons of former slaves and the sons of former slave owners will be able to sit down together at the table of brotherhood.
I have a dream that one day even the state of Mississippi, a desert state sweltering with the heat of injustice and oppression, will be transformed into an oasis of freedom and justice.
I have a dream that my four little children will one day live in a nation where they will not be judged by the color of their skin but by the content of their character.
I have a dream today.
I have a dream that one day the state of Alabama, whose governor's lips are presently dripping with words of interposition and nullification, will be transformed into a situation where little black boys and black girls will be able to join hands with little white boys and white girls and walk together as sisters and brothers.
I have a dream today.
I have a dream that one day every valley shall be exalted, every hill and mountain shall be made low, the rough places will be made plain and the crooked places will be made straight, and the glory of the Lord shall be revealed, and all flesh shall see it together."

Tony's beginnings were in Philadelphia where he was born, ordained, and married. His passion has taken him not only throughout the nation but to the far corners of the world where his message is welcomed, needed and absorbed by thousands. He is in great demand at colleges and universities as well as in the corporate and business community. His message touches a need, a hunger, in all of us regardless of our status in life–from those living in the ghetto to those working in the highest ranks of business or government.

Tony Campolo recognizes these needs in individuals, in families, in societies, and sets in motion the plans that help people to realize their greatest potential. To help those who feel defeated, lost, and hopeless. He enlists the help of those with the potential to be catalysts of change. He has established several organizations that are thriving and working toward building the best that humanity has to offer. He is founder and president of the EAPE-Campolo Ministries (Evangelical Association for the Promotion of Education). This organization is involved in educational, medical and economic development programs in various Third

World countries, including Haiti and the Dominican Republic, as well as extensive work among at-risk youth in urban America. According to Tony, "EAPE has touched, molded and challenged a lot of young people. Many of them have continued on to do great things for others in the name of Christ. This is what our ministry is all about." Each of the outreach organizations of EAPE is meeting the problems of our society in many different ways. To put it another way, these are all different expressions of Tony's passion for so many people with diverse needs.

Urban Promise, an outreach ministry founded and supported by EAPE, seeks to equip children and young adults with the skills necessary for spiritual growth, academic achievement, life management, and Christian leadership. Operating in Camden, New Jersey since 1985, this ministry includes after-school programs, a Street Leaders Program for teens, summer and sports camps, and a gospel choir that performs children's musicals. Printworks, a unique outreach of Urban Promise, produces high quality screen-printed clothing and cards in a realistic work environment that trains employees from surrounding neighborhoods and develops their individual potential. Discouraging numbers of dropouts in the Camden public schools might cause some to despair and feel a sense of hopelessness in our youth, but Urban Promise is making a difference. Growing numbers of students in the Street Leaders Program, who are gradually envisioning new possibilities for their lives, are now considering a college education.

The many faceted aspects of Tony's passion figuratively have propelled him to enhance educational needs in Haiti, even for the elementary need for reading. That's why EAPE family of ministries is Beyond Borders. This organization works to provide Haitians with the opportunity to learn to do two of life's most vital functions: to read and to write. Fewer than one in four Haitians can read. Although the current democratically elected government has shown commitment to making education available for everyone, years of neglect by past rulers has taken a heavy toll. Today, fewer than one-quarter of Haitian children complete grade school, and only one percent graduate from high school. The lack of educational opportunities has contributed to Haiti's many social problems. Haiti has the highest infant mortality rate, the highest level of malnutrition, and the lowest life expectancy of any nation in the Western Hemisphere. In spite of working tremendously hard, over half of all Haitians earn less than $100 a year. Haitians desperately want a better life, and they know that learning to read and write is absolutely crucial to combating their country's many social problems. Beyond Borders exists to meet that need. Within the walls of Literacy Centers, which are staffed by Haitian community members as teachers, thousands have learned to read, write and develop other skills needed to break the bonds of poverty. Tony Campolo reflects, "I like Beyond Borders because they help people in such a way that when the people do enter into a better life they can say, 'We did it ourselves.' That's what we want, not an organization that's out to bring honor and power to itself, but is out to empower indigenous people to solve their own problems."

The Transformation Travel initiative of Beyond Borders seeks to build relationships across borders and challenge people to look at their lives in a new way–a way that reflects global realities. Participating groups travel to Haiti for one or two weeks, meeting people from Haitian communities and learning about their faith, their struggles and their joys. They witness community organizations wrestling against great odds to make a better life for their people. They interact with both Haitians and expatriates who have spent years working for the justice and peace of God's kingdom. Emphasis is placed on learning and growing through new insights and awareness. Participants perform their most important service after they return home in the response they make to their experience and in their life choices that promote local and global justice and peace.

The Apprenticeship in Shared Living program of Beyond Borders places Christians in rural Haitian communities for 18 to 36 months. With Jesus and his incarnation as a model, the apprentice learns to share in the life of a Haitian community, learning their language and culture. The apprentice learns to live out the Gospel in a way that truly speaks to their community–demonstrating love by giving up privileges and power, laying aside their own way of doing things, their comforts and their very lives.

Kingdomworks is a unique Christian organization dedicated to empowering inner city churches to reach out to children and young people. Kingdomworks' mission is to help kids on the street build positive relationships with Christian adults, with one another and with God. Its goal is to develop solid urban ministries and to raise up a new generation of missionaries, proclaiming the hope of Jesus Christ. Through its summer camps and outreach events, internships, youth workers, weekend retreats and training programs, this goal is being met.

The Cornerstone Christian Academy, founded in 1988, is a Christ-centered elementary/middle school with high ambitions for itself and it's over 300 students. As part of EAPE, this school's mission is to become a beacon of hope–a place where the vision has been defined as, "To educate the children we serve from public housing and the surrounding Southwest Philadelphia community in an environment that provides high standards for academic achievement and spiritual development." Cornerstone has become an anchor of stability for the community, helping to provide service for the working poor and lower-middle class families. Cornerstone is committed to standing with the community and against the political and social-economic forces that continue to strip it of its dignity. Over the years, Cornerstone has grown from four classrooms with fewer than 60 students to 13 classes with more than 300 children. Major renovation of the urban campus has been required to keep pace with this growth. Betty Wright Riggins, B.A., M.A., head of the school noted, "Our faculty is made up of qualified, dedicated, Christian teachers. Each is committed to teaching children more than academics, more than reading, writing and arithmetic, more even than science, art, and computing. Each is also committed to teaching children respect–respect for God, respect for others and respect for themselves as unique persons with unique talents. Teachers are assisted in class by interns recruited for a year of missionary work in Christian education." She added, "God has determined that we will educate, evangelize and emancipate."

EAPE-Campolo Ministries also helped to establish the Evangelical University of the Dominican Republic, the Nueva Esperanza-Hispanic Clergy of Philadelphia, and a new initiative, Orthopraxis, a student volunteer movement working to unite thousand of college students and inner-city ministries to provide meaningful volunteer summer internships. These are some of the many ways m which Tony Campolo and his organizations have touched the lives of so many, many people.

It is clear that Tony Campolo's passion and enthusiasm have led him to find ways to help individuals and society as a whole: "If you say that the world can't be changed, you're wrong! Together with Christ we can become a movement so powerful that the gates of Hell shall not prevail against it." He was captivated and motivated by the realization that in the heart of God there is a special love for the poor and oppressed. He believes that his mission is to challenge, train, and deploy college-aged young people to minister to those society has labeled "the last and the least of these." Through ministries in urban America and in Third World countries, EAPE-Campolo Ministries carries out this mission.

Tony Campolo is a best selling author and has 25 books presently in print. He has articulated his perceptions of Christian-based realities and has inspired leaders in government, business, and education to re-evaluate their goals and missions. Through his writing, he has motivated people in all walks of life throughout the world to raise their expectations and has guided them to experience God's love. He currently hosts a weekly television program, "Hashing It Out," that is carried by cable television to 28 million homes. He and prominent preacher Steve Brown of Orlando model the ways that Christians can disagree, learn from each other, and use the Bible in working through the hot issues of our society.

Tony Campolo's focus on the future is expressed through his conviction that a personal relationship with Christ will transform us into a new person. In an article in Prism May/June 1995, he wrote, "Nobody doubts that what has happened in by-gone days, especially in the formative days of childhood, heavily influences what we are and who we are today. What we have to question is any claim that the past determines who and what we are. So many of us bear the scars of traumas and painful relationships of our pasts. When I talk with the ghetto kids we try to reach through our ministries, I would despair for them if I believed that the past was of ultimate importance. For most of them, the past has been so ugly, and so filled with horrendous abuse that if who and what they are lay with the past, they would be hopeless.

"The good news is that for each of them there are great possibilities. In counseling them, I do not so much pay attention to their pasts as I help them believe in what God has in store for them in the future. Once they see what they can be in Christ, then the hold of what they once were is broken. Their dreams and vision of what they might become, nurtured by the Holy Spirit, impacts their lives more than anything demonic in days gone by. Christ will set us free from what we have been and we will sense Him inviting us to believe that in His plan for our lives. This is what it means for us to enjoy salvation by grace through faith. For in essence, our faith is wrapped up in our hopes and dreams of our future in Christ."

8

Impartation

The Power of Influence

Featuring

David Wardell, Ph.D.

Co-Founder, Promisekeepers

"If Shakespeare should come into
this room, we would all rise;
but if Jesus Christ should come in,
we would all kneel"

-- Charles Lamb

Webster's New World Dictionary defines the word "impart" as: "to give a share or portion or; give, to tell, reveal." How perfectly it fits into the overall picture of leadership development. For as passion is the power of enthusiasm, it tends to consume a leader's entire body, soul and spirit with the vision and mission before him. Impartation is the sharing of that vision with the leaders who follow the leader. I like to think of it as the "passing of the torch" as portrayed in the Olympics. Imparting or sharing is the eloquent transmission of one's vision and mission. It is the power of influence from the very heart.

By association with one another, leaders already have a lot going for them. In their leadership roles, these individuals influence the lives of others. They impart intended influence that becomes lasting influence. The deeper meaning of this principle can be more greatly appreciated by a brief study of other words that have the same basic root word, but different prefixes. For instance, let us look at the word "depart." The meaning is totally different from the word "impart." Yet, it is common for many leaders to be tempted at least, if not actually to leave–quit–get away from it all: to depart.

Next, let us look at another word with a different prefix: rampart. This word means fortress or ornament for defense purposes. Clearly, the last thing a leader wants to develop in people is defensiveness. That is just another form of selfishness and self-centered manipulation. If we just change the prefix of the root word a major difference in the meaning occurs! The point I'm trying to make is that if you really focus on imparting your vision, mission and passion to others, you will never have to worry about departing, or being defensive (rampart). Leaders who share or impart to others are truly giving persons. They tend to be giving of self, as well of time, talent and money. Without a doubt, giving is at the core of imparting, and is the antithesis of a person who is only looking out for number one.

There is a great price to pay on the part of the leader of leaders who wants this form of power of influence. That price is a life of giving: giving away of yourself to others as freely as God has given to you. As leaders, we must realize that what we have is of value and that it is graciously received from God and others.

Jonathan's noble friendship with David before he became King of Israel serves as a classic illustration of the power of imparting. The essence of this genuine friendship was a primary ingredient in the leadership of others, when the stakes were high. Saul, the reigning first King of Israel, had disqualified himself. Because Jonathan was Saul's son and also David's friend, he had a conflict of loyalty. He resolved this conflict by maintaining an honorable attitude toward his father, King Saul, but was not blinded by his loyalty.

Jonathan did not condone his father's disqualification, nor his subsequent jealousy and violent rage that drove Saul to try to murder David. At one point, Jonathan gave totally of himself when defending David and ended up being pinned against a wall by the spear of his own father. What were the ingredients of this relationship that could lead to such sacrificial love and loyalty? To answer these questions, we need to go back to the original source of the Hebrew Old Testament in the Holy Scriptures. In I Samuel, Chapter 14, Jonathan and his armor bearer slew 20 enemy soldiers. A bit against the odds, was it not? You see, this is significant because David slew the giant, Goliath, yet Jonathan's father, Saul was too frightened to fight. So, you see, the respective victories shared by David and Jonathan were the basis of their friendship because they had a mutual respect for one another.

A true leader does not need to have the affection of his followers, but there must be mutual respect. Mutual respect must be cultivated as the absolute foundation in any relationship. In a marriage, mutual respect means one can continue to live unconditionally even after the emotional and physical love of the relationship has burned out. Mutual respect serves the married couple as adequate reason to remain true to their marriage vows. Indubitably, mutual respect is the bedrock foundation for all precious relationships.

Once mutual respect was established between David and Jonathan, it created an emotional love that existed between the two of them. We must all work hard at cultivating emotional love for one another within relationships: married couples, friends and leaders. In the case of Jonathan and David, the emotional love came about by overcoming the barrier of abuse, as evidenced in Saul's persecution of David after he was anointed by God to be the next King of Israel and to replace Saul.

Let us take a closer look at emotional love. I do not mean a syrupy emotionalism, nor do I mean uncontrolled or extreme feelings. I am referring to the definition of "feeling" as defined in the Webster's New World Dictionary. Note the progression below:

1. Feeling is the interpretation of reality through the five senses of seeing, smelling, hearing, tasting and touching.
2. Emotion is strong feeling.
3. Passion is very strong feeling.

When I speak of emotional love in this book, I am referring to friendship and how we develop strong feelings for each other to compliment the already established logical, intellectual and mental respect we have for one another. Clearly, this requires a building process as we see in the example of 1 Samuel, 14-19. The price of building such a friendship may be summarized as, "the knitting of their two souls together." One of the problems in the modern day is that we do not have enough intimacy amongst men. I suppose this is a result of World War II when it was frowned upon if men or boys cried because it thought to be a feminine trait. Intimacy is simply and wonderfully being chained together, feeling joy and sorrow together. Intimacy is figuratively the consistent, persistent application of the second commandment of Lord Jesus Christ, "Love your neighbor as yourself." Jonathan did this by voluntarily giving up the throne to which he was entitled through inheritance so that his good friend David could be king.

There is a distinct graduation of intensity. Doctors, psychologists and psychiatrists advise us to trust our feelings or emotions, for many times they are the most accurate monitor we have. Our instincts are the "monitor" or "judgment" factor that signals our decision making process. Often when reason falls short, our emotions come to our aid. We must remember that humans are composed of three basic parts: intellect, emotion and will, all of which should work together efficiently and spontaneously as an organic whole. To downplay or over-emphasize any of the three is foolish.

Jonathan's commitment to David was great and he did not give up his rights to the throne grudgingly. He understood that God had anointed David to be king. I think the power in Jonathan's actions tells us that "second fiddles" of the world may be many times more secure than we think. They have their act together well enough to serve as a stepping stone for the more insecure, so that in the edifying relationship, the person who is the most insecure is made more secure.

We see in I Samuel, 16 that David had low self-esteem because of his father. He had been omitted from the anointing when the Prophet Samuel visited their home. It was only through the supernatural grace of the spirit of God that Samuel persistently sought out David as the "not so considered one."

When David came on the scene to slay Goliath, his older brother, Elias, treated David in the same condescending manner as his father. He asked, "What are you doing here?" An indication of how much he despised David. As if that insult was not enough, he continued, "Why aren't you tending your few sheep." God compensated David by giving him a real friend Jonathan. Real friends also act as leaders. The Christian Business Men's Committee, International defines leadership as: "A leader is one who helps those who follow to take one step closer to his/her goal." This definition surely fits Jonathan, for in addition to accepting and understanding David as he was, Jonathan also helped David to become greater. The third and last major ingredient in "the essence of genuine friendship" as modeled in the story of David and Jonathan is a genuine commitment. Notice how the components of friendship parallel with the three basic parts of the human personality.

Human Personality	Friendship Components
Intellect	Intellectual Respect
Emotion	Emotional Love
Will	Genuine Commitment

Clearly, it is by our will that we choose to make a genuine commitment. This is the agape, unconditional love spoken of in the New Testament. This kind of love is not based on what another thinks, says or does. It is the ultimate love which God has for us, and is the love we should have toward our neighbor as Jesus commanded. Jesus also commanded, "Love one another as I have loved you. Greater love has no one than this one lay down his life for his friend." This is precisely what Jonathan did for David. He loved David so much that he laid down his own ambitions, his kingship, his life in defending David. He virtually risked his life, time and again for David and in doing so, jeopardized his father-son relationship with Saul. He was loyally committed to David until the end when he laid down his life in battle.

"A real friendship is one in which both are mutually committed to the best interests of each other."

Genuine commitment requires that one must first give of self. One gives of thoughts, feelings and will until death itself. Our scriptural example implies that a friend always speaks well of a friend. Jonathan interceded for David; he was courageous; he sacrificed for him. While jealousy and rage drove his father, Jonathan remained loyal to his father, but did not compromise his genuine loyalty to his friend. He honored his father by not retaliating against him. Furthermore, this genuine commitment included encouraging David when he knew of his fear. A true, committed friend puts the friend before himself.

The fact is that most of us have been abused in some way in our lives. As a result, unless we are privileged to have a special friend like Jonathan, we still carry around the extra baggage of depression and anger.

Unfortunately, other leaders disqualify themselves as leaders, as did Saul, for selfish reasons. They do so when they take on an egotistical attitude that says: "I can handle it," or "Leave me alone," or "It's my problem," or "It's none of your business." The best leaders qualify themselves by being vulnerable, humble, and accountable to their followers and co-leaders. To a team, there is nothing more refreshing than when a leader humbly acknowledges to all that he "blew it" or frankly states, "I'm having a tough time;" or "I need your help;" or "Would you forgive me?"

Some leaders fear that if they admit to weaknesses, people will lose confidence in them. Actually it works just the opposite. People, especially fellow leaders, admire honesty for it indicates courage. Why is it that we have so many things backwards or upside down? No wonder the world thought the early Christian Church made such incredible and miraculous progress in the first century and then said the Church "turned the world upside down."

As we approach the coming millennium, it would be wonderful to have another worldwide reformation that "turned the world upside down." The kind of modern day man who is doing just that is Dave Wardell, co-founder of the Promise Keepers movement that is sweeping our country today. Dave is a modern day version of Jonathan. He is a person of integrity who is willingly taking the initiative to befriend fellow leaders. Although both Dave and Bill McCartney co-founded this movement, Dave acknowledges Bill as the founder. Usually leaders are vying for each other's positions, but here, as with Jonathan and David, we see leaders working together.

Like Jonathan, Dave Wardell honors his Christian brother and special friend, Bill McCartney and gives him all the credit for creating Promise Keepers; yet, he is equally responsible for this Million Man Movement. While giving thanks in prayer that Dave had agreed to be our guest speaker, a wonderful insight hit me that a person greater than Jonathan is coming to Valley Forge, the birthplace of America, in the person of Dave Wardell. I remember that he would phone to encourage me while he was on a vacation and hunting trip. Note his sacrificial spirit to call me while on vacation. He suggested that I choose a speaker more established than he, such as Dr. Howard G. Hendricks or Dr. Charles Swindoll. I almost had to fight to convince him that I wanted him. Once Dave and I made a covenant over the phone, I felt a great burden lift from me. Then I knew. This is a man of God, sent by God to serve as our leader of leaders, to do for us what Jonathan did for David. I was so excited!

While still on my knees giving thanks, I also realized that Dave is being used in a miraculous way to serve as leader for the first Leader of Leaders Premier Celebration. At that time, 5,000 leaders will be gathered at Valley Forge. What could be more beautiful than to think of thou sands of modern day Jonathans returning home after they came to be led by such an example as Dave?

Some leaders fear that others may get too much credit, recognition or praise, but this is not the case with great leaders. It is the generous leader who gives credit to others and considers it a compliment if one of his fellow leaders becomes a greater leader than he. Like Albert Einstein, he challenges his students to "Stand on my shoulders and go higher."

Samuel continued to portray the fond memories David has for Jonathan after his death. I am also reminded that Lincoln served us as a wonderful Jonathan role model. As Reverend Henry Eisenhart wrote in an article, "Lincoln was great because of goodness." With Eisenhart's permission, I include his article here: "Many years ago, a sick woman, with but a few days to live, lay down on a pallet dreaming a golden dream. Calling her only son, a lean, lanky lad, to her bedside, she gazed into his deep dark eyes with her own dim sight and communicated to him her glowing vision and hope. Her own years had been few and unflavored. Her life had been occupied by the limitations of a pioneer life. Her castle, a log cabin; her hopes were bounded by forest-clad hills and mighty streams. Her paths led only to deeper enclosures and darker dells. She had hoped and dreamed in vain. Life offered little or no rewards. The days brought few actual joys. Her boy shall know no such imprisonment. He shall break the barriers that enclosed her, and crash the gates of her imprisonment. In him her dreams shall come true, her hopes enjoy the highest fulfillment. Drawing the boy close to her bed, she noted the print of the woodland life, and the crudities of their pioneer existence stamped upon his face and form. She despaired for a moment. Touching his brown, coarse cheeks with her soft, white fingers, she caught his gaze and held it with her deep meaningful eyes. Drawing his face close to her own, she whispered the magic words–words that held her dreams: "My boy, be somebody."

Thus, Nancy Hanks Lincoln planted a golden dream in the soul of Abraham Lincoln. The world knows the result. Her magic words were the golden stairs upon which the son of Nancy Hanks Lincoln climbed to fame. Out of a mother's fear and disappointment, Lincoln realized a cherished dream. This challenge to her nine-year-old son was not easy to achieve, but dogged persistency won. When Abe Lincoln was a young man, he ran for the legislature in Illinois and was trounced. He entered business, but failed. He was in love with a beautiful, young woman to whom he became engaged. Then she died. Entering politics again, he ran for Congress and was badly defeated. He then tried to get an appointment to the States Lane Office, but failed. In 1856 he became a candidate for the Vice-Presidency and was again defeated. Then, in 1858 Stephen A. Douglas, a popular and skillful orator for the United States Senate, defeated him. "It's about time you quit trying, isn't it?" Inquired a friend. "No time to quit," was Lincoln's reply, "I'm too busy preparing to make another attempt." He wrote his name indelibly in the history of the United States by easily winning the presidential election of 1860, receiving 180 electoral votes to 72 for John C. Breckinridge, 29 for John Bell, and 12 for Stephen A. Douglas. The keynote of Lincoln's greatness is given in his own words: "I am not bound to win, but I am bound to be true, I am not bound to succeed, but I am bound to live up to what light I have." He was great because he was steadfast, patient, far-sighted, honest, true. Combine these qualities into one comprehending word. He was great because he was good. Nancy Lincoln's dream came true. Her boy became "somebody" one of our best and most beloved presidents. In grateful humility, he added: "In all that I am or ever hope to be, I owe to my angel mother."

My own mother, Helen was just as much a "Jonathan" to me. She always told me, "Son, keep your word. Your word is the most valuable asset you have. Without it, you're nothing. Even if it hurts, keep your word, for in the end, you'll hurt yourself and others a lot more if you don't. Make me proud of you son." Little did I then realize how biblically based my mother's advice was. Later when I went on to seminary and doctoral studies, I discovered what theology calls the "doctrine of commitment" and realized it as exactly what my mother's advice was all about.

God in His perfect timing brought Dave Wardell into my life to surround me with an ongoing support system, whereby I keep on keeping on as a man of his word, a man of integrity. Yet, I must conclude that time spent in giving to others is not enough in itself, for who wants a mediocre Christian rubbing off his faults onto some new Christian? My friend Dick Varnum states, "One of the principal shortcomings of people today, in giving service to others, is how to care enough to give our best." Another friend, Darrell Lind said, "The main reason why I was afraid to share my faith in Christ was because I had no real life message of any value." How do we keep it working? How do we keep that snowball rolling? In order for the glorious reality of discipling to be a continuing reality, everyone has to impart his life to others. Certainly the answer is not an academic one. Giving of one's self pays off. Now, here we are 22 years later, and Darrell and his wife, Carol, are leaders of leaders in their own right . . . through their home life, through their church and through their community, helping others to help themselves so they in turn can help others to become leaders of leaders.

When we make the genuine "Jonathan" kind of commitment to another, we are living up to the true standards of imparting. We must bear in mind that the power of imparting is the power of influence. Whether we are aware of so doing or not, everything we say or do influences those about us. Not only must we make a commitment to our fellow men to give the best we have to give, but we must remember that we must also commit to being the best we can be at all times. As always, it is the act that speaks louder than do the words themselves and it is by those everyday acts that we are judged by other people, co-leaders, and team members. When leaders hold themselves to the highest of standards and performance, so too do they encourage others to do the same. Let us sow seeds of the highest quality as we influence others. Then we must tend to those seeds with loving care so that they may grow and bring forth that which is excellent in every way. Thus do we contribute to and improve our own cycle of life, influencing the other cycles yet to come. For as we have seen in the examples of Jonathan and Abraham Lincoln. The power of influence continues to influence others for many generations to come.

9 INCLUSION

THE POWER OF SYNERGY

FEATURING

RAYMOND COLEMAN
EXECUTIVE SECRETARY, SUBURBAN 1 LEAGUE

"A good spirit
attracts friends."
-- Anonymous

Inclusion is the power of synergy. "Synergy" is a word from the Greek synergos, which means "working together with" or "working harmoniously." It means that the outcome or results are multiplied through the act of working together as a solid unit. Therefore, 1 + 5 = 6 becomes incorrect and is replaced by 1 + 5 = 10, 15, or 20; or the total number of the parts is greater than the whole. When each and everyone who is included in the inclusion group, task force, committee, official board, or mastermind group, determines to follow the leader, they then give themselves to the project at hand, and synergy is achieved.

There is a power when people commit to working with synergy. It is exciting to see it happen, and even more exciting when you are a part of making it happen!

That is why Ray Coleman is such an amazing person! At age 72, Ray Coleman is still touching the lives of youth in 25 districts of the Suburban One League using the principles of inclusion and the power of synergy. As executive secretary of the sports league, his passion for children and his joy from his work overshadows any thoughts for a more leisurely retirement lifestyle. Reflecting on his many years of being involved in with the school system, he said, "As an educator, I always felt the bottom line was what is best for the young people that we worked with. What was best for them was not always best for you maybe, but again as an educator you were there to help young people to go into the real world."

As athletic director of Abington High School, Ray Coleman's influence on youth extended beyond student athletes. Since I graduated from Abington High School, I knew him well. He knew I excelled as a diver on the high school swimming team and was blessed with five college scholarships. But he also knew I needed something more. He invited me to his church one Sunday evening and for the first time I encountered a mass of people as excited about God as a gymnasium full of spectators get about sports.

Ray recalls some other students he has helped. "Vo-Tech students were special people to me. I tried to encourage them and show them their worth. They would always stand up for me—no one dared give me a hard time, or else—but I respected each one." He remembers that as a teacher he could be quite blunt, which prompted many students to respond. Because he was candid in what he wanted from them, it helped them make it in life. Ray truly believed that a good education should provide lessons that had a lifetime of value. Reflecting on this, Ray said, "I never taught a subject, I taught people and hoped and prayed what influence I had on them would make a positive impact in their later development in life."

Regarding drugs he was hard-nosed and laid it on the line. "I'll help you, but if I have to go the record and you reject my help, you have a problem."

Ray gave one deserving student money for college text books so "he could make something of himself." The student graduated and now teaches youth himself. Another student's mother, an abusive alcoholic, eventually asked Ray to give her away at the occasion of her second marriage. Ray got her son involved in the church and in so helping, became a part of the family. Another student, a football player was short a grade point in obtaining a college football scholarship. Ray agreed to help him if he helped himself. For six months, the student had to study for each class and bring progress reports to Ray signed by each teacher. Both Ray and the student were proud when the work resulted in a full scholarship.

"You were the best teacher I ever had," wrote one student. Another tells Ray that she will never forget him. He told her she was capable of anything and so she believed it.

"I realized every day I worked with a student, I had a responsibility to that student. A teacher (or leader) must realize that he or she has a tremendous impact on the people they instruct."

Ray Coleman

Therein, in a nutshell, is inclusion's main principle: Working with others for the good of others, produces stellar results. Inclusion is a group effort. A leader knows he must be selective about who is involved in the group effort. He knows how to choose the right people to do the job. He knows to avoid including those who are egotistical, self-centered or arrogant because they are so self-focused, they are unable to contribute to synergy. To include such individuals would drain the very life from synergy, making it non-existent.

Such leaders are always on the alert for other leaders and followers who desire and aspire to make the fullest use of their potential. To be sure, they are hard to detect, let alone select from the crowd, but sooner or later, the cream rises to the top. He realizes that even though he labors from sunrise to sunset, he cannot do it alone, it takes a group effort to do the job.

We know we need people on our team who are givers, not takers. We want those who have vision, mission and passion, those who realize that association and importation are all necessary ingredients. These ingredients create the chemistry of synergy. Not everyone gets to experience the thrill of synergy, but many desire it. It has a magical quality all its own. Ray Coleman would often tell the teachers under his supervision, "Always be aware that you have a responsibility that you are making an impact on the students that are in your charge. You may never know, but make sure all that you do will be a positive influence."

"In inclusion, I purposefully include serving you. My hope is to be a good, positive and constructive influence on you personally as you and I serve in the project publicly," states the astute leader. I say, who would choose not to follow a leader like that? This leader of leaders believes that life and work are best experienced as a community. That is why people like Ray Coleman are respected and loved long after their work with an individual is complete. Synergy (working together in harmony with efficiency) results in a multiplied fruitfulness of unified teamwork. In his wisdom, he knows that people are more important than projects. For that matter, he says that without the right people involved, there are no projects worthy of their salt.

Ray Coleman believed that the bottom line of his job as teacher or athletic director was "doing what is best for the young people." As an educator, he was there to help them make the transition from the school world to the real world.

The leader goes on to emphasize responsibility, expectation from and for all concerned, acceptable behavior, unacceptable behavior, examples of good sports ways to promote good sportsmanship, ejection from an athletic contest, and right of appeal. The fact is that right now in the greater suburban area of our Delaware Valley, this phenomenal influence exists on a daily basis for our youth. That is why we focus on Ray Coleman here as a leader of leaders in athletics, because he is exemplary of the kind of character and personality that makes up this kind of leader. So to get to know Ray Coleman is also to gain a better appreciation for such leadership qualities that we tend to take for granted.

Leaders recognize that the sum of the parts is greater than the whole. It may be difficult put all together in the beginning, but once the work begins, it is like a snowball rolling down a hill that picks up more snow along the way. It gathers momentum until its ever-increasing weight propels it powerfully along in a multiplied fashion. Ray believed in the potential of all students.

On a business level, inclusion requires a more intimate relationship between leader and leader than does delegation. Inclusion begins at the beginning of a new project or movement. The real leader of leaders "feels" his way to other leaders who will share his vision, mission and passion. In this way, inclusion is a natural result of well-established relationships. Inclusion does not involve only the most gifted or talented, but rather the most trusted. The precious qualities of unity, harmony and compatibility create the synergy of inclusion. When such affinity is present amongst the team, greater are the results. For example, have you ever seen a basketball team of five individual champions play against a lesser talented, but more harmonious team? The five champion players act like lone wolves with each going his own separate direction, thus each one looks good individually. However, the more harmonious team works together to overcome the frailties of the other team.

Inclusion restores and upholds the all but lost art of compassion, which all leaders of leaders tend to have in common. It is true that a plurality of leadership is best enhanced by a diversity of personality temperaments, spiritual gifts and vocational talents. At the same time, there are certain main attributes the team must have in common, one of these is compassion. The compassionate person has a keen sensitivity for the hurts of others and has the urge to extend a helping hand. When one person within the master mind group reaches out to help one, such actions tend to multiply themselves until all within the circle have given and received help. Our compassion shines through differently based on our personalities, but nevertheless it will reveal itself. Ray Coleman's compassion can best be described in his words:

"I have a strong faith in God, but I always felt that faith should be demonstrated in the way I treat people. It is not what I say, but rather how I walk."

Winston Churchill believed strongly in the power of a four- or five-person committee. He was rather emphatic about the number because he felt that when the number of people was less than four, it lacked the necessary synergy. On the other hand, when the number of people grew to more than five, the project became difficult to manage. This is the reasoning behind his statement, "With a four- or five-man committee, we can win the war and rule the Kingdom."

Inclusion requires simultaneous actions from separate team players, which creates the greater total effect than the sum of individual efforts. Inclusion is the power of synergy because it acts as a spontaneous combustion of the greatest power in the world: love. The resourcefulness of love knows no boundary, for there is no fear in love because perfect love by its very nature casts fear aside. That is why the very heart of this book is a demonstration of love in all of its life messages. Love is not just an option for the weak and feeble; love is the *summum bonum* of the wise and mighty.

To create synergy, a wise leader knows that each individual must be aware that he is a respected, valued part of the whole. Clearly, the magic lies in a leader's knowledge of the intricacies of inclusion that have made him such a highly respected leader among leaders. That is why the life of a leader in inclusion is like the life of an athlete. With Ray Coleman, inclusion means, "I enjoy life and I'm content with who I am. Because I love others as myself and care about team effort, I include you."

Inclusion is the power of synergy. "Synergy" is a word from the Greek synergos, which means "working together with" or "working harmoniously." It means that the outcome or results are multiplied through the act of working together as a solid unit. Therefore, 1 + 5 = 6 becomes incorrect and is replaced by 1 + 5 = 10, 15, or 20; or the total number of the parts is greater than the whole. When each and everyone who is included in the inclusion group, task force, committee, official board, or mastermind group, determines to follow the leader, they then give themselves to the project at hand, and synergy is achieved.

10

DEMONSTRATION

THE POWER OF LIFE MESSAGE

FEATURING

JESUS CHRIST, THE LORD
THE LIVING WORD OF THE NEW COVENANT

"Do good to thy friend
to keep him,
to thy enemy to gain him."

-- Benjamin Franklin

If there is ever a word with many meanings, demonstrations and connotations it is "demonstration." It could mean everything from a "demonstration" of a vacuum cleaner on your carpet by a door-to-door salesman to a Million Man March in Washington, D.C. It could denote proof of evidence, or it could connote explanation by example. Even Webster's New World Dictionary lists six definitions. However, there is no more pure meaning of the word "demonstration" than "The Power of Life Messages."

The world is constantly crying out for leaders whose lives overflow with the walk of their talk. Talk by itself is cheap. The world is full of politicians who make promises they cannot keep. The world is fed up with the multitude of words from the mouths of its leadership, which the Book of Proverbs refers to as the height of folly. "A fool is known by his multitude of words." "Vanity, vanity, vanity," said Solomon, "all is vanity."

The world needs more than just an allegiance to a leader. The world needs the example of its leaders. Followers and fellow leaders need to know how the leader's life experience is maintained and shared if it is to be perpetuated to the development of greater leaders. Of course, in a technical society, life precedes action, but from a thoroughly practical point of view, we live by what we do. One must breathe, eat, exercise and carry on work if he is to grow.

If those functions of the body are neglected, life will cease to be. That is why the effort of the leader of leaders to convey to his fellow leader and followers the secret of his exemplary influence or the power of life messages needs to be considered as a deliberate course of his master strategy. He knows what is important, especially the reality of love.

In light of this, there is one vital clarification, about what was said above concerning what we must do to stay alive, for in the case of the care and nurturing of a baby, this is not enough. Laboratory tests have proven over and over that unless a new born baby is cuddled with love, it will die—no matter how much you feed, cover and help it rest. It must be provided plenty of love. Truly an adult may possibly exist without love, but that is all that it is—mere existence. It is not living. It may be surviving, but it is not thriving or living.

Thus, what good is leading at all if it doesn't flow from a life of love? What does the leader have to offer his follower if not a loving supporter, a loving life message for "his little corner of the world"? As the song says: "What the world needs now, is love sweet love."

So in keeping with the dedication of this book to the youth—the future leaders of America and the world, I do my best to focus your mind "forward to the fundamentals and back to the basics" by directing your attention to the greatest chapter on love ever written - 1 Corinthians 13. I offer you my absolute best both in scholarship, where I have employed the wonderful tools of my doctoral residence in Greek, and in "street smarts" which I gained through 33 years of publishing books and magazines, the wonderful essence of love in its 17 "life messages."

You see, we came to that crucial point in the book where we need to stop, back up and think about: "Who am I really?" "What am I doing?" "Where am I going?" "Why do I think, say and do what I do?" "How do I find a better way?"

Dear leader, that better way is the way of love. Any other way will be filled with phonies, bores, and robots. Yes, you can be an effective leader by mastering the methods, manuals and models of the previous chapters. But, if you really want to be leader of leaders, you also need to cultivate love. And the practical value of doing it here is that love is shown by what love is and by what love does. In not one of the 17 life messages is there an instance of what love says. That is why this kind of love is not cheap, for it is the real thing. "Coke" is not the real thing, as the words of the Coca-Cola commercial say: Love is the real thing. Better yet, reality for this love here is the love that *is* and *does*. Hence, since God is love and Jesus Christ the Lord is God, the Son in flesh, these 17 Life Messages are in essence His own. Isn't that awesome!

To be sure, you won't "speed read" this section of the book very well, for it is the heart of the book. Hence, just like heart surgeons, we also shall take much time and carefulness with it. Hopefully, you will not just read it, but also reread, mark, underline and highlight, reverently memorize, meditate in and internally digest these 17 life messages so that they become *your* life messages. And don't worry about getting religious, but rather be grateful that it will make you more real.

Really, aren't you, as well as the rest of the world, sick and tired of the artificial, superficial and commercial? And wouldn't you really prefer to go through the rest of your life with most of the real, sincere and genuine?

Then dive in! Come on in, the water's fine! Immerse yourself in the one reality which no one will ever criticize you for having too much of, love. Have you ever really wondered what the secret is for the phenomenal, almost supernatural, charisma of the most outstanding leaders unto whom people literally gravitate? Well, here it is. So, go for it!

INTRODUCTION

Here is another exposition on love. Why? First, because there are very few books that give substantial devotion to the subject. By substantial, I mean books that are based upon the Bible, which alone portrays the pure essence of love.

Yes, I am well aware of Henry Drummond's "The Greatest Thing in the World;" Granville T. Walker's "The Greatest of These;" Eleen "To Live in Love;" and I highly recommend them to you. I am also well aware of the many commentaries on I Corinthians that relate to the chapter on love. Yet, at the same time, having studied just about every solid commentary on this book, I was amazed to find how little space was given to the thirteenth chapter.

So, although there are other books and commentaries on this subject, I believe the greatest subject in the world deserves many more books. Surely, if we accept as the truth the words of the saying, "What the world needs now is love," then, whatever books we can write to encourage love will not be in vain.

Furthermore, in addition to the above objective reason for another book on love, I also have several subjective reasons growing out of my own life which has changed through the love of God.

With the hope that some of the events from my life will open your heart and mind to read this book, I would like to share with you how love has changed me. The people who have been the greatest help to me suffered from the same problem themselves, but found a solution and shared their discovery with me. So that is my motive; to help you the same way someone helped me.

You see, by nature, I am a very unloving person due in part to my upbringing. I was raised in a very unloving environment. In my home there was much tension, strife, frustration, and division. Because of the lack of love in my home, one by one the members of my family split. Dad left home when I was eight, my older sister left home when I was 12. When I was 14 my older brother left home two months before he graduated from high school to go into the army. Even my younger sister left home when I was 22 to get married one month after she graduated form high school.

Why not leave? There was little holding them there. Then why did I stay until I was 25 when I married? Because God was teaching me how to love in that environment. I also saw and deeply appreciated the good points of my loyal mother who, regardless of her faults, lovingly poured her life as a living sacrifice into her children, so that unlike her, we wouldn't be raised in an orphanage or foster home.

Another facet of my life that related to the theme of this book is my education. Probably the biggest reason why I went to college and graduate school for 12 years full-time was insecurity. Yes, I had different reasons then, but I was not conscious of the real reason. For instance, I went to the Philadelphia College of Bible for my Bachelor of Science Degree because I wanted to learn the Bible. I went to the Reformed Episcopal Seminary for my Bachelor of Divinity degree because I wanted to systematize my Bible knowledge into a theological framework. I went to Westminster Theological Seminary for my master's degree in apologetics because I wanted a broad perspective of philosophy and non-Christian theology. Along the way, I went to Ohio State University and the Community College of Philadelphia because I wanted a broader outlook on the arts and sciences of the world. Lastly, I went to Dallas Theological Seminary for my Doctorate in New Testament Greek and exegesis because I wanted to complete all of my studies on the basis of the original languages of the Bible (Hebrew and Greek), so I could be an expert in the original sources of the Hebrew culture and Christian faith.

Nevertheless, underlying all these conscious reasons was an unconscious one, my insecurity. This hit me suddenly when a group of professors at Dallas told me that after I completed my doctoral residence work and before I finished my dissertation, I should get into the ministry and prove myself. They had serious questions about how much my 12 years of full-time education had helped me where it counts - in the heart, not the head.

I'm also writing this book partly as an outgrowth of my success in business. During my last seven years of graduate schools, I worked as a salesman and manager for the Southwestern Company of Nashville, Tennessee. I had two conscious reasons for doing this: (1) to develop myself practically for the ministry by selling books door-to-door in over 10,000 homes, and teaching other students to do the same; (2) to support myself through all these years of school without going into debt.

By God's grace I accomplished those two goals, but it was not until later that I found out the underlying, unconscious reason why I went into sales: insecurity. I was an unloving person and deep down inside of me I knew it. So I tried to solve the problem by positive thinking programs and selling techniques, all of which I later found were inadequate in themselves to envelop me in love, although I still gained much from them. Even though I was the number one salesman for three consecutive years, number one student manager of the Bible Library Division for five consecutive years and even number one organizational manager in the whole company, ahead of more than 5,000 men from colleges all over the country, from Harvard and Yale to Dallas Seminary and UCLA, still I was insecure. Despite the tens of thousands of dollars that I made in that job over those seven summers, I still was insecure!

But what really shocked me was my first year in the ministry. There are many ministers who refer to the first year of ministry as the "honeymoon year." Man! That was not true for me at all. It was my worst year. There I was, beginning my lifetime of ministry, attempting to blend together my 12 years of education and my seven years of selling and managing into a dynamic ministry. As I started in the fall of 1970 in Valley Forge, I felt confident that I had so much to offer. My attitude surely came across as "you people in Valley Forge are very privileged to have me." What a shame.

From October 1970 to June 1971 the church grew from nothing to about 70 people. However, I was blindly unaware of the trail of offenses, mistakes and blunders that I was leaving behind me. But in the first week of June they caught up with me and clobbered me in the head. Seven families left the church. They said I was egotistical, arrogant, cocky, and unloving. Oh, how right they were.

It was then that I began to understand I Corinthians 13. How I could enter into those first three verses of the chapter! "If I speak with the tongues of men and of angels, but do not have love, I have become a noisy gong or a clanging cymbal." I must confess that is what I was. In spite of my study of languages, Greek for eleven years, Hebrew for nine years, German for five years and French for three years, I sounded like a noisy gong!

Then I began to understand verse two: "And if I have the gift of prophecy, and know all mysteries and all knowledge, and if I have all faith as to remove mountains, but do not have love, I am nothing." I discovered that in spite of my ability to preach and teach and even motivate people; in spite of my 12 years of higher education and the resultant degrees; in spite of my self-confidence that was developed during seven years of success in the dog-eat-dog business world, I was *nothing*, a *big zero!*

Likewise, I came to understand verse three: "And if I give all my possessions to feed the poor, and if I deliver my body to be burned, but do not have love, it profits me nothing." In spite of my leaving the prosperity of the business world; in spite of giving away all of our earnings to various charitable institutions; in spite of being willing to die as a martyr for Christ, I still agonizingly discovered that it profited me nothing. What a hard truth to swallow! But I did accept it.

Is it any wonder, then, that since June 1971 I have devoted myself to a pursuit of love? Is it any wonder that I would be more consumed with this pursuit than with any other? My very own life, meaningfulness in life, usefulness in the ministry, and sense of fulfillment to justify my existence in this world were at stake. Is it any wonder that I would write this book to share with you something that I have learned in love, so that you, too, can be kept from a life of waste?

The pure motive and earnest prayer behind this book is to serve you, the reader, with some insights into the greatest thing in this world, and the only thing that we shall carry with us into the next.

In the words of Browning, I implore you to learn love: "For life with all it yields of joy and woe and hope and fear, is just our chance o' the prize of learning love—how love might be, hath been indeed, and is."

Part One

God's Explanation of Love

The book, "In His Steps," written by Charles M. Sheldon, challenges the Christian to visualize himself in the footsteps of Christ. The author exposes what many Christians really are compared to what they ought to be. From this standpoint the book is hardly an enjoyable one. However, for the Christian who is really sincere about being his best for God, it is a welcomed challenge.

Unfortunately, such a spirit of openness to a candid presentation of truth is not too common. For instance, what if Jesus were to visit your church this Sunday? Would He really be welcome?

In essence, of course, Jesus is everywhere by means of His spiritual presence, but what I mean is, Is He welcome at your church in a personal way. Would your church feel comfortable in His presence. Would you?

Many people would have to say no in answer to these questions. I suppose there are many reasons for this, but one in particular is that they do not understand the nature of the love of God in Christ.

Therefore, in Part I, we plan to introduce you to the love of God in Christ as portrayed in I Corinthians 13. In verses 1-3 we are going to see the necessity of love; in verses 4-7 the functions of love; in verses 8-13 the permanence of love.

I Corinthians 13 is one of the greatest chapters of the Bible. Adolf Harnack says it is "the greatest, strongest, and deepest thing Paul ever wrote." Other authorities acclaim that although Plato did a great work on lone in his "Symposium," A.D. 107, Paul in I Corinthians 13 has surpassed him and all other writers on the subject. So let us see what he has to say.

I. THE NECESSITY OF LOVE (VV. 1-3)

In the opening paragraph, Paul sets forth the necessity of love by comparing love to spiritual gifts. His point is that love is more important than any, or all of the most coveted gifts.

A. More Than the Gift of Tongues

In verse one he specifically singles out the gift of tongues. It is interesting that although Paul apparently recognized the gift of tongues as the least of gifts, he mentions it first. The reason is that the Corinthian believers were so immature in their Christian experience that they considered tongues to be just the opposite, the greatest gift. So Paul begins at their point of need and pierces through their false notion by stressing that without love, their speaking of all the foreign languages in the world made them at best like noisy gongs. They were perhaps something like Cleopatra.

Cleopatra was a great linguist. She could speak the languages of the Ethiopian, Hebrew, Arabic, Syrian, Median and Parthian ambassadors, says Plutarch. She could turn her tongue to whatever dialect she pleased. But without the love of God even she was nothing.

B. More Than the Gift of Prophecy.

Paul moves from the gift of tongues to the greatest gifts. He shows that love is more important than the gifts of prophecy and faith. His point is that even if one could know all the deep counsels of God ("mysteries") and possessed all knowledge, and if one even had faith to move mountains, without love he would be nothing. That is, he is nobody, nothing, zero.

C. More Than Charity and Martyrdom.

Paul continues the same line of logic, comparing love to the sacrifices of one's possessions and life itself. He mentions giving up of goods and the body, but not the soul. The reason is that the soul is the sphere of love. Although the sacrifice of goods may be commendable, without love it profits one nothing. Likewise, even giving up one's body in martyrdom—without love—profits nothing at all. In the time of the Roman Emperor Diocletian, some of the early Christians actually courted martyrdom. How foolish without love! Some think Paul's reference here could be to an Indian, Zarmano Chegas, who burned himself in public on a funeral pyre and had the inscription say that he was immortal. But without love, this act helped him not at all.

Paul's key emphasis in this first paragraph is that our gifts and deeds, no matter how great, are worthless unless we use them in a loving way. Next, in verses 4-7, he shows "the way, the truth, and the life" of love as personified in the Lord Jesus Christ (cf. John 14:6).

II. THE NATURE FUNCTIONS OF LOVE (VV. 407)

In this paragraph Paul portrays the functions, or conduct, of love in a marvelous rhapsody. Love here is seen as a person, and that person is none other than Jesus Christ the Lord. the Greek work agape (love) reflects the nature of love as a beautiful, steady, flowing stream. But that picture is not adequate; the portrayal is only fulfilled in Jesus.

So we are going to visualize ourselves going through an art museum where there are 15 portraits of the life of Christ. We are going to pause for a moment at each one to admire the beauty of the love of God in Christ.

A. Love is Patient.

In the first portrait we see the title, "Love is Patient." This portrait depicts Christ weeping with deep longing, anguish and passion over the people of Jerusalem. "Oh Jerusalem, Jerusalem! How often I wanted to gather your children together, just as a hen gathers her brood under her wings, and you would not have it!" (Luke 13:34). Here we see that love is patient because Jesus was patient with the capital city of Israel. How long He waited so patiently for Jerusalem to repent, but her people would not. What unbelief on the part of Israel, but what love on the part of Christ!

B. Love is Kind.

The second portrait is entitled, "Love is Kind." We see Jesus with children gathered around Him, sitting on His lap. "Let the children alone, and do not hinder them from coming to me, for the kingdom of heaven belongs to such as these." (Matthew 19:14). His kindness was seen in His compassion not only for children, but also for the despised, the outcast and the downtrodden.

C. Love is Not Jealous.

The next portrait presents Christ speaking with the rich young ruler. His features strikingly indicate that He is not jealous of the young man's worldly goods. All we see is genuine concern for the young ruler's soul. That is true love.

D. Love Does not Brag.

In the next picture Jesus is being pressured by the Pharisees. Having done great miracles by the power of the Spirit, Jesus was asked about the source of His power. He answered, "The Son can do nothing of Himself, unless it is something He sees His Father doing; for whatever the Father does, these things the Son also does in like manner." (John 5:19). Love does not brag, and neither did Jesus.

E. Love is Not Arrogant

We see Jesus now in the Garden of Gethsemane, praying on His knees. He wrestles with the will of God the night before His crucifixion. The devil tries to put Him to death there in seclusion. It looks like Satan will be successful, because Jesus is sweating drops of blood. In His humanity, Jesus cannot understand it. He cries aloud, "Father, if Thou art willing remove this cup from me; yet not my will, but Thine be done" (Lk. 22:42). Even in the face of death in what appeared to be the wrong place, in the garden instead of the cross, Jesus was willing to submit to the will of God. Why? Because love is not arrogant and neither was Christ.

F. Love Does Not Act Unbecomingly.

Now we behold Jesus in a debate with the Pharisees. They are trying to trap Him, trying to trick Him, doing their best to get something on Him. But no matter what they think, say, or do, Jesus does not act unbecomingly because love does not.

G. Love Does Not Seek Its Own.

This is a picture of Jesus suffering from great loss of sleep. He has given Himself to others all day, but instead of going to sleep, He goes into the woods, kneels down, and prays all night. Why did He do this? Because love does not seek its own.

H. Love is Not Provoked.

In the next hallway, as we turn the corner, the first picture on our left is of Jesus with His 12 disciples near the end of His ministry. The disciples look perplexed, confused and frustrated, because they still do not understand Him. But is Jesus upset? No, He is not provoked.

True, He does say, "Have I been so long with you, and yet you have not come to know me?" (John 14:9). Yet this was an expression of grief and earnestness, for love is not provoked at all.

I. Love Does Not Take Into Account a Wrong Suffered.

This picture is difficult to fully appreciate because it is of Jesus being betrayed by Judas. In spite of such a low blow, Jesus is not angered. He accepts the whole matter with serenity and peace that surpasses all human understanding. Love does not take into account a wrong suffered, even the wrong of a betrayal.

J. Love Does Not Rejoice in Unrighteousness.

We are moving forward to Calvary and on the way we see a portrait of Christ at this unfair trial before the Sanhedrin. However, instead of being alarmed about the possibility of His innocence being mistaken for guilt, Jesus is rather grieved over the unrighteousness of His accusers. Jesus cared for them and yet at the same time He was grieved because of their unrighteousness. He knew God was working out His will through their unrighteousness.

K. Love Rejoices in the Truth.

Now we see Jesus hanging on the cross, with the words above His head, "King of the Jews." The words were placed there by an ungodly man. They were ridiculed by the crowd. But yet Jesus could rejoice in the truth of them, although dying a criminal's death He did not deserve. Why? Because love rejoices in the truth.

L. Love Bears All Things

As He hung on the cross, Jesus cried out to God, "Father, forgive them for they do not know what they are doing" (Luke 23:34). Oh, to what lengths love can go! As He bore the sins of the world, He paused for a moment to show His concern for His mother, saying, "Woman, behold your Son." (John 19:26). With His dying breath He saw to His mother's welfare, for love bears all things.

M. Love Believes All Things.

In this picture Jesus turns to John, His beloved disciple, and says, "Behold your mother. And from that hour the disciple took her into his own household" (John 19:27). He believed in John, but He also believed in the other disciples whom John symbolically represented. He believed in their potential, although they had forsaken and fled from the cross, for love believes all things.

N. Love Hopes All Things

At the end, Jesus cried out, "It is finished!" By these words He confessed that He hoped in the eternal value of His mission. He did not despair, for He hoped and knew that His death accomplished the redemption of all who believe. His death was satisfactory completion of His life's work, because love hopes all things.

O. Love Endures All Things

We gaze upon Jesus in this last picture as He walks down the road to Emmaus with two disciples. He expounds the Word of God to them from the Old Testament Scriptures. He warms their hearts by His abiding ministry. He had endured all things with His triumph over the grave. Love endures forever. Why? Because love endures all things.

III. The Permanence of Love

Actually, there are 17 characteristics of love in verses 4-13, if we include "love never fails" and "love is the greatest." In the following chapters all 17 characteristics shall be treated separately. But here we shall consider these last two characteristics in contrast to the gifts, and in connection with perfection.

A. In Contrast to the Gifts.

This third and last paragraph of I Corinthians 13 begins with the words, "Love never fails." This is a new term for the perpetuity of love. Here love is seen as surviving everything. Love is never to be out of use. Love always holds its peace. Love even outlasts those three greatly appreciated gifts of prophecy, tongues, and knowledge. Paul's perspective on all these things is that whereas the greatest and the least gifts of man will fail, love will not.

B. In Connection with Perfection.

It is difficult to know for sure what the word "perfect" means. Some think it refers to the completed canon of Scripture. I cannot agree with that, because the idea seems so foreign to the context. Others think it means Christ's second coming. This is a good possibility. Still others believe that it refers to that realm of reality that God will set up in the future after Christ's return. I lean toward this last view

When such perfection comes, especially in the new heavens and the new earth in which righteousness shall dwell, the partial things shall be done away; immaturity, childishness, and ignorance shall be gone, having given way to maturity, vision and understanding. The enduring qualities of faith, hope, and love will abide, but even among these three, love is the greatest. This is the love of God in Christ. This can also be the love of God in you, as you acquaint yourself with it in the succeeding chapters of this book.

No wonder the immortal words of the great martyr, Elizabeth Folks, live on. She said her last words at the stake. "Farewell, faith; farewell, hope." And taking the stake in hand, she exclaimed, "Welcome, love!"

PART TWO

GOD'S EXPLANATION OF LOVE

LIFE MESSAGE ONE

LOVE IS PATIENT

If you have ever watched a beam of light striking a prism, then you know the experience of seeing the different rays of color: red, orange, yellow, green, blue, indigo and violet; all the colors of the solar spectrum. It's truly a sight to behold. One beam of light, but many rays of color.

That is the way we can best approach I Corinthians 13:4-13. For as Granville Walker says, "The Holy Spirit used the inspired intellect of the Apostle Paul as a prism through which he radiated the beam of light of love and had it come out the other side in all its rays of color."[1]

As we look at the first color, we see that love is patient. Patience is one of 17 rays of color of the most magnificent force of all the world, the force of love. Now we have to take that one ray of color and send it through another prism to understand something of what it is all about. What is meant by, "love is patient"? We want to answer that question in three ways, by looking at patience in attitude, in words and in actions.

I. PATIENCE IN ATTITUDE

To get the force of Paul's meaning, we should translate his description, "Love bears patience, or love produces patience." This must first take place in the realm of the attitude, the realm of the subconscious as well as the conscious within us, the inner man, that which we call heart. This is where patience begins. As Proverbs 23:7 puts it, "For as he (the man) thinks within himself, so he is." Or, as the riddle goes: "You are not what you think you are, but you *think*, you are." What you are thinking, that is what you really are.

A. The Basis of Patience

If a person is going to build a life of patience, he must have a foundation. The foundation of our attitude of patience must be the fact that God is God. For instance, Paul had this foundation when he described his ministry at Corinth. He said that although he planted and Apollos watered, God gave the increase. God made the church grow.

If I have as the basis of my attitude a recognition that God is God, that all that happens God causes, and that all He wants for me is good and for His glory, and if I trust Him regardless of what comes across my path, I can be patient because I'm letting God be God. That's the attitude of patience.

B. The Definition of Patience.

Paul did not write long definitions. He did not create a dictionary of terms, but rather he described what love produces. When he said that love produces patience, or perhaps more literally, love suffers long, he meant that quality in a person that knows no limit to restfulness in the fact that God is God. Patience is the attitude that says, no matter what comes, "I will not get ruffled, because I know that this is for my good and for God's glory." Regardless of what happens, whatever touches a believer, he must do right, not wrong, in the face of it. He must think right in the face of it, regardless. Even if this means suffering l-o-n-g. He must be patient rather than become angry, impetuous, hasty and later regret what he forfeited of his character in Christ in the face of a trial.

C. The Confidence of Patience.

Perhaps the best way to describe the confidence of patience is to tell you about the Trail Ridge road in the Rocky Mountains of Colorado. This is called the highest road in the world through mountain ranges. On this road you almost become lost in a world of mountain peaks, but when you come to Long's Peak, you enter a problem area. That problem happens to be fog, or clouds, so that you can't see anything ahead of you, hardly even the road itself. All you can hope for is that as you drive very slowly, soon the clouds will lift. Of course, you drive with the confidence that the road is there and that the mountain tops are all around, even though for the moment you cannot see them. But they are there. Then suddenly the clouds lift, not by your power, either. You did nothing to move those clouds. They just lift and you say, "Oh, how beautiful! How beautiful!" That helps us to understand the confidence of patience.

Who hasn't gone through some clouds of circumstance, clouds you cannot control? All you know is that the road is there; the most you can do is take one step at a time, step by step, and pray and hope that God will lift the clouds. That's the confidence of patience.

In our local prayer meetings, we have asked God to make His power known in our church, that He would raise up a mighty church for Himself, that He would so do such great work through our ministry that the world would have to say, "God did it." Sometimes it's hard to come back week after week and not see all the things we want to see in the lives of people and in the growth of the work. But, perhaps far more important than God giving us numbers is God giving us patience. God sends the clouds for a period of time because love and patience are far more important to Him than a packed church building. Our attitude is all-important; we think not just in terms of the church, but in terms of our own lives. The question, therefore, comes: Are you willing to be patient as a Christian? If so, suffer long. Remember, winners never quit and quitters never win. Remember, hasty action never promotes the purposes of God. And remember that if you don't suffer long with love, you'll probably wind up suffering in other areas anyhow.

II. PATIENCE IN WORD

Next we come to patience in word. This is our response to how life affects us. Threatening circumstances often expose what a person is really like inside. Hear the words of an individual in response to a threatening situation, and you have a revelation of what that person is really like.

These kinds of situations often occur in the church among God's people. We regret the impatient words we speak. Before we speak hastily, we must suffer long. If we don't, we shall suffer after we have said those words, in a different way. The quality of long suffering must condition what we say. If a brother offends us, dare we slash back and retaliate?

Let's leave the church scene and go to the home. Does your wife, your husband or your children do things that threaten you and your own estimate of yourself? Do you, as a result, slash back with your words? Do you say something that you ought not to say because you do not suffer long in the face of those circumstances? These situations are involved in patience in word.

The basic rule is this: whatever happens to you, your words should never reflect impatience. If they do, you are not acting in a loving way to yourself, to God, to your loved ones, or to others. Again, let that quality of suffering long condition your words as well as your attitude.

May I encourage you to read the Psalms. The Psalms over and over again admonish us to stop hasty action, hasty words and hasty thoughts and to wait upon the Lord. Oh, but waiting is so hard to do! That's why God says love suffers long. Wait, yes; suffer long, but wait patiently.

III. PATIENCE IN ACTION

This refers to our relationship to our fellow men, especially to three different kinds of our fellow men.

A. Towards Difficult People

Do you know any people who are hard to get along with—besides yourself, I mean? What should be your action toward them according to the Bible; not according to your own thoughts, not according to even the mixture of the thoughts you had before you were saved and the ones that you presently have now that you are saved, but according to the Word of God purely? Should you rid yourself of them as the Pharisees did with their "holier than thou" attitude? Should you split from somebody because you can't get along with him? Is that really what God says? No! Your conscience as well as the Holy Spirit, I'm sure, convinces you that that is not the way. So much of the New Testament, even this very chapter, aims at keeping believers together, not making them split apart. But what do you do about a difficult person? Let me teach you by way of contrast.

The Greeks taught different kinds of virtues, but patience was not among them. As a matter of fact, Aristotle said that one of the greatest virtues was the strength of a man to retaliate when he was wronged, even to the point of death. This is where you get the idea of having a duel when a man had said something wrong to you.

But by contrast, the Lord Jesus Christ says virtue is having somebody hurt you, even 70 times seven, and then refuse to retaliate. Why? Because God is God. I know Christians I can't even hurt once without their slapping me back in the face, so to speak. But the truth is, love suffers long; even towards different people.

B. Towards Impossible People

Let me illustrate with a story. Robert G. Ingersoll, the brilliant atheist of the 19th century, in the midst of one of his profound lectures said all kinds of things against God and then added, "I will give God five minutes to strike me down dead for all things I have said against Him." For five minutes he arrogantly waited for God to strike him down. The five minutes passed and he went on with a smile and a smirk of satisfaction.

When Theodore Parker, the great man of God of the day, heard about it, he said, "Did the man really believe he could exhaust the patience of the eternal God in five minutes?"

Our actions toward even the impossible people, who would think and perhaps say all kinds of things against us should be, after five minutes, patient like the eternal God.

C. Towards Nice People

What about nice people like your wife, your husband, your parents and all the ones you call your loved ones? I personally find that the ones with whom I am most impatient are the ones whom I love the most. It is not the impossible person. It is not the difficult person. It is the one I love the most, especially God. I am not pleased about the fact that God is not doing what I want fast enough. And, of course, right down the line with my wife and children.

Love suffers long. Love takes daily count of what you must do to your loved ones, especially in being one who bears patience. If you bear patience towards the ones you love the most, you will have no problem dealing with anybody else.

I have to conclude, therefore, when someone is impatient toward me, it is because he is impatient toward God.

Application

How can you begin a new and fresh today being a patient Christian? It's as simple as your ABC's. Look at James 1:2,3: "Consider it all joy (consider, that's attitude) my brother, when you encounter various trials, knowing that the testing of your faith produces endurance." In the King James Version it says "patience," but a more accurate word is endurance. Endurance is patience stretched over a lifetime, patience stretched out. The way you get patience, in simple terms, is "Be joyous in every trial". Let no trial ruffle you in thought, word or action. Rejoice before God. say, "Thank-you, Lord". Be happy in it, even if somebody calls you a bad name, even if they hurt you in some way, even when you get setback financially. Whatever it is, say, "Thank-you, Lord." Rejoice in it and say "Thank you, because you have sent this trial to teach me patience if nothing else." That's how to get it.

Life Message 2

Love is Kind

Perhaps you know the old fable about the wind and the sun. The wind and the sun debated back and forth about which of them could first cause a man to take off his coat. The wind tried first; it blew, it stormed and it raged, but the more it did, the tighter the man held his coat. Finally, the wind stopped and in despair let the sun have a try. The sun radiated its warmth on the man. It was not long before the man loosened and took off his coat.

Each one of us has a choice, whether in our marriages, our homes, our churches or our communities of using the method of the wind or of the sun. The results will be the very same for us, depending on our choice.

Perhaps you say, "I want to use the method of the sun, but, oh, the windy, stormy, blasting treatment I get from other people who take advantage of my warm and kind treatment of them! Do I not have to fight wind with wind, or fire with fire? The answer comes from God's words, "Love is kind." Love offers no exceptions to the rule. Regardless of how others treat you, is it not better to choose the method of the sun?

We need a fresh bath in the "Son-shine". I do not mean the s-u-n shine; I mean the S-o-n shine, from God's Son, the Lord Jesus Christ. To help us get such a bath, we examine the Apostle Paul's words in I Corinthians 13:4.

Paul himself had to learn that love is kind. He was at least 40 years of age at the time of his conversion. He was a great hater of God's people and poured out all sorts of windy blasts against the Christians of his day. He especially had to learn this lesson. God only knows how long it really took him. We know that he spent at least three years in Arabia after his conversion, but there were an additional 14 years after that, silent years, about which we just don't know anything concerning the apostle. So, there were at least 17 years between the apostle's conversion and the time he was able to write these words.

Kind? What does that word really mean? It is a word you rarely hear in our present day society. Have you ever stopped and asked yourself, what really is the definition of kindness? What does it really mean? Of course, once you saw what it really meant, did you ever really face honestly the complications that you found involved in being kind? Once you've done that, have you been bold enough to endeavor to apply love that is kind?

I. THE DEFINITION OF KINDNESS

A. The Contextual Meaning

As you look at the definition of kindness, you will notice, first of all, the contextual meaning. Many commentators bring that out in verse four: love is patient, love is kind; you have what is known as a couplet. They say that this couplet actually summarizes the next 13 ingredients of love in the latter part of I Corinthians 13. Therefore, when you look at the other different ingredients of love; that it is not jealous, does not brag, is not arrogant, etc., these are all different aspects of either love suffering long or love being kind. Of course, other scholars do not feel that way, but most of them think that at least they go together, love suffers long and is kind.

Why do we make this point? Well, for this reason: It's one thing for a Christian to suffer long. And, of course, some Christians do just that and no more than that, and they sure look like it. Did you ever see the martyr complex? Some believers just sit there enduring. Do you know a Christian who sort of makes you feel like all he is doing is enduring you, suffering long with you? But is it not true that the person who receives such "love" will miss the total impact of a positive manifestation of love? That is why "and is kind" must go along with "love is patient." It is one thing to endure, but it is something else to be kind in the positive sense as well. That is the idea of the contextual meaning of being kind.

B. The Literal Meaning

As for the literal meaning, I want to quote John Short as follows: "The word as used here denotes to be good natured, gentle, tender, affectionate. Love wishes well. Kindness is not harsh, sour, morose or ill-natured; kindness is being courteous. The idea is that under all provocations and ill-usage, kindness is gentle and mild. Hatred prompts one to harshness, severity, unkindness of expression, anger, and a desire for revenge. On the contrary, love is the reverse of all these. A Christian who truly loves someone will be kind, desirous of doing that person good, will be gentle not severe, not harsh, will be courteous not morose, because he desires that other person's happiness in all circumstances and would not dare to pain his feelings. Love is constantly kind in this manner."

This description reminds me of those Christians in the first century. They died at the hands of Nero; they were cast into the arena and fed to the lions. What impressed Nero and the Romans of that day was not that the Christians were willing to die for Christ, and even sing as they walked out into the arena, but that they went to death with a smile of kindness on their faces. Over and over again as he went from one part of the arena to the other, the smiles, kind and gentle smiles on the faces of these Christians. They did not only suffer, and even suffer long unto death, but they were kind to the end as well; kind even in the face of the worst enemy of all: death itself.

But what about the person who turns you off? What about the person who wrongs you? What about the person who is cold to you? What about the person who provokes you? And what about you when you're just plain tired? Are you not justified to be unkind in situations like these? Don't these complications mean anything at all to God?

Doesn't He understand that we're only human?

The answer is that "love is kind" is in the present tense, the durative tense, the tense of continuous action, which sees in it no kind of imperfection or discontinuance of the act. It is something that endures, is constant and on-going, something that is consistent. Therefore, there are no exceptions.

You see, love is something; love is kind. If we have that love in our hearts, regardless what anyone is to us on the outside, our behavior does not change. To express kindness, our love on the inside must be bigger than that force or influence upon us from the outside. So, whether a person turns us off, is cold to us, offends us, or provokes us because of repeated mistakes, the answer always comes back: love is kind!

Kindness is being nice to someone, regardless of their treatment of you. Kindness is what flows out of you without any thought of the other person's action. If Christ is in us, and if we let His love, His unconditional love, flow out of us like a stream down a mountainside, no obstacle along the way will be a complication.

I want to ask you before the end of this chapter to renew your commitment to God in this matter of being kind. Maybe it never entered your mind to do so, it never did mine. With all my years of preparing for the ministry, with all my years of serving the Lord, I never thought deeply about what it means to be kind, and to commit myself to that action, but I want to do so, and I hope you will too.

Will you try this for at least one week? Say no unkind word about anybody. Don't talk about their mistakes, don't about their problems, don't mention anything negative about them for a week. I challenge you. Just say only positive things, only kind things, only tender things, only compassionate things, only tender-hearted things for a week. I challenge you to see what kind of a person you will be after one week of this.

II. THE COMPLICATIONS OF KINDNESS

What if she says...? Forget it. What if he says...? Don't retaliate. Just gaze at the following scriptures, realizing that they represent God's will for us:

James 3:17: "But the wisdom from above is first pure, then peaceable, gentle, reasonable, full of mercy and good fruits, unwavering without hypocrisy."

I Peter 3:8-9: "To sum up, let all be harmonious, sympathetic, brotherly, kind-hearted, and humble in spirit; not returning evil for evil, or insult for insult, but giving a blessing instead; for you were called for the very purpose that you might inherit a blessing." Therefore,

(1) When someone wrongs you, realize: love as kindness acts with goodness towards those who ill-treat it. It is gracious and kind as opposed to malice and ill will. It is one of the softer graces of God.

(2) When someone is cold to you, realize: kindness is being nice to someone. It is tender and compassionate in itself, and does not depend on outward circumstances. It is mild and obliging to others.

(3) When someone turns you off, realize: love as kindness is full of gentleness and considerateness. It extends good to others. In commenting on Ephesians 4:31, Martin Luther explained it this way, "We should love God so much that we will not purposefully tell lies about anyone, nor mention his mistakes, nor talk concerning him, but we should defend our neighbor and say the best we can about him."

Just think of that! These are the words of the man who remained steadfast in court when asked by the Roman Catholic officials to recant his position that salvation is by faith, who was fearless about standing for the truth, to the point of declaring: "Here I stand. God helping me, I can do nothing else, for it would not only be against my conscience, but also against my very sanity; and therefore, I cannot recant and will not."

How we often justify our unkindness by emphasizing that we are only being honest, straightforward and open. Yet, as true as Martin Luther was, he did not allow his stand for truth to negate his responsibility of being kind.

(4) When someone doesn't empathize with your tiredness or sickness, realize: our Lord Jesus Christ did not mistreat people in return for their mistreatment. He did not let self-pity get the best of Him at a time like that. The Christ-like individual also is one who will accept such a situation as an opportunity to be tested by the Lord; that even in tiredness and sickness he may show you kindness.

III. THE APPLICATION OF KINDNESS

You probably raise the question, "Man, this is unreal! This is too far beyond me. I'm human. Yes, I'm a Christian but... Surely God doesn't require this of me on this earth now, does He?" We can see from

Ephesians 4:32 that He does. Notice what Paul says, because he is interested in the application of kindness in our lives, not just its definition in our brains.

A. The Goal

He says, "And be kind." That's in the imperative mood, it's a command. He does not say, will you please, if it is at your convenience. No! He does not say think about it, or pray about it and than do it. He does not say do it once in awhile, either. He gives a present command: "Be kind." Be kind all the time because love is kind; not love "was" kind or love "shall be" kind but love "is" kind. Because love is kind, you should be kind because you have God's love in you.

"Be kind to another, tender-hearted, forgiving each other, just as God in Christ also has forgiven you." This verse gives me direction I need. With my choleric temperament, it is not easy for me to be kind. I can become so goal-oriented that I step on people's toes. I can be so full of truth, and tell all kinds of true things, and hurt people's feelings in the process. I speak truth, but I do not do it in love; I do not do it in kindness, and oh, how I hurt people. I have to confess that, but I'm so glad for a verse like this, because I find hope in it. Regardless of how people think of me anymore, regardless of what the past has been for me, I have hope because of what this verse says.

I see a goal in this verse.

B. The Starting Point

Regardless of the spiritual level you are currently at, you have a goal —to be kind. You may think you are so far from that goal. If you do, that is great because now you have a starting point. After Paul says, "Be kind one to another," he adds, "Be tender-hearted". That's the starting point. How is being tender-hearted a starting point? Simply this: What really motivates you about loving anybody? Begin, for example, with the love of God and keep on telling yourself, "God loves me, God loves me, God loves me." Keep telling yourself this until you begin to believe it and let your heart become tender, anew and afresh with the love of God?

Why does God love you? Because He sees something good in you? Because you are handsome or beautiful? Because you are intelligent? Because you are spiritual? Because you are rich or poor? No! He just loves. Oh, how that should make you tender in your heart. Because He loves you like that, and because you are a Christian and a child of

God, you can be like Him. You can resemble your Heavenly Father and begin to let that same kind of feeling be communicated to other people. Just love them for the sake of loving them, just love people and let that love also have a quality of kindness, just for the sake of kindness. Let it come out of a tender heart because of how God loves you. That is your starting point. Yes, the goal may seem far, but do not worry about that; see the goal and pursue it.

Many times in my past, especially working with salesmen who did not learn quickly enough under my teaching, I would get angry. Spencer Hays, my boss, repeatedly said to me, "Don, you have to be more kind! Be gracious!" Every time he counseled me like that, I would feel mixed emotions. On the one hand, I knew in my heart he was right, but on the other hand, I felt a horrible sense of insecurity. Where do I begin? I did not know where to begin, so I didn't! But you do not have to be at such a loss, for in Ephesians 4:32 I am showing you from my own past experience where to begin. If it works for me, it can work for anybody.

C. The Means

The means by which you can attain that goal of being kind is this: "Forgiving each other, just as God in Christ also has forgiven you." Many times Christians disobey this command with various excuses: "I'll forgive you, but I won't forget," or, "I'll forgive you, but I won't trust you anymore," or, "I won't forgive you, I can't forgive you." The question comes: How did Christ forgive? How did God, for Christ's sake, forgive you?

First of all, He did it *freely*. There was no reason why He had to forgive you; you did not earn anything. You did not somehow bribe God to forgive you. He forgave you freely.

Second, He forgave you *completely*. He said, "Not only will I forgive all your sins, but I'll put them behind Me and remember them no more. And as far as the east is from the west, as deep as the deepest ocean, that's how far your sins shall be removed from Me." That's how we should forgive. Have you ever had the experience of being forgiven by somebody, a Christian, and then seeing them later and feeling, "Oh, no, he really didn't forgive!" ? That is not forgiveness. That is just a diluted, carnal kind of forgiveness. Forgiveness is forgetting also.

If you hold bitterness, and you just cannot forget, God can give you the power. He will help you at least to put it out of your mind each time it comes in. That you can do. You do not have to think on it, and surely you don't have to talk about it.

Third, He forgave *liberally*. He forgave all the many sins we have done. That is the standard by which we should forgive others. This is the means for our growth in kindness. The only thing that complicates our being kind to people is our not forgiving them. If somebody is severe toward you, harsh, morose or hard, they have not forgiven you. It's that simple. If you forgive them, it flows.

Ian McClaren, the author of "Beside the Bonnie Briar Bush," and one of the greatest orators of the Christian gospel who ever lived, attempted to preach in his first church without notes. In the midst of his sermon, he would sometimes have to stop and say to the congregation, "Friends, that is not very clear. It was clear in my study on Saturday, but now I will begin again." One day when this happened, a gaunt elder came forward after service, took him by the hand and said, "When you are not remembering your sermon, my son, just give out a song to us and we will be singing that while you are taking a rest. Just sit down and rest in that chair, remembering what you were going to say, for we are all loving you and praying for you." With such elders and parishioners, he went on to become a great preacher, and a great master of the deep things of the heart. That first church made Ian McClaren. Years afterward he said, "I am in the ministry today because of the tenderness and charity of those country folk, those perfect gentlemen and Christians." If love is kind, we can experience this same depth of spiritual growth and power in our churches today.

Life Message Three

Love is not Jealous

Oscar Wilde, writing about a trip of Satan through the Libyan desert, describes a very interesting situation in which Satan was watching his demons tempting a holy hermit. All during this period of time they were tempting him with sins of the flesh. One by one the holy hermit victoriously handled each temptation. As time wore on the devil became more and more impatient. Finally, he went up to his demons and said, "Move aside, let me show you how it's really done." Then he approached the holy hermit and said, "Your brother has just been appointed the monarch of Arabia." The holy hermit responded with a scowl of jealousy, and the victory was the devil's.

I. JEALOUSY CAUSES HATRED TOWARD OTHERS.

Would to God that each of us would realize that in God's eyes the greatest sins are not necessarily the sins of the flesh. Equally great in God's eyes are the sins of disposition, like jealousy. Jealousy is a poison that eats away at the being, character and personality of the individual and destroys the highest relationship of human beings in life. Unfortunately, we, like the demons, put a higher sense of disapproval on the sins of the flesh. But does not the message of the Spirit come to us afresh to challenge our value system in terms of the gradations of sin?

A. The Predominance of Jealousy

Jealousy is near the top of the list. In the apostle's description of love his first thoughts are about two positive aspects of love. In verse four he says that love suffers long and love is kind. But when he describes what love is not, the first thing that comes to his mind is not something to do with sins of the flesh, but with sins of the spirit. "Love is not jealous." That is amazing to me, but it is not new. Think about what happened after Adam and Eve were thrown out of the garden. Their sons, Abel and Cain, were born. Then Cain became jealous of Abel, and because of his jealousy, Cain slew Abel. The first crime committed in all of human history was done out of a premeditation fostered by a feeling of jealousy. In God's book, jealousy heads the list of sins.

Jealousy? What really is jealousy? I want to quote a description from Barnes' notes on the New Testament that I think is relevant to our understanding of this problem:

"To be jealous or to envy is to feel uneasiness, mortification or disconnect at the sight of superior happiness, excellence or reputation enjoyed by another. To repine at another's prosperity and to fret oneself on account of his real or forced superiority. Of course it may be excited by anything in which another excels or in which he is more favored than are we. It may be its accomplishment, reputation, success; it may extend to any employment or rank in life. But one thing is for sure, envy or jealousy lies commonly in the same line of business, occupation and rank. We do not usually envy a monarch, a conqueror, a nobleman unless we are aspiring to the same rank. The farmer does not usually envy the blacksmith, but another farmer. The blacksmith does not usually envy the schoolmaster or the lawyer, but rather another blacksmith. The clergyman does not envy anybody else really, but another clergyman. The physician, another physician; the housewife, another housewife; the businessmen, another businessman and on and on it goes. This is something of what jealousy is all about."[2]

Even kings are disturbed by it! You mean a king would actually be jealous? He has so much, so much power, so many riches, so much of everything. And yet he would be jealous? Yes, and if there was ever a king who should not have been, it was King Saul. He was head and shoulders above all the people in Israel the time. He was God's gift to the nation, so to speak. If there ever was a man who was competent to rule a nation, it was Saul. But one day he had a seed of jealousy developing in his heart toward a young man called David. That seed of jealousy grew into a root, and that root of jealousy sprouted forth in all sorts of blossoms until it brought about Saul's destruction. His empire fell. He himself fell, and it finally led to death itself. Another man took his place, all because of jealousy.

B. The Power of Jealousy

Jealousy is recognized by psychologists, psychiatrists, medical doctors as well as by ministers. It is a vice that grips the disposition of an individual and so keeps him within its clutches that his own good is hindered. Jealousy controls him because of his feelings towards someone else. What a pity! That is jealousy, the power of it, so powerful that it robs people of their joys in life. But where does it come from? What really is the root of the thing?

II. Jealousy Is Caused by Self-Hatred

What kind of chain reaction really occurs in this process? May I describe to you how it starts? Jealousy is caused by self-hatred. It is not hatred toward others that causes a person to be jealous of another, but self-hatred, me hating myself that causes jealousy toward others. Hatred toward others is the effect—self-hatred is the cause.

A. The Root of the Problem

Why would you be jealous of someone anyway? Is it not because you do not really feel fulfilled within yourself for what you are? When you look at yourself from the inside, are you really satisfied? Have you learned to recognize yourself for what you are and to be thankful for it? If you are jealous, it is because you have never accepted how God has made you. You have not learned to rejoice for what you are. Many people do not like the way they look. Many are dissatisfied because their intelligence is not as high as they want it to be. Many feel that their skill level in their job is not where they would like it to be. Basically, they suffer from a lack of self-worth. They have not learned to accept themselves. That lack of self-acceptance can be defined as self-hatred.

Harry Emerson Fosdick described it this way. In his psychology of the human personality, he portrayed jealousy as hypersensitivity in someone who has an inferiority complex. It is the expression of a person whose ego is so small and so threatened by other people that it thrashes out in negative feelings, words and actions. By way of contrast, the superior person; the person who is fulfilled, the person who really accepts himself for what he is, and who has learned to live with and be happy with himself, is described as a banquet for others to attend and eat. But that kind of a banquet is poison to a person with an inferiority complex, because it manifests how small he is.

B. The Chain Reaction

Self-hatred: how does it progress into hatred for others? Here's how: we really despise what we lack. We have all these inner feelings of inferiority, and then we meet someone who somehow has excelled beyond us in our same rank. We see him, we interact with him a little bit, and our self-hatred causes a feeling of resentment, unthankfulness, lack of appreciation, or jealousy. This jealousy leads to a feeling of bitterness, because we are projecting to that person our own lack. We are bitter about the fact that they are what we want to become, and we hate ourselves for not being that. This bitterness grows and grows into hatred for other people. That finally leads to strife and violence. What is the source of quarrels and conflicts among us? "You lust and do not have; so you commit murder" (James 4:2). Murder, as referred to here, may be physical murder, but it could also refer to character murder. You will easily find an envious person, a jealous person very active in character assassination, gossip, and slander. "You hate yourself for what you are not," is what James is saying. You lust to get it and when you find somebody who has it, you murder them in your thoughts, you are envious and cannot obtain, so you fight and quarrel.

"You do not have because you do not ask," James declares. This reminds me of that gala festival held in Milan, Italy, in honor of the great composer, Verde. Two of the leading composers of the day were invited to present some music in his honor. Toscanini was the one, Mascagni was the other. But interestingly enough, Toscanini had great feelings of envy toward Mascagni. So he said to the management of the festival, "I'll compose anything for Verde that night, in his honor, if you'll pay me more than you'll pay Mascagni." The management thought it over and agreed. The festival went beautifully and after it was over, Toscanini was given one lira. He looked at it with amazement. "What's this?" he demanded. The manager explained to him, "Mascagni did it for free."

Oh, the fools we make of ourselves by being jealous towards someone else. How we reveal how small we really are, how selfish we really are, when we express jealousy. Because the biggest thing we express is how miserable we are inside with self-hatred. Such a power like this can only be cured by love. How so? Well, the opposite of love is hatred. Therefore, the only cure for hatred must be the presence of love. But how can you really cure jealousy in the human heart toward someone else? It has to begin in the human heart?

III. JEALOUSY IS ONLY CURED BY LOVE

Now I want to offer the solution to the problem—and, may I say, it is a universal problem. It is not just Toscanini's; it is not just Saul's; it is not just mine, but it is yours, too. Granville Walker, in his book about jealousy, says he cannot imagine anybody reading his book who does not have a problem with jealousy once in a while; neither can I imagine anybody reading this book who is exempt from the problem of jealousy. Therefore, you should be very much aware of what the cure is. It's the love of God in Christ for you. I know of nothing else that can solve a problem of self-hatred than the love of God. Why? Because of this:

We have tried for years to overcome our problems by ourselves. We have tried positive thinking, and that did not work; we have tried getting busy at work and hobbies to get our minds off our problems, and that works only to a certain degree. We have tried all sorts of other things; we have listened to advice and tried to apply it. Even prayer and Bible reading alone are not the answer. What it all comes down to is a personal relationship with a loving God. It begins with the realization that God loves us through Christ, not for what we are not; but if God loves us and accepts us for what we are not, surely we can learn to do that, too. As soon as we allow that fact to saturate the very core of our being, we can eliminate self-hatred.

The first and greatest commandment of all is, "Thou shalt love the Lord thy God with all thy heart, with all thy soul, with all thy mind and with all thy strength." But we cannot love God without His first loving us. John makes that very clear in his epistle, "We love because He first loved us." By ourselves, if we cannot love ourselves or anyone else properly, we cannot love God. But when we receive God's love, then we learn to love Him in return, because it is a cause and effect relationship. As soon as we learn to love Him, ascribe worth to Him and praise to Him for who He is, then we have already begun to act the same toward people. That is why the second commandment is like unto it, "Love thy neighbor as thyself." It is only when the love of God in Christ floods the human heart, and makes our hearts feel a sense of acceptance, recognition, security and stability in God, that we can learn to love ourselves as well as love God. Only when we learn to love ourselves can we love our neighbors. God based His command to love our neighbors on this fact—love your neighbor as yourself. The reason why we are jealous toward people is because we are really jealous towards ourselves. We are really hateful to ourselves. Jealousy is hatred. Jealousy is not love. "Love is not jealous," the Bible says, therefore, hatred must be jealousy, and jealousy must be hatred. So, when we are jealous of someone, we are automatically showing hatred. Hatred comes from inside ourselves, from our attitude toward ourselves. When we learn to love God and to feel His love for us, and learn how to love ourselves because of how He loves us, then we can love our neighbors. Perhaps it can be illustrated like this:

Hawthorne should have written about human psychology, but he did not. Yet, he did write a book called, "The Bosom Serpent." In it he gave his views, on jealousy. It is a story about a man who lost his wife and separated from her because of ill-founded suspicions about her. The suspicions came out of a heart that felt inferior toward itself. He was so gripped by jealousy that it became a serpent in his breast. So gripping was this vice within him, that when he walked down the streets of his town, people asked him, "What's the matter? What's the matter with you? Aren't you feeling well today?" He would say in return, "It gnaws! It gnaws!" That bitter spirit of jealousy was like a serpent gnawing away inside of him and he looked at everybody through the posture of that jealousy. But one day after he was just about at the end of his rope, his wife came to him again and said, "Honey, why can't you forget yourself and love me?" Hear her words: Forget yourself and love me. With those words he dropped to the ground, and suddenly there was a sound like the hissing of a snake passing by. It appeared to leap out of his breast, and in a moment there was ripple in the fountain as it disappeared. When he stood back up again, he forgot himself and loved her.

Beware of that serpent of jealousy in your bosom. Let it pass away. Get rid of it and drown it in the nearest fountain.

Leonardo DiVinci is a great example to us, not only in his paintings, but also in his character. He is known not only for his own work, but also for the way he praised other men. Although he had occasional problems with his enemies, he knew how to praise his friends, especially his fellow craftsmen in the field. In describing one of his friend's paintings of the gates of the temple in Florence, Italy, he called them to "Gates of Paradise," thus the coining of the expression, "the gates of paradise." His expression became as great as the painting itself. Let that kind of feeling toward other people be ours. What kind of a life are we painting before others? What kind of details in the masterful strokes of Christ in our lives are we portraying? Let them be tempered by the strokes of the love of God which tells us: love is not jealous.

Application

We have already alluded to I John 4:14: "We love, because He first loved us." This verse appears in the context of a Christian hating another Christian. That is why the following verse says, "If someone says, 'I love God,' and hates his brother, he is a liar; for the one who does not love his brother whom he has seen, cannot love God whom he has not see."

Interestingly, the Apostle John utilizes I John 4:19 as the solution to such a problem. Likewise, this verse can be the solution to anyone's problem of jealousy. "We love because He first loved us." The key obviously is that we must get to work on convincing ourselves that *God does love us!* The rest shall be automatic.

But this is not all. In John 17:23 we read: "That the world may know that thou didst send me, and didst love them, *even as thou didst love me."* Isn't that amazing? See how much God loves us, as much as He loved His only begotten Son! Should not such a realization overwhelmingly cause us to love also?

We close this chapter with the helpful words of Goethe:

"Against the superiority of another, the only remedy is love. The psychologically healthy person rejoices in the excellence of others. Objectively interested in whatever he is giving his life to, he is glad when a musician, teacher, administrator appears who is better than himself. Thereby the world is enriched and if he can admire and so share in the excellency he is enriched himself." As another put it, "a superior character is a public banquet to which we are all invited."

LIFE MESSAGE FOUR

LOVE DOES NOT BRAG

I knew a certain Christian years ago who seemed to have a vice of forgiving people and he really seemed to enjoy it. As a matter of fact, after you asked his forgiveness, he would say something like the following, "Oh, I certainly will forgive you," and then he would add, "I was just praying this morning and God showed me all the different sufferings I must endure for His glory and the means by which I can grow to grace." That type of attitude alone was bad enough, but more than that, in the presence of other people he would refer to that forgiveness again. Numerous times the little incident that was supposedly forgiven by him was brought up in a sort of casual way. The meaning was plain. He seemed to take a double delight, on the one hand, in showing his great spirituality by forgiving people, and on the other hand in exposing the restricted, hidden, secret things a person does wrong and in betraying the confidences. This person did not really know how to forgive and he also was a braggart.

I. THE RAMIFICATIONS OF BRAGGING

Bragging takes all sorts of forms in life. It is not just saying, "I did this great thing," or "I did that great thing." That is only one form of it. There are many other subtle ramifications, as we shall discover from I Corinthians 13:4, where Paul used a very interesting word to describe bragging. The fourth ingredient of love is a negative one. "Love does not brag." The word used for brag does not have one single meaning. John Calvin in his commentary on this passage says this word means, "to display oneself; it means to boast; it means to brag; it means to talk about oneself repeatedly; it means to misbehave; it means to act unruly; it means to trouble people; it means to be inconsiderate." You will find a similar list of meanings in other commentaries and lexicons.

What does this mean? It means that bragging is something that has many ramifications. Consider some of them:

For example, self-deception. A little girl went to her priest in the confessional booth and said, "Oh Father, I have to confess that I must be very, very proud." He said, "Why?" She replied, "Well, every morning I wake up and I look into the mirror and I see my face and I think to myself how beautiful I am." And he said back to her, "Now just calm down, little girl. Don't worry, that's not so much pride as it is self-deception!"

Think this principle through and apply it. Perhaps we do the same thing once in a while, too. The mirror is God's Word. Sometimes we look into it and we don't see what we should see. We go away, forgetting what good we think we saw, or what bad we saw.

Another ramification of bragging is vanity. One time Goethe and Beethoven were going for a little stroll through the park. They were talking about music. As they were walking together, people would come along and tip their hats, or give them a nice gesture and bow. This continued on throughout their walk. Finally, Goethe said, "this is too much for me to bear, all these people doing all this kind of homage." Beethoven just gave him a little word of rebuke by saying, "Perhaps a few of those are for me?"

Bragging is also self-seeking. A self-seeking individual is a braggart. The way people pursue status symbols is a definite form of bragging. They don't say, "Look at what great things I have done." But, by the houses they live in, by the cars they drive, by the clothes they wear, by whatever they do to grab on to symbols that set forth their status in life, they are bragging.

Once an African Christian went to the village shoemaker and said he wanted a pair of shoes. He had them fitted exactly to his feet. He walked away very happily, and for weeks he wore those shoes. However, then he came back and said, "I want to return these." The shoemaker asked him, "What's wrong with the shoes?" He said, "Nothing, they fit perfectly."

"Well, then why don't you want them?"

"It's because they don't squeak."

The shoemaker couldn't understand the man's reasoning. Obviously, it appeared to be that this Christian wanted to wear a pair of shoes that squeaked as he walked down the church aisle so that everybody would turn and look at him. It was a subtle way of bragging.

Another ramification of bragging is concept. Some people do not openly brag about themselves, but they show an attitude of coldness. You do not dare upset them in any way, because if you do, all sorts of words will come forth from an injured, conceited attitude. Many of those words will be about how you hurt him. On the other hand, if the Christian gets to the point of realizing that he has no rights at all, you really cannot hurt him, because he cannot stand up for rights he does not have.

Bragging is also a form of self-defensiveness. For example, a husband and wife both have learned to do things well. They never talk about their accomplishments, but if there is a slight hint of criticism in their conversation, something the one did not like in the other, before you know it, they are defending themselves from attack. In defending themselves, they really are telling each other how great they are. Is that also not another form of bragging?

What about being contentious? What about the person who always has to prove his point, or champion an issue? What really is the motive behind this? Is it perhaps a deflated ego, a person who wants to become inflated by winning an argument? Of course, often this person finds that when you win the argument you so often lose the sale: when you win the argument, you lose the person involved. So what good does it do?

John Short brought out in his work on the passage that the most unpopular person in the world is a braggart. The person that people want to avoid the most is the one who talks about himself.

II. THE REASON BEHIND BRAGGING

There are reasons why people brag.

A. The Apparent and Surface Reason - Superiority.

At first glance, you would think that a person brags because he is superior to other people. This is true of many people who brag; they do accomplish big things and good things. Of course, they never learn that a person who has the right to brag does not need to, as Ben Franklin said. But, nevertheless, they go on.

B. The Subtle and Real Reason - Inferiority.

But there is another, more subtle reason why people brag. It is for the opposite reason. Instead of having a superiority complex, they have an inferiority complex. Why is it that a person really needs to talk about how good he is? Why? Is it not because of his terrible feelings of inferiority, or inadequacy, and insecurity and fear? These people feel inadequate in the presence of other people who have superior talents.

1. Feeling of inadequacy before others.

They have a psychological need to talk, to make up for their own deficiencies in contrast to what they see in the other person. They raise their own egos and do not feel so inferior after bragging.

2. Feeling of insecurity before God.

Some people also have great feelings of insecurity before God. A person who really does not know the love of God, and who really does not know how to trust in the Lord, needs to talk about himself and display himself, even in status symbols. By the way of contrast, think of Jesus Christ. He did not need more that one coat to wear; He did not have a place to lay His head; He did not need to have any of this world's possessions or riches. He walked by faith and not by sight, and yet He never felt insecure. But today there are so many Christians who have to get so many things for themselves just to feel a little bit of security.

3. Feeling of fear towards oneself.

Another aspect of inferiority in a person who has to brag is a feeling of fear toward himself. Listen to the person who has to brag; look at the person who trusts so much in status symbols, and mark it well that that person is afraid of himself. Afraid, for example, that what he is, underneath all of his talk and all of his status symbols, will be exposed if he stops talking and displaying himself. He is afraid, most of all, that he will see himself as he really is.

It has been well said, "The show-off is the one most shown-up in a showdown." There it is. The person with a great fear toward himself is always afraid that will happen.

Then there is Don Marquis' story about Wattie the Toad. He is the toad who felt that the world owed him everything. Finally, when the world provided a toadstool for him to be under, he said, "What did the universe do to deserve me?" Of course, that is perhaps rather extreme, but Wattie the Toad illustrates the attitudes of many of us. "Why did this church deserve me?" "What did this home do to deserve me?" On and on we go. Of course, the person who thinks that way, even to a certain degree, is nothing really more than a "toad."

III. THE REMEDY OF BRAGGING

We go on to the remedy for bragging. May I suggest three ways to solve the problem?

A. Reflect on the past Experiences.

First of all, think about yourself. At least one of the above ramifications of bragging applies to you. As it has well been said, there is no vice that is more common with the average person, and yet more overlooked in his life, than the vice of bragging in one of its forms or another. So do not think of anyone else—think of yourself right now. Reflect on your past experience. Think clearly about how many experiences you can add to those I have already listed. See yourself as you really are.

B. Remember the Scriptures.

Second, remember the Scriptures. Look at Proverbs 25:27, for example. This is a very significant text with regard to the matter of bragging. "It is not good enough to eat much honey, nor is it glory to search out one's own glory." That is a paradox, is not it? Why do we do it? Why do we display ourselves in any form at all? Because we are seeking some glory; we are seeking some recognition to fulfill a great psychological need we have. But God says it is not glory to search out one's own glory.

Consider Proverbs 27:2, "Let another praise you and not your own mouth; a stranger and not your own lips." We are afraid that if we don't speak and tell how good we are, we'll be overlooked; and yet the Bible says even a stranger will recognize how good we are. Let them do it; don't do it for yourself.

In Matthew 23:12 Jesus says, "And whoever exalts himself shall be humbled or abased; and whoever humbles himself shall be exalted." That is a law of the universe. If in any way, shape or form you brag, mark it well that you have already abased yourself; rather God will abase you because of it, and other people will too. There is no greater bore in all the world than a person who talks about himself. If you are like that, you will bore people to death and that is why they will avoid you. But, the reverse is true; if you humble yourself, you shall be exalted.

We read in I Peter 5:5-7, "The younger men will likewise be subject to your elders and all of you clothe yourselves with humility toward one another; for God is opposed to the proud, but God gives grace to the humble. Humble yourselves, therefore, under the mighty hand of God that He may exalt you at the proper time. Casting all your anxiety upon Him because He cares for you." How important this is! Are you afraid or are you worried about uncertainties in this life? Are you afraid you will be recognized for who you are? Cast all that on Him and realize it is God's job to exalt you; it is not yours, nor does it belong to anyone else.

C. Realize the Essence of Love.

The last point is, after reflection on past experiences and remembering the Scriptures, realize the essence of love. Turn to Philippians 2:1-5 and look carefully at the portrait of Jesus Christ found here. Notice what the apostle says in exclamatory terms: "If there is any encouragement in Christ, if there is any consolation of love..." Love is the only cure for a braggart. Love is the only cure for a person who has feelings of inferiority, insecurity and fear. Just as there are many ramifications of bragging, there also are many ramifications of love to solve the problem of bragging. All the ramifications are found in verse one. What is the answer? "Make my joy complete by being of the same mind, maintaining the same love, united in Spirit, intent on one purpose. Do nothing from selfish or empty conceit but with humility of mind, let each of you regard one another as more important than himself. Do not merely look out for your own personal interests but also for the interests of others. Have this attitude in yourselves which was also in Christ Jesus."

There it is. We violate the Scriptures when we start talking about ourselves instead of others. We violate God's laws when we think of ourselves before the other person, when we think more of ourselves than we do of the other person. If we do this, we will wind up feeling all the more insecure, all the more inferior, and all the more afraid. Therefore, if you are a person who has feelings of inferiority, may I suggest the way to feel more superior? If that is what you really want, God's way is to think more highly of the other person and talk about him instead of yourself. Do you feel insecure? God will exalt you; you abase yourself and humble yourself. Do you feel afraid? There is great security, trust and peace in the love which casts out all fear.

Love would correct bragging because it produces a desire for others to be happy. Love regards others with esteem; it teaches us to treat them with affectionate regard. No man who has affectionate regard for others is disposed to boast of his own qualities over them. Besides, love produces a state of mind just the opposite of a disposition to boast. It receives its endowments with gratitude, regards them as the gift of God, and is disposed to employ them not in vain boasting, but in purposes of utility, in doing good to all others on as wide a scale as possible. Christian love is humble. A truly great person never makes a display of his greatness. On the contrary, as John Short has phrased it, they "are so sure of themselves in their humble, gentle way that they do not need to attract attention to themselves. They indulge in no self-advertisement. If they are Christian, they are always willing and even anxious that their life and service should express not themselves but the spirit of the Master. Love's humility is its greatness. It is never boastful."

As Henry Drummond put it, "Love is our only salvation. Love which is superior to eloquence, to spiritual insight, to knowledge, to faith and even to charity and martyrdom; love which suffers long and is kind, is the only power in the world which can save a man from ridiculous swagger of boastfulness or from indulging himself in the bitter sneers of envy, for it neither grudges others of their gifts nor is it eager to show off its own. Love has not only the positive virtue of being patient and kind, but it also saves a man from making a fool of himself by pompous conduct.

"And then, having learned all that, you have to learn this further thing: humility, to put a seal upon your lips and forget what you have done. After you have fruitfully used your gifts, after you have accomplished something great, after you have been patient and kind, after your love has stolen forth into the world and done its beautiful work, go back again into the shade and say nothing about it. Love hides even from itself. Love waives even self-satisfaction. Love does not display itself.

"Love destroys boastfulness. When love really goes to work in a Christian, it so takes possession that it transforms pride into humility, insecurity into security, selfishness into selflessness. And this is not so amazing because what has happened is that the center of spiritual gravity has been changed from self to Christ. Love, true love, will limit our esteem for ourselves and prevent the tumors of self-display."[3]

Application

A young man was in the theater of Athens, during the days of the great Greek philosophers, standing around saying, "I have become wise because I have talked to so many wise men!"

But Epictetus stood up, and with his great years of wisdom and age said, "Young man, not necessarily so, for I have talked to many rich men, but I'm not rich."[4]

Reading these words alone will not stop you from bragging. As the old saying goes, "Talk is cheap. Listening is better, but practicing is best of all!"

Life Message Five

Love is not Arrogant

"Love is patient, love is kind, and is not jealous; love does not brag and is not arrogant" (I Corinthians 13:4). In the King James Version the words "puffed up" are used for arrogant. Those words remind me of the first fish my friend caught when his dad took him deep-sea fishing. As a boy of eight, it was a big thrill for him, even though he only caught a blowfish. Do you know what a blowfish is? When you pull it out of the water and scratch its belly, it puffs up like a balloon. This is the mental image I get when I read, "Love is not arrogant". Of course, what we are really talking about here is pride. In this chapter we want to consider from God's Word how pride causes us to be arrogant, how it causes us to be puffed up just like a blowfish. Our pride puffs us up because we seek to protect ourselves, too. Our study on love at this point forces us to think about the whole matter of pride.

When you think of a person who is arrogant, you probably think of a very outgoing person, a braggadocio, one who is very forceful and overbearing, and this is true in many cases. However, other kinds of people can be just as proud. There is not one of us who does not have some degree of pride in our lives. Since God's Word says, "Love is not arrogant," we cannot allow pride to be in our lives if we want God's love to fill us.

It is necessary to look at arrogance from four viewpoints: 1) the root of arrogance; 2) the ramifications of arrogance; 3) the results of arrogance; and, 4) the removal of arrogance.

I. THE ROOT OF ARROGANCE.

Pride works within us to shut us off from God. It shuts us off from the kind of love that God seeks to pour into us. Pride really strives within each one of us, blinding us to the fact that we really are sinners. Many people, of course, recognize they are sinners. That is why they accept Jesus Christ. And they know that they still commit sinful acts. But the question is whether we really consider ourselves to be sinners. "Yes, I commit sins," we say, but are we sinners? Or does our pride blind us to that fact that we really are sinners?

A. Inner Striving of Pride.

Many times we center our attention on the things in our lives that are wrong, that are an affront to God, the things that are sinful. But we need to realize the root of sinful acts, that we are in a state of being sinful people. This is what Jesus Christ came to redeem us from, from the state of being sinful people. We are still sinners, even though saved by grace. All of us are by nature sinners. It is pride in us that strives to cause us to overlook this fact. Consequently, to some degree, we are all proud and arrogant, because we do not really recognize the fact that in and of ourselves we are sinners. This is part of our nature; this is part of our being. Pride strives to blind us to this fact.

B. Deception of Pride.

Pride also deceives us and causes us to be arrogant. Often when we do recognize sin in our lives the guilt comes. But the guilt comes when we experience the consequences of our sin, rather than the sin itself.

One of the things that holds back God's blessing in our lives is the fact that we really do not fear God. If we really did fear God, we would call sin "sin" when we see it in our lives. We would call it sin and not wait until the consequences set in. We would refrain from sin, because it is an affront to God. Pride causes us to feel guilt about the consequences of sin, rather than the sin itself. This is because pride stirs up our concern about our appearance before other people. Pride puts up a front and keeps other people from seeing us as we really are.

C. Inner Distortions of Pride

In many ways, pride distorts our image of God. Because God is the creator of the universe, He also wants to be King in our lives. There's a logical deduction. But pride many times causes us not to allow God to be God in our lives. Pride tricks us into thinking that God is really King in our lives, when in reality we are on the throne and we are calling the shots. We are having our own way. That is arrogance.

In Galatians 5:19-21, we see some of the visible symptoms of pride: "Now the deeds of the flesh are evident, which are immorality, impurity, sensuality, idolatry, sorcery, enmities, strife, jealousy, outbursts of anger, disputes, dissension, factions, envyings, drunkenness, carousings and things like these of which I forewarn you just as I have forewarned you that those who practice such things shall not inherit the kingdom of God." That is a portrait of our nature. It is a description of every one of us, whether we are practicing these things overtly or not. These things are characteristic of every man. That is why God says there is none that is righteous; we have all gone astray; no one seeks God, because by nature we are sinful (Romans 3:11,12). We do not need to be reformed, we need to be liberated from ourselves, so that Jesus Christ can flow through us.

D. Final Consequences of Pride.

Pride produces these visible symptoms because we allow self to have its own way. That's arrogance. The final consequence of pride is that it causes us to be hardened to sin. When we allow ourselves to be on the throne of our lives, when we satisfy ourselves, we begin to grow hardened even to the sin that the Spirit of God convicts us of. When He reproves us, we turn our backs. As we continue to turn our backs, we become hardened to sin. Our arrogance before God hardens us eventually to the point where we will call right wrong, and wrong right. That is what pride does. Such is an arrogant person.

II. THE RAMIFICATIONS OF ARROGANCE.

Now let us consider some of the ramifications of arrogance, so that we can identify it in our lives.

A. Pride

At the top of the list is pride itself. Pride is the essence of arrogance. Pride is excessive self-esteem, putting myself above all else, even above God Himself.

B. Haughtiness

Another ramification of pride is a haughty spirit. What does it mean to have a haughty spirit? It means to be conscious of your own superior birth or your own superior power. It means looking down at other people because they are not of the same social class as you, they do not have the same means as you. Because you perceive yourself as powerful and influential, you have a haughty attitude toward those of a lower status.

C. Lordliness

An arrogant person is a lordly person, one who pompously displays his power. All of us have others who look up to us. But how do we display this relationship? Are we lordly with our power? Are we like possessive little children? You take your children to visit Johnny and suddenly little Johnny becomes very possessive with his toys. You do not have to teach him that. He lords it over his playmates; he lets them know what they can have and what they cannot have. This is part of our sinful nature. This is the way we are without God and without Christ.

D. Insolence

Arrogance makes us insolent. Often we become insolent to the point of actually despising other people. There are people we just do not like to be around. There are people with whom we are not comfortable. Maybe you consider yourself above them! This is insolence.

E. Forcefulness

An arrogant person is overbearing, he forces himself on other people, and he is tyrannical in his manner.

F. Supercilious

Another ramification of arrogance is the supercilious expression as seen in the uplifted eyebrow and the permeating attitude of a cool, condescending spirit.

G. Scorn

Arrogance makes us disdainful of others. It leads to scorning other people because of the way they are, because of the way they look, because of the way they act. This attitude often comes out when we talk with our husbands and wives and our friends about other people.

H. Conceit

Conceit is another ramification of arrogance. This is an excessive appreciation of our own virtues, our own abilities. It centers in ourselves and elevates ourselves.

I. Self-righteousness

Self-righteousness is another ramification of arrogance. If we look at this list of nine ramifications of arrogance, we are sure to find something that applies to some degree. It is our nature to be arrogant; it is our nature to be proud. This is an indication of the fact that we are sinners.

III. THE RESULTS OF ARROGANCE.

What are the results of arrogance in our lives? How does it affect our relationship with God?

A. In our Relationship with God.

Allow the Scripture to speak for itself:

"In pride the wicked hotly pursues the afflicted . Let them be caught in the plots which they have devised. For the wicked boasts of his heart's desire, and the greedy man curses and spurns the Lord." (Psalms 10:2,3).

"May the Lord cut off all flattering lips, great the tongue that speaks great things." (Psalms 12:3).

"No one who has a haughty look and an arrogant heart will I endure." (Psalm 101:5).

"For though the Lord is exalted, yet He regards the lowly, but the haughty He knows from afar." (Psalm 138:6).

"Everyone who is proud in heart is an abomination to the Lord. Assuredly, he will not be unpunished." (Proverbs 16:18,19).

"A rich man's wealth is his strong city, and like a high wall in his own imagination. Before destruction, the heart of man is haughty, but humility goes before honor." (Proverbs 18:11,12).

The word of the Lord speaks very clearly that God does not honor a haughty spirit; God does not honor pride. Pride cuts us off from God. Pride shuts us off from the free flow of God's Spirit. Love is not arrogant. Love opens us up to God and allows God to be God in our lives.

B. In Our Relationships with Others.

Another result of arrogance is the fact that it cuts us off from other people. It causes us to think poorly of them. We begin to devalue them as people. It causes us to think poorly of them. We begin to devalue them as people. We begin to devalue their gifts, because their gifts may be a threat to us, to our being esteemed by others.

Pride also causes us to devalue other people's needs. God has placed us on this earth to be ministers to one another, but pride keeps us from being sensitive to other people's needs. It cuts off our awareness of their needs. God wants to use us to meet other people's needs, but if we are self-centered we can't be used. We become more interested in satisfying our own desires because of arrogance.

Pride causes us not to be transparent with people, not to be open with them, because we are afraid they will see us as we really are. But love is not that way. Love is allowing yourself to be seen as you really are, by God's grace. On the other hand, arrogance shuts us off from what God is seeking to do in other people's lives. Every acquaintance we have is a "divine encounter". This is because God is seeking to work in the lives of others through us. When I come together with another person, I should ask myself, "What is God doing in this person's life, and what can I do to help God accomplish this?" But if there is arrogance in our lives, we cannot minister to other people, because we are more interested in our own needs being met.

C. In our Relationship to Ourselves.

Arrogance also keeps us in bondage to ourselves. That is the opposite of humility. Real humility is being full of God, but if we are arrogant, we are full of ourselves. We are in bondage to ourselves when we do not allow God to be God in our lives.

Being arrogant means being unable to give up our rights to God, because we must protect them. We must do all we can to see that our needs, wants and desires are met. This is why being arrogant keeps us from experiencing the joy of surrendering our rights to God. If we are arrogant, we do not allow God to take over our lives and to protect us. This is His responsibility, once we give our rights back to Him. So, the root of arrogance is pride; the ramifications involve all of us; the results of arrogance cut us off from God; they cut us off from other men; and we are in bondage to ourselves.

IV. The Removal of Arrogance.

But how do we get rid of arrogance?

A. Abasement before God.

Before we can experience freedom from ourselves, before we can experience freedom from arrogance, we must abase ourselves before God and recognize that indeed we are sinners. Recognize that without Him we are nothing! We are truly nothing. Our lives are empty without Him and we must abase ourselves before Him.

B. Attitude of Christ.

One of the ways we can remove arrogance is to seek the kind of humility that Jesus Christ had when He came to John the Baptizer. John said, "Behold, the Lamb of God who takes away the sin of the world." The kind of disposition that God is looking for in each one of us is the disposition of a lamb, willing to be shorn. A lamb does not complain when he loses his wool. He is willing to give up his rights. We need to get a vision of Jesus the Lamb if we are going to rid ourselves of arrogance. We need to have the kind of spirit He had. When He was baptized, a dove came down and rested upon Him, a picture of gentleness and peace. This is the disposition God expects in each one of us, if we are going to remove arrogance. He wants us to have the disposition of a lamb, of a dove, so we can be gentle and peaceable.

C. Rule of Peace.

In Colossians 3:15 Paul says, "And let the peace of Christ rule in your hearts to which indeed you were called in one body, and be thankful." The Spirit of God came upon Jesus as a symbol of peace. Because we are baptized by the Spirit into the body of Jesus Christ, the peace of God ought to be in us. Because we have peace with God, therefore, we ought to know the peace of God. When the peace of God stops flowing, it is an indication that arrogance has come in somewhere. God expects His peace to rule in our lives. When it is not there, something is wrong; the lamb-like disposition of Jesus is not in us. If we yield to His peace, we shall find that love is not arrogant. But if there is arrogance, we cannot experience His peace. Where do we start to experience the removal of arrogance from our lives?

D. Begin in Your Home.

The best place to start is in our homes. This is where it is most difficult to give up our rights. This is where it is most difficult not to display pride. This is where we react most often to selfishness and pride in other people. But we can start by recognizing qualities that God wants in our lives; those lamb-like, dove-like qualities. Perhaps our rights will be violated when we seek to be humble, when we seek to abase ourselves before God, when we seek to yield to others in our homes. Perhaps God will put us to the test to see how sincere we are about giving up our rights and removing pride and arrogance. Perhaps He will not change others in your family first. You may have to take the first step. We cannot wait for perfect situations to develop. We must look at each situation as an opportunity to develop the kind of qualities that God wants in our lives. This means being a true servant of others in our families. Rather than react to them, respond to them and allow the love of God to flow through you.

E. Willingness to Serve.

Another way to remove arrogance is to adopt the attitude of a bondslave. Jesus took that attitude toward His disciples. Therefore, we also ought to look for ways to serve others. There was no arrogance when Jesus Christ washed the feet of the disciples. Did he not deserve esteem? Yes. Did He not deserve to have His abilities recognized? Yes. Did He not deserve to have His right honored? Yes. But Jesus Christ was a servant. He was a bondslave to the will of God in His life. He set an example for us to be bondslaves as well. This means allowing God to be God in our lives, not ourselves, not our pride, not our arrogance. Being a bondservant means allowing ourselves to be taken advantage of by others in the family. If we are practicing "love is not arrogant," we will get some responsibilities thrown on us that normally are not ours. We can expect not to receive a thank you when we do things out of love for people, because love is not arrogant, love is not proud and love does not seek its own.

We are bondslaves and we have no rights as bondslaves, because we have given up our rights to Jesus Christ. This will mean being stretched to the limit. It will mean allowing our rights to be violated, while we maintain a dove-like, lamb-like quality. It will mean not lashing back at someone, not reacting.

We have been saved to be servants. And when we are anything else but servants, we are not fulfilling God's will for our lives, but we are thwarting the love of God in our lives. We are not allowing our lives to be opened to the free flow of God's Spirit. We are not allowing our lives to be open to the flow of God's love through us.

F. Appropriate "the Blood"

We noted above that we must abase ourselves before God and recognize that we are sinners. Then, we accept God's love in Christ by taking to ourselves the blood of Jesus Christ which cleanses us from all sin, even the sin of arrogance. The blood of Jesus Christ, a fountain that still flows, can cleanse us from all the ramifications of arrogance. Therefore, we must allow ourselves to be set free by appropriating the blood of Jesus Christ. Jesus Christ not only saved us for heaven after this life, He also saved us from the present power of sin. After we recognize our sin and call it sin, we can be purified. God purifies us with the blood of His Son. His blood cleanses us day by day, hour by hour, moment by moment, whenever we sin. This is the way to rid ourselves of arrogance.

Application

Then we can appropriate the free gift of God's love in Jesus Christ. I Corinthians 12 lists some of the gifts that God offers to His body, the Church. But I Corinthians 13 talks about His greatest gift: the gift of love. These attributes of love can be true in our lives. But we need to appropriate that gift. When Jesus becomes Lord of our lives, then His nature becomes part of our nature, and we begin to manifest the fruit of God's Spirit in our lives. Our lives are characterized by humility, not by arrogance. God offers each one of us that free gift of love in Jesus Christ.

Allow the conviction of God's spirit to come upon you. Appropriate the blood in Jesus Christ to rid yourself of arrogance and pride, so you can be the kind of person described in I Corinthians 13: "Love is not arrogant." Love is humble, love is being a bondslave, love is being willing to serve.

Life Message Six

Love does not Act Unbecomingly

There he is, standing in the snow. The snowflake destroyed his world power. He was a great man, and he still remains great in the eyes the world. But this great man and his armies were defeated by a snowflake. Was he really the man he thought he was? No. That's why he was an arrogant man. That's why he stands in that famous posture. Napoleon stands with all his arrogance and pride.

Napoleon? The great general, the great leader, the world emperor an arrogant man? Yes, he was a great man in many ways, but also, among other things, he was arrogant. Because he was arrogant he also was very discourteous. Many times he acted very unbecomingly, he knew very little about how to live in style. He could force people out of duty, but not inspire them inwardly. That is why he treated his soldiers the way he did.

In the previous chapter we dealt with arrogance. This is not another chapter on that subject. But arrogance is intimately related to things like courtesy, acting becomingly, having style in the way we come across to people.

Our understanding of the apostle's description of love is hindered by the break between verses four and five of I Corinthians 13. The last word of verse four is "arrogant" and verse five goes on "does not act unbecomingly." One would think that because of the verse break that there is not logical connection between being arrogant and acting unbecomingly. But we cannot make that conclusion, the opposite is true. Arrogance and acting unbecomingly are very intimately related. A person who is arrogant, a person who has a puffed up estimation of himself, cannot be sensitive to the feelings, interests and rights of other people. Arrogant people think so highly of themselves that they cannot condescend to little old people like you or me. It is very difficult for an arrogant person to act in a becoming way. Arrogance is the cause of discourtesy, the cause of bad manners, the cause of a lack of style.

We use words like courtesy, good manners, kindness and style because they are all related to the idea of acting unbecomingly. I want to use the word "style" as an umbrella word for all these concepts. The dictionary says style means "a distinctive, particular mode of behavior or deportment." When we say, "That person has style!" what we mean is "he has a good way of coming across that really turns us on."

But how does a person get that? This way of coming across in a becoming way is something that we ought to have as Christians. Paul says, "Yes, love does not act unbecomingly." I want you to note three dimensions in life concerning style. There are three kinds of Christian responses to this word. First of all, there are some Christians who deny style. They live as though it has nothing to do with their Christian lives. Second, there are some who doubt style. And third, there are some who develop style. This third category should be the goal for all of us.

I. DENYING STYLE

We must begin by asking ourselves which dimension we are in. Do we deny style; not by our thoughts, but by the way we talk, by the way we come across, by the way we are observed by other people? Do you go through life denying style? Are you one who goes through life doubting style? Or do you want to go through life developing it?

A. The Relationship of Arrogance and Rudeness.

First, let's take the one who goes through life denying style. This person evidences a relationship between arrogance and rudeness. There is arrogance in his life. He has never overcome the basic problem of puffed up pride, a high opinion of himself. Because of this he cannot possibly be sensitive about people's feelings, their interests, their rights and his obligations to them. He is the center of his own world, which has the consequential effect of turning people off. Do you have that problem?

In I Corinthians 13:11 Paul says, "When I was a child, I used to speak as a child, think as a child, reason as a child, but when I became a man, I did away with childish things."

B. The Relevance of Childishness and Rudeness

A second reason why people go through life denying style is because they are childish. A child of four, rushing into a room, screaming at the top of his lungs, demanding instant attention, cannot understand that he is wrong for doing such things. He cannot possibly be aware that he his actions unnerve adults and cause instant tension. A child sees himself as the center of his universe; everything in life revolves around him and his demands. A little child cannot understand that other people are as important, if not more important, than he.

Paul said, "When I became a man I put away childish things." Yet, many Christians have not put away childish things; they wonder why they upset people.

C. The Realization of True Greatness and Rudeness

A third reason why Christians go through life out of style is because they do not understand what true greatness is. What is it? Stand back from I Corinthians 13 and try to get an overall view of the chapter. What do you see? You see a portrait of living Christ. When Paul, inspired by the Holy Spirit, wrote those qualities of life, he must have thought of the one whom he adored above all: the Lord Jesus Christ.

Jesus represents true greatness. It was not until my sixth year of graduate school that I realized that I Corinthians 13 wasn't a beautiful exposition on love, but rather a portrait of Christ Himself. Why? Because I was tuned out as to what true greatness was. My eyes of perception could not grasp what was really out there.

As Henry Drummond put it, "Love is so great that it never calls attention to itself; so much so, that after it has done its great task, whatever its task is, it not only hides from the praise of others and response of others, and the recognition of others, but it even hides from itself as it goes back into the shade into total humility and self abasement."

One reason we go through life denying style, turning people off instead of turning them on, is because we do not understand true greatness.

What a contrast. Napoleon stands in history with all his great posture of arrogance. But where is Jesus? We have to be told that His portrait is in I Corinthians 13. Why? He doesn't draw attention to Himself. That is true greatness. When we get to that point in our Christian lives, that whatever we think, say and do, we do for the glory of God instead of other people, then we will have learned true greatness and we shall be on the road toward living in God's style.

II. DOUBTING STYLE.

But perhaps you are the kind of Christian who goes through life doubting style. Why should a Christian go through life doubting style? There are two basic reasons: (1) because of a great concern for truth; and (2) because of an undue concern about testing, temptation and trials.

A. Because of a Concern for the Truth

There are some Christians who are so concerned about accuracy of truth that they lose all Christian grace. For instance, a lady just arrived home from church. She walked into her house very hurt. Why? Because she was troubled by two seminary graduates whom she loved very much. After the service she had said something that was perhaps a bit untheological. In response, the two seminary men smiled and looked at each other knowingly. They knew her terminology wasn't quite right. They acted as though they were entertained, or perhaps even offended by it. And so the woman went home very hurt. Later, she wrote of these two young men, "They lacked style." They were so concerned for the truth and its accuracy that they failed their duty of love to this woman.

A second reason why some Christians are so concerned for the truth is that they want to be accepted by the in-crowd. An unfortunate thing that often happens to a new Christian is that he loses the freshness of his prayer expressions when he realizes his prayer method is not identical to that used by the in-crowd. So he gradually adapts, and before long he sounds like the rest of the Christians, the in-crowd. If we are concerned about conforming our ways to that of the in-crowd, we will lose our unique style, a style that God wants to use to bless the hearts of people.

Some people are overly concerned for the truth because they are afraid of becoming liberal. In my own education for the ministry, I have often heard professors say that liberals emphasize love and conservatives emphasize truth. I began to think that if I would actually become more loving, I would be mistaken for a liberal! So, I avoided it like a disease. That is a fact.

A marvelous cure for all this can be found in John 1:14. This is another portrait of Christ penned by John. "And the Word became flesh and dwelt among us, and we beheld His glory, glory as of the only begotten from the Father, full of grace and truth." The word "grace," by the way, is the word that can also be translated to "charm." "Charm" is what we mean by the use of the word "style." Christ was full of style and truth, full of charm and truth. He attracted people so they craved what He had. In the Greek, the word is in the emphatic position: "full of grace (charm, style) and truth." Christ did not emphasize love, grace or style at the expense of truth, but neither did He emphasize truth at the expense of losing love, charm and style. He was a balanced man; He was full of both. He was full of style of truth. What a tremendous corrective for us. We become so overly concerned about truth that we neglect to be loving.

B. Because of a Concern for Testing.

When it comes to testings we sometimes go through life doubting the importance and priority of style. Sometimes we get so overly preoccupied with the test, or trial, or temptation that we miss the importance of love. We pass the test to the letter of the law, but lack love. "I can't lie." But in not lying we can be very ungracious. Or, "I can't steal. I can't do a thing like that." In saying that very thing, we can be so arrogant that we forsake love. Even in our obedience to witnessing correctly we can be very unloving.

In stressing perfection we often ignore style. Or if we have a melancholy temperament, we excuse ourselves for a lack of love. Or if we have a bad temper.

In James 1:2, we find a corrective concerning temptations and tests. "Consider it all joy, my brethren." Some Christians, when they face a temptation, trial or test, pray for patience. God sends them that test to give them patience. But God also says, "Consider it all joy." This is the style of love. "Brethren, when you encounter various trials knowing that the testing of your faith produces endurance." Endurance is nothing more than love having style to the end. Whatever the test is, it is for the purpose of increasing your love, not just to have you put up with it, but to do so with grace and style. "Let endurance have its perfect result that you may be perfect and complete, lacking in nothing," especially in style.

So whatever the test, you can meet it in style, being courteous and mannerly. Let me give you a specific about style. I quote Henry Drummond, who said, "Courtesy or good manners is nothing more than love in tiny things." Try that and see the style of the Spirit of God with all His fruit flow through your life in abundance. Acting becomingly is loving people in small things.

III. DEVELOPING STYLE.

There is a third group: those who are developing style. To see something of what we mean by this, look at the beloved poet, Robert Burns. He was called the "Plowman Poet" because he was loved so much by ordinary people. It was said that he could walk into a cottage of a widow, or the mansion of a king, and be at home and in style in both realms. Why? Because he loved the mouse whose nest was plowed up in the field. He loved the daisy on the hillside. He loved every little thing and every big thing that God created. Robert Burns was called the greatest gentleman in Europe. He knew what it meant to cultivate or develop style. Thank God for some Christians who actually have matured so much that they have developed style. Of course, the most mature Christian will tell you he has never arrived in his manners, courtesy, kindness, love and style, so that he can stop developing. He is always involved in cultivating his love and style. Regardless of what level you are on today, if you want to continue to develop your love beyond where you are now, you should consider the four steps below.

A. Process of Growth.

Step number one: realize the process of growth. II Peter 3:18 commands us, "But grow in the grace and knowledge of our Lord and Savior Jesus Christ." Believers are expected to grow spiritually just like children physically. This means good manners, courtesy and kindness, among other things. Having style involves growth. II Peter 1:5-7 lists the building blocks of growth, or the baby steps of faith to grow up in Jesus Christ. If you want to grow step by step, and learn how to walk better as a Christian, may I suggest these little steps mentioned here.

"Now for this very reason also, applying all diligence, in your faith, supply moral excellence, and in your moral excellence, knowledge and in your knowledge, self-control, and in your self-control, perseverance; and in your perseverance, godliness; and in your godliness, brotherly kindness; and in your brotherly kindness, Christian love." If you follow these steps, you will have a developing style. This is growth.

B. Practicality of Decisions

Step number two: The practicality of decisions. Proverbs 3:5,6 says, "Trust in the Lord with all your heart and lean not to your own understanding. In all your ways, in all your decisions. Decisions, decisions, decisions. In one day there are a thousand decisions to make. Whether to go be kind or cruel. Whether to work hard or take it easy. Whether to drive fast or slow. In all your decisions, acknowledge Him. Realize the practicality of your decisions; realize your love and your style will increase as you learn to decide between style and self.

C. Power of Willingness

Step number three: You may say, "Look, I am the way I am. This is how I was made, and if you don't like it, leave it!" Have you ever heard anybody talk like that? I have. Anyone who talks like that is arrogant, especially in God's eyes. There was a time when I thought that way. A person who speaks like that knows nothing of Christ. On the other hand, II Corinthians 8:12 says, "For if the readiness is present, it is acceptable according to what a man has, not according to what he does not have." If you tell me, "I just don't have those niceties. I can't be kind like that. I can't be loving in little tiny things. It's not me," then I say to you, as long as you are willing to change, God does not expect you to be something that you are not. The important thing is not what you do not have, it is what you are. In other words, just begin where you are, and be willing for God to change you. You cannot make yourself over. But if you are a Christian, the person of the living Christ is in your being and He wants to burst into your life and make you a new creation.

Paul writes in II Corinthians 5:17, "Therefore if any man is in Christ, he is a new creature, the old things passed away, behold, new things have come." When a person is born again, he is not only saved from hell, he is also saved from himself. If you feel you can't be kind, courteous, gentlemanly and mannerly, then claim that as an area in which Christ will save you. God is concerned with our being saved from the ugly sins in our lives that upset our wives, our husbands, our friends and our children. He is also concerned if unbelievers are not impressed by our Christian profession, if they are not attracted by style.

After counseling four hours with a new couple, I learned what really attracted them to Jesus. It was not being saved from hell. They knew that was involved, but there was more to it than that. When they heard that Jesus saves us from the power of our sins, as well as from the penalty, that registered with them. When they realized that Christ could save them from their pride, from their stubborn wills and from whatever sins in their lives from which they could not save themselves, they wanted to receive Him. They said, "We will pay the price to get that." And yet some Christians are still touchy about some things in their lives. Why?

Because they have never let Christ come into that area to save them from that sin.

How about you? Will you let Christ save you? Are you willing to say "All right. I am miserable this way, but I am willing to let Christ save me from it, because I cannot do it myself."

D. Practice of Obedience.

Step number four: The practice of obedience. In John 14:15 we read, "If you love me, keep my commandments." After we experience salvation from sin, death and hell, we can know the joy of being saved from our sins day by day. This victory comes by practicing obedience. Jesus Christ said, "My sheep hear my voice, and I know them, and they follow me." Do you hear His voice? Do you obey His commands? This is the way to develop a genuinely Christian lifestyle.

Application

There is a very simple conclusion to all of this. Those who lack good manners, etiquette, courtesy, style, love in the tiny things, need to be "saved" in those areas. George Washington must have known this truth. One day when he was walking down the path with Lafayette, he was greeted by a black slave, who said, "Good morning, General." General Washington actually took off his hat, did a bow, and said, "Good morning to you." Noticing the quizzical smile on Lafayette, he turned to him and said, "My colleague, could I really let a black slave outdo me in good manners?" That is a mark of greatness. That is style, that is love. So great was Washington that he would not think of offending a slave. Christ was like that. Are you like that? Love does not act unbecomingly, for love has style.

Life Message Seven

Love does not Seek its own

There he is, walking cockily into a multitude of people gathered around the Lord Jesus. He brushes people as he walks past them, trips over a few feet, hurries past some others in need of beings healed, and ignores the compassion he owes them. He stomps right into the presence of the disciples themselves, pushes them aside and walks right over the Lord and Master Himself. With the arrogance of wealth and youth, what does he care about the rights of others? He demands of Jesus, "Sir, what must I do to inherit eternal life?"

To this rich young ruler our Lord answered, "Keep all the commandments. You know them. Keep them."

And the rich young ruler said back to him, "But I have kept all these commandments since the days of my youth."

Then Christ said, "Oh, you have in so many words, then why do you ask Me, 'What must I do to inherit eternal life'?"

"Because I want to know from You what You think I should do to inherit eternal life."

Jesus made it clear. "All right, I'll tell you in so many words. Go, sell all your riches, give them to the poor, and then follow after Me."

The rich young ruler thought for a moment, bowed his head, and walked away with great shame, because he knew that where his treasure was, his heart was also. His treasure happened to be his riches, not his faith in God.

We see a man insisting on his own way, but we also see the love of our Lord. Perhaps there were tears in His eyes, because the Scripture says, "He pitied him because of how greatly He loved him."

What a tragedy for the Lord Jesus Christ to love anyone; rich young ruler or not, only to have that person go his own way. Insisting on one's own way is not just peculiar to a rich man, rather it is a universal problem of human nature. All of us to one degree or another have a problem with insisting on our own way. We hold very closely to ourselves, not necessarily our riches, but our rights; what we think we deserve. We, to some degree, actually feel that the world owes us a living, that our wives owe us something, our children owe us something, our husbands owe us something, our parents owe us something, or the community does, or our friends. We all basically have that inner problem of wanting our own way. We look out for ourselves, even at the expense of others.

There are two basic kinds of selfish people. There are those who are overt in their selfishness, very crude, known by their rudeness, lack of manners and arrogance. When we meet them, we're glad we're not like them. The second type of selfish person is the one who is very subtle about his selfish desires. He knows that publicizing his selfish aims will turn people off, therefore he will be more quiet about it. He devises ways of secret maneuvering, manipulating people and things until he gets what he wants. On the surface this person could appear to be the sweetest, kindest and most loving person, but underneath what is the real motive? Is this person not also selfish?

I. SINCERE CONFLICT BETWEEN SELFISHNESS AND SELF-INTEREST

The problem of selfishness is further compounded by another question: Is it always wrong to think of my needs? Don't I have any right to think of what I need in life, or to think about what I myself must be in order to help other people? We are caught on the horns of the dilemma. On the one side, is the problem of selfishness, and on the other, the problem of self-interest. These two sides constantly conflict with one another. "Selfishness" is defined as wanting your own way at the expense of other people or God. "Self-interest" is defined as wanting your own way for the benefit of God and other people. This may be illustrated, for example, by a lifeguard. He has to learn how to swim before he can save another from drowning. He must also learn life-saving skills so he will know what to do when a person is drowning. To save his own life, he needs to learn defensive procedures, in case the drowning person tries to grab him and pull him under. Is the lifeguard wrong for thinking of himself?

The Bible says in I Corinthians 13:5, "Love does not seek its own." What about the housewife? Is it wrong for her to want proper sleep, proper food and proper love from her husband? Is it wrong for her to expect tender care from him, so that she in turn can be a good wife and mother? Is it wrong for the breadwinner of the family to expect his wife to treat him right and his children to make him happy? Is it wrong for him to want his food, clothing and shelter all cared for when he comes home from work?

All these questions, you see, crop up in this conflict between selfishness and self-interest. How do we resolve them? Have we really sat down with the Word of God and looked for the answer from God to this problem of selfishness? I have found this to be a very difficult chapter. I have the problem of being basically selfish myself. I have been selfish in the ministry many times, and right in my own home. I need to learn from the Holy Spirit how to be less selfish. I'm writing, not because I have overcome all selfishness, but because this truth has to be presented.

II. SOLUTION TO THE PROBLEM

The answer is found in four Scriptures. Those simple words, "Love does not seek its own way," must be expanded by other Scripture texts. The greatest commentary on them is to be found in the Bible itself.

There are people in my congregation who have come to Christ through the truth of these Scriptures about denying self, letting self die and taking up one's cross and following Him. There are four accounts in the Gospels where the same basic truth is taught, that if any man would like to follow Christ, he must first of all deny himself, pick up his cross, and follow Him. That same truth appears four times in the Gospels in different contexts, and in answer to different questions. Taken together, they will help us solve the problem of selfishness.

A. Mark 8:31-38.

First, Mark 8:31-38. "And He began to teach them that the Son of man must suffer many things and be rejected by the elders and the chief priests and the scribes, and be killed, and after three days rise again. And He was stating the matter plainly. And Peter took Him aside and began to rebuke Him. But turning around and seeing His disciples, He rebuked Peter and said, 'Get behind Me, Satan; for you are not setting your mind on God's interests, but man's.' And He summoned the multitude with His disciples, and said to them, 'If anyone wishes to come after Me, let him deny himself, and take up his cross, and follow Me. For whoever wishes to save his life shall lose it; and whoever loses his life for My sake and the gospel's shall save it. For what does it profit a man to gain the whole world, and forfeit his soul? For what shall a man give in exchange for his soul? For whoever is ashamed of Me and My words in this adulterous and sinful generation, the Son of Man will also be ashamed of him when He comes in the glory of His Father with the holy angels.'"

Notice especially that the answer, "...deny yourself, take up your cross, and follow Me," was given to Peter in response to his rebuke of Jesus. In the face of Peter's thinking of man's interests, and not God's Christ gave this statement, that a man should deny himself, take up his cross and follow Him. Jesus added to that, "And whoever wants to save his life (his own way) shall (in essence) lose it, and whoever seeks to lose his life for Christ's sake shall find it."

B. Luke 9:18-26.

Second, Luke 9:18-26. The words are essentially the same, but the situation is different. "And it came about that while He was praying alone, the disciples were with Him, and He questioned them saying, 'Who do the multitudes say that I am?'" The occasion here was one of prayer, and Jesus used a question to teach the disciples something concerning His identity. "And they answered and said, 'John the Baptist; but others say, Elijah; and others, that one of the prophets of old has risen again.' And He said to them, 'But who do you say that I am?' And Peter answered and said, 'The Christ of God.' But He warned them, and instructed them not to tell this to anyone, saying, 'The Son of Man must suffer many things, and be rejected by the elders and chief priests and scribes, and be killed, and be raised up on the third day.'" Jesus prophesied His suffering, but He was praying before He told them these things. In Luke's account, Peter passed the test with the proper answer about who Christ was, but yet on the other hand, he flunked it because he rebuked the Lord. The rebuke is not recorded in Luke's account. Jesus continued, "If anyone wishes to come after Me, let him deny himself, and take up his cross daily and follow Me."

Jesus must have known that we would have such a difficult time with ourselves, trying to solve the problem of a selfish life. He uses the word "daily." If we want to have victory over ourselves, our self-denial must be a "daily" part of us.

My wife's father says that every morning when he gets up he repeats these words to his Lord: "I beseech you therefore, brethren, by the mercies of God, that ye present your bodies a living sacrifice, holy, acceptable, unto God, which is your reasonable service. And be not conformed to this world, but be ye transformed by the renewing of your minds, that you may prove what is that good and acceptable, and perfect will of God" (Romans 12:1,2). After he quotes those two verses, he says, "Lord, I give you my eyes today so that I don't sin with them; and I give you my lips so that I don't say the wrong thing to somebody; and I give you my hands so that I don't do anything wrong; I give you my feet, Lord, so that I don't walk in the wrong place." He denies himself daily, every new morning. If you have a problem with self, may I suggest, deny yourself.

C. Matthew 10:24-39.

Third, Matthew 10:24-39. "A disciple is not above his teacher, nor a slave above his master. It is enough for the disciple that he become as his teacher and the slave as his master. If they have called the head of the house Beelzebul, how much more the members of the household. Therefore, do not fear them, for there is nothing covered that will not be revealed, and hidden that will not be known. What I tell you in the darkness, speak in the light; and what you hear whispered in your ear, proclaim upon the housetops. And do not fear those who kill the body, but are unable to kill the soul; but rather fear Him who is able to destroy both soul and body in hell. Are not two sparrows sold for a cent? And yet not one of them will fall to the ground apart from your Father. But the very hairs of your head are all numbered. Therefore, do not fear, you are of more value than many sparrows. Everyone therefore who shall confess Me before men, I will confess him before My Father who is in heaven. But whoever shall deny Me before men, I will also deny him before My Father who is in heaven. Do not think that I came to bring peace on the earth; I did not come to bring peace, but a sword. For I came to set a man against his father, and a daughter against her mother, and a daughter-in-law against her mother-in-law; and a man's enemies will be the members of his household. He who loves father and mother more than Me is not worthy of Me; and he who loves son or daughter more than Me is not worthy of Me. And he who does not take his cross and follow after me is not worthy of Me. He who has found his life shall lose it, and he who has lost his life for My sake shall find it."

Notice, there are different circumstances. First, Jesus said that the servant is not greater than his lord. Second, he talked about their worries. They were worried about where their next meal was coming from, their next robe, the shelter over their heads. He referred to the birds of the sky and said, "You are of more value than many sparrows." He talked about the family. A wife, husband, mother, father, daughter or son can keep a Christian from following the Lord. Jesus said, "Regardless of what any member of your family does, that is no excuse for you to be unspiritual and un-Christ-like. That is no excuse for you to exert your self-interest, just because they stumble before you." If we let any member of our own family hinder us from serving Jesus, we are not worthy of Him.

D. Matthew 16:24-27.

Fourth, Matthew 16:24-27. "Then Jesus said to His disciples, 'If anyone wishes to come after Me, let him deny himself, and take up his cross, and follow Me ... For what will a man be profited, if he gains the whole world and forfeits his soul?'" Some Christians forfeit the joys of the Christian life over something far smaller than the whole world.

One of the consequences of being selfish is that we sell short God's marvelous plan for us in exchange for a very small thing; a car, a boat, a house, a family member. We deny ourselves what God wants to give us: love, joy and spiritual vitality; because of something between us and Jesus, because we want our own way.

Jesus added, "And He will recompense every man according to his deeds." Christians will give an account of all their deeds at the judgment seat. Therefore, is it not wise to avoid the selfish ones?

In summary, Jesus said, "Deny that self which exerts itself, so that Christ will be first, others second, and you last." He wants you to eat, for He promised to provide for you. He wants you to sleep. He wants you to be healthy. He wants you to be strong. He wants you to be happy, to be at peace with yourself. But He wants you to do this His way, not your way.

Perhaps many of us are like the two little boys on a hobby horse. One of them said to the other, "If only you would get off, I could ride much better." A young woman left a suicide note saying, "I am killing myself because I have never sincerely loved any human being all my life." Many people love in order to be loved in return. We treat others nicely, because we know we will be treated kindly by them. We do not act out of sincerity. There is a big difference. Happiness is evasive. Try to grab it and it avoids you, but forget it and just give it without any thought of return, and God will flood you with it like an ocean wave.

John Calvin brought out this important truth when he said, "Even though we are degenerate and sinful men, still we are so constructed in the image of likeness of God that we will never be fulfilled in life, if left to our own selfish ends. That even in our depraved state, even in the light of our imperfection, we still cannot be satisfied and fulfilled in life, wanting our selfish desires. Even unsaved man feels better when he gives without any thought of return. How much, therefore, the Christian."[6]

An elderly lady sat in the back of her chauffeur-driven car and went to the cemetery parking lot. She stayed in the car because she was too weak to walk. The chauffeur said to the cemetery manager, "Will you please speak to the lady, because she is too weak to walk." He went to her and she said to him, "I am the lady who has been mailing you the $5 a week." He said, "Oh yes, for the flowers." She said, "Yes, for my husband's grave. I have just been told by my doctor that I only have a few more days to live. I don't care, because I have nothing to live for. I want to make arrangements that $5 a week will still be used for flowers on that grave." He said, "Ma'am, it won't do that much good." She was shocked. Then he explained to her: "Please understand what I mean. I have been a member of a visiting society that goes to mental asylums and state hospitals. Those $5 worth of flowers would be so much better for people there who can see them, smell them, and feel them." She was totally taken aback. She ordered her chauffeur to drive away.

Two months later the woman drove her own car to the cemetery office and walked up to the manager. With a bright happy smile, love beaming out, peace just bursting in her breast, she said, "You were so right two months ago. The reason I am still alive; the doctor does not know it, but I know it, is because I found a purpose for living. I did not send those flowers to hospitals and asylums, I brought them. And the joy I have found in bringing joy into other people's lives has given me a new purpose for living."

APPLICATION

Isn't that our purpose for living? If we could just stop seeking things for ourselves, and instead give to others what they need, we too would surprisingly find our happiness.

"But you, are you seeking great things for yourself?" asked the prophet Jeremiah (Jeremiah 45:5). "Do not seek them." Why? Because there is no greatness in things or in self-seeking people. But there is greatness in unselfish love, so seek that. As you do, be ever cautious that even self-denial can be a subtle form of self-seeking, and therefore nothing. So be cautious by double-checking that your motive for self-denial is selfless love.

Do you think this is not only difficult, but perhaps impossible?

Perhaps you do not understand the true nature of love. Nothing is a hardship in love. Jesus said His yoke is easy and His load is light (Matthew 11:30). If you don't think His promise is true, perhaps it because you have not found Christ Himself! You must do what He says, "Come to me and I will give you rest." Do that right now and you will find the reality of this truth. Remember the words of Henry Drummond, "There is no happiness in having, or in getting, but only in giving."[7] Although the rest of the world is going in the wrong direction, we do not have to follow. Jesus in His sermon on the mount said, "It is more happy to give than to receive."

Life Message Eight

Love is not Provoked

The words of our Lord Jesus Christ from the Sermon on the Mount are equally fitting here at the beginning of this chapter as they were at the end of the previous chapter!

"You have heard that the ancients were told, 'You shall not commit murder,' and 'Whoever commits murder shall be liable to the court,' but I say to you that everyone who is angry with his brother shall be guilty..."

These are troublesome words to us because we all have a problem with anger, with getting provoked. Anger is a universal problem that has been around since the beginning of the world. That is why one of Adam's sons committed murder.

I. The Character of Anger.

"Love is not provoked." This truth in I Corinthians 13:5 rings in our ears as we hear the words of the first murderer echoing through the ages, "Am I my brother's keeper?" Cain's lying lips were attempting to cover up his fatal offense against his brother, Abel. What provoked Cain to murder his brother? Was it a momentary loss of composure, a fleeting fit of anger or rage, or was there an inward attitude that displayed itself in this moment of rage?

In Genesis 4:4-5, we have an answer to these searching questions. Two brothers came before God with their offerings, "And the Lord had regard for Abel and for his offering; but for Cain and for his offering He had no regard." Why did God accept one offering and reject the other? God not only looks at the outward act, but also at the inward heart attitude. God saw that Abel's heart was repentant before Him. He had a heart of love for God. But there was not true repentance in Cain's heart. He was not willing to humble himself before God in repentance. Cain's heart was selfish. Consequently, "Cain became very angry and his countenance fell." His anger manifested itself in the murder of his brother, Abel. An outward act cannot be divorced from an inward attitude. Anger is an inward attitude of the heart. Thus, the true character of anger is murder in the heart toward someone. Yes, we can get control of ourselves, so our anger does not go as far as murder. Nevertheless, murder is its true characteer. That is why Christ equated the two in Matthew 5:21-22.

Why is it that we can hear the story of Cain and Abel over and over again, and each time be horrified at the gross sin of murder, and yet hardly wink an eyelash at the inner attitudes that led up to this murder? Is it because we have excused anger as a weakness and say it is just our temperament? Can we excuse it that way? The Bible speaks about these inner sins of attitude just as much as it does about murder and adultery. Why does the Bible speak so much about them? Is it because we so readily tolerate them?

In Galatians 5:19-21, we read a list of sins, "Now the deeds of the flesh are evident, which are: immortality, impurity, sensuality, idolatry, sorcery, enmities, strife, jealousy, outbursts of anger, disputes, dissensions, factions, envyings, drunkenness, carousings and things like these." Strife, jealousy, outbursts of anger, disputes, dissensions and factions are listed along with the worst carnal sins, and yet we treat them so lightly.

II. THE CAUSE OF ANGER.

In his book "Spirit-Controlled Temperament," Tim LaHaye wrote the following: "Although we love to excuse our weakness and justify them to ourselves as we nurse our grudges and indulge in anger, violated, bitter feelings, they are all motivated by selfishness. When I am angry, it is because someone has violated my rights and I am interested in myself. When I am bitter against someone, it is because they have done something against me, and again I come back to selfishness. Vengeance is always inspired by selfishness."[8]

Observe a group of children playing at a playground, and it will not be long before you see selfishness and anger in action. Two little girls playing, the one yells, "It's my doll! I want to play with my doll. It's my turn!" Two little boys with a bat and ball, and one says, "It's my turn. I want the ball and bat now!"

The root cause of all these things boils down to one thing: selfishness. It is interesting that being provoked comes right after "love does not seek its own." This selfishness is not only evident in the lives of children, but in the lives of adults as well. Husbands and wives often become angry with one another because they are more concerned with their own problems than they are with reaching out in love and sympathy toward their partner. When a husband comes home after a hard day's work, he is feeling tired and unaware that his wife had a hard day, too. Each can be self-centered, so that when they tell each other about their own problems, the other one thinks, "I had a harder day than her/him." We are selfish people. We think of ourselves. But love is not self-regarding. "Love is not provoked."

When we look at the basic cause of anger in all its forms: arguments, loss of temper, irritations, touchiness; it all boils down to selfishness.

III. THE COST OF ANGER.

What is the high price we pay for pent-up bitterness and anger stemming from selfishness? Paul writes in Ephesians 4:30-32, "And do not grieve the Holy Spirit of God, by whom you were sealed for the day of redemption. Let all bitterness and wrath and anger and clamor and slander be put away from you, just as God in Christ has also forgiven you."

Let us consider the high cost of anger in four areas: emotionally, socially, physically, and most important of all, spiritually.

A. The Emotional Cost of Anger.

Suppressed anger and bitterness will cause tremendous emotional strain. We are designed by God to be intensely emotional creatures, but if we permit anger to dominate us, it will squelch the rich emotion of love.

Dr. S. I. McMillen, in his book "None of These Diseases," makes an interesting statement about the emotional effects of anger: "The moment I start hating a man, I become his slave. I cannot enjoy my work anymore because he even controls my thoughts. My resentment produces too many stress hormones in my body and I become fatigued after only a few hours' work. The work I formerly enjoyed is now drudgery. Even vacations cease to give me pleasure...the man I hate hounds me wherever I go. I can't escape his tyrannical grasp on my mind. When the waiter serves me porterhouse steak with french fries, asparagus, crisp salad and strawberry shortcake smothered with ice cream, it might as well be stale bread and water. My teeth chew it and I swallow it, but the man I hate will not permit me to enjoy it...the man I hate may be many miles from my bedroom, but more cruel than a slave driver, he whips my thoughts into such a frenzy that my innerspring mattress becomes a rack of torture."[9] What a price to pay for anger!

Anger takes many forms. Many people do not think they have a problem with anger. When Paul warned that "love is not provoked," he had in mind anger in all its variations. Consider the following to find out if you are an angry person: bitterness, malice, clamor, envy, resentment, intolerance, criticism, revenge, wrath, hatred, seduction, jealousy, attack, gossip, sarcasm and unforgiveness. Several of these are in Ephesians chapter four and the rest of them are are found in Paul's other writings. Many are under the misconception that only the one who shows a physical outburst is an angry person.

B. The Social Cost of Anger.

The social price of anger and bitterness is exclusion from enjoyable times with other people. People do not want to be around an angry person. Many families have been torn apart and many friendships have been ended by outworkings of anger. In Proverbs 22:24 there is this warning, "Do not associate with a man given to anger, or go with a hot-tempered man." The Bible warns, "do not even associate with an angry person."

C. The Physical Cost of Anger.

The physical cost of anger is also a financial cost. Anger and bitterness produce so much stress that often a person gets sick and spends much money for doctors to cure his problems. The physical problems are caused by inward anger. Doctors and medical associations say that from sixty to ninety percent of physical problems are emotionally induced. The majority of these sicknesses stem from either fear or anger. Because of the great physical cost, to yourself, beware of harboring anger.

D. The Spiritual Cost of Anger.

We pay a high price in the spirtual realm for tolerating anger. Anger grieves the Holy Spirit. Jesus Christ said, "I have come that you might have life and that you might have it more abudantly" (John 10:10). Abundant life can only be experienced when we are filled with the Holy Spirit. This cannot take place when we are grieving the Holy Spirit with our bitterness, wrath, anger, clamor or malice.

If we grieve the Holy Spirit, we cannot expect to have the fruit of the Spirit in our lives. The presence of anger indicates the absence of love. If love is absent, we cannot experience peace, joy, patience, kindness, goodness, faithfulness, gentleness and self-control.

IV. THE CORRECTION OF ANGER.

Having seen anger in its true character, and the high price we pay for it in every area of our lives, how we can correct it? How we can we stop grieving the Holy Spirit?

Paul writes in Phillipians 2:5-8: "Have this attitude in yourselves which was also in Christ Jesus, who, although He existed in the form of God, did not regard equality with God, a thing to be grasped, but emptied Himself, taking the form of a bond-servant, and being made in the likeness of men. And being found in appearance as a man, He humbled Himself by becoming obedient to the point of death, even death on a cross."

Christ's attitude was one of meekness. Meekness is the opposite of anger. We get angry when someone infringes on our rights. Yet, meekness means yielding personal rights to God. This is the only way to respond when we are tempted to get angry. This is the only way to correct anger—to give your rights to God, to humble yourself before God.

Look at the trial of Jesus Christ. He stood before Pontius Pilate, and the chief priests and elders accused Him falsely. He made no defense. He did not answer their charges. Pilate was amazed at Christ's attitude, because the natural reaction would have been for Him to strike out in anger and self-defense.

They took Him away, they beat Him, they crowned Him with a crown of thorns, they mocked Him, they spit upon Him, they nailed Him to a cross! What was his reaction? "Father forgive them, for they know not what they do." For "Love is not provoked," even to the point of death.

Application

In applying this to yourself, you may have an objection similar to the following. You may feel that your outbursts of anger are part of being human and God understands. He knows you can not be perfect, so you excuse yourself. However, anger can be the vice even of the best as well as the worst people. Often, it is the one blemish on an otherwise excellent character. It is the one thing that can even make the best of people unappreciated. If we are angry, people tend to forget all the good we have done.

That may not seem fair, but that is the way it is. Mario Lanza was one of the greatest singers who ever lived, but he could offend people by his temper. We all know people who are so refined, except for their quick temper. They are easily offended and have short fuses. The striking compatibility of anger with high moral character is one of the strangest and saddest problems of ethics and religion.

No, none of us, no matter who we are, can afford to get provoked. Let us be as diligent in getting rid of it as we are in dealing with what we think our worst sins may be.

Life Message Nine

Love Does Not Take Into Account a Wrong Suffered

Rudyard Kipling, in his great poem, "If," wrote:

If you can keep your head
When all around you are losing theirs
And blaming it on you.
Or being lied about; don't deal in lies.
Or being hated; don't give way to hate.
Yours is the earth and everything that's in it;
And what is more—you'll be a man, my son.

Perhaps you've heard these words before, but find they are hard to apply in your life. Perhaps you have often felt as the woman who poured out her problem to her pastor.

It seemed to be a very trivial matter, but as the counseling session progressed, the minister discerned that she was under great nervous stress. Her problem had begun years ago when she was living with her sister, an invalid. She ministered to her day after day, week after week, month after month and year after year. She seemed to enjoy it; but deep down in her heart she hated her sister. Although she tried to justify and explain away her feelings, this did not alleviate her suffering internally. The minister gave her some practical suggestions, and then prescribed the only medicine that really could solve her problem: "You *must* forgive and forget."

I. THE PROBLEM

Forgive and forget, we say. We can perhaps work ourselves up to forgiving a certain individual, but how can we forget? Years ago a teacher of mine said, "Only God has the power to forget, not man. Man can forgive, but only God can forgive and forget." I raise the question, Is that really true? Perhaps it is not, especially in light of the fact that so often our forgiveness seems so personally unsatisfying when we do not forget as well as forgive. But the real question is, How can you forget when the hurt is so deep? The answer is in I Corinthians 13:5: "Love is not provoked, love does not take into account a wrong suffered."

In the previous chapter we discussed the fact that love is not provoked. There is an important connection between this and the subject of this chapter. We have to take the two together. There are two basic surface problems: Christians being provoked and Christians bearing resentment. But what is the relationship? Being provoked is the outward manifestation of anger. Many Christians do not show outward bursts of anger, but within them they are keeping records of wrongs suffered from other people. These are both expressions of anger. Both find their root in the problem of anger. The person who does the latter hurts himself just as much as the person who does the former.

My father had a friend who, whenever he was provoked, blew his top. But once he did, he forgot about it, he had no resentment. He walked away, free from the ulcers of the problem.

But some people are like the magician on a ship going to Europe. As he entertained the people with his tricks, a parrot belonging to one of the passengers said, "You're a faker!" The people applauded his tricks, but the parrot kept saying, "You're a faker!" This went on for some time, but the magician, of course, did not blow his top, because he would lose the respect of his audience. He simply tried more fantastic tricks, trying to think of some way to get even with the parrot. Finally, as he attempted one last trick, the ship struck a mine and exploded. The magician and the parrot survived by clinging to a raft. The parrot studied the situation and then said, "OK, buddy, you win. But tell me, what did you do with the ship?"

When we allow resentment to build up, we lose the whole ship, so to speak. Benjamin Franklin once put it this way: "Doing an injury puts you below your enemy; revenging one makes you even with him; but forgiving the offense sets you above your enemy."

Keeping records of wrongs done is another way of expressing anger, just as much as getting provoked and blowing your top. Inside, we can become like a closed steam kettle. If it boils without any kind of release of steam, there's an explosion.

Not all twins are identical, even though they are born at the same time from the same parent. Being provoked and carrying resentment are not identical twins, but they come from the same parent, anger. Many people learn to control bursts of anger, but they keep records of wrongs done against them and they brood over those records. They read and reread those records until they make a mountain of hostility out of a molehill over some small offense. They get steamed up inside, even though they do not express it outwardly. That is resentment.

The word "resent" is an accounting term that mean to mark down something like an item on a ledger so that it can not be forgotten. That is exactly what we do when we are resentful. We mark down; we keep records. We take into account items; that is, the slights, injuries, offenses, harms, and wrongs that people do to us. On the surface we may try to respond in a gracious manner, but inside we keep records and this leads to a terrible problem. What is the solution?

II. THE HUMAN SOLUTION.

There are two basic solutions, the human and the divine. First, the human.

A. SELF-JUSTIFICATION (NO ANGER, BUT NO FORGIVENESS)

There is the solution of self-justification. We justify ourselves by saying, "I did not get angry with that person." Think about the last time you had a conflict with some person and you walked away with a victory, "I didn't get provoked." But in your heart you harbored the wrong. You did not forget. There is something there on the ledger of your heart toward that person. You justify yourself because you did not blow your top and get angry. Is that really a solution? Such a human solution, although it is practiced by many Christians, is very inadequate.

B. Self-Rationalization (forgiving, but not forgetting)

The other human solution is self-rationalization. This is saying, "Well, I'll forgive him, but how could I ever forget?" That attitude is very common. Perhaps you have resigned yourself to that solution, so far as getting along with your husband, wife, parent, child, or friend is concerned. Is that really the solution God wants us to practice? No, God has a better way in store for us. Some clues to this better way are found in these quotations:

"What a grand world this would be if we could forget our troubles as easily as we forget our blessings."

Is it hard to forget when we were wronged? We do not seem to have a problem forgetting our blessings. Why can't we forget our wrongs just as easily as we forget our blessings?

Another, "Always remember to forget the things that made you sad, but never forget to remember the things that made you glad." That is a good one to memorize.

Also: "If you were busy being true to what you knew you ought to do, you'd be so busy, you'd forget the blunders of the folks you met."

III. THE DIVINE SOLUTION.

This leads to the divine solution. God has the real answer for us. To help you remember and apply God's way, write these three lines on one side of a 3 x 5 card:

- Forgive and forget;
- Forgive without regret;
- Forgive to beget.

If you do your forgiving that way, there will be an exciting change in your life. You will be clean and free with other people. Forgive and forget; forgive without regret; forgive to beget. We will consider them in that order.

A. Forgive and Forget.

In Psalms 103:11 we read, *"For high as the heavens are above the earth, so great is His loving kindness toward those who fear Him. As far as the east is from the west, so far has He removed our transgressions from us."* This is God's way of forgiving. He moves our sins from Himself as far as the east is from the west. He forgets as well as forgives. This is the pattern for us.

Isaiah 43:25 declares: *"I, even I, am the one who wipes out your transgressions for My own sake; and I will not remember your sins."* That is beautiful! And the very next words are, "Put Me in remembrance." If we are busy remembering the Lord, we will have no problem forgetting other people's sins against us.

In Jeremiah 31:34 we read, "And they shall not teach again, each man his neighbor and each man his brother, saying 'Know the Lord,' for they shall all know Me from the least of them to the greatest of them, declares the Lord, for I will forgive their iniquity, and their sin I will remember no more." We must not only agree with this teaching about God's forgiveness, we must do it ourselves. We are to be like God in His forgiveness. He is our Heavenly Father and we are His children. Therefore, we are to resemble him in His character.

Then there is the command of Ephesians 4:32: *"And be kind to one another, tender-hearted, forgiving each other, just as God in Christ also has forgiven you."* Just as God forgives and forgets, so should we. We can not escape it; we are committed to it, there is no other way.

If we find this command difficult to obey, we can find help in the second part of God's three-fold solution: forgive without regret.

B. Forgive Without Regret.

Why do we not want to forget so many times? Because we are afraid that if we do not remember, we may be wronged again. Another reason why we remember instead of forgetting is because we think the peson who wronged us has not had chastisement from us. We want him to feel how hurt we really are. We can not face the fact that he may go scot-free, so we do not give up our regrets.

We must learn instead to leave that person in the hands of the Lord. I Peter 4:8 tells us how to do it. *"Above all, keep fervent in your love for one another, because love covers a multitude of sins."* If we do not forgive without regrets, our love can not cover even one sin, let alone a multitude of them. When we cover something the way God means it here, you can not see it—it is almost as if it's not there. This kind of love means giving no room to feeling sorry for yourself.

James 5:20 says, *"Let him know that he who turns a sinner from the error of his way will save his soul from death, and will cover a multitude of sins."* Peter says that by loving him we will cover a multitude of sins. James says we can actually turn him away. When a person who has wronged you feels that you have forgiven him freely without personal regrets, he opens up to you and receives your corrections by your example. You can turn him from his sin by the way you respond to him, by forgiving without regrets. You can be the instrument that God uses to turn him to Himself and away from a multitude of sins. This is why wives, in I Peter 3:1, are commanded to win their unsaved husbands by the power of their deeds and attitudes.

C. Forgive to Beget.

The third part of God's three-fold solution is to forgive to beget. Forgive to beget what? First, forgive to beget the confidence that you are forgiven by God.

1. The Confidence That You Are Forgiven By God

Let that flow into you; let that saturate into your consciousness. If we find it hard to keep from being resentful. It is perhaps because we have not fully accepted forgiveness by God. As the Lord's Prayer directs us, we are in a position to forgive because God has forgiven us. No one can really forgive another unless he has been forgiven by God Himself. His forgiveness gives us the capacity to forgive and forget. If you make it your intent to forgive to the point of forgetting, it gives you renewed confidence in and appreciation for God's forgiveness.

2. The Influence on Others to Forgive Like You.

Second, forgive to beget the influence that you can have on other people to forgive and forget also. Do not be an island to yourself. Do not be so selfish that you think you live unto yourself. The way that you forgive and forget will encourage and influence others to forgive and forget in like manner.

In that great drama, "Quo Vadis," we are told of Chilo and Rucus. Chilo was a very wicked man, the right-hand man of the Roman

Emperor, Nero. So loyal was he to Nero that when his good friend Raucus became a Christian, Chilo thought nothing of selling his friend's wife and children into slavery. He betrayed Raucus to the Roman soldiers, who tortured him and put him to the stake to be burned. Raucus was asked to deny his faith and to recant his position, but he did not. And so he was burned alive. Nero, with Chilo by his side, went down the long line of people being burned alive. They finally came to the stake on which Raucus was burning. As they looked at the human torch that was Raucus, the wind blew the smoke away from his head. Chilo looked and saw him. He was struck in his conscience with a horrible sense of guilt. Caught up in the pain of such guilt, he cried, "Raucus, will you please forgive me?" He saw Raucus's head near the top of the stake tilt a little bit. Then came the words with a groan, "I forgive," and his head fell. Chilo was cut to the heart. With a beam of light in his face, he turned to Nero and said, "You are the wrong one!" Within an hour or so, Chilo found himself in the midst of a crowd of Christians. Among them was also the Apostle Paul. Paul said to him, "Oh, the truths of infinite forgiveness!" Chilo believed them and was baptized on the spot. The next day, he too, was seized by the Roman officials and he, too, was asked to recant his faith, but he would not. But Chilo asked, "May I please die the same way the Christians did, especially Raucus?" They bound him to the stake and jabbed him with iron bars. But while they were doing so, he kissed the hands of those who were binding him. With a look of love, he said to all of them, "I forgive you, for you don't know what you're doing." He was put on the stake, the stake was lifted up, and he was burned alive.

Application

Chilo did it because he had been forgiven. He did it because he learned to forgive. His Christian faith gave him the power to forgive and forget. Love means to forgive and forget. Love is not resentful. Love does not keep records of wrongs suffered.

Now take your 3 x 5 card and on the other side write the names of people whom you must go to and forgive, with the intention of forgetting their wrongs as well. Write on your card, "Love forgives and forgets." Now ask God for the power to forget as well as to forgive.

Perhaps there are two or three people whose offenses you have not forgotten. Be honest with yourself and with God. What good is truth about love unless it is practiced? Perhaps there is something that you have done wrong yourself, for which you have not forgiven yourself—that's very common among Christians. God wants you to forget the sins He has already forgiven in Christ. Perhaps some of your own unforgotten sins should be on your list. Right now you can ask God for the power to forget as well as to forgive.

Life Message Ten

Love Does Not Rejoice in Unrighteousness

Clarence MacCartney's mother told him many moral tales that made striking impressions on him that he carried through life. One of them was about the army general stationed in India who had a pet tiger cub. He was a very affectionate tiger, just like a little kitten. As the days, months and years went by, the tiger became strong, full in strength and stature.

One day the general was doing some research in his study and fell asleep at his desk. His tiger was so affectionate, even when full grown, that he started to lick the general's hand as it dangled from the desk. There was a slight cut on his hand, and the tiger licked it. Before long, having licked the scab clean, the tiger liked the taste of blood. Suddenly, the once little, tiny playful cub became a wild beast. The next thing the general knew the tiger was on top of him. He awakened and looked into the eyes, not of his pet, but of a raging beast ready to devour him. Just in time, he grabbed his pistol and shot the tiger.

In the moral realm, the story never ceased to influence MacCartney's conduct through life. He compared it to making pets of "affectionate sins" that perhaps seem totally harmless, sins we cuddle, enjoy, and play around with, so to speak. MacCartney knew such pets would grow to be raging beasts that would one day require his life.

Something like this is in the Apostle Paul's mind in I Corinthians 13:6, where he writes, "Love does not rejoice in unrighteousness, but rejoices with the truth." That is the literal translation of the passage. Traditionally we have been taught that this verse means that we should not be happy with wickedness itself, as an abstract thing in life. As we shall see; however, the meaning is far deeper. Love goes beyond that.

We want to make three observations about love in this verse: love does not rejoice in unrighteousness (1) because love knows the deceitfulness of sin, (2) because love grieves over sin, and (3) because love hates sin.

I. BECAUSE LOVE KNOWS THE DECEITFULNESS OF SIN.

A. Defining not Rejoicing in Unrighteousness

How can love know sin's deceitfulness? Try to imagine what it means not to rejoice over some unrighteousness. No doubt it means that we should not be happy when we hear about something going wrong with a friend, even if that friend somehow offended us and we were tempted to rejoice over the fact that God is getting even with him for our sake. It also means that we should not rejoice over what happens to our enemies, our own and our country's.

Going a bit deeper, it means we should not be happy when we get a report about some friend or some foe who has fallen into some fault, mistake or sin. But, more deeply, it also means we should not take pleasure in what we may think are secret sins. We should not rejoice in such unrighteousness.

Love does not rejoice over the vices of other men; does not take delight when they are guilty of crime; or when in any matter they fall into sin. It does not find pleasure in hearing others accused of sin, and in having it proved that they committed it. Love does not find malicious pleasure in the report that they have done wrong; or in following up that report and having it established.

Perhaps you have heard of the little boy's prayer. He was taught by his mommy to pray and ask God to take away his sins, those "naughty things" as she called them. So he said, "Dear God, please take away the naughty things I did today. But, dear Father, in case you don't, I won't mind because I enjoy them anyhow." He was being very sincere and honest as children are. He really meant it. He spoke the way many Christians feel, because of their own self-deception.

B. Departmentalizing Such Rejoicing.

Yes, we must admit certain sins we take pleasure in. We can begin to change our lives, however. Begin by looking at the Word of God. Romans 1:32 shows the logical conclusion of the tolerance of sin in our lives. *"And although they know the ordinance of God, that those who practice such things are worthy of death, they not only do the same, but also give hearty approval to those who practice them."* "Them" refers to all the sins of the flesh that are listed in verses prior to verse 32.

Christians, of course, are not in the category of being condemned by God to hell. However, human nature in the Christian is the same as human nature in the non-Christian. Although the believer has a new nature in Christ Jesus, there is still the potential of the old self exerting itself, just like the general's pet tiger. That "tiger" of self will linger until the day we die and go to heaven. Potentially it is ready at any point to devour us, if we let it. Therefore, there is the potential within us to do whatever sins the world does, if we don't watch and keep a check on that old beast in us day by day. This means that we must bear our cross and deny self, until we meet Jesus face to face.

In Romans 12:1-2 we are commanded by Paul, *"I urge you therefore, brethren, by the mercies of God, to present your bodies a living and holy sacrifice, acceptable to God, which is your spiritual service of worship. And do not be conformed to this world"* (Why would God have to command us not to be like the sinners in the world unless He knew we had the potential to be like that, Christians or not?), "but be transformed by the renewing of your mind, that you may prove what the will of God is, that which is good and acceptable and perfect."

All of you reading this book have the potential to murder, we all have the potential to lie, cheat, steal, to commit adultery, and to break the commands of God. That is why St. Augustine said, in such fitting words, *"The Christian has the potential to do the very sin he watched his brother do, apart from the grace of God."* Beware, the Scripture says, let him who stands take heed lest he fall.

C. Discerning Such Rejoicing.

There is another dimension to this matter of rejoicing over evil or unrighteousness. What happens to you when you actually take pleasure in the sin, mistake or fault of someone else or yourself? Does it not encourage you to do it again? Does it not make you go in the opposite direction to which Christ has called you? Does not it make you sow to the flesh, and therefore reap more to the flesh? Yes.

A person who rejoices in unrighteousness is affected in three ways.

1. In terms of Pride

When we hear about someone falling short in something, especially someone we do not like or who has offended us, we have a certain sense of pride that we are at least as good as he is, if not better. That feeds our ego. What does the Bible say about that? Look at Proverbs 6:16. "There are six things which the Lord hates, yes, seven which are an abomination to him: Haughty eyes" (Eyes that are just looking for things that can feed pride.) "A lying tongue and hands that shed innocent blood, a heart which devises wicked plans, feet that run rapidly to evil, a false witness who utters lies and one who spreads strife among brothers." I want to focus on "a heart that devises wicked plans." A person who rejoices in unrighteousness is devising wickedness in his heart. Love does not do that.

In Proverbs 15:25 we read, "The Lord will tear down the house of the proud, but He will establish the boundary of the widow." If we rejoice over evil, it is because we are proud. If we are proud, we can be sure that God will tear us down, because God resists the proud and gives grace to the humble.

2. In Terms of Selfishness

What else happens to me when I am rejoicing over unrighteousness? What else would cause me to smile to a wife, husband or friend when another person goes wrong? It is selfishness. I Corinthians 13:5 says, "Love does not act unbecomingly." Love does not seek its own. But whenever we take pleasure in the failings of another, is that not exactly what we are doing? We are seeking to satisfy, gratify and fulfill our own ego, ourselves.

3. In Terms of Hate.

The third thing that causes us to rejoice in unrighteousness is hatred. Since love does not do this sort of thing, then what does? There's only one alternative: hate. Outwardly you do not hate the person. You are not emotionally angry with that person; you do not have any kind of violence toward him. But that does not mean that you do not hate him. Hatred really is the absence of love. Love is absent when we get pleasure over somebody's sin. Therefore, we hate that person. It is said of Moses that he chose to suffer with the people of God, rather than to enjoy the pleasures of sin for a season. There is lots of pleasure in staying home from church when you should be at the Lord's House. There is a lot of pleasure in transgressing against the laws of God, but that does not make it right. Enjoying such pleasures that make you deviate from the ways of Christ is really self-hatred. It makes you go against what God has created you to be in all your fullness.

Put a frog into a pot of hot water and he will jump right out again.

But put that same frog into a pot of cool water and he'll stay there. Turn on the stove and let that water get warm, and the frog will stay there. He will endure gradually rising temperature, hotter water than he would if he were dropped into it. He will stay there long enough to get boiled. Many Christians are like that. They are not aware of the degree of temperature that the sin in their life produces. They are so comfortable that they are engulfed in the pleasure of sin. They do not know when to get out.

The little boy walked down the church aisle with his class, followed by his teacher. He got into trouble by tripping on a few choir robes. He got in the way of a few people and really acted up in general. But he had his alibi: "The devil was so fast he got me to do wrong before I knew it." Not really! The boy did certain things with great pleasure before that point, and then he did more overt acts. The devil was not fast. The boy was slow. That is the truth about us, too.

II. BECAUSE LOVE GRIEVES OVER SIN

Love grieving over sin? Yes, love does not rejoice over evil, because it grieves over sin. This is foreign to us because so many of us are too close to sin in our lives; we do not want to grieve over it. We do not even feel the necessity of grieving over it.

First of all, the word "grief" means regret or disappointment or great disheartenment over something. That is, when you hear the report of someone who gets fouled up in sin, perhaps even an enemy, or yourself, rather than taking pleasure in it, love does just the opposite. Love grieves over the stumbling. That is what love does for us. If we practiced that response to sin, we would not keep on practicing the sin. If we practiced grieving over whatever sin we commit, or someone else commits, we would not have the problems that we ourselves have with other people. We need to learn how to grieve. There once was a country newspaper editor who got tired of being told he was biased in his news reports. Some of his disgruntled subscribers charged him with being a liar. In angry retort he announced that in the following week's paper he would tell the full truth about everybody and everything. As human nature is, they were looking forward to it. But he outguessed them. When it came off the press, this is what the villagers found: "Dave Conkey died at his home last Friday evening and there was a big funeral Sunday afternoon. The minister said it was a loss to the community, but I doubt it. The community is better off without him. The doctor said he died of a heart attack; nonsense, whiskey killed him. The Wednesday Literary Club met in the home of Mrs. Gadabout. The program stated that they were going to study Shakespeare's play, "Much Ado About Nothing." Well, they did not. The lady who was assigned to present the paper had never read the play, and so they had no program. But they made up for it by gossiping about every member who wasn't there, and the whole afternoon was really like the play, "Much Ado About Nothing."

Winifred Jones and Jim Smith were married Saturday afternoon at the Methodist parsonage. The bride is a very ordinary girl who does not know any more about cooking than a jack rabbit and never helped her mother three days in her life. She is not a beauty by any means and has a gait like a duck. The groom is an up-to-date loafer. He spends most of his time hanging around a pool hall. He has been living off his old folks at home all his life and is not worth shucks. It will be a hard life for both of them." We get the point, don't we? People like to hear the truth, so long as it is about someone else. But, how we fear the truth being told about ourselves. Love is so greived over the sin of someone else, it produces compassion toward that person, even though the sin itself is not accepted.

Chrysostom, the great early church father, was arrested by the Roman emperor for his faith. In the court hall, the Romans maliciously were involved in figuring out what kind of torture to administer. The emperor turned to his counselors and said, *"What shall we do with him? Shall we put him in the dungeon?"* The counselors said, *"No, because he would love, he would enjoy, he would have pleasure in being in solitude like that in which he could meditate upon his God. We can not put him in a dungeon."* The emperor said, *"Shall we put him on a stake and kill him?"* The answers from the counselors came again, *"No, he would love to die, because he knows that when he dies he will be with the presence of his Heavenly Father forever. We can't even give him death." "Then what shall we do?"* said the emperor. This is what they said: *"If you want to make Chrysostom pain, cause Chrysostom to sin. that's what makes him pain."*

Would it not be wonderful if each of us were so Christ-like that we could think the same way? Practice grieving over sin and that will be your attitude, too.

III. BECAUSE LOVE HATES SIN.

Love also hates sin. Love does not rejoice in unrighteousness because love hates sin. In Zachariah 8:16,17 we read, *"These are things which you should do: Speak the truth to one another; judge with truth and judgment for peace in your gates. Also let none of you devise evil in your heart against another, and do not love perjury; for all these things are what I hate, declares the Lord."* The word perjury means dishonesty, bearing false witness. This is what some people do when the preacher calls on them to find out why they are persisting in their sin. They must think preachers are stupid, because of all the excuses they give for why they are not doing what they should be doing. In Psalm 5:4 we read, *"For thou art not a God that takes pleasure in wickedness."* That's why love does not rejoice and take pleasure in wickedness, because God does not. God is love. God who is rich in love, mercy and grace, does not take pleasure in wickedness. He will not coddle you in yours, either. He is not that loving, that would be a denial of what He is. *"No evil dwells with Thee. The boastful shall not stand before Thine eyes: Thou dost hate all those who do iniquity."* That upsets the applecart of those who think *"God hates the sin but loves the sinner."* In Psalm 45:7 we read, *"Thou hast loved righteousness and hated wickedness."* God loves the one and hates the other. Speaking of the Lord Jesus, Hebrews 1:9 says, *"Thou hast loved righteousness and hated lawlessness."* Revelation 2:6 *"Yet this you do have, that you hate the deeds of the Nicolatians, which I also hate."* Not only does God hate sin, but He also commends believers who hate sin. Do you hate sin? Do you hate the sin of other people because it makes you grieve over them, instead of having pleasure in it? Do you hate your own sin so much that you are broken over it, or do you persist in having pleasure in doing wrong and then excusing yourself for it?

F. Application in Paul

In Romans chapter seven we find a portrait of the Apostle Paul. In verse 15, he writes, *"For that which I am doing, I do not understand; for I am practicing what I would like to do, but I am doing the very thing I hate."* Paul learned to hate sin, but that in itself did not make him stop doing it, did it? Note verse 16, *"But if the very thing I do, I do not wish to do, I agree with the law, confessing that it is good. So now, no longer am I the one doing it, but sin which dwells within me. For I know that nothing good dwells in me, that is my flesh; for the wishing is present in me, but the doing of good is not. For the good that I wish, I do not do; but I practice the very evil that I do not wish. But if I am doing the very thing I do not wish, I am no longer the one doing it, but sin which dwells in me. I find then the principle that evil is present in me, the one who wishes to do good. For I joyfully concur with the law of God in the inner man."*

He adds in verse 24, *"Wretched man that I am!"* That is one of the most Godly things you can do, frustrated over your sin, if you go on to ask: *"Who will set me free from the body of this death? Thanks be to God through Jesus Christ our Lord!"* Do you have that feeling toward a neighbor or brother. It is been well said, *"The biggest trouble with sin is the 'I' in the middle of the word."*

Henry Ward Beecher made a very interesting comment when he said, "For every hundred preachers that are hacking away at the branches of sin, there is at best only one preacher hacking away at the root of it." I trust we have hacked away at the root. For every hundred preachers who hack away at the branches, there are a thousand average Christians playing around with the fruit of sin and having pleasure in it. Let us get to the root, shall we? Let us learn to avoid pleasure in sin.

Application

In his powerful short story, "The Minister's Black Veil," Nathaniel Hawthorne portrays the time when a church in New England had a minister come to the congregation. Everybody was excited. They had been many months without a preacher. Finally, came the morning in which the new preacher walked into the pulpit. But to the amazement of everyone, he walked in wearing a black veil. The people looked and wondered. Some conjectured that he had a diseased face and was covering it up so as not to offend the people.

Others thought he was in bereavement because of the loss of a loved one. Others went a step further and said he was using the veil as a symbol of his own penitence over some sin he had done. But the thing really remained secret. The preacher did not reveal that day why he was wearing it. Weeks, months, years went by; finally his entire ministry was there. Every Sunday and every day the minister wore the black veil. Wherever he went he wore it, until finally one day he grew ill and was found dying. A neighboring preacher went to his home and inquired, "What is the secret behind the black veil? Please tell me, so you don't go to your grave taking the secret down into it with you."

With his dying strength, the preacher with the black veil sat up in bed and turned to the other preacher and said, "Why are you so concerned about my black veil? Oh, how men have avoided me. Oh, how women have shunned from pitying me. Oh, how children have screamed and run from me, all the years of my ministry because of this little piece of cloth, when in their own lives they have a black veil behind which they treasure their own pleasure in sins, secret sins and never change. Don't worry about my black veil," said the preacher to the neighboring preacher, "Worry about you and your people's veils."

What about yours? What kind of black veil are you hiding behind? Love takes no pleasure, even in the secret sins behind your black veil.

Life Message Eleven

Love Rejoices the Truth

It was a wintry Christmas morning. The family gathered inside the house was not very happy. The mother was dead; a wayward son was not yet home. His sisters and brothers were gathered around the tree. Finally their brother walked in. He had been out all night drinking. He walked in rather ashamed, because it was Christmas morning.

It was the last straw for his sisters and brothers, and they pressured their father to put him out. As the day progressed, the father came to the conclusion that he must appeal to his family. After a long discussion the vote was unanimous, expulsion was the only solution. So the father turned to the boy and there in that little home in Manchester, England, the young lad heard the words, "Your sisters and brothers have unanimously voted that you be expelled from our house. You have been coaxed; you have been threatened; you have been punished and you just refuse to change. They have asked you to leave and yet, my son, I love you. I believe in you. Yes, in spite of all the things you have done wrong, I believe the potential within you and for that reason, I cannot let you go." Hearing such words of love and confidence, the boy broke into tears. His soul melted. He experienced for the first time the living Jesus Christ. That boy became none other than the great Henry Morehouse of Manchester, one of the greatest preachers who has ever lived.

Such a story helps us to understand the truth of I Corinthians 13:6, *"Love does not rejoice in unrighteousness but rejoices with the truth."* The father of that young man rejoiced in the truth of the potential in his life, even when everything else looked dark.

How many Christians could really be like that? For so many, when someone rubs us the wrong way, especially in our families, we get irritated and hurt. We miss a traffic light and lose our peace. We get behind schedule and become irritated toward our loved ones. We know so little about rejoicing in truth. As parents, we quickly get impatient with our children, especially when they are trying to do something right and they can not do it. We jump on them and forget to rejoice in the truth of their attempt and potential. We men so often criticize our wives for what they do wrong, but we do not rejoice about what they do right. Wives many times nag their husbands and do not rejoice in their accomplishments. One reason we do not win more souls to the Lord is because we do so little rejoicing in the lives of others, rejoicing in the truth that is in them, even though they are unbelievers.

Love rejoicing in the truth introduces the whole matter of what a truly positive personality is like. There are three categories of personalities: (1) the minus personality; (2) the middle-of-the-road personality; and (3) the marvelous personality. There are three types of personality, but only one type fits the words of I Corinthians 13:6, "Love rejoices with and in the truth." In order to appreciate that truth, we have to see by contrast what the alternatives are.

I. The Minus Personality.

Consider the minus personality. As you do, be honest and ask yourself, Am I like this one, or am I more like this one, or am I like the third?

A. His Career.

The minus personality makes a career of emphasizing the faults of people, that is picking them to pieces. This is his life style.

B. His Contagion.

Such a personality is contagious. This is because so often we as human beings are so much more alert and curious about hearing negative things. We like to hear minus things instead of plus things; things that tear people down instead of build them up. Such influence spreads much faster than good influence does. A minus person is very good at this, "Did you know? I don't mean to gossip but..." "I don't mean to be a backbiter, but did you know...?" "I haven't told him this because I'm not really sure it's right, but did you know?" "I wouldn't go to him because it would hurt his feelings, but guess what he did the other day?" These are typical of how the minus person talks. Unfortunately, he sets off a chain reaction that spreads to many other people.

C. His Commonplace.

The minus personality has a career, he is contagious, and he has a commonplace about himself. The reason so many of us respond to hearing negative things about other people; the reason we sit around and talk about other people; the reason why we have "roast preacher" for dinner on Sunday is because by nature we have a gravitational pull toward the nature of a minus personality. We all have this minus potential within us. We all realize that going downhill is much easier than going uphill. Even though we know it is wrong, we continue. During the days of Lincoln, a man went to such an extreme that he even criticized Lincoln for making friends out of his enemies. He said, "I thought you were to treat your enemies by destroying them, not by kindness and love and thoughtfulness and other virtues."

Lincoln replied, "By making friends out of my enemies, have I not destroyed my enemies?" The minus person destroys even the good that a positive person would do. Barnes says, "Minus people are people who rejoice in the vices instead of the virtues of others." But a truly loving person rejoices not in the vices but in the virtues of people.

II. The Middle-of-the-Road Personality.

By definition, the middle-of-the-road personality does not really tear down people, because after all, that is not nice, but on the other hand, he does not really build up people either. He is just a person who does not want to get involved. He shies away from anything that looks like an issue. He is a middle-of-the-roader. He has a way of playing it safe, of being non-controversial.

A. Danger.

Unfortunately, however, there is a very great danger in this kind of a personality. Such a person usually compromises truth because of his tendency toward false love. I was eating lunch with the township manager, and he brought out something that I have felt for a long time, but could not verbalize because of my lack of experience. He said, "I get so upset with people, Christians especially, who think love is always namby-pamby, that love doesn't preserve and protect truth, and rejoice in truth. Rejoicing in truth doesn't always mean being kind and gracious, but it may mean standing up for the truth, and calling a spade a spade, and letting a person know when he is wrong, not to tear him down, but to let him know where he's wrong to build him up. That's also rejoicing in truth." How important that is. So many of us under the guise of love, overlook wrongs in others. We quote the verse, "Love covers a multitude of sins," without understanding what it means. It really means to go to a person and expose his sin in love, spiritually, meekly, with lowliness, with the intent of building him up, and getting him beyond it. That is how you cover the multitude of sins. If he repents of it, you will save him from a multitude of sins after that. That's what it means for love to cover a multitude of sins. The great danger for a middle-of-the-road Christian is to compromise the truth. Such a middle-of-the-roader was Lot.

B. Description.

Go back to the time when Abraham and Lot split because their servants could not get along. Lot, the aggressive, young, ambitious man, chose the plains of Sodom and Gomorrah. He thought it was a land of promise. Abraham took whatever was left. Lot lived right there in Sodom. But first he pitched his tent towards the city and then he lived in it. Down he went. He was a real believer, because the Bible calls him "righteous." But what happened? He certainly did not want to insult anybody in Sodom. Out of compromise he overlooked their homosexuality, their beastly way of living. He compromised truth so he became of no use to God. But he was so far from the world that he was no use to the world either. He was in the miserable middle-of-the-road. He escaped by the very skin of his teeth when judgment came to Sodom and Gomorrah. His wife looked back and he lost her, for she became a pillar of salt. His daughters committed adultery with him. That was the cost of Lot's middle-of-the-road position. We must count the cost of continuing in a middle-of-the-road Christianity.

C. Doom.

Such a middle-of-the-road life leads to doom. If a car goes down the middle of the road, one of three things will happen: (1) it will go backwards, especially with oncoming traffic coming around the curve: (2) it will break right down; or (3) it will boom right into a collision. Staying in the middle-of-the-road requires so much effort that it's like going uphill in the Christian life. You wind up just going backward. The "engine" of the Christian life can not take such pressure. It breaks down because your life is constantly involved in not tearing people down or building them up, not making any kind of personal contribution to anybody. Life becomes a series of "flats" and emptiness, like being in the desert and breaking down, without water. Being in the middle is a collision course because you are headed for a collision with the condemnation of God. In Ephesians 5:11, Paul says something about the middle-of-the-road Christian, the person who does not want to get involved, who wants to be neutral about everything, *"And do not participate in the unfruitful deeds of darkness,"*. If we say nothing about sin, we have participated in it. It's only a matter of time before your life becomes equivalent to it. The solution is spelled out; *"But instead even expose them."* Love that rejoices in the truth and with the truth does not circumvent and detour around that responsibility. We are to expose the evil works of darkness. In Proverbs 28:13 we read, *"He who conceals his transgressions will not prosper."* This person will break down, he will fail, he will never reach his destination. *"But he who confesses and forsakes them will find compassion."* Consider Proverbs 17:15, to paraphrase it, *"He who justifies the wicked is also one who winds up criticizing the righteous, and because of such receives the condemnation of God."* That verse makes it clear that the person who tries to be in the middle of the road by over-looking or justifying wrong will also attack the person who does right. In doing so he is under the condemnation of God. Some Christians are so tolerant of unsaved people, of wicked people, and of sinning Christians, and yet they can get angry at a Christian who does right. This is because being in the middle of the road is an impossible situation. Such people criticize the righteous, and live like the unrighteous. They will experience the condemnation of God. This is a more devastating type than the minus personality, but it is more common among Christians. The majority of Christians fall into the middle category, not being too hot for Christ or too cold.

III. The Marvelous Personality.

Now we must move on to the marvelous personality. Marvelous personality? Does that not sound far-fetched? Yes, you can actually be a marvelous person. Let us define it first.

A. He is the Plus Personality.

He is a plus person. If the minus person tears down, the plus person builds up. If the minus person criticizes and picks to pieces, the marvelous person or the plus person, puts people together and adds to their lives. He knows how to encourage. He not only sees where a person is wrong, he encourages him how to do it right.

"What I need most," wrote Emerson, "is something to make me do what I can." One of the most rewarding experiences you can ever have is to be that something for someone, to be the catalyst that dispels inertia and brings out the best in someone you know.

The thing that brings out the best in people is encouragement. No matter what your circumstances are, you can provide those around you with precious morale plasma. Think encouraging thoughts, speak encouraging words, and most important of all, adopt an air of confident expectancy toward those you are trying to help. Be genuinely interested, let your attitude be more eloquent that your words. In this way you can be a "best friend." There is no rejoicing quite comparable to the rejoicing you can earn in this way.

The plus personality is one who encourages. It is finding out what a person needs. It is finding good in him, to give him the courage to get over the difficulties. Are you minus, middle-of-the-road, or plus? Did you open this book with a suspicious attitude to find out what you could find wrong with somebody? Do you sit there with the attitude, "Now I'll sit down and read this book to see how he tries to bless me. I dare him to bless me!" Or did you open the book with an expectation of God's blessing you as you read it? Did you feel like you were going to put your best effort to your reading? Can you test your spirit right now? Is your spirit right now that old minus or middle of the road? Do you want a plus spirit? Would you move in that direction?

B. Every Human Heart Yearns for this Treatment.

Think of Jesus. He believed in a Samaritan half-breed and gave her the way to eternal life, the kind of life that can destroy all the racial, marital, social, and political strife between people. Jesus Christ believed in a Roman soldier. Although he was not a Jew, yet his deeds of kindness shamed those who would dare name the name of God. Jesus saw even in a prostitute the potential of a powerful love. She came to love Him so much that she washed His feet with her tears. He saw the potential of latent stability and greatness in Peter, a very impetuous and impulsive man. He was not rated very high on the scale of successful people. He was a minus personality. We would not have chosen him to be the leader of the Apostles. But Jesus saw the potential and He brought it out. He did not tear him down. Every human heart needs and yearns for that kind of love from somebody. All of us want people to look for and find the potential in us.

John Short had it right when he talked about little children: "Even little children bloom in the sunshine that is of the spirit that encourages and helps them whenever they try to do well. There is a child in every heart." He tells of the Scottish preacher who long years ago died and of whom it was said, "There is no one left in our village to appreciate the triumphs of ordinary folks." That tells all that we need to know about him. He truly understood the spirit of the Master, a spirit which our world needs so desperately, for there is so much bitterness, hatred and suspicion in our time.

Who of us needs a reminder of more importance than this, namely that love is always so eager to believe the best, that love is never glad when others go wrong, that love is only gladdened by goodness? Yes, a truly positive personality is one who underscores the best in every man.

C. Even the Demon-Possessed Turn On.

Even a possessed man with a legion of demons responded to that kind of love. *"And as He was getting into the boat, the man who had been demon-possessed was entreating Him that he might accompany Him. And He did not let him, but He said to him, 'Go home to your people and report to them what great things the Lord has done for you, and how He had mercy on you.' And he went off and began to proclaim in Decapolis what great things Jesus had done for him; and everyone marvelled."* (Mark 5:18-20). May I tell you two reasons why they marvelled? One because of his absolute change. The man was demon-possessed and he was delivered of his demons, he was a new man, no longer a raging, beast-like individual. That would make anybody marvel. Second, he must have tasted of such love from the Master, that when he went back to that town, there was not a person who felt his problem could not be overcome by Jesus. He went back to that town and told people the great things God did for him. Someone might say "Oh, yes, but you don't know how bad my situation is." The healed demonic could empathize with them and say, "Oh, yes, I do! But look, it's still possible. "

Application

This is a story about twins. One was an extreme pessimist; the other was an extreme optimist. The problem became so bad that their parents had to take them to a psychiatrist. His solution was to put the pessimistic boy in a room full of toys, candy, ice cream and cake and everything that makes a child happy. They were to put the optimistic boy in a room with only one thing, a large pile of horse manure. They put them in their rooms for an hour and checked on them. The parents went to the room of the pessimistic boy hoping to find him very happy, but he was doing nothing. They said, "What's the matter, Johnny? Why don't you ride the horsey?" He said, "I was afraid of falling off the horsey and breaking my leg."

"Why didn't you eat the ice cream?"

"Oh, I was afraid of getting a tummy ache!"

"Well, why didn't you do this...?" For everything he had a negative response. It did not solve his problem.

They went to the room of the optimistic boy. As they walked toward his room, they heard this, "Splat, splish, swish, splash, splash, bang." They opened the door very carefully and they saw him bent over the manure pile. "What in the world are you doing, Jimmy?" they shouted.

"Mommy and daddy, with all this horse manure around here,

there's bound to be a pony somewhere!"

No matter how difficult life becomes, no matter how much the lives of others even smell and stink to us, love does not rejoice in unrighteousness but rejoices with the truth. By God's grace we can rejoice in truth. We can give ourselves to those who are the most deeply involved with sin, knowing their potential to love Christ more.

Life Message Twelve

Love Bears All Things

Viewing 37 movies in one week, believed to be the typical filmfare showing around the country, a University of Utah psychologist and his research team saw 59 murders, 89 justifiable killings, 76 attempted murders, 11 massacres, six bombings, three assault rapes, 168 nude scenes, 19 acts of explicit intercourse, three acts of masturbation, seven scenes of oral-genital activity and a variety of seductive exhibitions. According to Victor B. Cline, that is 23 acts of violence and 15 episodes of sex per film. He believes movies and TV are headed for an era of unrelenting violence and exploitive sex. "By making violence appear glamorous and exciting and illicit sex normal and desirable, these media are setting the stage for a society based on aggression and irresponsibility," he said.

Other findings: two-thirds of the films took a fatalistic view of life and human destiny; 22 percent of the protagonists were killed or in some way destroyed. In 57 percent of the films dishonesty was presented in a heroic light or justified; in 83 percent, criminal activity actually paid of—there were no negative consequences; in 43 percent, the heroes were lawbreakers or anti-social figures; in 60 percent premarital sex was normal, acceptable, desirable; 70 percent of the heroes were to some degree sexually promiscuous.

In the TV ads for children, 20 salesmen per hour talk to them, half the time with sweets in hand. Robert Choate, Chairman of the Council on Children, Media and Merchandising, estimates that a moderate TV-watching child views more that 5,000 commercials for edibles every year. "Fifty percent of the advertising directed to children is on edibles. And the ethic is buy, spend, eat and consume," he said. The harm goes deeper than arguments over nutrition. The essential harm is the materialistic value it promotes. "Our free enterprise system considers it fair and proper for competition to advise kids to be materialistic and acquisitive, to keep up with the Joneses, govern health by artificial means, and to live in a world of fantasy," Mr. Choate says.

Mental depression increases. "If the 1950s were the age of anxiety, then the 1970s are the age of melancholy," says Dr. Gerald Klerman, Professor of Psychiatry at Harvard. Depression paralyzes the will, saps energy, drives some to suicide. Doctors divide on cause; some blame stress, others say it is malfunction of the chemistry of the brain. Depression can hit several times during a lifetime and last up to six months at a time. Women sufferers outnumber men, two to one. It is twice as common among married people. Depression hits students especially hard and is a major cause of dropping out. Anti-depressant drugs do not work with many people. Suicide rates with depressives is 30 times that of the general population. Very successful people are often subject to depression. Sexual and marital problems are the most common types of stress.

Divorces went to 80 percent between 1960 and 1971, according to the U.S. Bureau of Census. Divorces averaged slightly more than 400,000 in the 1960-1962 period, but there were 768,000 divorces in 1971. The study indicated that about 29 percent of the marriages of women now between 27 and 32 years of age will end in divorce. The average age for woman's first marriage is now 20.8, compared to 20.3 in 1960.

Ralph Sorcom said, "The roots of responsibility run to the ends of the earth, and we can no more isolate our consciences from world issues than we can fence off our oyster beds from the tides of the ocean." Yet that is exactly what most people are doing today, including those in the church. The church has a major problem because Christians tolerate too many things. They are too permissive. This destroys the spiritual fiber of the church and degenerates its witness. Christians can hide their eyes and pretend these problems do not exist. They can interpret I Corinthians 13:7 - "Love bears all things", to mean that we just bear those things we can endure, we cover them over. We close our eyes to them, we do not pay attention to them. Therefore, Christians shirk their responsibilities and live self-centered, egocentric lives. However, Paul's statement, "Love bears all things" really means we must bear the responsibility of all things. I'm embarrassed that although I checked 20 commentaries on this passage, I did not find one that spoke to this issue. Therefore, we must approach this text with three basic steps: observation, interpretation, application. Observation answers the question: What is it?; interpretation: What does it mean? application: What does it mean to me?

I. Observation of "stegay" ("bears")

To observe we ask six questions, who, what, when, where, why and wherefore.

A. Who?

Who bears all things? Love. Love can also be a person. God is love. I Corinthians 13 is also a portrait of Jesus Christ Himself. The "who" could also be Christ. But because every Christian should be Christlike, the "who" is every believer.

B. What?

What here? All things. Love bears all things. It does not mean negative things only. Of course, love does bear somebody's stupidity, ignorance, or some irritating ways. But the text does not limit love to that. Love bears good things, too.

C. When?

When does love bear all things? Well, if you look at the word "bear", it is in the present tense. It is durative action. It is constantly going on without any thought of beginning or ending. The implication, of course, is love does not bear all things sometimes and not other times. Love is consistent.

D. Where?

Where? Love bears all things everywhere. If love bears all things at all times, then all places would be included. Love, for example, does not act one way inside the home and another way some other place outside the home.

E. Whence?

The word whence means how. How does love bear all things? This verse does not say how. Why does not it tell us? Because Christ said, "You shall do and then you shall know." To obey is to know. In the doing is the knowing.

F. Why?

Why? Why does love bear all things? Because it is the very nature of love. It is unnatural for Christ, God, or the Christian to act in an impatient, unenduring way.

II. Interpretation of "stegay" (bears")

We must go to the second step, interpretation. What is the interpretation of "stegay?" The word "stegay" is the Greek word for "bears".

A. "Cover"

There are two basic meanings of the word. The one meaning is "cover." It comes from the word for roof or covering. The idea is to protect people, to protect things. But this does not mean that love simply glosses over sin, for example. Covering a multitude of your brother's sins does not mean ignoring them, but rather ministering in love and humility to him, so that he will repent. A person covers a multitude of sins by sparing his brother from successive sins, by spreading the link in the chain of sins. Love does not actually cover sin, because the Bible says in Proverbs, "He who covers a transgression shall not prosper." We cannot apply this meaning of the word to love. Love does not cover bad habits but rather corrects them and exposes them.

B. Endure.

The second meaning of the word "stegay" is endure. This means enduring something or somebody for a long period of time. This is passive. It leaves a person unfulfilled. Then, too, some things I enjoy so much that I don't have to endure them. Other things I do not endure at all, because the Bible says to repent of certain things.

C. Bear.

A third meaning of "stegay" is "bear," the idea of holding fast or containing, the idea of bearing responsibility. This meaning rings the bell here, meaning to bear one's responsibility in all things. If we use the meaning of bearing responsibility in light of the six questions above, it fits all of them beautifully. It means controlling the selfish drives. It means being responsible in all things of life, whether at home, school, work, church, wherever we go.

III. Application of "stegay".

There are three priorities in life: our personal relationship to God, our relationship to our family, and our relationship to our life's work. The idea of love bearing all things must be applied to every one of these relationships.

Matthew Henry says "Hearing all things in life means passing by and putting up with injuries without indulging in anger or cherishing revenge; will be patient upon provocation, ill-usage, curses, contumacies, slander, prison, exile, bonds, torments and even death itself. But all these things imply only the negative things we should bear. Let me add a few positive things, because all things means all positive as well as all negative things. Things like this: prayer, Bible reading, meditation, soul-winning, serving, punctuality, diligence, loyalty, faithfulness, discipline, faith, hope, love, food, clothing, shelter. Love bears all things."

A. Our Relationship to God.

Love bears all things to God. Tithing money, for example. The Bible teaches at least 10 percent of our income should go to the Lord, without any excuses. Beyond that are offerings, love gifts, and grace giving, as the grace of God enables us to give liberally and hilariously. What about our relationship to God in time? It has been well said that if a Christian would tithe his time, that would be 16.8 hours a week. If believers do that, every church would run beautifully and smoothly. How many Christians give 16.8 hours per week to serving God in the local church?

What about our talents? Christians can use a variety of talents for the Lord. Some of them never think of doing this. Yet this is something that love bears for the sake of Christ.

B. Our Relationship to Family.

Do Christians "bear all things" with regards to their families?

Do husbands love their wives as Christ loved the church? Do wives really submit to their husbands and husbands to their wives? Do children really honor their parents in the Lord? And do parents honor their children?

C. Our Relationship to Work.

Bearing all things at work means doing your best at your job. Love does not just put in time. The believer should be really excited about his employer's success. He does not simply get his money the easiest way he can, with the least amount of effort.

Application

A child was born into a Christian family, but it became apparent that he was suffering an incurable illness. As the little boy got older, the family had to decide whether or not they should put him into an institution. After discussion, the vote was unanimous; the child would remain at home. He was loved tenderly in spite of his mental and physical retardation. Finally, at the age of 13, he died. But all the family members turned to each other and said, "We have gained so much by giving so much. We have all learned how to be much more loving and kind, compassionate and understanding in treating other people as well as Tommy." Love bears all things. There are many weak people in the church. In the society there are people who are spiritually dead. They are dead in trespasses and sin; they are bound for hell. Love bears a responsibility for all of them.

Life Message Thirteen

Love Believes All Things

Some very interesting words have been said down through the centuries about faith. Our Lord Jesus Christ said, "Nothing shall be impossible to you" (Matt. 17:20). Augustine said, "Faith is to believe what we do not see, and the reward of this faith is to see what we believe." Others have said, "The greatest victories are the victories of faith. It is not so much what we can do that counts, but what we can trust God to do." "Small faith may take you to heaven, but great faith may bring heaven to you." "We do not know one millionth of one part of one percent about anything. We do not know what water is; we do not know what light is; we do not know what electricity is; we do not know what gravity is. We do not know anything about magnetism. We have a lot of hypotheses, but that is all" (Thomas A. Edison). But the Bible says, "Through faith we understand." Faith is exercised in relation to the world, to the church, and to the Christian.

I. In Relation to the World.

An article by Gerald H. Train, Chairman of the Community Inter-Faith Emergency Service, Norristown, Pennsylvania, says in relation to our world:

"Our nation today stands on the brink of disaster. Its communities from the Atlantic to the Pacific, from Canada to Mexico, are being disrupted by the great drug epidemic which is breeding crimes of all types in order to feed the insatiable appetites of the addicts. Fear and hate stalk our villages and cities. Hunger and racial tensions weigh heavily in the ghettos and slums. Our elderly are living in dark forbidden times, instead of in the fulfillment of their golden years.

"Look with me for a moment in your imagination into a large transparent sphere where exist our communities. Here is what you'll see. The churches burdened with seemingly unsolvable inner problems of departing clergy, dropping membership roles, and drastically reduced giving, and lament entangled with the materialistic values of life. The social agencies running in ever tightening circles of frustration and desperation as the stream mounts swiftly to a flood of human misery, daily moving through their doors, seeking answers to problems that threaten their very existence. The community at large, splitting out of control, while being fragmented by corrupt politics, crimes of all degrees, growing drug problems, fear, hunger, sickness, racial tension and violent death itself. All these things comprise the world in which we live."

These insights arouse within me a great consternation. We have problems enough to solve among ourselves as Christians, let alone trying to solve the world's problems. Yet our responsibility is still there, because the Bible says, *"Love believes all things"* (I Cor. 13:7).

How can a Christian "believe all things" in a world like this? Is it not unreasonable of God to expect us to believe all things in the face of a very troubled society, nation, and world? Do the words, "Love believes all things" in relation to the world include every Christian? Yes, even though humanly it is an impossible task, God still expects you to fulfill it! It is unreasonable if you try to do it without faith. How can I solve the word's problems? By believing all things.

I used to say, "It's not great faith in a big God, but rather it's small faith in a big God. That's all it takes." But now I am beginning to see where we are responsible for great faith. Although we may start by having faith no bigger than a mustard seed, faith has to grow. As our Lord told the story, that tiny seed grew into a mighty tree. So we must face the ideal. Nothing is impossible unto him who believes all things, even in relation to a troubled world. Christians, therefore, by love must make some impact on the world.

II. In Relation to the Church.

In that great 14th chapter of John, verse six, the Lord Jesus not only shows the way to heaven, but also the way through our life in this world. He is the way through the problem of a fruitless, ignorant, weak and foolish Christian life. He is the way to a more fruitful, powerful, glorious life for Him in this world.

One of the most beautiful experiences a person can ever have traveling in Norway is to sail through the majestic fjords. You sail past the sheer cliffs, with cascades of water splashing down, echoing their beautiful musical tones. You see high mountains and verdant green slopes. But when you approach the end of the fjord, as you get closer and closer, you are filled with fear because you think the ship is going to collide with the cliff. But at the last moment, in the nick of time, a whole new beautiful way opens up to another fjord.

Life is like that, isn't it? The mountains are seemingly unmoveable in our lives. Circumstances make us stop dead in our tracks. We either want to jump off the boat, or stop the boat. We seemingly never reach the place where there is a way around it, under it, or through it. We never find out the way, because we do not believe there is a way.

Faith finds a way always. The Lord Jesus Christ is that way. He never fails. The same Jesus Christ who said He is the way, the truth, and the life, also said, in Matthew 16:18, *"Upon this rock I will build my church and the gates of hell will not prevail against it!"* The iron gates of a fjord will not prevail against the assaults of the devil, but will destroy his gates as it progresses forward.

David Livingston said, "I'll go anywhere, as long as it's forward." That is the spirit of a real Christian. No wonder he went to Africa in all its darkness to bring light to that continent. That is the kind of spirit the church needs. Faith finds a way. Christ promised, "I will build my church." He did not start to build until after He went to heaven. On the day of Pentacost He preached through Peter to that crowd of thousands. That was the way He began to build His church. Three thousand souls came to Christ and were added to the church; days after that, more came, 5,000, and it went on and on and on. Jesus Christ from the Father's right hand is still building His church. His only requirement is "all things are possible unto him who believes." For love believes all things. Our Lord Jesus Christ wants to build His church. Can we believe that in the face of all the problems in this world, we can be used by Him to build His church?

Jesus has chosen to build His church with foolish, weak, and inadequate building stones. According to I Peter 2:1, we are all living stones. He chooses to use us, but He does it by transforming us into building blocks in His kingdom. Unfortunately, because we persist in our folly, in our weakness, in our nothingness, we become stumbling blocks instead of building blocks.

On one occasion, John Wesley was walking down a country path with a friend. The friend shared how he had lost his faith over the years of Christian life, and how despondent he was over the problem. As he was talking they came to a cow. Wesley turned to his friend and said, "Brother, do you see that cow looking over the wall?"

"Yes."

"Why is that cow looking over the stone wall?" Wesley asked.

"I don't know. Tell me why."

"Because the cow can't see through it, that's why!"

Too often Christians are looking at the wall, trying to look through it. They can not see anything. What a predicament. The answer is just a matter of looking over the wall, and faith does that sort of thing.

Faith is so great that it causes those who are really spiritual in the congregation not to leave when a brother transgresses or stumbles. The ones who are spiritual are bolstered by faith to pick up and restore those who stumble. The church should be a place of security like that. When we stumble we should be surrounded by a cloud of dear, loving Christians, who in meekness and gentleness pick up and restore us. That is what faith does as it builds the church.

Faith enables a congregation of people really to believe that they can reproduce spiritually by going out and winning souls. The Founding Pastor says "We at Christ Church of Valley Forge have just passed our fourth anniversary. We are also just about filling a 275-seat auditorium. But as long as we keep seeing empty seats, no matter how big the building, we are seeing a stone wall. In our churches, all believers must look above the wall and so do their part in leaping over it, to bring in others to fill the empty chairs."

You know the story Jesus told about the wedding feast. The King himself made invitations for all the neighbors to come to a lovely wedding feast, but only a few came. What did he tell his servants? He told them to go into the highways and byways and hedges to seek people, to bring in the poor, the blind, the maimed, the weak and the sick. Many people are maimed, blind and sick spiritually. They have lost their hope. Their hearts are sick and burdened with heavy cares. Christians must reach out to them. Can love motivate you to go out to your neighbors and bring them the feast of a message of hope in Christ? Faith believes and makes you believe you can do that.

III. In Relation to the Christian.

There is another realm of love that believes all things, that is in relation to the Christian: (1) The Christian in relation to another Christian; (2) The Christian in relation to himself.

Regarding the first aspect, the Christian should unsuspiciously believe all that is not palpably false, all that he can with a good conscience believe to the credit of another (James 32:17). On the surface this appears as though love is soft and credulous, easily taken in by any doer of evil. But the truth is that one must live either in a state of trust or in a state of suspicion toward his fellows and himself. There really is not a middle ground. Either we go through life cynically suspecting everybody and turning out to be wrong most of the time, or basically we go through life believing in the good of others and turning out to be wrong part of the time.

We can take our choice, but from a purely practical standpoint our happiness is at stake in the way we go. If we are basically cynical, we do not want to be wrong about anything, for to be wrong is to prove the folly of our cynicism. And if we are right, which on occasion we will most certainly be, what satisfaction can we possible get out of that?

Really, distrusting people does not do us any good. There is a story about a woman who used to say complacently, "I'm very frank. I always believe in being honest and open." She was, in fact, frank to the point of untenderness. If there was a weakness in the character of any of her friends, she pointed it out with the most devastating bluntness. She was fond of telling others what she thought they ought to do. Her frankness was a camouflage for being mean. When it came to those not equally blunt, she always said, "I wouldn't trust her as far as I could see her, too mealy-mouthed." We tend to put our trust in our own strong points rather than in the Lord. As a result, we distrust everyone whose strength lies in something else.

You may be an introvert and therefore, say, "But there are certain people who make me feel uncomfortable." Then look at the words of A. B. Simpson, "You will never learn faith in comfortable surroundings." Some of the very people we do not believe in, and consequently avoid, are the very ones whom God will reveal to you at the judgment seat as the very "instruments" that He chose to shape you more into His own image. Do not pass up such an opportunity of growth.

The truth is that to love men in the sense in which Paul is using the term is to believe in the best in them and often to believe in the best to help it come into being. Many a young man has done fine things with his life because others believed he would and he knew it. Many a fine girl has accomplished fine things with her life which she never would have accomplished except that their were those who loved her and believed she would.

Of course, it works the other way around also. To hold someone in contempt is to run the risk of making that person worthy of our contempt. More than one husband living with a suspicious wife, and more than one wife living with a suspicious husband, has seriously raised the question, "Why not? I am believed to be guilty anyway, and I cannot possibly prove that I am not." Many a person has rationalized and justified behavior of an evil sort in advance of performance on the ground that he might just as well be guilty as to be accused and believed by others to be so.

The other side of the coin is the skepticism with which we view our own weaknesses. It is possible to be entirely immobilized because we are so sure of our failure. Or to say of someone else, "He won't stick to it, of course, he has never been able to see anything through." In short, it's very difficult for us to believe either that we will come crashing down some day in one of our strong areas or that we can succeed in the weak ones. Our trust is in ourselves, not in Christ at all.

Perhaps it's a good thing that we all fail once in a while, in the very area where we've been most successful; and that we see unexpected triumph in places of defeat. Human nature is unpredictable, we say at such times, but the truth is that the way God works is unpredictable and He does not intend for us to be too sure of anything but Himself...it is too dangerous for us.

Handel had to face failure in his musical career, as well as financial bankruptcy. He was even threatened with prison. He faced such serious sickness that his right side became paralyzed. In that condition, at the point of despair, God finally came to him. As a result, he produced ***"THE MESSIAH"*** with its great ***"HALLELUJAH CHORUS."*** Failure may teach us not to be too sure of our strengths, especially, or to be too unbelieving about our weaknesses. It can bring us to that point where only God Himself will bolster us up, carry us on, and teach us the lesson that He is in everything.

But why stop at this? Why not believe all things just like Eileen Guder, who lost her husband shortly after the roof of their house caved in one night during a storm. Eileen Guder's son died at an early age. Her financial future crashed before her. She said, "Believing all things about life in a baseless optimism helps me not at all. Being naive like that helps me not one single bit in my agonies of life." But she added, "Believing everything because God is in it, that strengthens me!"

Such an attitude is similar to that of another exceptional individual, who believed all things even when his only son was killed. When Sir Harvey Lauder's only son was killed in World War I, he said to a friend, "When a man comes to a thing like this, there are just three ways out of it. There is drink, there is despair, and there is God. By His grace, the last one is for me."

Let us move on to the Christian in relation to himself. Here is where the real problem lies. After many years in education, business and especially in the ministry, I am convinced that the average Christian has a difficult and almost impossible time believing all things about himself, just as he has a great difficulty loving himself. Satan does such a good job of deceiving the Christian that he actually feels it is a sin to have confidence, or belief, even in his new self in Christ. Many Christians do not know how to believe for their own benefit. I want to share with you an acrostic on the word BELIEF that has helped tens of thousands of people both in the secular and religious world.

We will assume that we are sharing this little device with a person whose faith is either shattered, or is not at all developed. We shall start at zero. The key question is, how does one grow in belief from zero? Whether it is to believe in Christ Himself, or in one's God-given ability and talents by which to serve Him, how does one grow in belief?

To answer this question, we shall take the word belief and form an acrostic, so that:

B *stands for boldness*
E *stands for excellence*
L *stands for liability*
I *stands for insistence*
E *stands for endurance*
F *stands for faith*

Obviously the purpose of this acrostic is simple memorization by the reader, so he can carry it with him wherever he goes.

Now let us go into more detail.

B stands for boldness. Here is the starting point. If one ever intends to believe in anything, he must eventually be bold enough to make that leap of faith! This is necessary whether it is to believe in the Lord Jesus Christ as one's Savior and God because of His purchasing heaven as a gift by His death on the cross, or whether it is to believe in accomplishing some seemingly difficult or impossible work. This boldness should be one of the first things that people see in a Christian. In Acts 4:13, Luke says, *"Now when they saw the boldness of Peter and John, and perceived that they were unlearned and ignorant men, they marveled; and they took knowledge of them, that they had been with Jesus"* (King James Version).

The early Christians were "dumb enough to be bold in their belief." They did not complicate it like we do, but rather they were childlike in their faith. Being uneducated was not an obstacle. Believing in Jesus was all they needed. As a result, people marveled that they had been with Jesus! So can it be for you and me.

We lack boldness because we have our eyes too much upon the obstacles of our belief.

Think on this anonymous poem:

Doubt sees the obstacles,
Faith sees the way,
Doubt sees the darkest night,
Faith sees the day!
Doubt dreads to take a step,
Faith soars on high,
Doubt questions, "Who believes?"
Faith answers, "I!"

Do you see the possibility of budging your inertia of doubt? Believe and it will grow. One of the names for a Christian is "believer." Yet it is so unfortunate that so many who have been born again are for the most part mediocre in faith. We say, on the one hand, that we believe in the God of miracles. Yet, on the other hand, our lives deny that belief. Faith without works is dead.

Too often we are communicating to the world that our God is the God of mediocrity, not the God of miracles. We say Amen to the words, "Love believes all things," but we do not make changes regarding our doubts.

Some aspirants who desired to scale Mount Everest were examined by a psychologist at Nepal before they began their climb. They were asked, "Will you get to the top?" One said, "I certainly hope so." Another said, "I'll try." Another, "I'll do my best." Only Jim Whitaker replied, "Yes, I will." And only Jim made it. He was the first American to reach the summit of Everest. "Mountain climbing brings out the best in a person," said Whitaker. "It forces him to try something normally beyond his reach." Browning said, "A man's reach should exceed his grasp, or what's heaven for?"

Is it not time that Christians, by faith in God, claim their heritage in boldness and move forward from spinning wheels in the mudhole of mediocrity to springing zeal in the mountain of miracles.

E stands for excellence. There is no reason to move out of mediocrity unless we go all the way to excellence, for that should be the believer's only standard. The Lord Jesus Christ commanded, *"Therefore you are to be perfect, as your heavenly Father is perfect"* (Matt. 5:48). Yes, He said these words in the Sermon on the Mount to Jews who were about to enter the Kingdom of God, but His words contain a principle that can be applied to all of us. That is why the Apostle Paul also commanded: *"Let us therefore, as many as are perfect, have this attitude; and if in anything you have a different attitude, God will reveal that also to you: However, let us keep living by that same standard to which we have attained. Brethren, join in following my example, and observe those who walk according to the pattern you have in us"* (Phil. 3:15-17).

An anonymous individual put it this way, "There are peaks of holiness and Christian virtue which ever beckon and challenge us in our upward path. Let us not be content to hang on to a cliff halfway up. Let us get to the top." Solomon in the inspired writings of Ecclesiastics put it another way: "Whatever your hand finds to do, verily, do it with all your might."

Where is the Christian who will do his best in his work and strive for excellence in all that he does? Where is the person who should be a Christian, but is not because of the bad advertisements of Christianity he has seen in other Christians? Is it not time for all of us to ignore the obstacles and progress towards excellence, which comes through our belief in the Lord Jesus Christ? Do we not all realize that we are responsible to be perfect, whether Christian or non-Christian? If not, we are left to our hell in hell as well as in our hell on earth! It is true that in ourselves and of our selves we are inadequate. But we can be made perfect as well as excellent through Christ. That is why God reveals though the Apostle Paul, *"Just as He chose us in Him before the foundation of the world, that we should be holy and blameless before Him"* (Ephesians 1:4). This holiness and blamelessness is nothing less than God's standard of perfection for man.

Well, then, how does one get it? Look at Ephesians 1:7. *"In Him (Christ) we have redemption through His blood, the forgiveness of our trespasses, according to the riches of His grace."* That is how. Look at it this way. When you first believe in Christ, you accept the fact that Christ Jesus the Lord sacrificed His perfect life on the cross for your rather imperfect (sinful) life. In response to your faith, God graciously forgives you from all your sins and positions you in Christ. Thus, in Christ, you are positionally perfect. He also promises you that you will be perfect in heaven forever. In the meanwhile, between the time you first really believe in Christ and the time you go to heaven, you are to work at matching your practice with your position. That is to say, that one day at a time you are to surrender your thoughts, words, actions, to the standard of perfection that is in Christ. Yes, you will stumble, but you will get up and continue. Living in such a style, your trend is upward and certainly higher than any other lifestyle you would have otherwise.

If you do not know how to overcome your past at this point, listen to the words of the Apostle Paul: *"Not that I have already obtained it, or have already become perfect, but I press on in order that I may lay hold of that for which also I was laid hold of by Christ Jesus. Brethren, I do not regard myself as having laid hold of it yet; but one thing I do: forgetting what lies behind and reaching forward to what lies ahead, I PRESS on toward the goal for the prize of the upward call of God in Christ Jesus."* (Phil. 3:12-14).

Every believer can rise above the soft and mediocre environment of our materialistic age and press on toward God's true mark of excellence!

L stands for liability. Just what do we mean by the liability of faith? Webster defines liability as "the state of being exposed to danger." Such a definition is pertinent to our point here, because living by faith certainly does expose us to danger. Thus, a great caution from God's word, *"Therefore let him who thinks he stands take heed lest he fall."* (I Cor. 10:12).

Instinctively, we are all afraid. We are afraid to move ahead because we do not know what is there, and is our fear well founded? Is it not true that most things we fear never happen? A young businessman addressing a sales convention somehow came up with the figure of 90%, but certainly it makes the point that we fear too much. On this point I highly recommend Tim La Haye's book, "Spirit Controlled Temperment," which has an excellent chapter on fear, showing the great costs of fear.

It is important, however, to stress what we should really fear. Martin Luther said, "My greatest enemy is not the people who try to assassinate me, not the demons, nor even the devil himself, but rather my greatest enemy is my own deceitful heart." Our greatest liability is our own deceitful hearts. No wonder the prophet Jeremiah said: *"The heart is deceitful above all else and is desperately sick; who can understand it?"* (Jeremiah 17:9).

I stands for insistence. It is not intelligence, but rather insistence. I do not minimize the necessity of intelligence, but neither do I maximize it. This priority fits together in I Corinthians 1:26-29: *"For consider your call, brethren, that there were not many wise according to the flesh, not many mighty, not many noble; but God has chosen the foolish things* *of the world to shame the wise, and God has chosen the weak things of the world to shame the things which are strong, and the basest things of the world and the despised, God has chosen, the things that are not, that He might nullify the things that are, that no man should boast before God."*

The question could well be raised, How does God shame the wise and mighty by choosing the foolish and the weak? There are two ways:

(1) By His choice of man, which is based upon His unconditional love and not the ability of man.

(2) By His synergizing power by which He transforms the foolish into wise and the weak into might. There is a dynamic potential in this for every believer.

Although God chose; foolish and weak, He does not intend us to stay that way! On the contrary, he desires to transform us by His power from foolishness into wisdom, from weakness into might. When people who know you see your changed life, they will be amazed, confounded, and shamed by what they see, realizing that only God Himself could have changed you like that. If this is not true of all of us, it is because we lack insistence. There is the quality of faith that Christ had in mind when He commanded, *"Have faith in God. Truly I say to you, whoever says to this mountain, 'Be taken up and cast into the sea,' and does not doubt in his heart, but believes that what he says is going to happen; it shall be granted him. Therefore, I say to you, all things for which you pray and ask, believe that you have received them, and they shall be granted you."* (Mark 11:22-24).

True belief in Christ is an insisting belief that will not doubt. Do you pray like that? Do you move toward your goals like that? Do you work like that? Unfortunately, most Christians pray with the pestilence of doubt, not the insistence of belief.

To be sure, your faith is according to God's will. Begin with God's word and insist by faith that God be true to His promises, that He perform miracles in your life, things like changing your behavior, your witnessing, your godly presence as salt of the earth and light of the world. You are on safe ground, believing that these things are God's will, because the Bible says so. Second, obey the above Scripture by really learning how to pray. Notice that little clause in verse 24, "Pray and ask." It reminds us of James 5:16-17, describing the praying of Elijah: "The effectual prayer of a righteous man availeth much. Elijah was a man subject to passions as we are, and he prayed earnestly." (King James Version). This is the key to faith. In the words of George Muller: "The great point is never give up until the answer comes. The great fault of the children of God is, they do not continue in prayer; they do not persevere. If they desire anything for God's glory, they should pray until they get it!"

That is the only way you can know what God's will is in the circumstances of life outside the pages of the Bible. But beware of even the subtle doubts once you know. Dr. Samuel Zwemer said, "Faith is the outstretched hand of the soul, taking what Christ offers. Faith is what made the little girl take an umbrella to the prayer meeting called especially to pray for rain! The grown-ups wore sun glasses."

Only by earnest, fervent belief and prayer will you move mountains and accomplish great things for God.

E stands for endurance. Our Lord said, "But the one who endures to the end, it is he who shall be saved." (Matt. 24:13). This passage has dispensational overtones that I accept, but I also accept the principle that is inherent in it for all of us. Taking the verse at face value, we must apply it to ourselves in solemn self-examination. What it simply means in principle is that unless we endure our belief in Christ, we will not be saved by Christ in this life or in the next.

At the end of His sermon on the Mount, our Lord further clarified this point: "Not everyone who says to me on that day (Judgment Day), 'Lord, Lord' will enter the Kingdom of Heaven; but he who does the will of My Father, which is in Heaven." (Matt. 7:21). He exposes the true nature of faith, which is not just the ability to say words like 'Lord', but also the ability to do the will of the Father even to the Day of Judgment. This is what John Calvin meant by the doctrine of perseverance of the saints. The true believer cannot lose his salvation, for he is eternally secure (Phil. 1:6), but the true believer also endures to the end by shaping his behavior according to the Father's will. It is true that a believer cannot lose his salvation, but it is also true that while many people profess to be believers that does not mean that they are. We have no right to give assurance of salvation to anyone, unless he keeps enduring to do the Father's will.

What about the carnal Christians? There are such Christians, but I do not believe that the popular notion of the carnal Christian is what Paul meant in I Corinthians 3:1-3. The popular notion of a carnal Christian portrays him as a backsliding idler, and an apathetic believer. What a contrast this is to the carnal Christian portrayed in I Corinthians

3:1-3. There he is presented as progressive, active and energetic in the flesh instead of in the Spirit. Those carnal Christians at Corinth were playing favorites between the great Christian leaders of their day. Therefore, they caused divisions. That is why Paul called them carnal. We have no right to give assurance of salvation to a backslidden, idle, and/or apathetic person who professes to be a believer, as though we viewed him to be a "carnal" Christian. That is not a carnal Christian.

There is a great danger in robbing some believer of his assurance, but there is the greater danger in robbing some believer of his assurance to a person. Love does not give a person false assurance. Even though love believes all things, love is not so naive and presumptuous as to tell a person he is going to heaven, when in reality he is going to hell.

If a Christian stumbles into sin: (1) It is the responsibility of the spiritual believer to restore him (Gal. 6:1); (2) It is the responsibility of the sinning believer to get up and go on, even if he falls seven times (Prov. 24:16); (3) It is the responsibility of God to come to his aid (Psalm 37:23, 24; Jude 24); (4) It is the responsibility of angels to minister to him (Hebrews 1:14). With such a four-fold force keeping the real believer on the straight and narrow path, I seriously question any believer who stays off the path too long.

What about discouragements? Meditate on the words of George Muller: "I have not met with many discouragements; but at all times my confidence has been in God. On the word of Jehovah's promise my soul rests! Oh, it is good to trust in Him; His word never returns void! *'He gives power to the faint and to them that have no might, He increases strength' .*" (Isaiah 40:29).

True, George Muller was an exceptional man of faith, but listen to his exhortations. *"Does the Lord love you less than he loves us? Does He not love all His children with no less love than that with which He loves His only begotten Son, according to John 17:20-23? Are we better than you?"*

Why did I go to such lengths about endurance? Because in these last days, there appear to be many people professing Christ, but they do not possess any kind of quality of enduring Christ. The slightest demands of discipleship cause them to avoid the local church. The slightest touch of persecution triggers them into compromise. The slightest hint that their sinful lives must be changed into holy lives make them retaliate. "I thought salvation was through faith and not works?" they say. Such people, no matter what they say, are not really believers.

What a contrast such professors are to the possessor, Paul, who declared:

"Thou, therefore, endure such hardness, as a good soldier of Jesus Christ. Therefore, I endure all things for the elect's sake, that they may obtain the salvation which is in Christ Jesus with eternal glory." (II Tim. 2:3, 10, King James Version). The kind of love that believes all things, also believes that endurance must be a supreme characteristic for the believer.

F stands for fight. The last step in the development of one's belief is "fight." The Christian, having been justified through faith, has peace with God. But the Christian life is also a fight. The Bible declares, *"Finally be strong in the Lord, and in the strength of His might. Put on the full armor of God, that you may be able to stand firm against the schemes of the devil. For our struggle is not against flesh and blood, but against the rulers, against the powers, against the world forces of darkness, against the spiritual forces of wickedness in the heavenly places. Therefore, take up the full armor of God, that you may be able to resist in the evil day, and having done everything to stand firm."* (Ephesians 6:10-13).

You do not have to be a Christian long before you fight against the above realities. As a matter of fact, the new believer or the revived believer who grows enthusiastically in his faith will quickly face opposition by Satan. Consequently, Paul appropriately exhorts us to take up *"the shield of faith with which you will be able to extinguish all the flaming missiles of the evil one"* (Ephesians 6:16). Furthermore, to the degree that the believer grows in faith, to that degree he will have to fight for every inch of ground he attains. Nor does such a fight cease, for at the end of his life, Paul said, *"I have fought the good fight; I have finished the good fight of faith."*

APPLICATION

BELIEF! ***B*** stands for boldness; ***E*** for excellence; ***L*** for liability; ***I*** for insistence; ***E*** for endurance; ***F*** for fight—**B-E-L-I-E-F.** This is important because love believes all things. Do you believe like that? Let me give you a final secret about acquiring such belief.

Centuries ago, in the land of Greece, a young man walked up to

Socrates, the great philosopher, and asked, "Socrates, will you share with me the secret of wisdom?" Socrates, in reply, said, "Young man, do you realize that for which you are asking?" The young man said, "Yes." Then Socrates stood up, began to walk toward the lake, and said, "Follow me." The young man did. The next thing he knew he and Socrates were walking deeper and deeper into the water until they were shoulder-deep. Then, Socrates said, "Turn around and face away from me." As soon as the young man did that, suddenly Socrates with his 210-pound body, swept out of the water and over the lad. Squeezing a death grip on him, Socrates held him under the water until he saw bubbles floating to the surface. Then he let the young man go. As he came struggling and choking to the surface, he cried out, "What were you trying to do to me?" Then came Socrates' secret for wisdom. He said, "Young man, when you seek for wisdom like you sought for air, you shall find it. That is the secret for wisdom!"

Likewise, believer, when you seek for belief like that young man sought for air, you too shall find it. That is also the secret for developing belief.

LIFE MESSAGE FOURTEEN

LOVE HOPES ALL THINGS

Sir Winston Churchill stated, "I am an old man. I have lived a long time. I have never seen days like these. I am tired of it all. I see no hope for the future. Our problems are beyond us." Those are the words of one of the great men of our century, a man who well understood the condition of our world.

Words like "hope, love and faith" are very difficult to understand, even by the greatest of men, because we have drained them of their content. They have become empty words because of world wars and because of many personal disappointments. It is hard to recover their meaning, to once again be inspired by their reality.

Winston Churchill's pessimism is a common attitude today held by more than a few people. Why? Because what the world calls hope is not true hope. What many Christians call hope is not true hope. True hope can be found only in the Lord Jesus Christ. It is not something based on anything other than Christ. Whatever we want to console ourselves with, we can be sure it will not stand the test of trials in our time.

Apart from Christ, we finally come to the place reflected in the words of Churchill.

Hopelessness is a real problem in our time. But it has always been that way. In every age there have been trials that test faith and hope. Where does that lead us? What can we say in answer to the question, "So why hope about anything, anytime?" How many times have you been disappointed, when you had hope? We raise the question many times, if we are honest. How well are we grafted into Christ, whereby you live everyday believing and hoping all things? If that is not your normal Christian experience, then I Corinthians 13:7 is a message for you.

LOVE IS OPTIMISTIC

"Love bears all things; love believes all things; love hopes all things." Why? How can we really say that? How can we honestly, courageously, boldly, confidently, and even dogmatically say there is hope, hope for me, my family, and everybody with whom I share this wonderful truth?

Notice first of all that we are to hope in the meaning of life itself. Secondly, there is hope in the mode of life that God has ordained through Christ. Lastly, there is hope in the motive of life.

I. Hope in the Meaning of Life.

Let us first consider hope in the meaning of life. The text emphasizes that love hopes all things. In other words, love is invincibly optimistic, for even when it suffers defeat it will not quit, lest it fall short of hoping all things. Love never knows when it has lost a battle, so it keeps on hoping.

Such an attitude reminds me of a ten year old boy who was very optimistic about his baseball ability. His father was curious to find out just how optimistic he was, so one day he decided to play ball with him. He teased him, saying, "I'm going to strike you out the first time you're up to bat." His son replied, "Oh, no you're not! I'm a good batter!" The father pitched the ball over the plate. The boy swung and missed. The father shouted "That's strike one!" Again the father threw the ball over the plate. This time the boy swung harder, and missed again. And the father shouted, "That's strike two!" He threw the ball for the third time over the plate. This time the son gave it all he had as he swung with all his might, but again he missed. He heard his father shout, "That's strike three!" as he fell to the ground, having swung his bat so hard.

Then came the crucial moment. His father, as he stood there looking at his son on the ground, asked himself, "Was I too hard on the boy? Did I hurt his spirit?" Within moments the boy got right back up, dusted himself off, and said, "Boy am I a good pitcher! Come on, Dad, you're up to bat!" That is being invincibly optimistic.

A. Not Because the World is a Nice Place to Live In.

But we cannot think for a moment that Christian optimism is a Pollyanna buoyancy of good spirits. Christians do not have hope because the world is a nice place to live in. Christians do not have optimism because society is basically good. Nor do Christians have hope because they reinforce themselves with positive thinking, or with all sorts of pills and drugs.

B. But Because There is a Point to Living

On the contrary, the Christian keeps on hoping on the basis of the conviction that because God is God, all fine ideals will some day become reality. For the Christian there is hope because there is a point to living, and that point is the assurance that God lives and works in men and in the world. The Christian optimistically looks forward to that which God is doing in history. With absolutely optimistic enthusiasm the Christian hopes in God, who has a purpose for all things, even though the Christian doesn't always understand the times of men and things. That is why Paul wrote in Romans 8:28: *"And we know that God causes all things to work together for good to those who love God, to those who are called according to His purpose."*

The Christian does not live in a world of fantasy, but rather he is convinced that regardless of what may go wrong, regardless of what sufferings he must go through, one day it will all be worth it.

"For I consider that the sufferings of the present time are not worthy to be compared with the glory that is to be revealed to us. For the anxious longing of the creation waits eagerly for the revealing of the sons of God. For the creation was subjected to futility, not of its own will, but because of Him who subjected it, in hope that the creation itself also will be set free from its slavery to corruption into the freedom of the glory of the children of God. For we know that the whole creation groans and suffers the pain of childbirth together until now. And not only this, but also we ourselves, having the first fruits of the Spirit, even we ourselves groan within ourselves waiting eagerly for adoption as sons, the redemption of our body. For in hope we have been saved, but hope that

is seen is not hope; for why does one false hope for what he sees? But if we hope for what we do not see, with perseverance we wait eagerly for it" (Romans 8:18-25).

Some people disdain such hope by saying that Christians are dreamers. But I cannot imagine a more realistic outlook on life than that expressed above. The Apostle Paul encourages Christians to be constant in doing good without losing heart, not because things might work out well in this life necessarily, but because nothing they did would ever be lost or wasted in the eternal purpose of God. As Eileen Guder says it, "There would be a final solution, and all patient waiting would be rewarded, in God's time." That is why Dorothy L. Sayers is correct in observing, in her preface to "Man Born to Be King," that no Christian tragedy is possible! Tragedy implies no hope, inevitable, unalterable doom. But that is not the message of the Bible. That is not the meaning of life.

"For in Him all things were created, both in heaven and on earth, visible and invisible, whether thrones or dominions or rulers or authorities, all things have been created through Him and for Him. And He is before all things, and in Him all things hold together. He is also the Head of the body, the church; and He is the beginning, the firstborn from the dead; so that He Himself might come to have first place in everything. For it was through the Father's good pleasure for all the fullness to dwell in Him, and through Him to reconcile all things to Himself, having made peace through the blood of His cross; through Him, I say, whether things in earth or things in Heaven." (Col. 1:16-20).

II. Hope in the Mode of Life

Let us move on to the Christian's hope in the mode of life. The question logically arises, what should be the life style, or the mode of the Christian's life? The answer is rest.

A. Rest in the hope that is God.

If the reason to hope is that there is a point to life guaranteed by God, then we can relax or rest in the realization that our hope, above all things, is God himself. *"Who through Him (Christ) are believers in God, who raised Him (Christ) from the dead and gave him (Christ) glory, so that your faith and hope are in God"* (I Peter 1:21).

B. Rest in the Hope that is Good.

Such a hope is good and genuine, because it comes from God himself. It is not one of the vain hopes of the world that comes to us from political speeches, unloyal friends or overly positive promises of prosperity. We can rest in the hope that is good because God gave it to us: "Now may our Lord Jesus Christ Himself and God our Father, who has loved us and given us eternal comfort and good hope by grace, comfort and strengthen your hearts in every good work and word." (II Thess. 2:16, 17).

The "rest" of the Christian does not make him lazy or passive, but rather calm and restful in attitude. As a matter of fact, the restful hope of the Christian strengthens him to work harder in the will of God, because energy he would spend in worry and frustration is channeled into his life's work.

How different this attitude is in contrast to that of Jean Paul Sartre, as expressed in quotation from him which I once memorized, but have since forgotten the source from which it came. Nevertheless, expressing a widely prevalent and increasingly popular belief among intellectuals—negative existentialism—Jean Paul Sartre once said, "Man can count on no one but himself. He is alone, abandoned on earth in the midst of infinite responsibilities, without hope, with no other aim than the one he sets for himself, with no other destiny than the one he forges for himself on this earth." How hopeless and purposeless life is for those who embrace this negative belief. How worthy and satisfying life is for those who live for Christ and others.

C. Rest in the Hope that is Growing.

It is a growing hope because it is a living hope. It is a growing hope because it begins with a rebirth, with being born again, with spiritual regeneration of God's life into ours. It is a growing hope because we grow into it daily. But do not forget, growth requires growing pains. *"Blessed be God and the Father of our Lord Jesus Christ, who according to His great mercy has caused us to be born again to a living hope through the resurrection of Jesus Christ from the dead."* (I Peter 1:3).

A long time ago, Robert Bruce, the King of Scotland, was forced to hide from his enemies. He found refuge in a cave deep in the forest. He was downhearted and discouraged. He had tried to save Scotland from her enemies, but he had lost every battle. His soldiers had been killed, wounded, and forced to hide. "It is of no use to fight any more," he said, "our enemies are too strong for us." Just then he saw a spider weaving its web. She was trying to spin the web between two rocks. She had fastened one end of her thread to a rock and was trying to swing herself across, but each time failed to reach the other side.

Bruce sat watching her for a long time. He wondered how long she would keep on trying. The spider tried and failed seven times. "You are a brave and patient spider," thought the king. "If you try once more and succeed I, too, will fight again." She did. "Thanks for the lesson you have taught me, little spider," said Bruce. "I will try once more to free Scotland from her enemies."

So King Robert Bruce went forth once again at the head of his army. He and his men fought as they had never fought before. Bruce won the battle and his country was freed.

D. Rest in the Hope that is Groovy.

Really, I can not think of a better word to describe I John 3:3. "And every one who has this hope in him purifies himself, just as He is pure." That word "purifies" can certainly mean to groove our ways into God's ways. Is not the whole method of God in our lives to groove our life style into His? The hope that God gives us is groovy.

E. Rest in the Hope that is Girded.

Peter tells us to be *"Sober and hope to the end."* (I Peter 1:13). Gird your minds for action. The cold, dark world is no match for the Christian, who is girded by hope.

The Irish essayist and lecturer, George Bernard Shaw, sums up the hopelessness of his own barren life and philosophy in the epigram: "There are two tragedies in life. One is not to get your heart's desire. The other is to get it." But Shaw is talking about the desire of the heart of the natural man, who knows not God nor Christ, and whose life is only death. He speaks truly when he says that, when such a man has gotten his heart's desire, he finds in it only disappointment, emptiness and dissatisfaction. That is why so many today, both old and young people, having won their heart's desire, commit suicide.

F. Rest in the Hope that is Gratifying.

Paul tells us in Titus 2:13: *"Looking for that blessed hope and appearing of the glory of our great God and Savior."* This blessed hope is gratifying because it floods our subconscious through our eyes of hope. This is significant because psychologists tell us if we meditate on anything three different times with real concentration and earnestness, our subconscious receives the effect of such meditation equally as it would the actual event itself. That is to say, our subconscious does not know the difference between that which is meditated on in such a threefold manner and that which actually has happened. Both effect the subconscious in the same way. Is this not hope that is gratifying? So hope on, my friend, hope on!

G. Rest in the Hope that is Glorious.

In the same verse we see that our hope is also glorious, for it shall be consummated in the literal appearing of our great God and Savior, Jesus Christ. All history is moving toward a consummation point, so history is really His story.

If love proves wrong, if believing in the best, the worst is nevertheless done, and if the offense proves to be a fact which can no longer be overlooked or condoned, love still does not give up. Love bears all things, it believes all things, and when proved to be wrong, then it resorts to hoping all things, ever allowing for the possibility that the penitent will do better. Hope sees the bright side of things; it doesn't despair.

It is certainly remarkable that both faith and hope are here predicated of love. This implies that hope and faith arise from love. When we love somebody, we trust him fully, we expect nothing but good things in return from him even though appearance be against him.

Love as far as it can with any reason will hope for the best and will stretch its faith beyond appearance for the support of a kind opinion; it will go into a bad one only with the utmost reluctance, and force against it as much as it fairly and honestly can. And when, in spite of inclination, it cannot believe well, it will hope well and continue to hope as long as there is any ground for it. With such a God-given, good, growing, groovy, girded, gratifying and glorious hope, how can we not hope?

III. Hope in the Motive of Love.

True Christian love produces hope in the motive of life. Why is it of all of the wonderful traits of love in I Corinthians 13, faith, hope, and love alone abide and yet the greatest of these is love?

Because it is only love that fully motivates us to do our best in life for God and man and ourselves. In II Corinthians 5:11 we see that the fear of God is a great motive for life. Even the Apostle Paul needed this type of motivation. When our love for God ceases to motivate us to do God's will, then we would better fear, for *"the fear of God is the beginning of wisdom."* (Prov. 9:10). Paul stresses fear as a proper motive for our lives.

But look also at II Corinthians 5:14: *"For the love of Christ controls us."* The word "controls" is a powerful word. It certainly means to motivate, but it also means to constrain, to dominate, to consume. To be sure, any Christian who is under such an influence as this will be filled with hope.

The greatest motive in life is the love of Christ. Let's hope in this motive. Hope in the love of Christ and you will have a life that hopes all things. It is an unfailing law. Try it and see.

Love hopes all things, and "all things' includes anything, no matter how despairing. Just take note of some of the following inspirational gems:

Harriet Beecher Stowe once said: "When you get into a tight place and everything goes against you until it seems you cannot hold on a minute longer, never give up then, for it is just the place and time when the tide will turn."

Lord Byron in "The Bride of Abydos" said of hope: "Be thou the rainbow to the storms of life, the evening beam that smiles the clouds away and tints tomorrow with prophetic ray."

Le Rochefould said: "We promise according to our hopes and perform according to our fears."

Peter describes the Christian's inheritance as a *"living hope."* (I Peter 1:3). That is in striking contrast to the hope of the world, for the worldly hopes men set their hearts upon fail them.

California for many years had a higher percentage of suicide than any other state. At first that seems strange when one reflects upon its beautiful scenery, its blue skies, and bright sunlight. Life, one would think, ought to be easier there than anywhere else. Why then so many suicides? The reason ascribed is that many have gone to California with what has been a last hope, either as to their health or their personal fortune, and when this hope failed them, life had nothing left for them. But the believer according to Peter has been begotten, born into a living hope.

Application

When Abraham Lincoln was a young man he ran for the legislature in Illinois, and was overwhelmingly defeated. He next entered business, failed, and spent 17 years of his life paying up the debts of a worthless partner. He was in love with a beautiful woman to whom he became engaged, then she died. Later he married a woman who was a constant burden to him. Entering politics again, he ran for Congress, and again was badly defeated. He became a candidate for U.S. Senate, and lost again. In 1856 he became a candidate for the vice presidency, and was once more defeated. In 1856 he was defeated by Douglas.

One failure after another, bad failures, great setbacks. In the face of all this he eventually became one of the greatest men in America, a man whose memory is honored throughout the world. When you contemplate the effect of a series of setbacks like that, does it not make you feel rather small to become discouraged?

Life Message Fifteen

LOVE ENDURES ALL THINGS

There are all sorts of humorous, as well as serious, sayings about endurance. I'm sure you have heard the one so often used by the late Vince Lombardi, "Winners never quit and quitters never win."

Another football coach, Frank Lee, said, "When the going gets tough, let the tough get going." On one occasion, a preacher was asked by an evangelist how his endurance quotient was concerning his church. The pastor said, "Not too well, brother." The evangelist asked, "Why not?" "Because my church is an active church," replied the preacher. The evangelist scratched his head and tried to figure out how it could be difficult to endure an active church. The pastor explained, "It's this way: half of my congregation is active for me, and the other half is active against me! And that's hard to endure at times."

There's the story of the optimistic frog put in poetic structure:

Two frogs fell deep into a cream bowl.
One was an optimistic soul;
But the other took the gloomy view.
We shall drown he cried, without more ado.
So with a last despairing cry
He flung up his legs and he said good-bye.
Quote the other frog with a merry grin:
"I can't get out, but I won't give in;
I'll just swim around till my strength is spent;
Then I will die the more content."
Bravely he swam till it would seem;
His troubles began to churn the cream.
On the top of butter at last he stopped;
And out of the bowl he easily hopped.
What of the moral? 'Tis easily found;
If you can't hop out, keep swimming around.

Of course, endurance is a serious business. I think of our forefathers who crossed the continent on foot in pioneer days. One thing alone got them across: endurance. They traveled day after day, mile after mile, through the barrenness of the desert, the roughness of hills, all the seemingly insurmountable obstacles. What got them to their destination? It was not genius, personality, or talent, but simply endurance. That is why one of the greatest mottoes of the preachers in those days was, "Lord, give us a through trip." A through trip, that meant, of course, get us through.

Today, life is a rough journey for many people. They feel overwhelmed by the waves of difficulty. They hurt from many wounds and they want to give up. The winds of resistance leave them without a breath of air.

What does God say about this? The answer is I Corinthians 13:7. *"Love endures all things."* From this marvelous vantage point, we can get new strength, courage, and dynamic to revolutionize our lives. Why? Notice, first of all, the test of love. Second, the tenacity of love, and third, the triumph of love.

I. The Test of Love.

With regard to the test of love, consider, for example, the matter of your family life. Through persecution, Jesus warned, *"And brother will deliver up brother to death, and a father his child; and the children will rise up against parents, and cause them to be put to death. Do not think that I came to bring peace on earth; I did not come to bring peace, but a sword. For I came to set a man against his father, and a daughter against her mother, and a daughter-in-law against her mother-in-law and a man's enemies will be the members of his (own) household. He who loves father, mother more than Me is not worthy of Me"* (Matt. 10:21, 34-37).

If we do not believe these words we will never pass the test of love. The test of love means loving Christ supremely, so that I am willing to lose my father, mother, husband, wife, sister, brother, son, daughter or anyone else. This does not necessarily mean that a man will have to lose his wife physically. But it does mean we cannot allow a human relationship to block what we know is the will of God for us. Too often we passively allow the ones who are closest to us to divert us from following Christ. We can not let their pressure hold us back from serving Jesus and loving Him. We must endure whatever pressure they put upon us in their efforts to keep us from living for God. Sometimes, of course, our loved ones can be used by the Lord to correct us where we are wrong. Love would dictate that we know the difference. But if we are faultless, and we are still being pressured by a loved one, we must learn to love Jesus supremely.

For example, if a girl finds love for a fellow, and he does not love Jesus supremely, if she continues to love him, she is not worthy of Jesus. That is a test she must pass. It is not worth even dating a fellow or a girl who is unsaved. Even more, do not even date someone who does not win souls. What about winning an unsaved girlfriend or boyfriend to Christ? God can use many other means to bring them to Christ.

What about the fear of man? There is a test of love in the family life also because of the fear of man. *"And you will be hated by all on account of My Name, but it is the one who has endured it to the end who will be saved. And do not fear those that kill the body, but are unable to kill the soul; but rather fear Him who is able to destroy both soul and body in hell."* (Matt. 10:22,23).

There is a common error abroad today. It is the belief that a Christian should not fear God, but only reverence or respect Him, and that only unsaved people should fear God with trembling. The Scripture does not teach that. Jesus said we are to fear Him who can cast our soul into hell. That refers to professing Christians, as well as outright unbelievers.

In Acts 5, we find the account of the lie and punishment of Ananias and Sapphira. They were Christians, not unbelievers. But they lied to the Holy Spirit, and as a result, they were both chastised to the point of physical death, in the presence of other people who faltered. Notice as a result of this: *"And as he heard these words, Ananias fell down, and breathed his last; and great fear came down upon all who heard of it."* (verse 5). Not just the ones who witnessed it. After the death of Sapphira, *"great fear came upon the whole church"* (verse 11). Great fear does come upon a church and believers. May God help us to have that same kind of fear. After Ananias and Sapphira died so suddenly, fear also came upon the unbelievers. A church that truly fears the Lord will not only influence and purify its own members, it will also influence the community. If a person does not fear God, he will fear man. He will fear circumstance. He will fear himself, his wife, and his boss. Such people are stunted, hampered, frustrated and they are miserable. They would not be bound by the snare of fear if they truly feared God. They would have liberty and power in their lives.

Love is also tested by the temptation to quit. Matthew 10:22 gives a wonderful assurance to the Christian who trusts in Christ. *"Let him who stands take heed lest he fall."* Until the day we die, we should be diligent about our salvation. The one who has endured to the end will be saved. That does not rob us of eternal security, the assurance, but it does mean this: it means that the person who is really saved, who has eternal life in Him, will live every day of his life to the end. If he does not live out his new life in Christ, he ought to question whether or not he was ever truly saved.

Some people have the idea that if they do not really stand true to Jesus at a time of persecution, surely God will understand. Beloved, no He will not. They can plan on going to hell if they think they can deny Christ at the threat of physical death. Jesus warns us: "Take heed; behold I have told you everything in advance. Take heed, keep on the alert, for you do not know when the appointed time is. Therefore be on the alert, for you do not know whether the master of the house is coming, whether in the evening, at midnight, or cockcrowing, or in the morning, lest he come suddenly and find you asleep. And what I say to you, I say to all, *'Be on the alert!'* (Mark 13:23, 33, 35-37). A Christian who obeys this will never have any worry about trusting Christ and being true to Him when facing death, or any other trial.

Love is tested also in the matter of our self-discipline. Paul declares in I Corinthians 4:2, *"In this case, moreover, it is required of stewards* (that is, every Christian) *that one be found trustworthy (or faithful)."* Note his words also in II Timothy 4:2: *"Be urgent in season and out of season."*

Christians should be characterized by faithfulness in giving out the Word of God to their neighbors, relatives, and friends. It should be their number one priority and their supreme love. It proves their love for Jesus. But many Christians fail this test of love. They do not love other people and they are not faithful in witnessing. Churches have problems getting people to learn how to win souls. If a Christian is undisciplined in this, he is failing the test of love.

Look also at the matter of enduring hardness. Christians are to endure hardship as good soldiers of Jesus Christ (II Timothy 2:3). Instead of complaining when hardships come, they should stand ready to endure them. Christians are supposed to endure joyfully (James 1:2). We are to praise God, because hardship is the stuff out of which our Christian lives are made. Note this aspect of love in II Thessalonians 1:4: *"Therefore, we ourselves, speak proudly of you among the churches of God for your perseverance and faith in the midst of all your persecutions and afflictions when you endure."* It is the mark of a true mature Christian that he stands strong in the face of all his hardships. He even says, *"God, thanks for the compliment of all these problems, hardships, sufferings, persecutions and tribulations because you must think an awful lot of my strength to endure it to give it to me. And if you want to, God, give me more."* That is Christ in you, beloved. That is what the love of Christ is all about.

The Athenians in their games had a very special kind of race. Those who won the crowns in the race were not necessarily the fastest, but those who endured. They gathered torches and the winners finished with their torches still burning. This typifies Christians who, when they go through problems and pressures, wear the fire and glow of the love of God in their faces. You see them smiling the more intense it gets. That torch of the Christian in trial is the smile that reflects a deep-down joy of the love of God.

II. The Tenacity of Love.

Next, consider the matter of the tenacity of love. I just have three things to say about this: a paragraph, a portrayal and a point.

A. The Paragraph.

The paragraph is simply this. The word tenacity means strength, and the strength of love is endurance. Why? Because in the easy things of life anybody; unsaved, carnal or whatever, can be loving. It is only when the rough things come that the storehouse of love of God can be unlocked and opened. It floods out to show other people just what is in you.

B. The Portrayal.

The portrayal is of a soldier. During the Civil War he walked from Manchester to Gettysburg. The toughest thing was not the battle itself, but rather that march of 34 miles. He said it was the most difficult thing he ever faced in his life. He walked through clouds of dust, mile after mile, seeing men with stubs for hands and crutches of legs, seeing cowards dropping off, seeing others wanting to turn back if someone would get the ball rolling. All these things were so difficult. He said the one thing he needed was endurance. That was the inspiration of a few that kept the others going. They were not going to quit.

More Christians should be emulative of this; Christians who will be tenacious at witnessing and at holy living. Take it a day at a time. I do not know how to live a holy life, but I can grasp living a holy day. I can take that much. That is all God expects of me, for Jesus said, "Daily bear your cross."

That is the ultimate characteristic of love. This means enduring, not simply with a passive indifference. "I'll just endure my lot in life. Poor me! If you only knew how bad I had it. If you only knew the cross I had to bear. What will be will be." Enduring love is an active, victorious, triumphant attitude. Confident of victory, the Christian sticks it out until the end. That is what endurance is.

III. The Triumph of Love.

That leads to the triumph of love. There are two kinds of people: those who allow circumstances to make them, and those who make their own circumstances by the grace of God, into His synergy, power and love. So make your circumstances. "I can't win souls. Poor me!" Make yourself win souls. "I can't be at evening service." Make yourself be at evening service.

Realize also, that when all else fails, love abides. No one really knows how precious love is until all of life has caved in.

That happened to Eileen Guder in the fall of 1966. She and her husband anticipated a golden opportunity in business. The children were raised. The expenses of their college education were behind them. They looked forward to some freedom from bills and pressures. But her husband got sick and it was diagnosed as leukemia. The night he died, the rain-soaked ceiling fell on her, literally. She saw the falling of the ceiling as only the echo of the spiritual hammer-blow of her husband's death.

How did she react? "How could God do that to me? How could a loving God do this to a person like me?" No! She said, "Sickness and even death are not really the stuff that real life is made of. For God used that to show me that the real stuff out of which life is made is love, that strengthens you to endure at a time like that." She then realized her mission was to share such reality with millions of people through her writings and her lectures.

Application

As a result of this teaching about the endurance of love, you can do only one of two things, become bitter or better. That is your choice. What shall it be?

There is an anonymous poem called, "Don't Quit."

When things go wrong as they sometimes will;
When the road you're trudging seems all uphill;
When funds are low and debts are high;
And you want to smile but you have to sigh.
When care is pressing you down a bit;

Rest if you must, but don't you quit.
Life is queer with its twists and turns;
As everyone of us sometimes learns.
And many a failure turns about;
When he might have won if he stuck it out.
Don't give up though the pace seems slow;
You may succeed with another blow.
Often the goal is nearer than it seems;
To a faint and faltering man.
Often the struggler has given up;
When the might have captured the victor's cup.
And he learned too late
When the night slipped down;
How close he was to the Golden Crown.
Success is a failure turned inside out;
The silver tint of the clouds of doubt.
And you can never tell how close you are;
It may be near when it seems afar.
So stick to the fight when you're hardest hit;
It's when things seem worse that you mustn't quit.

LIFE MESSAGE SIXTEEN

LOVE NEVER FAILS

The Upper Room was used on more than one occasion. One of the most important occasions was when our Lord taught what is called the Upper Room Discourse. (John 13-17). He shared all His plans with His disciples. If there was ever a man who had goals in life, it was Jesus Christ and He was not afraid to share them with His followers.

Among other things, Jesus said to His troubled disciples, *"Greater things shall you do than I have already done because I go to the Father."* (John 14:12). I've often wondered what really was in their minds when they heard Him say those words. "Greater works"? Probably they would have been glad enough to do the same kind of works, or even a little bit less, than what Christ had done. But He said, "greater works." Many of them. Of course, as we know, those very apostles later on raised the dead, healed the sick, cured the blind and preached to great crowds.

But the truths Jesus taught in the Upper Room were not just meant for the apostles, they were also meant for us today. However, I do not see Christians raising people from the dead. I do not see multitudes flocking to become Christians.

The big question comes, Why? Is it a lack of faith? Or did Jesus Christ expect this only of the apostles? If this promise is only for them, we have a problem because other truths in the same discourse obviously refer to all believers. For example, heaven. *"Let not your heart be troubled, you believe in God believe also in Me. In My Father's house are many mansions. If it were not so, I would have told you. And I go to prepare a place for you."* (John 14: 1-3). Surely heaven is not just for the apostles.

The answer is that the "greater works" just could not include only miracles, but something else as well. Perhaps something even greater than raising people from the dead. After a person is raised from the dead, he's got to live for a period of time. If he does not have something to live for, what good is being raised from the dead? After a person is healed from a sickness what good is it if he can not have love, joy, and peace in his life? So what is greater than healing? Jesus reached the climax of all those "greater works" when He said, *"Greater love has no man than this, that a man lay down his life for his friends"* (John 15:13). That is the greatest work, love. That is what the Apostle Paul describes in I Corinthians 13.

In this chapter we want to see the absolute supremacy of love. Paul proves this supremacy by three facts: The partial is to be done away (vv. 8-10); the process is to be done away (v. 11); the perfect is here to stay (v. 12).

I. The Partial is to be Done Away.

Paul says, *"We know in part, and we prophesy in part, but when the perfect comes the partial will be done away."* What does he mean?

A. The Place of the Partial.

He explains in Ephesians 2:20-21, *"Having been built upon the foundation of the apostles and prophets Christ Jesus Himself being the corner stone, in whom the whole building being fitted together is growing into a holy temple in the Lord."* Paul refers not to a building of brick and mortar and stone, but rather the church, the individual members who make up the body of Christ. The church is a building made up of spiritual stones. Notice, the foundation is already done. It stands firm so we can rely upon it and build upon it, knowing it will not crumble beneath us. Christ is not referred to here as the foundation in the church. Paul says the apostles and prophets are the foundation, and Christ Himself is the cornerstone. The ministry of the apostles and the New Testament prophets is what Paul means by, "the partial." They spoke the Word in prophecy because there was no written New Testament, they got knowledge fresh from heaven, and they even spoke in tongues. These were the things by which the apostles and prophets laid the foundation of the church.

B. The Period of the Partial.

Their miracles, their greater works were the foundation. There was a reason for that. Whenever God did an unusual work, He blessed certain messengers, whether they were prophets or apostles, with unusual gifts to perform miracles. This was so that when they preached the message of God, people would believe them, if for no other reason than the miraculous works. There were three great periods of miracles. One was during the time of Moses. Moses needed miracles to confirm his message to Pharaoh, because Pharaoh would not change his mind.

The second period of miracles was when Elijah and Elisha had to revive Israel. During that period of time, there was a great outpouring of miracles. The third period of time was the time of Christ, which included the apostles and New Testament prophets. All of these miraculous works, raising the dead, healing people, speaking in tongues, prophecies, special revelations from heaven, were done at the foundation. Why? Because God was about to initiate another work, the work of the church. In order to establish it in the eyes of the people, and give it credibility, miracles were necessary.

C. The Purpose of the Partial.

Notice, however, that "the partial will be done away." "The partial" refers back to verse nine, "For we know in part and prophesy in part." Why must the partial "be done away" Because you do not keep building a foundation. There comes a time when you stop building a foundation, you build the superstructure, and ingredients that go into the foundation do not go into the superstructure.

This refers not only to the foundational gifts of the apostles and prophets, but also to all the gifts listed in I Corinthians 12-14. When God brings about a new heaven and a new earth, we will not need any one of the 18 or more gifts mentioned. Even those gifts in a sense are partial. But Paul says "the perfect" is coming and it will remain forever and ever. What is the "perfect"?

II. The Process is to be Done Away.

In verse 11, Paul speaks about a child. He does so because he wants to illustrate the necessity of love. He illustrates what we are to be doing during the time between the foundation of the church and the coming of the Kingdom. He calls this a period of childhood. In other words, Christians are to grow up and put away childish things. *"When I was a child, I used to speak as a child, think as a child, reason as a child."*

These verbs; speak, think, reason,are directly parallel to speaking in tongues, the gift of prophesy, and the gift of knowledge. These three "childish" ways of behavior are compared to three spiritual gifts that went into the foundation of the church. The child referred to here in verse 11 is the church. Beyond Paul's own testimony, there is a figure of speech. He represents the whole church. The church is supposed to be putting away childish things.

A. Speaking as a Child

What is the implication? Tongues are the baby talk of the church, not the adult talk. How do I know? Because the word "child" is not the word for a boy of growing age, say from six to twelve, it is the word for baby, infant. How does an infant talk? "Da-Da, goo-goo, ge-ge." It does not make sense. That is how Paul describes tongues. How does a baby talk? Out of turn, many times. You see that in tongues. Baby talk is cute, but it is certainly not a sign of maturity. It certainly is not edifying.

In I Corinthians 14:18, 19, Paul says, I thank God, I speak in tongues more than you all. However, in the church I desire to speak five words in my mind, that I may instruct others also, rather than ten thousand words in a tongue." By A.D. 50 or 55 at the latest, Paul was already putting away tongues, putting away "the baby talk." Paul also commanded, *"Be imitators of me just as I am of Christ."* (I Corinthians 11:`). I get the impression that Paul was saying, "You put away the baby talk, too."

B. Thinking as a Child.

Let us move on to the next one: "Think as a child." What else did Paul put away? "Thinking," or prophecy. You must think to talk correctly; you must think to be able to preach, to prophesy, especially to convey some revelation that God gives you on the spot. Direct revelation through a messenger to people is prophecy. But, according to Paul, that was the baby thought of the early church. Think about a baby. A baby doesn't think for itself. A baby depends on the thinking of its parents. A baby is helpless and can not think in terms of helping itself. That is what is meant here.

The Apostle John explains in Revelation 22:18, 19: *"I testify to everyone who hears the words of the prophecy of this book; if anyone adds to them, God shall add to him the plagues which are written in this book; if anyone takes away from the words of the book of this prophecy, God shall take away his part from the tree of life and from the holy city, which are written in this book."* The last book of the Bible was written by the end of the first century. Therefore, there is no more revelation coming to us in the character of prophecy, as it did in the infant church.

C. Reasoning as a Child.

Paul's next phrase is, "Reason as a child." How does a child reason? The reasoning is self-centered and self-excusing. Sometimes children are logical, but most of the time they are unconvincing and inconclusive. Paul compares this to the gift of knowledge in the early church. If a person doesn't have a Bible, he needs a special kind of knowledge that comes directly from God. The early Christians needed that during the time, but we are not in that kind of situation. We have the complete Bible. We are mature in the sense we have full knowledge of God in His Word. We need nothing else. We do not have to say, "I wish God would tap me on the shoulder." That is baby reasoning. The answer is in Scripture. Paul says when he became a man he put away childish things. So should we.

Paul exhorts in Philippians 2:12, 13: *"So, then, my beloved, just as you have always obeyed, not as in my presence only, but now much more in my absence, work out your salvation with fear and trembling; for it is God who is at work in you, both to will and to work for His good pleasure."* Even when Paul was not present, he expected the Philippians to follow him. He is not around today, but we should still follow him, in terms of Scripture. God is at work in us, willing to do and to work for His good pleasure.

So we have the power to do so. Every Christian can walk on his own two feet. There is no need to talk baby talk, to think baby thoughts, and to reason as a baby.

III. The Perfect is Here to Stay.

Sir Isaac Newton, just before his death, made this remark, "I do not know what I appear to the world, but to myself I seem to have been only like a boy playing on the seashore and diverting myself now and then finding a smoother pebble or a prettier shell than the ordinary, while the great ocean of truth lay all undiscovered before me."

We can move on to something more than that, because we have the power in Christ, a power greater than the creative power Newton had. The key is found in I Corinthians 13:12, "For now we see in that mirror dimly."

A. Not the Medium of Knowing.

The word "mirror" translated can mean either a mirror or a window. In the original Greek, the preposition "in" is not used; it is the word "through." I think a better translation is this, "For now we see through a window dimly."

"The most natural idea is that of seeing objects by an imperfect medium," said Pliny, the ancient philosopher and scholar, "by looking through something in contemplating them." It is, therefore, probable that Paul refers to those transparent substances which the ancients had and which they had used in their windows occasionally such as thin slates of horn, transparent stone, etc. Windows were often made by lapis specularis which was pellucid and which was split into thin laminae or scales, probably the same as mica.

It is not, therefore, unlikely that such material was used in Paul's day. Paul is describing people inside the house looking out the window. It was not a clear transparent window such as we have. It was like frosted glass, but they could still see the figures of people outside. However, they could not tell for sure who the person was coming to the house. That fits the context here better than "mirror" because you can not see through a mirror. The point is, we don't see through a window like that. We can see face to face, just like you see a friend face to face, and see him clearly.

B. But the Reality of Knowledge.

The word "know" is the word that refers not to theoretical knowledge, but to experiential knowledge. Added to that experiential knowledge is the idea of being fully known and knowing fully. It is the word for such an intimate knowledge of a person that it is used to describe the experience of Isaac and Rebecca on their wedding night. The Bible says, "And he knew her." Paul says love never ends, so one day we shall know even as we are fully known by God already. God describes our knowing Him and His knowing us as the result of unfailing love.

APPLICATION

We are to respond to this truth by growing up. Whatever gifts we have, let us use them. Let us not emphasize the foundational ones. Some people still persist in baby stuff.

As for me, I do not need baby talk, baby thought, and baby reasoning. I want to build a superstructure, not a foundation. The foundation is finished. I want to stand upon it and I want to build upon it with preaching, teaching, prayer, and faith. Even all these gifts will be put away one day, and by the grace of God the one thing that is going to last for eternity is love. As I am growing up, I want to love people, really love them, and I want them to love me. I want to know God as He knows me.

That is Christian maturity. May you have it.

Life Message Seventeen

LOVE IS THE GREATEST

Gift, estate and income taxes have not significantly decreased the financial tide going to the rich, says a report by the Carnegie Institute. On the other hand, welfare, Social Security and other payments from the government to the poorest one-fifth of the people have not caused any significant improvement in their financial situation. The Institute, which specializes in social research, concludes that there has not been any significant redistribution of either income or wealth in the U.S. for the last generation. Other findings in the report include:

1. The dollar-gap between the richest and poorest one-fifth of the population is increasing.

2. Some 45 percent of all salaried income which goes to the top one-fifth of the population is increasing.

3. Over 60 percent of income from personal businesses and property goes to the highest one-fifth.

4. The top one-fifth owns 77 percent of total personal wealth.

5. One percent of Americans own between 20 and 30 percent of all personal wealth.

6. Only 5 percent of the population reports a substantial inheritance; however of those whose wealth is over $500,000, 34 percent report a substantial inheritance.

7. From 1950-1970, the bottom one-fifth's share of total personal income rose only one percent - from 4.5 percent to 5.5 percent.

8. In 1968, the average family in the poorest one-fifth had an annual income of $3,085 per year, while the average income for a family in the highest one-fifth was $21,973 per year.

When you see statistics like that, you become convinced that money is a problem. If they tell us nothing else, they show that the greatest nation can not solve money problems.

I. It is not Money.

This is one reason we are told by God that money is not the greatest investment we will ever make in life. This chapter is about the greatest investment you will ever make. The first point simply is, it is not money. But why not?

In Matthew 6:19, 20, Jesus says, *"Do not lay up for yourselves treasures upon earth, where moth and rust destroy, and where thieves break in and steal. But lay up for yourselves treasures in heaven, where neither moth nor rust destroys, and where thieves do not break in and steal." Notice also verse 24, "No one can serve two masters; for either he will hate the one and serve the other, or he will hold to one and despise the other. You cannot serve God and mammon* (money)."

What does money have to do with a book on love? Very much, because although people in general are willing to say love is the greatest investment they can ever make, in truth men serve and love money far more than they serve or love God, or love. It is serving the "almighty buck" instead of the almighty God. That is really where America stands as a nation today.

It is very important to get this point clearly in mind in order to understand what really is the greatest investment we can make in life. We are all a part of this society in which the pursuit of money is so prevalent. We are unable to clearly appreciate what love is really all about unless we first remove whatever cobwebs are in our thinking with regard to money.

Is money really bad? No, money in itself is good. Money is a wonderful thing. It is a convenient, efficient medium of exchange. It represents power, but so often it is used for wrong goals. That is why Paul told Timothy to spread the word throughout the churches that the love of money is the root of all evil. That is why we should not make money our greatest investment in life. Even if there were not so many evils in the misuse of money, it would still not be the greatest investment you could ever make, because even properly used money is subject to the "moth" and "rust" that destroy, and the thieves that break in and steal. Even if those things were not a threat to your money, one day your money will completely disappear and in your eternal state the only currency will be the money of love.

A financial investment is certainly not the greatest investment you can ever make, and yet how hard it is for people to learn that lesson well. Practically, we have a problem. The rich man in the story told by Jesus said to himself, *"Soul, you have many goods laid up for many years to come; take your ease, eat, drink and be merry. But God said to him, "You fool, this very night your soul is required of you; and now who will own what you have prepared?"* (Luke 12:19, 20).

II. It is not Humanitarianism.

Would to God we could learn that lesson. Would to God that we could also realize that the greatest investment in life is not humanitarianism.

A. Whether it is for Family.

Erotic love in its proper perspective is wonderful in the bonds of matrimony and family. But as wonderful and powerful as it is, it is not the same as the Christian love spoken of in I Corinthians 13. Romantic love can not compare to Christian love, neither can a man's love for his wife or children. The love of a man for his wife and children, which causes him to give his life for them and which causes him to dedicate his whole being to their provision, protection and preservation, as great as all that is, is not Christian love.

B. Whether it be for Friends.

May I go a step further? The love spoken of in this chapter is greater than the love of a friend for his friend. No matter how great a friend's love may be for his other friends, it can not compare to Christian love. A man can love a friend so much that he'll die in his place, but that still is not the love spoken of in I Corinthians 13. That is why the apostle says, *"Though I give my body to be burned and give all my possessions to feed the poor, but have not love, it profits me nothing."*

C. Whether it be for Strangers.

There is also philanthropic love that embraces strangers, the poor and the needy. If we provide for them and care for them to the point of giving up all we own, even our very lives, even that is not the love spoken of in this chapter. Such love is not the greatest investment a person can make. Humanitarianism in the world, no matter how great it might be, is not love as the Bible speaks of it here. Therefore, it cannot be considered the greatest investment you can ever make. It is not money, it is not humanitarianism, then what is it?

III. It is Love.

Having considered what the best investment is not, not let is consider what the best investment is. What is it? *"But now abide faith, hope, love, these three; but the greatest of these is love."* The greatest investment we can ever make in life is the love of God. It is so great that even faith and hope cannot be compared to it. Love surpasses all that went into the foundation of the church, all the miracles of raising the dead, healing the blind and the sick, speaking in tongues and all the other miraculous gifts. All the gifts of preaching and teaching are not to be considered the greatest investment in life. Even sharing Christ with someone else is not the greatest investment. No, it is love, self-giving love.

To define love once more; it is what you do to someone else without any thought of return. It is what you give to someone without any consideration whether they deserve it of not. It is unconditional in character. It is all-inclusive. It is giving your life for people for their highest good and for God's highest glory. That is love.

That is the only thing in this world worth investing in. Why? Because it is the only thing that will last beyond death. Look at the text: "But now abide faith." Now, the present time. Even faith and hope are now. We will use them and they are great to invest in now, but even faith and hope will not go beyond the grave. Why? Look at verse seven: "Love is so fulfilling, so self-containing, and so complete and central that it has all it needs within itself. Love is everything, absolutely, and it will even carry us through eternity. It is the atmosphere of heaven as well as the currency for earth for the believer in Christ.

Application

Augustine had it right when he said this: "Love is so inclusive that it even takes the four cardinal virtues of Greek philosophy and supersedes them as well as fulfills them. Temperance, fortitude, justice and prudence." Temperance is nothing more than love keeping itself entire and uncorrupted for God. Fortitude is nothing but love bearing readily everything for the sake of God. Justice is serving God only and therefore fulfilling well all else as subject to men. Prudence is love making a right distinction between what helps it toward God and hinders it from God. Love even fulfills faith because love hopes all things.

In the days of Archibald Rutledge, a preacher died, but his widow kept on serving people, helping the poor, nursing the orphans, helping other widows. Archibald Rutledge was so pleased and thrilled with this widow's service for the Lord that he built her a beautiful home in his own backyard. The first day it was open, she invited the most disreputable woman of the community. Rutledge took her aside and said, "What did you do that for? Why did you have this woman in your home on my property?"

Her answer was, "Jesus would, that's why!"

Our hearts agree with the answer, Jesus would. Jesus would. That is just like Jesus, that is unconditional love, the only thing worth investing in for time and eternity.

Part Three

God's Exemplification of Love

The disciples are gathered around the Lord Jesus, listening to Him teach the Upper Room Discourse (John 13 through 16). One of the most important truths he taught was this: "Greater love has no man than this, that he lay down his life for his friends." What love that is, that would actually drive a person to give his life for someone else. Such love is applied love. Such love is love in action. But the question comes, how did the disciples who learned this truth apply it? What record do we have in God's Word that shows just what these men did?

In the book of Acts, we find that God has given just such a record. Luke writes, *"The first account I composed, Theophilus, about all that Jesus began to do and teach."* (Acts 1:1). The link between the Upper Room teaching and how the disciples applied it later is found in the word "began." Luke was the author of both the Gospel of Luke and the book of Acts. Referring to his gospel, he says it simply is what Jesus Christ began to do and teach. In the gospel of Luke we see Christ doing and teaching in His earthly body, whereas in Acts we see what He does and teaches from the Father's right hand, in His glorified body, through His disciples. In the book of Acts we see the unfolding of the obedience of the earthly disciples to the teachings of Christ.

For that reason I have chosen to use this book to review the 17 characteristics of love as we have already discussed.

Notice in I Corinthians 13 that there are three dimensions of love: negative, positive and superlative. There are eight characteristics of love in the negative, indicating what love is not. Love is not jealous, boastful, arrogant, discourteous, selfish, provoked, unforgiving or unseemly. Then there are seven characteristics of love in the positive; love is patient, kind, rejoicing, responsible, believing, optimistic and enduring.

In the third place, there are some superlatives about love in I Corinthians 13:8 and 13. It never ends and it is the greatest. Now consider the book of Acts and see how the disciples applied all of these dimensions of love.

I. The Negative Dimension.

A. Love is Not Jealous (2:14).

"But Peter, taking his stand with the 11, raised his voice and declared to them: 'Men of Judea, and all of you who live in Jerusalem, let this be known to you and give heed to my words.'"

The day the church began there were 11 other apostles with Peter as he preached. But there was not a trace of jealousy. That was love in action. They all were not preaching, although the others had listened to Jesus Christ teach in His earthly life. Only one did the preaching. Note how it is described: *"taking his stand with the 11, he raised his voice."* The rest, I'm sure, were praying, supporting, and loving. They were not jealous.

B. Love is Not Boastful (3:11-13).

"And while he was clinging to Peter and John, all the people ran together to them at the so-called portico of Solomon, full of amazement. But when Peter saw this, he replied to the people, 'Men of Israel, why do you marvel at this, or why do you gaze at us, as if by our own power or piety we have made him walk? The God of Abraham, Isaac, and Jacob, the God of our fathers, has glorified His Servant Jesus, the one whom you delivered up."

Peter made the point that he had not done a thing, that John had not done a thing, that none of the apostles had done a thing in the healing of this man. They gave glory to God. They boasted in the grace of God, if they boasted at all. Love did not boast in this case, because they gave God the glory for the great things He had done.

C. Love is Not Arrogant (4:13).

"Now as they observed the confidence of Peter and John and understood that they were uneducated and untrained men, they were marveling, and began to recognize them as having been with Jesus." The power of the love of God in Christ did not puff up these men with pride or arrogance, but rather it enabled people to see Jesus puffed up in them, so to speak. That was true, even in the midst of the great works done by these men.

D. Love is Not Discourteous (5:40, 41).

"And they took Gamalie's advice and after calling the apostles in, they flogged them and ordered them to speak no more in the name of Jesus, and they released them." The occasion for such flogging was the evangelism by the Christians in Jerusalem. The response of the apostles to the flogging is what we want to see in verse 41: *"So they went on their way from the presence of the Council, rejoicing that they had been considered worthy to suffer shame for His Name."* Being so positively absorbed in rejoicing, and in considering it a privilege to suffer for Jesus, there was no chance for any sort of discourtesy.

E. Love is Not Selfish (6:37).

"But select from among you, brethren, seven men of good reputation, full of the Spirit and of wisdom, whom we may put in charge of this task. But we will devote ourselves to prayer, and to the ministry of the word. And the statement found approval with the whole congregation." Such unselfishness really won the hearts of the whole congregation, which by this time included at least 8,000 people. Note in verse 7: *"And the Word of God kept on spreading."* When Christians are unselfish, the Word of God spreads. That is an unfailing law. When Christians stop being selfish, the church increases.

F. Love is Not Provoked (15:37).

"And Barnabas was desirous of taking John, called Mark, along with them also. But Paul kept insisting that they should not take him along who deserted them in Pamphylia and had not gone with them to the work. And there arose such a sharp disagreement." Even in the early church, men disagreed. The disagreement was so bad that Barnabas took Mark and

went on to Cyprus, while Paul went a different way with Silas. The reason for the disagreement was that Paul was not loving in this case. Paul was provoked with John Mark. On the first missionary journey he turned back and went home. But does that mean that the Apostle Paul should have held it against him? Note what finally happened because Barnabas loved John Mark and gave him another chance. In II Timothy 4:11 Paul says, *"Only Luke is with me. Pick up Mark and bring him with you, for he is useful to me for service."* Thanks to the love of Barnabas, John Mark was redeemed for the Lord's service. This is a lesson to learn.

G. Love is Not Unforgiving (16:19-25).

"But when her masters saw that their hope of profit was gone, they seized Paul and Silas and dragged them into the market place before the authorities, and when they had brought them to the chief magistrates, they said, 'These men are throwing our city into confusion, being Jews, and are proclaiming customs.' And when they had inflicted many blows upon them, they threw them into prison, commanding the jailer to guard them securely; and he, having received such a command, threw them into the inner prison, and fastened their feet in stocks." Did Paul and Silas demand their rights? As a result of such treatment, did they cry for revenge? No! *"But about midnight Paul and Silas were praying and singing hymns to God."* The next time you are unjustly treated, do what Paul and Silas did, pray, praise God and leave any kind of retribution to Him. Do not try to justify yourself; do not try to get even.

H. Love is Not Unseemly (16:26-34)

After the earthquake, *"Immediately all the doors were opened and everyone's chains were unfastened. And when the jailer had been roused out of his sleep and had seen the prison doors opened, he drew his sword and was about to kill himself, supposing that the prisoners had escaped. But Paul cried out with a loud voice, 'Do yourself no harm, for we are all here!' And he called for lights and rushing in and, trembling with fear, he fell down before Paul and Silas. And after he brought them out, he said, 'Sirs, what must I do to be saved?'"* When we learn to be so loving to people that we do not even laugh inside when they are wrong, and hurt, and harmed, they will leap out of the kingdom of darkness and beg us to show them the way to salvation. Love does find a way.

When we exert our self-control in our actions, endeavoring to be loving, people get saved, even through our lives.

I. Love Never Acts Like a Failure (16:35-17:9)

In this passage we see the officials at Phillipi begging Paul and Silas to leave the city because they discovered they were Roman citizens. But they did not fail to fulfill their ministry before they left. Paul and Silas with sorely beaten backs, rebuked the chief magistrates by their boldness. They left the prison, but not as yet the city. Because love never fails, they went to the believers in the city and strengthened them in their faith. Finally, they departed but only to go on to Thessalonica where they kept on ministering the Word of God. What a portrayal of love never failing in such indefatigable men of God!

II. The Positive Dimension.

Now we pass on to the positive dimension of love.

A. Love is Patient (18:24).

"Now a certain Jew named Apollos, an Alexandrian by birth, an eloquent man, came to Ephesus; and he was mighty in the Scriptures. This man had been instructed in the way of the Lord; and being fervent in spirit, he was speaking and teaching accurately the things concerning Jesus, being acquainted only with the baptism of John." Apollos was limited in his teaching. As a result, Priscilla and Aquila *"took him aside and explained the way of God more accurately."* The key phrase is, *"they took him aside,"* and in patience and love showed him the more accurate way.

How love works! Note the effect it had upon him: *"And when he wanted to go across to Achaia, the brethren encouraged him and wrote to the disciples to welcome him; and when he had arrived, he helped greatly those who had believed through grace; for he powerfully refuted the Jews in public, demonstrating by the Scriptures that Jesus was the Christ."* Apollos could preach that way, thanks to loving, gracious, patient Priscilla and Aquila.

B. Love is Kind (20:7).

"And on the first day of the week, when we were gathered together to break bread, Paul began talking to them, intending to depart the next day, and he prolonged his message until midnight." The first act of kindness here is the congregation. They let Paul preach until midnight. Only a kind

congregation will let you do that.

Second, Paul was kind. We see his kindness in what followed. A man called Eutychus fell asleep while Paul was preaching. I cannot imagine the Apostle Paul letting anyone fall asleep in his preaching. "And there was a certain man named Eutychus sitting on a windowsill, sinking into a deep sleep; and as Paul kept on talking, he was overcome by sleep and fell down from the third floor, and was picked dead. But Paul went down and fell upon him and after embracing him, he said, 'Do not be troubled, for his life is in him.' And they took away the boy alive, and were greatly comforted." Paul was upset by John Mark's failure, but this case he healed the young man. Only love can change a man like that.

C. Love Rejoices (20:18-25).

"And when they had come to him, he said to them, 'You yourselves know, from the first day that I set foot in Asia, how I was with you the whole time, serving the Lord with all humility and with tears and with trials which came upon me through the plots of the Jews; how I did not shrink from declaring to you anything that was profitable, and teaching you publicly and from house to house." Here is a commentary on what it means to rejoice in truth. It does not mean saying, "I am happy for my Bible and here is the reason why." It means giving out the word of truth in all kinds of persecution, and still being happy for the privilege. It means giving your all and spending yourself in every house in town. Paul did this all through the city of Ephesus, a city of 500,000 people. But even when the people of Asia turned against him (II Timothy 1:15), he was practicing love. He could have recalled the words of Jesus, in the great Sermon on the Mount, that when you are persecuted for righteousness sake, you are to rejoice and be exceedingly glad. That is what rejoicing in truth means; that is part of being loving.

D. Love is Responsible. (20:26-27).

"Therefore I testify to you this day, that I am innocent of the blood of all men. For I did not shrink from declaring to you the whole purpose of God." Love bears responsibility. It does not hear only the command, "Reach your neighbors for Christ," and then forget. It hears it and then does it. The Christian who does not win souls is an unloving Christian. It is not a lack of knowledge, it is not a lack of confidence, it is not a lack of gifts, it is a lack of love. If Christians take this truth and put it into action, we

would see tremendous church growth.

E. Love is Believing (21:14).

"And since he would not be persuaded, we fell silent, remarking, 'The will of the Lord be done!'" A person, convinced of the truth of the Scriptures, finds it very difficult to watch believers grow so slowly. We get impatient with their lack of growth. However, even after we do our best to help them, we have to say with those disciples who did not convince Paul, *"The will of the Lord be done."* God can give us that conviction, that expression of love, after having done all we can. Once we have done that, and still there is no response, we must believe that God's will shall be done. Therefore, do your best and commit the rest.

F. Love is Optimistic (23:10-24).

Paul was not persuaded by the Ephesian elders to stay away from Jerusalem. At first he was greatly welcomed by the people. He told the Christians about all the great works God had done in the difficult cities of Asia and Europe. So great was the report that the Jews found out; and the Jews maneuvered to get him arrested. They wanted to have him executed. Paul tried to defend himself before the council in Jerusalem, but such a dissension among the council members broke out, that the commander of the troops was afraid for Paul's life. So he *"ordered the troops to go down and take him away from them by force, and bring him back into the barracks. But on the night immediately following, the Lord stood at his side and said, 'Take courage; for as you have solemnly witnessed to my cause at Jerusalem, so you must witness at Rome also.' And when it was day, the Jews formed a conspiracy and bound themselves under an oath, saying that they would neither eat nor drink until they had killed Paul. And there were more than forty that formed this plot. And they came to the chief priests and the elders, and said, 'We have bound ourselves under a solemn oath to taste nothing until we have killed Paul.'"*

Even at a time like this, love is optimistic. You don't have to worry about protecting yourself when you are secure in the love of God. You can be a tough-minded optimist in the most antagonistic circumstances. At such times God will even get an army on your side, so to speak, as He did to rescue Paul. Paul went along like a little lamb. Why? Because he had the power of the love of God.

G. Love is Enduring (28:16-18).

"And when we entered Rome, Paul was allowed to stay by himself, with the soldier who was guarding him. And it happened that after three days he called together those who were the leading men of the Jews, and when they had come together, he began saying to them, 'Brethren, though I had done nothing against our people, or the customs of our fathers, yet I was delivered prisoner from Jerusalem into the hands of the Romans.

And when they had examined me, they were willing to release me because there was no ground for putting me to death.'" Paul was not released. He was in that house for two and one-half years, but oh the people who came to Christ! Love caused Paul to endure in the proclamation of the Gospel.

III. The Superlative Dimension (Acts 28:25).

The superlative dimension of love is our conclusion. This is in Acts 28:25-28: *"The Holy Spirit rightly spoke through Isaiah the prophet to your fathers."* Paul then gives the quotation: saying, *"Go to this people and say, 'You will keep on hearing, but will not understand; and you will keep on seeing, but will not perceive; for the heart of this people has become dull, and with their ears they scarcely hear, and they have closed their eyes; lest they should see with their eyes, and hear with their ears, and understand with their ears, and understand with their heart and turn again, and I should heal them.' Let it be known to you, therefore, that this salvation of God has been sent to the Gentiles, they will also listen."*

One thing is for certain: The Holy Spirit stayed with Paul to the very end. The love of God in Christ through Paul was lasting. In the last chapter of Acts, love is going greater than ever.

APPLICATION (ACTS 28:30-31).

"And he stayed two full years in his own rented quarters, and he was welcoming all who came to him, preaching the kingdom of God, and teaching concerning the Lord Jesus Christ with all openness, unhindered." The love of God abides; that is how the Book of Acts closes. The book has no real conclusion. Why? Because the direction of the Book of Acts is that the

acts of love should continue through Christians today. Why? Because love not only acts the greatest, it is the greatest!

Part Four

God's Expression of Love

The captain of a ship crossing the Atlantic said to a minister aboard, "We have just crossed over the place where the Titanic, the alleged unsinkable ship, went down!" Later the minister said, "I thought of all the wreckage beyond the power of man to recover and redeem. I thought of the great bed of the deep sea, with its treasures that are too far down for man to reach and restore. Too far down!" And then he thought of all the human wreckage there is engulfed and sunk in the depths of nameless sin. "Too far down! For what? Not too far down for the love of God!"

And yet, why is it that more people do not avail themselves of God's love? What is it about people that makes them so unbelieving about God's love? Recently someone told me, "I really don't believe that God will heal me, because I'm not really convinced that He actually loves me that much."

Such a statement accurately expresses the feelings of most people. It reminds me of one morning years ago when I wanted to feed the birds. It was grey and cold, and the ground was covered with snow. I stepped out on the porch with a handful of crumbs, and called to them. But they did not respond. There they sat, cold, hungry and afraid. They did not trust me. As I sat and watched and waited, it seemed to me that I understood God's viewpoint more clearly than ever before. He offers, He plans, He watches, He waits, He hopes, He longs for all things for our good. But He has to watch and wait, as I did for those timid birds.

Does this sound familiar? Is it possible that you don't trust God's love? Yet, John 3:16 still stands. Perhaps you need to understand.

You recall the story. Nicodemus was the elderly religious man who was a ruler of the Jews. He approached Christ in the middle of the night. Why then? Probably for two reasons: (1) because he wanted to speak with Christ privately and confidentially, not during the day when the crowds might have interfered with his conversation, (2) because he felt embarrassed, for he had to ask questions of Christ, the answers to which he, a prominent and religious leader, should have known.

Nicodemus had all the religion a man could offer, but not the reality of God's love inside his heart, which only Christ could offer. After Nicodemus expressed his absolute confidence in Christ, Christ responded in very direct and emphatic words: *"Truly, truly, I say to you, unless one is born again, he cannot see the Kingdom of God"* (3:3). The following explanation reaches its zenith and climax in 3:16: *"For God so loved the world that He gave His only begotten Son, that whoever believes in Him, should not perish, but have eternal life."* Without these words, Nicodemus would have been left right where he was. But because of these words, his life was changed. Anyone's life can be changed if they are willing to go the way of this verse.

The verse opens with the expression of God's love, "For God so loved the world." The word "so" means "in such a way." In what way is that? God's answer is: (1) by way of super sacrifice; (2) by way of simple surrender; (3) by way of solid security. It is the way of super sacrifice because, "He gave His only begotten Son." It is the way of simple surrender because, "whoever believes in Him." It is the way of solid security because of the words, "should not perish but have eternal life."

I. Via Super Sacrifice.

God loved the world, that is, the whole cosmos of men, including the Gentile and heathen, the whole human race in such a way that He gave His only begotten Son for it. That way of love goes quite far and wide. The Lord reveals love as the one ground of the divine counsel in the gift of His Son to man. What an expression of love! It was this that prompted God to give man the Savior. God's love expressed the benevolent, merciful feelings that He had for man, that He was so earnestly desirous of man's happiness. That's why gospel means glad tidings. To be sure, it is good news, the best and happiest in this universe!

The expression of God's love in terms of the super sacrifice of His own Son vividly reminds us of the offering of Isaac upon the altar. Abraham loved God so much that he was willing to give up his son to die on the altar of sacrifice in order to prove his love. Likewise, God loved the world in such a way that He gave up His Son to die on the altar of the cross for the sins of the world; to have His dear Son's life blood shed to wash away as well as cover the guilt of mankind. Surely Nicodemus, possibly remembering the story of Isaac, was quite impressed by the love that such a sacrifice required.

God's love is a free gift, unmerited, undeserved. He gave us His Son as an absolute gift, an unconditional gift. Man had no claim; and when there was no eye to pity, or arm to save, it pleased God to give His Son into the hands of men to die in their place. It was the expression of His eternal compassion, and His desire that sinners should not perish forever.

Not only was the gift God's Son, but also God's only begotten Son. This is a very interesting term in the Greek. It means "unique," one of a kind. How is He unique? Very simple, but yet profound. He was the only eternally born Son of God. Men can be the created sons of God, but only Christ is the eternally born Son of God.

That is why the gift of God's Son to the world is the highest expression of love that we can imagine. Should a parent give up his only son to die, if this could or might be done, this would show the highest love. This is how God manifested His love. This shows something of the depth of the love of God.

In St. Paul's Cathedral, London, there is a life-sized marble statue of Christ writhing in anguish on the cross. The statue is inscribed: "This is how God loved the world!"

Ironically, however such an expression of the love of God shows the depths of the sin of man. The sacrifice of Christ was only the means by which the redemption of man could be effected. Christ's death alone was sufficient to accomplish this gracious design. It would have been inconsistent with the wisdom of God to have appointed a sacrifice greater than itself or less in its merit than what the urgent necessities of the case required.

Consider the startling implications here. Our sin, the sin of mankind, any and all of the sins of the world, is so indescribably evil and terrible that it required no less sacrifice to make payment for it than God manifested in the flesh.

Why? Human beings by nature have a hard time believing that anyone really loved them, especially God. So by giving us His Son, God manifested His love for us. It is inescapable! God loves us. We know He does because He proved it by giving His Son. He did not just send His Son as an ambassador to negotiate peace between heaven and earth, but rather He gave up His Son to the world. Even though the Son was powerful enough to prevent anyone from taking His life, God gave it away. Nor was this done on the spur of the moment (cf. Acts 2:23). Before the world began, God the Father planned His determinate counsel to give Him up. He was slain before the foundation of the world! Before you and I were born, Christ died for us in the mind of God. Oh, what love!

Is it any wonder that Peter MacKenzie said, "There are two striking things in my text: When God loves He loves a world; when He gives, He gives a Son."

That is why fond parents say to a child, "How much do you love me?" The answer is usually a kiss and a hug. If you put the same question to our Heavenly Father, the answer is the cross!

II. Via Simple Surrender.

As great as this sacrifice was, no man is saved through this sacrifice unless he believes. He needs to surrender himself to the simple yet profound realization that God provided all that was necessary for his salvation in Christ. He must give God the credit. He must rely personally upon what God has spoken regarding Christ, His sacrifice, the end for which it was offered, and the way in which it is to be applied in order to become effectual. That is the meaning of the second part of the verse, "whoever believes in Him."

A. The Implication.

The "whoever" does not include angels, for the good angels do not need salvation, and yet they desire to look into what it is like. The fallen angels do not even have a chance. One-third of the angels of God fell with Lucifer, that is Satan, at the beginning, and yet none of them have ever had a chance to be saved. Man was created a little lower than the angels, and yet the fallen angels have not been included in God's offer of salvation.

In the fifth chapter of Mark, there is a very striking insight. The demon-possessed man, Legion, was called such because he had a legion of demons in him. According to the Roman Empire's measuring standard, a legion is equivalent to 6,000 to 12,000 men; it is the largest single unit of an army. Just imagine, one man is more important to God than 6,000 to 12,000 fallen angels!

On the other hand, "whoever" does not mean Jews only. The conceited Jews vainly imagined that the Messiah should be sent in love only to their nation. But God tells us that He sent His Son in love to the whole world! Whoever in this whole world believes in Christ can be saved!

Whoever in this whole world who has revolted and rebelled against God and broken His commandments can be included in God's love. There is no sin, there is no mistake, there is no fault, there is nothing that a person has done that is so bad that it can not be forgiven.

B. The Condition.

All that anyone has to do to be saved from his sin is to believe. However, we must not overlook the real meaning of the word "believe." We must not confuse it with the shallow, empty, meaningless concept that many Americans have.

When the late Donald Grey Barnhouse went to South America on a preaching tour during the latter part of his life, he was approached by a missionary who had a problem in translation. He was translating the Gospel of John from the Greek into a tribal dialect. His problem was how to translate the word "believe." The only word in the tribal dialect that was even closely equivalent to it was the word "believe-obey." The missionary was reluctant to use it because he was afraid of misleading the tribe into a doctrine of salvation by faith plus works.

To his surprise, however, Dr. Barnhouse exclaimed, "That's exactly what the word means!" The word believe in the Greek is not a cheap faith, or easy believism. It is a commitment. Such is really borne out in John 3:36: "He who believes in the Son has eternal life; but he who does not obey the Son shall not see life but the wrath of God abides on him." Note how the words, "believe" and "obey", are used interchangeably. The point, therefore, is to believe in Christ in such a way that your obedient will is backing up such belief. He who believes in this way shall have eternal life.

A minister was discussing electricity with an electrician. "Is it true," asked the minister, "that electricity cannot get into you unless it can get out of you?" "That's absolutely right," answered the electrician. "Let me illustrate. When I worked in the coal mines of Pennsylvania, my brother operated one of the coal cars. I was standing on the rear of the car, singing in a carefree manner, coming to the point where the tracks divided, and my head got caught in the overhead 'frog.' There I dangled for a moment, my feet just clearing the ground. That explains my being here today. The high voltage current could not get into me because it could not get out of me."

God's love is like electricity, it cannot get into us unless it can get out of us and share itself with others. And only a believe-obey faith will get it out of you, so that is how we must believe in Christ.

III. Via Solid Security.

Just what happens to a person who believes in Christ as the highest expression of God's love? God promises that such a person "shall not perish but have eternal life."

A. The Negative Aspect.

On the one hand, he will not perish. What does this mean? Its meaning is twofold: (1) "to be lost"; (2) "to perish, to suffer destruction." Which is it? Both! There need not be any ambiguity here because both meanings may be taken together, emphasizing all the more the hopeless condition of man without Christ. Such a person is on a downward trail, and the further down it goes, the worse off he gets, for he gets closer and closer to ultimate destruction, to which he is bound. In real life, perishing is not always sudden destruction. It can be and most always is a gradual process. Nevertheless, all forms of this word lead to destruction, which is the inevitable fate of all things and persons separated from God and concentrated upon themselves. There is no neutral ground between perishing and eternal life. They are absolute alternatives. But do not misunderstand: this is good news to a weary mind and a guilty conscience. Christ saves him from this. This is healing to broken bones and bleeding wounds, that Christ came not to condemn us to this perishing, but to save us from it.

B. The Positive Aspect.

Obviously, the preferable alternative is the positive aspect of eternal life. Notice, God does not say future life, but eternal life. It is the kind of life that implies not only the pardon of the convicted traitor, but also the preference, the making of him as a favorite, as his treatment in kingly honor.

Neither does God say temporal life; He says eternal life. It is a life that begins on earth the moment you believe, but because it is eternal, it lasts forever in time and eternity. It is also eternal in the sense that you can never lose it. Once you have got it, you always have it. Oh, what blessed eternal security!

If the Lord had been pleased to kill us, He would not have sent His Son among us. He came with full powers to execute judgment, which He most definitely will use upon those who do not believe. He died so that dying people in this dying world might enjoy eternal life before they die for good. This is the good news or glad tidings to a guilty conscience, to a sinner, to a person who is fed up with himself, to a person suffering in depression, loneliness, sickness and even death, that whoever believes may have eternal life. Yes, it is good news to whoever wants to start life over again, whoever wants new life, whoever wants God's life, whoever wants the breath of God, by believing in the Lord Jesus Christ. Do you believe? I hope you do, but if you do not, do so now. In the best way you know how, just trust in what Christ has done for you as the greatest expression of love.

The late Donald Grey Barnhouse and his wife went out one evening and left their children in the care of a baby-sitter. When they returned about midnight, the girl was greatly concerned that the oldest child had been crying for about four hours. Nothing the baby-sitter could do would comfort her. Dr. Barnhouse went to the child's room and found her flushed and sobbing, her face red with weeping. When he picked her up, she threw her arms around his neck and sobbed, "Daddy, say it isn't true. You do love me." He replied, "Of course, I love you." His little girl said, "The baby-sitter said that if I was bad, you wouldn't love me, and I know I've been bad, so maybe you don't love me."

He pressed her to himself and said, "My dear child, I always love you. When you are good, I love you with a love that makes me glad; when you are bad, I love you with a love that makes me sad. But I love you, good or bad. I am always your daddy."

The child was already calm and the dawn of a smile came to her face. He began to cover her gently with kisses and then he told her that a good daddy had to be with her as the Lord was with him, and with all of us who have become His children. She smiled and was soon asleep.

If you are still not fully convinced, consider this story: An English businessman visited a mission hospital for lepers in India. He was deeply impressed with the nurse's loving care of the suffering, repulsive-looking patients.

"Your humanitarian sentiment and sacrificial service for these outcasts is praiseworthy indeed," he said.

She replied, "I can assure you, sir, that if my continuance here was based only on humanitarian sentiments, I would not have the will to carry on. I would leave before nightfall. The constraining love of Christ enables me to carry on day by day."

A sad, distressed little girl told her pastor, "I want to love Jesus, but I can't do it."

The pastor said, "My dear little girl, stop thinking about your not being able to love Jesus. Just keep saying, 'Jesus loves me!' Say it to yourself many times every day."

Later the little girl returned to the pastor with a happy smile on her face. The pastor said, "I know you love Jesus. Your face tells me that you do!"

Go and do likewise!

11 DELEGATION

THE POWER OF DIVERSIFICATION

FEATURING

LON WEBER, PH.D.
SENIOR VICE PRESIDENT,
FREEDOMS FOUNDATION

"Do you wish to be free? Then above all things, love God, love your neighbor, love one another, love the common weal; then you will have true liberty."

-- Savonarola

When we look at the word delegation we conjure images in our minds of a work environment where the manager or supervisor has a series of projects that must be completed. This manager, we shall call him, has a staff of subordinates under his supervision who carry out his directives as may be issued. The manager will make a determination of the amount of work that is invested in each of these projects and will then issue a directive to one or a group of individuals under his charge to complete the task assigned. This is otherwise known as delegation.

Delegation mainly occurs because there is a certain workload, task or project that must be completed, but which may be too burdensome for one individual to handle. To ensure completion, the project is delegated to another with a lighter workload who can assure proper execution and completion. The main purpose of delegation is transference of a task to someone with the capacity to execute that task. This capacity is identified because of necessary special skills that would make a person ideally suited to the task, or even because of available time.

When one looks at the word diversification, one thinks about a variety or cross-section of people from different backgrounds who are brought together in one setting or environment. With diversification, there is a pool of individuals from a variety of different countries, cultures, languages, technologies and life experiences who are sharing, caring and learning from each other. The benefit of this symbiotic relationship is that the lives of participants in the pool are enriched. They are able to grow and develop a sensitivity and better understanding of alternate cultures and lifestyles.

How are the concepts of delegation and diversification related? The answer is that they both deal in freedoms. As noted earlier, delegation provides a person with freedom to manage time and develop a sense of other people's attitudes and manners of interaction. Diversification provides people with the opportunity of choice, the freedom to choose with whom they may interact, whether in business relations or personal relations.

The Freedoms' Foundation is committed to the goal of understanding our liberties and freedoms so that we become better informed citizens. This ultimately affects "life, liberty and the pursuit of happiness" for us all. The Freedoms' Foundation is a nonpartisan organization that is committed to instilling a sense of patriotism in all Americans.

The Foundation was instituted by Gen. Dwight D. Eisenhower in 1949. His mission was to bring people to the Foundation to educate them on the Constitution and Bill of Rights in order to foster greater participation. The rationale for this is that an educated people is at the core or strength of a nation.

One individual who is crucial to the successful implementation and execution of the Foundation's mission and programs is Lon Weber, Ph.D. Lon Weber is the senior vice president for education at the Freedoms Foundation located in Valley Forge, Pennsylvania. In this position he is responsible for all educational programs for young students and graduate students.

Lon Weber is a native of Wisconsin, where he completed studies for his Ph.D. in educational administration and philosophy. Lon has a "diverse" background that has at its core a solid and laudable commitment to education: He has served in a variety of leadership positions in colleges and universities across America. Lon has also served in various capacities on national and international levels as well. As evidenced above, Lon Weber is a person truly committed to public service. What is truly commendable is the role he played in the Gulf War. Immediately following the Gulf War of 1991, Lon was in the country of Jordan accommodating expatriates to their home to become valuable, productive and contributing citizens to their native country.

Lon is truly excited about his role in the Freedoms Foundation and its strong educational purpose. When asked why he decided to become involved in education, he responded that education is the foundation of our country and that

> ***"the Freedoms Foundation is committed to and is a vehicle for providing a strong foundation for***
> ***the basics and fundamentals of education, which stress reading, writing, arithmetic***
> ***. . .but also citizenship."***

One of the most memorable events in the life of Lon Weber occurred on April 9, 1968, when he had the opportunity to represent the University of Wisconsin at the funeral of Dr. Martin Luther King, Jr. Lon was extremely honored and reflected on this:

> ***"Martin Luther King, Jr. represented a positive attitude through his method of passive-nonviolence and was committed to doing very important things for this country."***

The position of senior vice president carries with it great responsibility and excellent opportunities for exercising leadership skills. Lon described his leadership style as "inclusive." Lon said, "I try to avoid using the perpendicular pronouns." He avoids the use of "I" because all efforts undertaken and completed by the Freedoms Foundation are the result of team accomplishment and therefore others should receive credit. Lon explained,

> ***"Inclusiveness allows people to become excited about what's going on.***
>
> ***In the final analysis, people will say, 'Yeah, we really did achieve this.'"***

When asked further how he would summarize his ongoing leadership, he quoted his favorite Latin expression: "omnia ma tantur nas et mat in illus," which is translated as: "All things are changing and we are changing with them." What a relevant statement about his key role at the Freedoms Foundation! In this decisive role as senior vice president for Education, Lon constantly would delegate to his staff and students. He firmly believes that although he delegates the duties to his staff and assignments to his students, he cannot delegate his authority as their leader.

Furthermore, Lon regards these as excellent opportunities for exercising his leadership skills, both directly and indirectly. Obviously, the direct aspect refers to upholding the dignity of his own authority, whereas the indirect is the more subtle one with regard to the dignity of his delegates, whether staff or students. You see, Lon's principle of no "perpendicular pronouns" is vitally relevant to the whole gambit of delegation. By using the pronouns "we" and "you" he fertilized the good soil of the self image and dignity in his delegates. Because delegation is the power of diversification, he enhances the unique identities of each and every person under his authority without causing them to feel "lorded over" or worse yet ; "manipulated."

Lon Weber's style is one of security, because he must be, first of all, secure within himself in order to be free and generous enough to focus on the "you" and "we" pronouns which, in turn, "build up" his delegates rather than "puff up" himself. Lon also reproduces his sense of security in his staff and students in light of the age old proverb, "What you sow you reap." Lon has a lot to be grateful for because he is leading his staff and students to learn and to grow in wholesome character qualities and personality development, not just theoretical content. Yes, changed lives for the better along with everything else changing is the best we will get in this world. That's how to keep on top of the current of civilization.

A word of qualification is in order here, because we don't want to give the impression that the absolutes change. The possession of authority does not change in the course of delegation, consequently the absolutes of truth, liberty, choice, love, etc., do not change. As positive change happens in the multitudes of things that are relative, the absolutes stabilize us and actually are contributing factors to our much needed positive changes.

Likewise, the color of one's skin does not change, but it's a healthy, wholesome reality for students of all colors to be under the leadership of a leader of leaders like Lon Weber. Why? Because he will be so focused on guiding all the students on the real changes needed, that everyone will forget the things that do not matter. Clearly, this is what it means to be an American. Lon's leadership style causes his students to get back to the basics and forward to the fundamentals.

What a great time to have a leader of leaders like this at Freedoms' Foundation, when just 25 miles east and 25 days ago the Presidential Summit for America's Future was celebrated in Philadelphia. Timing, timing, timing ; location, location, location, say the professional target marketers. Because that's all so perfectly true, the future of our youth appears to be in good hands. True, Freedoms Foundation, for which Lon Weber does his thing, is a national institution, even though it's in a nearby location. Yet, the President, Lon Weber's boss, is entirely committed to being a "good neighbor" to the local community. That's why I had the distinct privilege and honor of having Lon accompany me in my car to a Leader of Leaders strategy dinner at White Dog Cafe on 34th and Sansom in Philadelphia on Tuesday, May 13, 1997. There were 18 leaders of leaders present who represented many of the key spheres of influence both in the city and suburbs. All of us were utterly committed to building a model in our region for the rest of the nation as well as for ourselves. So in that, Lon Weber must have equally felt that we all were a good neighbor to the Freedoms Foundation.

Beyond doubt, there are many mountains still to climb, but it's so encouraging to have leaders like Lon Weber with whom to synergize. There will be times when the problems will seem insoluble. But even at the end of the rope, when we ourselves may feel completely victimized, leaders of leaders like Lon Weber, not only discern the solution, but also disengage themselves from the problem in order to become a part of the solution.

12 REVISION

THE POWER OF REVISITING

FEATURING

ROMAN KUPECKY

SENIOR PASTOR, ABRAMS COMMUNITY CHAPEL

"Where your pleasure is, there is your treasure;
where your treasure , there your heart;
where your heart, there your happiness."

--St. Augustine

The word "revise" has several meanings according to Merriam Webster's Collegiate Dictionary: "To look over again in order to correct or improve; to make a new, amended, improved or up-to-date version of." "Revisionism" is defined as "the advocacy of revision (as of a doctrine, a policy or in historic analysis)."

Revision is the technique we should use to continuously improve ourselves. As we pass through the various stages of our lives, even as we attend to our daily responsibilities, we should revisit what we have done and critique ourselves so that we can improve ourselves and our outlook.

Often many of us choose not to look back for fear of what we may see. It is difficult to stand in the face of criticism, to learn and to grow. However, taking a step back allows one to undertake a self-analysis that need not be publicized, unless one so chooses. We can find our faults as well as our strengths and merge these into a formula for greater expectations.

Today King of Prussia, Pennsylvania is the regional hub of a giant retailing complex–the King of Prussia Mall–attracting people from all over the world. Traffic races down the main thoroughfare, Route 202, night and day transporting thousands to visit this huge retailing complex that houses some of the nation's most prestigious retailers. This was not always so. Years ago, King of Prussia was principally a pastoral oasis devoid of commerce, industry, (and houses of worship). Into this void strode a man with vision, imagination and energy. He acted as a catalyst to prod politicians, business people, fraternal groups, media executives and a host of civic leaders into action. They undertook the monumental task of activating the resources needed to make King of Prussia a thriving bastion of economic growth. That person with vision was Karl Schauffele, a man of humble origins. He was destined, as a public servant, director of planning for Lower Merion Township, to provide the leadership necessary to propel the Main Line and its surroundings into a position of national prominence.

Roman Kupecky discovered this when he came to this area in 1990. Today King of Prussia is a superburbia; with the King of Prussia Mall at its heart. Traffic races down the main thoroughfare, Route 202, which overflows from vehicles spilled onto it by nearby arteries. Night and day the Pennsylvania Turnpike, Interstate 476 and Interstate 76 transport legions of visitors to this huge retailing complex. King of Prussia is at the crossroads of yesterday and today.

"The functions of the church, do not change but the forms by necessity must and do, or else the church will die!"
Roman Kupecky

When Roman Kupecky first came to Abrams Community Chapel in King of Prussia, Pennsylvania, as the new pastor in April of 1990, he found that some needed changes would have to be inaugurated. Intuitively he understood that those changes could not occur overnight. Roman opted to begin by revisiting the mission of the church. He took time to rethink and revise its goals. First and foremost, he realized that he must begin by demonstrating his own love of God, and his work for the congregation.

By revisiting the mission of the church, Pastor Kupecky connected with the heart and soul of not only the church itself, but also its founding members. The original deep sense of love that enveloped and bound together the first congregation continues to do so today. Always strong, this demonstration of the power of love has not wavered since its inception in 1867.

This ability to make powerful revisions is what makes Pastor Roman Kupecky a leader of leaders. Realizing that long-lasting revision is a slow process, he began to turn the wheels of progress slowly, carefully and deliberately so that over time, his revisions would bring the church to where it is today. It did not happen overnight, nor was it meant to happen quickly. Under his direction, the changes were always well planned and then gradually implemented to ensure that all needs of his beloved congregation were met. This is not the end of his story, for change is a continuous process that occurs on a daily basis. He is constantly revising and revisiting. Pastor Kupecky, in his wisdom, knows that life itself means change. In time, nearly everything must change: the weather changes, emotions change, people change, needs change; there is a season for everything. If we go forward to meet the needs of today, we will be better prepared when we revisit yesterday, for only then can we make proper revisions. This is the power that comes from the act of revisiting the past.

"As we talk about the role of the church and the change in the community, we can't be satisfied with the status quo."
Roman Kupecky

It is the wise person, such as Pastor Kupecky, who takes time to revisit the past, so that he might become more knowledgeable. Once we have truth and knowledge, we have the power to revise and to create change. The past has much to offer and the leader who travels there has much understanding to gain. In his case, the past revealed a wealth of information about the history of the church that enabled Roman to understand the basic, underlying premises, hopes and dreams of his congregation. This basic understanding and knowledge then enabled Roman to make revisions to his own plans so that they might best serve the needs of his present-day congregation.

Roman is that rare human being who possesses an acute sensitivity when it comes to discerning that which is positive and that which is negative. While focusing on the future, he wisely took time to revisit the church's beginnings. He looked at those who were instrumental in establishing the church and then studied those who picked up the threads of a shaky beginning to pursue the development of the new church. In comparison to those humble beginnings, the achievements that have occurred over the past century are a stark reminder that many people pursued and helped with this development.

A sense of community and the willingness of individual members of the congregation to accept personal responsibility are key to continued success. Each one is prepared to yoke together for the greater good of the church. In this way, the church serves as a role model to all within the community and outlying areas. This church is a living example of the power of love; this congregation is a living model of the body of Christ.

Located at the crossroads of Henderson and Beidler Roads is Abrams Community Chapel. It bears the name of a Welsh family who settled in the area. This particular family received a parcel of land from William Penn and this land soon came to be known as Abrams, as did other areas such as Abrams Creek and Abrams Mill. The origins of the chapel date back to the mid-1880's. During that time, two women, Sarah Berry and Ann Eastburn, set up a private fund for the maintenance of a chapel and its grounds. During this era, as farmland was portioned out to new families settling in the area, the new chapel came to be known as Abrams Community Chapel. Aided by a land donation received some years earlier, the fund these two women established enabled community members to develop building plans for Union Chapel which was dedicated in 1867.

This early, independent church followed the lines of Baptist teachings; although to this day, the congregation is still not affiliated with any formal denomination. Prior to World War I, the building fell into disuse and remained that way for some time. In 1932, due to the continued and dedicated efforts of several area women, the building was reopened and renamed as Abrams Union Chapel. It was so named to embody the meaning of community, a meaning that is still at this church's heart today. It was a place where people of varied denominations came to worship together. The small stone structure was used for regular Sunday afternoon classes. In 1941 evening services were added.

As the numbers of the congregation grew, the building was again renamed. The First Baptist Church of Abrams debuted in 1945 and offered regular morning and evening services along with Sunday school classes. In 1957 there was another name change when the building was rededicated as Abrams Community Chapel. At that time, an addition was added onto the rear of the original structure and a new chapel was dedicated in 1962. Although the building's outer appearance remains basically the same, the windows were renovated to their present rectangular shape and the chapel now has two levels, whereas the original structure had only a partial basement. According to rumors circulating amongst the congregation, it is said that the building reopened only after the women of the congregation literally dug out the basement with their bare hands, using shovels and trucks to carry away the soil. This project took three long years and eventually was completed by the men who cemented the walls and floor. They followed this up by installing a stairway. The present day parking area at the back of the property once housed horse stables. A stone marker dated 1872 indicates that the building now used as the parsonage was originally a one-room schoolhouse.

Having gained a knowledge and understanding of the church's history by taking time to revisit the past, Roman realized how he could help his congregation fulfill modern-day needs. He knew that it would necessitate using new approaches, with new guidelines, while still drawing on the church's traditions. A man of great and endearing warmth, I find Roman's greatest attribute to be his understanding of his own role. He seeks to be a genuine servant of the people. In this way, he has enveloped the entire congregation in an atmosphere of love and understanding. He continues to put the congregation first by ministering to their needs. It is only after those needs are met that his projects receive attention.

"Everyone can make a difference with someone."

Roman Kupecky

Clearly taking the time to research and to study the history of the church allowed him to see that from the very beginning, its guiding principle was importance of community. This has been carried forward to the present. What could be more precious or Christ-like than the sense of honoring, loving, and caring for one another? This dedication to community is the very heart of Abrams Community Chapel.

Rather than demanding sudden changes, his enlightening sermons from the Word of God have shown the people over time that there are ways to both accomplish goals and fulfill needs. He offered suggestions; the congregation listened and learned. They understood and accepted that carefully planned changes could be implemented to meet their needs. Most of all they knew that, first and foremost, their pastor's concern was for the congregation and its members.

Today, in addition to Sunday activities, Abrams Community Chapel offers many opportunities for Bible study and fellowship throughout the week. For children ages four and five, there is *Discovery Hour*; while there is *Primary Church* available for first through fourth graders that provides a meaningful worship experience. Classes and activities are also available to support parents who wish to establish a firm Christian foundation for their children. The *Adventure Kid's Club* offers learning experiences through teaching, games, small group interaction and solid spiritual content in a physically active and inspirational context.

The children's choir and musical program provide a mechanism for teaching children through music, providing many occasions for joyful events and times for family sharing. *Crossfire* is a middle school ministry for fifth to eighth graders and is geared toward building relationships, while reaching students through outreach events and retreats. *Pierced*, the high school ministry, attracts and builds faith through relevant Bible teachings, worship, games and fun times. *People Advancing Christ* or PAC for short, is a program for college students and young adults that provides support and encouragement through interactive Bible study in a small group format.

Adult ministries offer opportunities to those dealing with similar issues in life. Small groups are built around love, instruction, fellowship and encouragement. All of the foregoing ministries are designed to cultivate a relationship with God through spiritual gifts and evangelism.

After serving for seven years as pastor of Abrams Community Chapel, Roman has no regrets. He is filled with joy and satisfied that his congregation has now reached a point where they are ready to grow after all these years of careful planning and revision. In helping them to revisit the past, he is patiently guiding, loving and teaching the word of God. In spite of the fact that his many responsibilities include preaching, teaching, administrative duties and counseling, his role of pastor remains his utmost concern.

Uncompromising in his dedication to his primary goals, Roman's total commitment has finally brought him and his congregation to its present stage of development. While, he is pleased that he has fulfilled his initial goals of revisiting old traditions and revising ways in which his flock can serve their fellow man, he knows that there will always be new goals to attain, new visions to achieve, and new missions to address. He also knows that meaningful change does not happen overnight. It takes carefully thought out planning. Vision is not enough. He knows that each step requires careful planning so the journey goes smoothly and the goal is realized.

While setting new goals, Roman continues to play the role of the faithful shepherd who welcomes new challenges. He is always expecting the unexpected, thus he is able to prepare for obstacles along the way. In this manner, he is able to sidetrack many problems because of his realistic, methodical approach. Today he prays for 20 acres of land on which to build a new place of worship, a facility of supervised recreation that would be a place to express God's love to thousands. He continues to envision worship services that would draw his flock ever closer to God. He envisions this church as a haven for those who seek meaning in their lives. His vision includes cutting-edge youth ministries, servant evangelism projects, Bible studies, and opportunities for fellowship. He sees a giving, caring congregation, one that welcomes those in doubt so that they may become new believers. Roman always keeps in mind that the purpose of Abrams Community Chapel is "to express love for God by obeying the command of the Lord to make disciples. Our goal is to develop people who demonstrate Christ."

Therefore, Roman is committed to encouraging Christians through gathered worship, consistent biblical teaching, united prayer, involvement in ministry training, personal evangelism, world mission and active practical service; "all to the glory of God."

"I talk a lot about grace."

Roman Kupecky

The congregation views its mission as creating a bonded community of believers to make and develop fully devoted followers of Jesus Christ, all to the glory of God. Their vision is based on four principles:

To be expressions of biblical Christianity by actively becoming involved in the needs of the church and community.

Expose each person to the reality of Jesus Christ through culturally relevant means.

Develop people who demonstrate Christ.

Facilitate every believer's ministry through the development and exercise of spiritual gifts.

These four basic principles have remained unchanged and are the very heart of Abrams Community Chapel. This deeply dedicated congregation's regional vision is to raise up community churches that reach out to the "unchurched community" (planting churches). Their continued vision for the world is to "facilitate ministry globally through support and training."

"Do you want to become difference-makers in people's lives?"
Roman Kupecky

This congregation sees the role of one who demonstrates Christ as one who participates in worship, in small groups, in ministry, and in outreach. In this sense they know that each and every member of the body of Christ and the church has its own function and is vital to the whole. Everyone is important at Abrams Community Chapel. The sense of community and family is their greatest strength. As a leader of leaders, Pastor Roman Kupecky is truly guiding his congregation to achievement and success–all for the glory of God.

13
Supervision

The Power of Supportiveness

Featuring

Jon D. Fox
U.S. Congressman

"Next to love,
sympathy is the divinest passion
of the human heart."
-- Edmund Burke

"Fifty percent of the women with cervical cancer in the United States have never had a pap smear. This (Women's Preventive Health Care Act) is an opportunity to improve the health of women by providing access to much-needed preventive care."

— Jon D. Fox, U.S. Congressman

The role of the supervisor is to guide and direct the trainee each and every step of the way. The supervisor serves in an almost parental role, for the supervisor must support and encourage the trainee from the time he begins to take those first hesitant steps and subsequently learns to walk on his own. With that accomplishment, trainees are likely to think they have conquered all, but people must learn to walk before they can run. The supervisor encourages and supports the trainee as he struggles to meet and overcome the challenges of each step along the way.

The great supervisor is able to lead, educate, train, oversee, discipline and organize with clarity. He is constantly aware of all around him, yet is able to maintain his focus on the achievement of the end goal. As his trainees develop and mature, he instinctively knows when to encourage them to take on greater responsibilities. His discerning eye spots the supervisory skills in certain ones and in time, he gladly passes the torch on to those who have proven themselves worthy to take on the role of supervision themselves. Thus, a cycle reaches completion and a new one begins as it was meant to be, for "there is a time and season for all things."

Supervision must be handled with clarity, discipline and organization. Not only must the supervisor clearly see the vision of the goal, he must see how to take the steps to achieve the goal. More than that, he must be aware that there will be twists and turns along the way. He knows in advance that this one or that one is likely to stumble and he must have the foresight to prepare himself to lead the way regardless of any and all obstacles. He knows to prepare for the unexpected and how to plan for detours when necessary.

Armed with foresight, the supervisor exhibits self-discipline and instills that same quality in all of his team players. He must be the "master of multi-tasking": able to simultaneously organize and oversee many people, roles and responsibilities. Above all, he is "guardian of the glue." He creates cohesiveness, perceiving when and how much glue needs to be applied to each part so that the pieces of the puzzle come together to form a whole.

A good supervisor has an innate sense of timing and intuition. He knows when each one on the team is ready and must be encouraged to take the next higher step. And while he must be adept at creating a sense of family and belonging amongst the trainees, he is keenly aware of each team member as an individual, noting the strengths and skills of each trainee.

Supervisors who keep their standards high demonstrate to their constituents the importance of so doing. High standards require that each one must reach deep inside to find and then give to others the best that they have to offer. They know nothing less will suffice.

The wise supervisor knows where and how to guide his team, even though the team members do not always understand either the intent or direction in which they are being led. The good supervisor always keeps his focus on the desired end result and is dedicated to fulfilling his role, for he, too is dedicated to giving his best. If the leaders have moments of doubt, they have only to look to Jesus as their own role model.

Those who bother to look, will see in the New Testament that although Jesus had entrusted the 12 disciples with evangelistic responsibility, he did not look upon them as finished products. He knew they needed further supervision, more examples and more encouragement. He knew that even in the limited amount of redemptive work in which they were engaged, they still needed consistent supervision.

Jesus continued to meet with them. He followed their tours of service. He heard their reports. He continued to share with them. He understood their difficulties, as well as their victories because of His own firsthand experiences. These incidents of supervision were not isolated events, for Jesus maintained constant fellowship with them, and in this way he was able to chart their progress and oversee their work at all times.

We can see, throughout his ministry, that Jesus used the experiences of the disciples, whether they represented personal successes or failures, as raw materials with which to constantly teach them more. He applied his principles to their daily lives so they could truly understand what he expected of them. His standards were high, yet he was the Supreme Supervisor, ever alert to their every action and reaction.

While they did not understand his role of supervisor, they knew that supervision was part of the process that eventually would equip them for the ministry that they would soon undertake on their own. In the end, when he did finally leave them to return to the Father, he promised them the Holy Spirit would continue to supervise and oversee their work.

Knowing the Great Comforter was at hand enabled the disciples to continue on with their work, for his presence meant they were not alone. They could feel his holy presence; they could call upon or lean upon him at any and all times. The presence of the Holy Ghost made it possible for them to accomplish what others saw as impossible.

And so it must be today. Leaders must equip people to deal with everyday life, on a personal level and within the business world. A supervisor cannot presume that he can merely show people what must be done. True leaders and supervisors realize that the successful completion of one task does not necessarily mean that a trainee is ready to be on his own. Each success that a trainee achieves today builds upon his success of yesterday. It is a building, strengthening process as each one continues to grow. Close supervision is what brings trainees into an eventual place of maturity.

Trainee leaders do not come into maturity overnight, any more than a little child becomes an adult overnight. It is a slow, steady, incremental process. The wise supervisor does not push his trainees beyond their capacities, nor does he burden them with impossible requests or assignments. He is astutely aware of each one's developmental stage and assigns tasks appropriate to each one's progress. He knows that a task successfully completed instills confidence and that each success prepares the trainee to reach higher levels of success. Nothing is left to chance, for the wise leader prepares his trainees well, giving them the best that he himself has to give. In so doing, he instills the same qualities and desires within each team member. He leads his team with his consistent examples and deeds, never faltering along the way. By choice he accepts responsibility and in turn, personifies the strengths of a real leader.

A supervisor must walk a fine line, serving as an exemplary role model at all times. He must not demand too much, too soon from the trainee. When the trainee stumbles along the way, the good supervisor is there to tend the scraped knee with loving concern. He must know when to say, "Job well done" or "Time to dust yourself off and try again."

The good supervisor never pushes his trainees beyond their own capacities or developmental abilities. He understands the growth process, knowing that there are likely to be those sudden spurts ahead, followed by little lapses along the way. He knows the process is not smooth nor always predictable, yet he is able to remain flexible to meet a need at any given moment.

After five years with Southwestern Company, I felt totally and completely satisfied that I had attained everything I could possibly desire from this experience and then some. And yet, my heart ended up persuading me to remain for two more years. Why? Because my boss, who had been such a tremendous help to me, now needed my help. He asked me to stay on for two more years to serve in a supervisory role for others.

After much discussion, we both realized it would take at least two more years to train certain key persons so they could eventually take my place. We knew that in spite of their optimism, they were not yet ready to take on the role. Thus I agreed to stay on and closely supervise eighty men to that end. I willingly devoted my time and energy, knowing that the end result would and could be achieved. Realistically I also knew it would take time and I pledged to give my all.

In this way, I provided supervision as it had been provided for me, while instilling that same quality of responsibility in my trainees. I knew that they must understand that in order to be successful, one must never forget two things: from whence one has come and where one is headed. One must never become so full of self that he forgets those who have helped him along the way and in turn, he must reach out to help those who come on board. One must always think of and remember that success is not a singular achievement attained by a lone individual; success is created with the help of many. In my case, my role as supervisor eventually bore the fruit I expected. But, as I realized, the reproduction of the fruit could not be hurried along. It could only develop and ripen in its own time.

Have you ever asked yourself what ever happened to the statesman in politics? We all remember Abraham Lincoln, Thomas Jefferson and George Washington. What about modern day statesmen? As we survey the present roster of politicians in our nation's capital, do we really see any great statesmen? I personally agree there is at least one and it is why my nomination for the Leader of Leaders Award in the political sector is for Congressman Jon D. Fox.

Webster's New World Dictionary defines a statesman as "a person who shows wisdom and skill in conducting state affairs or dealing with public issues." This eloquently describes Congressman Jon Fox. Jon Fox's wisdom is evident because he supports those he serves. As a public servant, Fox has dedicated 15 years to serving others. He has been involved in numerous pieces of legislation which include his authorship of recent anti-crime legislation that increases the penalties for those convicted of jury or witness tampering. He was also instrumental in reforming the Food & Drug Administration approval process which accelerated the approval process for life-saving and life-extending drugs to the public. Another piece of legislation which Fox supported provided educational benefits to the children and spouses of federal agents killed in the line of duty. He also fought to end the practice of pet theft by reforming the current system of buying and selling animals used for biomedical research.

As further evidence of his dedication to public service, Jon serves on a number of groups including the House Task Force on Reform, the Human Rights Caucus, the Organ Donor Caucus, the Task Force on Health and the Congressional Children's Working Group.

Prior to his congressional service, Fox served as vice chairman of the Montgomery County Board of Commissioners. While there, he led the fight to decrease property taxes and helped restructure local government to run more efficiently. He also worked to establish a first-time home buyer's program, a historic open space preservation program, a Commission on Women, youth intervention programs, to enhance the 911 emergency communication system and initiated a project to reduce government spending.

In recent months, the House passed an amendment offered by Fox that increased funding for the Foster Grandparent program. This program pairs low-income adults with "at-risk" children giving each a new lease on life.

> ***"We need to have citizens adequately trained to both identify the problem and to assist those who are victimized by it.***
>
> ***We need to lead a national rebellion against violence and abuse toward women, children and our senior citizens."***

Jon D. Fox, U.S. Congressman,
speaking on the subject of domestic abuse

Jon Fox definitely exemplifies supervision, the power of supportiveness in many ways. He supervises with clarity, discipline, and organization. His high standards and expectations serve as role models. These virtues are founded upon seven pillars of truth. These seven pillars are the seven channels of communication, characteristic of the New Testament church in the first century. These seven pillars are:

- **Worship**
- **Pulpit**
- **Education**
- **Fellowship**
- **Evangelism**
- **Missions**

Helen Leflar, a 78-year-old widow from Pennsylvania, was fed up with the stones that were washing up on her front lawn. The state told her it was the township's problem and the township advised her it was the state's concern. She called Jon Fox's office. Within a few days, Fox himself appeared on her doorstep, and within 24 hours after his visit, a contractor was at Helen Leflar's house fixing the problem.

"This vote in support of Legal Services is a vote in support of the American concept of equal justice for all Americans."

Jon D. Fox, U.S. Congressman,
regarding his efforts to save legal services funding for the poor

When I asked Jon Fox to accept the appointment as master of ceremonies for the Leaders of Leaders Premier Celebration, his response was, "Are you sure that there isn't a more appropriate leader than me?" I said, "No, the other potential candidate felt he was too busy for it." Then Fox said, "I would be happy to share it with him, if that would help." That is leadership style at its finest! Supervisor. Supporter. Champion of the elderly, the abused, the poor and the youth of America. He is a leader of leaders in the political arena as well as the personal arena.

14 REPRODUCTION

THE POWER OF GROWTH (PROSPERITY)

FEATURING

JAMES DOBSON, PH.D.
FOCUS ON THE FAMILY

"Nobody can inspire who does not have deep convictions; they are the results but also the feeders of the spirit."

-- Robert Ulich

As I keep on learning, the more I tend to put the "bottom line" at the "top line" and then proceed to explain why. That is exactly what I am doing here as we approach chapter 15, the final chapter of the book. You see, I refer to the conclusion as "The Power of Commitment" –not as the point of termination. No, it is not the "stopping point" or the "finishing line," but rather the "springboard" to the height of execution and the entry into the depths of the water.

For many years, from high school, college and various vocational pursuits until about the age of 40, I enjoyed springboard diving, platform diving, as well as diving off cliffs in the islands that were over one hundred feet. To be sure, it was a thrilling pleasure, but it was also a lot of hard work. If there was one fundamental that my diving coach, Paul Flack, drove into me, it was the "priority of the hurdle." It was the hurdle that brought you to the end of the diving board platform or cliff. Hence, I had to make sure that my hurdle was just right. If it was too low, the dive was low. If it was too hurried, the dive was mediocre. If it was too short, the dive was in jeopardy. But if the hurdle was high and in rhythm with the pendulum of the board, then the dive was highly conducive to execution.

So it is with the conclusion of our book. Hence, as we approach it, we really need to have our focus on where we are going. We need to have a clear picture in our minds of what is beyond the "supposed" end. We need to see now that "The Power of Commitment" is our springboard into action into the execution of reproduction, "The Power of Prosperity." In short, we move deliberately forward through conclusion into reproduction. Hence, our commitment is to prosper.

Now let's pause for a moment. You see, this sort of reasoning is not average or common, so therefore you may need to take some time to do more than just read it. You may want to think about it for a while. By all means, do not immediately disagree! Just because it is unfamiliar does not make it wrong. In fact, history proves that most of the time the majority is usually wrong anyway. That is mainly why for the most part we do not learn from history. As the Pennsylvania Dutch would say, "for once, let's learn": *a good conclusion is the power of commitment to a good truth, cause or in our context here, a good reproduction.* OK? By the way, do you know what OK means? It comes from two Greek words: ola kala, which mean "all is well." They are consistently used in Greece as a wholesome, uplifting greeting. We probably came by the phrase when a few American tourists went to Greece for a vacation, heard it said repeatedly, observed the positive effect and warm response it engendered in others and brought it back to America to share with us.

However, they forgot how to pronounce it, so they abbreviated it and very few people know what it means.

Yes, it is exactly like conclusion and reproduction, very few people know what they mean. Perhaps, we will. So let us "revisit" it all, and let's begin with the real meaning of OK–"All is well." This is actually the very essence of that to which we commit ourselves as a result of reading this book, "Leader of Leaders."

Now, let me document this reality on the basis of what I believe to be the most reliable book in the world, the Bible. The point is the Bible is still a reliable source for knowledge, wisdom and understanding. Hence, let's proceed to 3 John 2, written by the Apostle John:

"And I pray that you will prosper in all things
and be in good health,
even as your soul prospers."

WOW! I love that verse. It is one of my favorite sayings. It is loaded with meaning, so let's take it apart and analyze it: First of all, it's in three parts:

1. **Material prosperity**
2. **Physical prosperity**
3. **Spiritual prosperity**

How do I know? Because it says so:

1. **"that you will prosper in all things."–that is material prosperity because "things" are material in essence.**
2. **"and be in good health."–that is obviously physical prosperity.**
3. **"even as your soul prospers."–that is spiritual prosperity.**

Isn't that beautiful, yet so simple? The subtle key to these three dimensions of prosperity is that the material and physical forms of it are dependent upon the spiritual form of it. Note the emphatic conditional phrase: "even as" your soul prospers.

Now do not get the notion that I am trying to make you religious, as I qualified myself before. Again, I emphasize that I want you to be real, not religious. You see, just as material and physical prosperity are artificial and superficial without spiritual prosperity, so religion without reality is phony. The reality of prosperity is that all the money in the world is useless, if you lose your own soul to get it! Likewise, all the status symbols of materialism are worth nothing, if you ruin your health acquiring them. Once again, stupid and foolish is the man or woman who makes material prosperity a greater priority than his or her family priority. You see, the marriage bond and the genetic connection make your spouse and children an integral part of your soul. So to neglect your family priority or divine priority is the absolute height of folly.

Now, therefore, before proceeding to our vital emphasis on the priority of the family let me hopefully clear up whatever cobwebs of skepticism you still have left in your thinking towards me that I am trying to convert you. I refer to one of the greatest success scientists of the secular world, Earl Nightingale. I quote his definition for prosperity or success, which I memorized in 1963 and have practiced repeatedly for 34 years. Here it is:

"Success is the progressive realization of a worthy ideal!"

Earl Nightingale emphatically and categorically indicated that it took him 40 years to formulate this definition, and that he challenged anyone to contradict him about its comprehensiveness.

What is interesting is that I do not have the slightest notion of what were Earl Nightingale's religious beliefs. I do admire him for his grasp on "spiritual (worthy ideal) prosperity." Likewise, I respect him for his emphasis on realization, because it is not reality to lose one's health on his way to his wealth. Last, but not least, I applaud Earl Nightingale in that he does not even mention, "material prosperity." Clearly, in his own explanation of his definition in his speech "The Strangest Secret in the World," he vividly portrays that success is whatever your worthy ideal is. It may be money, but it may also be ministry, or if you please voluntary service. It is what you feel and believe to be your "worthy ideal." Isn't that awesome? But whether it is the Apostle John or Earl Nightingale or yours truly as Chairman of the Board of the Foundation for the Family, we must emphasize and caution that there is no "worthy Ideal" that leaves out the family priority, and there is no real prosperity or success if the family is neglected.

As President Ronald Reagan articulated in his Proclamation for National Family Week in 1984 when I was his National Chairman, "The family is the basic unit of society." Thus, with the breakdown of the family in America agitated by the 50 percent divorce rate, is the crumbling of the foundation for the American civilization. And as Rome surely fell because of the breakdown of the family, so will America.

Therefore, in the remainder of the chapter, let us focus on the family. This is a play on words because this is precisely the name of James Dobson's radio broadcast across the nation. James Dobson, Ph.D., is recognized as the number one authority on the family in the nation. Speaking of reproduction for instance, Dr. Dobson began his focus on the family in 1977 in Southern California. Today he has reproduced himself in more than 1,250 full-time workers at his international headquarters in Colorado Springs, Colorado. That is just for openers, because in only 20 years he has also magnanimously experienced "Reproduction: The Power Of Prosperity," thus:

- **His first book, *Dare to Discipline,* has sold over three million copies and was selected to be placed in the White House Library.**
- **His budget went from "scratch" in 20 years to $100 million per year.**

Now that we have your attention, let's learn more. James Dobson is the founder and president of Focus on the Family that is a non-profit organization responsible for international syndication of his radio programs heard on more the 2,900 radio facilities in North America and in seven different languages in over 70 countries worldwide. The organization is dedicated to the preservation of family life. Through various programs and broadcasting mediums, James seeks to influence those who hear his message and show them that the first step on the road to prosperity is through building solid familial relationships.

James has written a number of subsequent books that have continued on to become best-sellers. James began producing films on the family and his first series, "Focus on the Family," has reached 70 million viewers. He has also released two other series that have also had a large following. James is also responsible for producing the 90-second "Focus on the Family" commentaries that are broadcast on more than 200 secular radio and 39 television stations nationwide.

Already, it is quite apparent that James Dobson is an extremely busy person, but he also finds time to become involved in government-sponsored activities related to the family having served on numerous task forces, panels and commissions for both President Jimmy Carter and President Ronald Reagan.

Focus on the Family was founded in 1977 by Dr. James A. Dobson as a non-profit Christian ministry dedicated to the preservation of the home. Dr. Dobson, author of fourteen best-selling books, had previously served on the faculty of the University of Southern California and on the attending staff of Children's Hospital of Los Angeles. Alarmed by the societal, political, and economic pressures that were threatening the very existence of the American family. Dr. Dobson founded Focus on the Family to strengthen the primary component of civilization and to combat those factors that were leading to its erosion.

It is the firm belief of the staff of Focus on the Family that only a return to the concepts of morality, fidelity, and parental leadership can halt the continued slide of the family into marital breakup and all manner of interpersonal dysfunction. This belief unifies the wide array of outreach efforts that, together, compose Focus on the Family. These efforts include the primary radio broadcast (presently heard on 2,362 U.S. radio outlets), conveying the message of support and encouragement for individual family members and for parents in their respective roles. Consistent themes include husband/wife, parent/child relationships, advocacy for pro-life issues, discussions of the damage to women and children caused by pornography, a focus on abstinence education, the prevention of child abuse, and a host of other family issues. Supporting these efforts is a staff of over 1,250 employees, all dedicated to the overall purpose of strengthening the home. A partial list of other Focus on the Family ministries includes:

• Focus on the Family magazine, going to 2.1 million households monthly (TJ.S. & Canada).

• Citizen magazine, alerting and educating families in public policy matters, mailed to over 102,000 homes monthly.

• Physician magazine, going to 67,500 medical doctors every two months.

• Clubhouse and Clubhouse Jr. monthly magazines for grade school and pre-school children, going to 104,000 and 81,000 households respectively.

• Brio (for teenage girls) and Breakaway (for teenage boys) magazines sent to 173,000 girls and 91,000 boys monthly.

• Teachers in Focus magazine, mailed to 35,000 educators each month.

• Single Parent Family magazine, mailed to 51,000 single parent families monthly.

• Plugged In, designed to alert parents to disturbing trends in film, music, and youth culture while commending quality entertainment, sent monthly to 30,000 homes.

• Book publishing, with such titles as ""Mom, You're Incredible" - Films and videos including the popular "McGee and Me" (seen nationally as specials on ABC-TV), the "Adventures in Odyssey" series, and the "Last Chance Detectives." Focus on the Family basketball camps conducted in many cities every summer as an outreach to boys, primarily from single parent homes.

• "Adventures in Odyssey" dramatic radio broadcasts for children, heard on 1,473 radio facilities each week; hundreds of thousands of "Odyssey" audio cassettes have been requested around the world–"Family News in Focus" public policy news and commentary broadcasts, heard on over 1200 stations daily in the U.S.

• International broadcasting oversees the translation of Focus radio broadcasts into Spanish, Russian, French, Norwegian and Korean.

• Focus on the Family support for over 3,200 crisis pregnancy centers around the world.

Organized to strengthen families worldwide, the international ministry of Focus on the Family is syndicated over the airwaves. Focus broadcasts can now be heard in English, Spanish, French, Russia, Norwegian and Korean in more than 70 countries on over 1,500 stations from Vancouver to Melbourne, from Moscow to Buenos Aires.

He was appointed to Attorney General Edwin Meese's Commission on Pornography, 1985-86. Dr. Dobson was also appointed in the Spring of 1987 to the Attorney General's Advisory Board on Missing and Exploited Children, and to Secretary Otis Bowen's Panel on Teen Pregnancy Prevention, within the Department of Health and Human Services. In October 1987, he received the Marian Anschutz Award in recognition of his contribution to the American family. A videotaped message of congratulations was sent by President Reagan. He also consulted with President George Bush on family related matters. In December 1994, Dr. Dobson was appointed by Senator Robert Dole to the Commission on Child and Family Welfare and in October 1996 was appointed by Senate Majority Leader Trent Lott to the National Gambling Impact and Policy Commission.

Dr. Dobson is married, the father of two grown children, and resides in Colorado.

He was for 14 years an associate clinical professor of pediatrics at the University of Southern California School of Medicine, and served for 17 years on the attending staff of Children's Hospital of Los Angeles in the Division of Child Development and Medical Genetics. He has an earned Ph.D. from the University of Southern California (1967) in the field of child development, an Honorary Doctor of Laws from Pepperdine University (1983), an Honorary Doctor of Humanities from Franciscan University of Steubenville, Ohio (1988), an Honorary Doctor of Humane Letters from Seattle Pacific University (1988), an Honorary Doctor of Humane Letters from Asbury Theological Seminary (1989), an Honorary Doctor of Humane Letters from Mid America Nazarene College (1992), an Honorary Doctor of Letters from Liberty University (1993), an Honorary Doctor of Humane Letters from Campbell University (1994), an Honorary Doctor of Humane Letters from Point Loma Nazarene College (1994), an Honorary Doctor of Literature from Baylor University (1995) and an Honorary Doctor of Humanities from Abilene Christian University (1995).

His first book for parents and teachers, "Dare to Discipline," has now sold over three million copies and was selected as one of 50 books to be rebound and placed in the White House Library. It has now been revised and updated, and is entitled, "The New Dare to Discipline." His subsequent books for the family are also best-sellers: "Hide or Seek," "What Wives Wish Their Husbands Knew About Women," "The Strong-Willed Child," Preparing for Adolescence," "Straight Talk to Husbands and Their Wives," "Emotions, Can You Trust Them?," "James Dobson Answers Your Questions," "Love Must be Tough," "Parenting isn't for Cowards," "Love for a Lifetime," "Children at Risk," "When God Doesn't Make Sense," "Life on the Edge," and "Home with a Heart."

His first film series, "Focus on the Family," has now been seen by over 70 million people.

His second film series, "Turn Your Heart Toward Home," was released in January, 1986, and continues in circulation internationally. A third seven-part series, entitled "Life on The Edge," is designed to help late teens bridge the gap between adolescence and young adulthood was released in early 1994.

Dr. Dobson has been heavily involved in governmental activities related to the family. He served on the task force that summarized the White House Conferences on the Family and received a special commendation from President Jimmy Carter in 1980. He was appointed by President Ronald Reagan to the National Advisory Commission to the office of Juvenile Justice and Delinquency Prevention, 1982-84. From 1984-87 he was regularly invited to the White House to consult with President Reagan and his staff on family matters. He served as co-chairman of the Citizens Advisory Panel for Tax Reform, in consultation with President Reagan, and served as a member and later chairman of the United States Army's Family Initiative, 1986-88.

The revisiting of this phenomenal exposition of "Reproduction: The Power Of Prosperity," is to make three points:

1. That having God first, family second and vocation third is not an impediment to material prosperity. Just think of it. Dobson's budget is about $100 million a year. And on top of this, millions of people around the world listen to him daily on the radio.

2. Having succeeded with millions of people, he still is referred to by Howard Phillips, the former Reaganist who created the U. S. Taxpayers Party, as "One of the best-kept secrets in America." That is kind of humbling isn't it? What is so wonderful is that Dr. James Dobson, with all of his prosperity, is humble. Yet, he is a lot more than that.

3. That having progressed to being a revered public figure, he still retains his personable touch. Jim says, You can have very inti-

mate conversations with radio. People can be reached in a highly personal way. We just try to take mass media and turn them into a personal ministry that touches lives. We try to never drop a single request or lose a single person."

That should motivate you to remember the advice of your mother or father. For instance, my mother, to whom I have dedicated this book, died earlier this month on May 2, 1997. As I related to you in the Dedication section, the week before she died, she asked me to promise her, "Don't take issue with your brother and sister, just be nice." Clearly, this has not been easy, but I am working at it. Already I have experienced plenty of positive results and I am now trying to treat each and every personal encounter this way. While I was in Washington, D.C. for a visit to the White House by invitation on my 57 birthday on May 7, 1997, I remembered that my mother had put aside in her Bible just enough money for a book that she wanted to get me as a parting gift, but she was too ill to do it. So after church on the following day, I went to mom's house and had some communion with her for a while, both in her bedroom, from where she passed away and in the kitchen where she read her Bible, and prayed one to two hours each day. With that $20 I retrieved from the inside back cover of her Bible, I went to Gene's Bookstore at the Court and Plaza of King of Prussia, the largest bookstore in our region with over 50,000 titles and there Paul Riley, the general manager, guided me to the shelf where it was located. "If It's Going to Be, It's Up to Me," by Robert E. Schuller. You see, my mom was wise and knew that not just the book, but the very thought of it would encourage me to "not take issue, but be nice," as well as help me to fulfill my overall goals and mission in life.

"If It's Going to Be, It's Up to Me," is likewise a book, if not a thought that, likewise, will encourage you, too. (Remember "OK"?) "All is well" shall be your reality, too. So go for it! Prosperity–its power lies in your hands and yours only, for "if it's going to be; it's up to me."

By the way, as I was paying for the book, I asked Paul Riley to inscribe an inspirational message for me on the inside front cover. Being a special friend and in charge of the first bookstore to sell this book for its first three months on the market, the summer of 1997, he wrote these words, "Remember your purpose." Isn't that encouraging to you too! So let's both apply it, for "It will work."

Does all this sound familiar? "I pray that you may prosper in all things, and be in health, even as your soul prospers." Remember? I am convinced that the major reason for James Dobson's prosperity is his soul prosperity. Clearly, the only way he is able to exhibit such a personal touch over public radio is because he is personally and prosperously in touch with his own soul. It is no wonder then that he is a "soul mate" to so many!

It is because he still might be one of your "strongest secrets," that you may want to check him out at the library of Fairview Village Church of the Nazarene, Valley Forge Road and Germantown Pike between Collegeville and Norristown, Pennsylvania (Phone 610-539-3333). There, I know you will find all of his books and tapes. You see, he is the son of a pastor of the Church of the Nazarene and this particular church has been smart and wise enough to apply the prosperous principles of Dobson. So if you want first-hand exposure to all this, certainly, check it out.

Whether you do or not, get on with some sort of volunteer service to something. Be at least one of the Thousand Points of Light that President Bush portrayed. Respond to the "call to action" delivered by General Colin Powell in Philadelphia, "the City of Brotherly Love," as the Presidents' Summit for America's Future came to its end. Support at least one, if not all, of its five purposes.

15

CONCLUSION

THE POWER OF COMMITMENT

FEATURING

EDWARD RENDELL
MAYOR OF PHILADELPHIA

"A promise should be given
with caution
and kept with care."

-- Unknown

Commitment is an intrinsic feeling we all experience in at least some aspects of our lives. Whether it concerns our jobs, a specific task, or a relationship, all of us have spoken about our level of commitment in some aspect of our lives.

Of course, commitment is a relative term because it can be expressed in varying degrees based upon our motivations, attitudes and enthusiasms depending on the topic. However, commitment in and of itself is a positive trait for the leader of leaders to possess because it is an attitude that is easily recognizable by other people. For the leader of leaders this is important because once others detect this, some will also become inspired and committed to the same ideals.

Commitment results from an intrinsic belief that some ideal or task is very important and that a person has a responsibility to help to further or carry out the purposes and goals that stand for those ideals. Commitment is an attitude that is predicated upon all the other character traits that define the leader of leaders, as discussed in the previous fourteen chapters. The leader of leaders, for certain, must lead by example. If a person does not reflect commitment in his attitude and approach to the cause undertaken, others will be less inclined to follow. The core attitude of a group is defined by the individual attitudes of all participants, however, it is human nature to first look to the leader for guidance and direction. Unless the leader of leaders exhibits a positive commitment through his attitude, the others who look for leadership will become less enthusiastic about the causes in which they are participating.

For instance, that's one reason why the Presidents' Summit for America's Future was recently held in Philadelphia, Pennsylvania from April 27-29, 1997. The Presidents' Summit featured the participation of all the living, past and current, Presidents of the United States. April 28, 1997 was truly an historic date because it was on that date that Presidents Clinton, Bush, Carter and former First Lady Nancy Reagan, representing President Ronald Reagan, stood together in a display of true bipartisanship and issued a "call to action" to businesses, civic groups and citizens across this great country of ours to make a commitment to become involved.

The Presidents' Summit was originally a vision of the late Governor George W. Romney of Michigan. Governor Romney was disenchanted with the growing social problems that plagued our country. Believing that social problems posed a great threat to the nation and that governments could not tackle the problem alone, Governor Romney held that the conscience of every citizen should be awakened through a unified call to volunteerism. Governor Romney finalized his ideas for a Summit five days before his death. Governor Romney's concept was so unique and so inspiring that it captured the attention of many citizens across the country who expressed impassioned support for the Summit and desperately sought to participate in its planning.

The stated goal of the Summit was to mobilize citizens and organizations across the country to ensure that the nation's youths are provided access to five fundamental resources that are necessary in helping them to lead healthy, fulfilling and productive lives. These five fundamental resources are:

An on-going relationship with a caring adult, mentor, tutor, coach;

Safe places and structured activity during non-school hours to learn and grow;

A healthy start in the youth's life.

A marketable skill through effective education; and

An opportunity to give back through community service.

The other goal of the Summit was also to make volunteering an integral part of every one of our lives.

The city of Philadelphia was chosen as the site for the Presidents' Summit because it offered a historic context in which to hold the Summit. Philadelphia was the site where the foundation was laid for the guiding principles by which we govern ourselves today, over 200 years later. Our founding fathers were not paid representatives attending the Continental Congress, rather they were volunteers–individuals who were committed to formulating guiding principles that would not be static, but rather would transcend time.

As the mayor of the city of Philadelphia, Edward G. Rendell was honored and excited about the prospect of hosting the Summit in his city. Mayor Rendell himself is truly an inspiring individual. When he first took office as mayor of Philadelphia, the city was in a state of financial devastation. The city's bond rating was at its lowest point ever, reaching the bottom–"junk bond" status. To make matters worse, the city was losing many of its businesses. Historically, Philadelphia has been a city thriving with business, from mom and pop stores to large corporations. Over the last 10 years or so, the city has witnessed a mass exodus of businesses. They were either leaving the city for other locations that offered juicy tax packages or closing their doors forever. Also, the city was facing contract renegotiations with a number of its unions. The potential outcome threatened to place the city in deeper financial trouble. If that wasn't enough, the Pennsylvania Legislature was threatening to take control of the city's financial affairs.

Since he has taken office, Mayor Rendell has truly spread himself out in all directions, and as a result has brought the city back to financial vitality. He negotiated union contracts to ensure that workers received fair compensation and treatment, without breaking the financial back of the city. He worked with the City Council to produce a budget that held the line on unnecessary spending, yet funded those programs that were critical to the health, safety and welfare of citizens and businesses alike. He also made a commitment to retain businesses that still remained in the city and to attract new ones by offering enticing proposals for relocation into the city. It should be noted that all this was accomplished without any major adverse tax consequences to the citizens of Philadelphia.

The Presidents' Summit visited Germantown Avenue in Philadelphia on April 27, 1997. In an effort to show true volunteerism at work; citizens cleaned graffiti, planted shrubbery, painted murals and fixed playgrounds. Mayor Rendell once again revealed his commitment to improving the appearance of the city by declaring Germantown Avenue a "zero tolerance zone," whereby once the graffiti was removed along the avenue, any new acts of graffiti would be countered by immediate cleaning of the area.

Clearly, Ed Rendell has shown a level of commitment to the city that is readily apparent not only to the citizens of his city, but in other cities across America. As a result, he won reelection by an overwhelming margin and is now also known as "America's Mayor."

As Mayor Rendell has indicated, the Presidents' Summit did not end as of April 29, 1997; it continues on in communities across the country. America's Promise–the Alliance for Youth was established to carry out the goals of the Summit until the year 2000. This organization is committed to turning the tide for America's youth by insuring that by the year 2000, two million children will be provided access to the five fundamental resources mentioned earlier. Also, an additional five million will gain access to at least one or more of the resources.

This is based on the hope and assumption that if all children are provided with these five resources they will lead healthy and productive lives. The far reaching implications of this will be that America will be a stronger nation; that we will once again take pride in our rich heritage and place our faith and trust in the hands of our government and know that we are being provided exemplary service.

As a result, business and corporations have made tangible commitments to help achieve the goals of the Summit. From eyeglass donations, to time off for employees to do volunteer work, the business sector of our country has heard the call and responded loud and clear. It was leaders–the presidents and General Colin Powell who made the enthusiastic commitment to the Summit and the country followed. For three days the hopes, dreams and aspirations of a country were heightened together in anticipation that the Summit would play a major role in awakening the conscience of our citizens to plan for a better tomorrow. That's commitment of the highest level.

On June 5, 1944, the English Channel was a churning cauldron of water buffeted by one of the worst storms in recent history. Thousands of allied troops were poised to launch "Operation Overland," the invasion of the European continent. General Dwight D. Eisenhower, commander in chief of the Allied Expeditionary Force was confronted with a dilemma. His troops had prepared for months for this venture. But to launch the attack might result in a catastrophic failure. Thousands of lives would be needlessly lost. To delay the mission created its own set of problems. All the careful planning, logistical and air support, and the enthusiasm of his troops would be sacrificed. What should he do? Eisenhower reflected as he considered all sorts of advice from meteorologists and senior staff members. Only one individual could evaluate the myriad of meteorological, emotional and psychological factors, and make the pivotal decision to launch the attack or to wait until the elements were more conducive to success. No greater test of his mettle had confronted Eisenhower since his graduation from West Point when, as an aide to General Douglas MacArthur, he exercised leadership to quell insurgent, riotous World War I veterans seeking their service bonuses. That endeavor was not a great success. Controversy surrounded Eisenhower's performance in dealing with the angry veterans.

On June 5, 1944, he was confronted with the greatest challenge of his career. The invasion of Europe had to succeed! There is no honor in failure! All looked to him to provide the leadership, courage and decisiveness necessary to make this monumental decision. If he succeeded he would be associated with Caesar, Hannibal, Pershing, Roosevelt and a host of other leaders who had influenced history and earned the deserved plaudits of their contemporaries as leaders of the first rank.

Yes, leaders of leaders are who and what these persons are. It is the purpose of this book to inspire many to become such leaders.

Previously, we portrayed the essence of commitment, especially its significance in connection with results of the Presidents' Summit for America's Future, hosted by Philadelphia Mayor Edward Rendell. Now, let's relate that to the conclusion of this book, titled Conclusion: The Power of Commitment. We titled it that because: (1) in fact, it is the book's last chapter, but not one's average conclusion, and (2) because this ending chapter leads to opportunities to do something with our new enthusiasm, thus "The Power of Commitment."

Clearly, this is a time in our lives when we cannot be weak-willed, because the choice to do something is so powerful that it is life-changing. And, the more leaders of leaders there are who choose to "go there and do likewise," the more we will be able to make positive changes in our community, society, and country. Isn't the potential of this absolutely awesome?

At the beginning of this chapter, I emphasized that commitment resulting from an intrinsic belief in some ideal or task is very important. Clearly, on the very eve of the Presidential Summit, when General Colin Powell, appeared, large as life, with President Jimmy Carter and Ted Koppel, the Summit was of itself altered by the magnitude of the challenge. This challenge commanded my attention spontaneously, riveted my focus consistently and persistently throughout the entire celebration, and compelled me to commit myself to action.

Commitment results from an intrinsic belief that some ideal or task is very important and that a person has a responsibility to help to further or carry out the purposes and goals that stand for those ideals. Commitment is an attitude that is predicated upon all the other character traits that define the leader of leaders.

Hence, when Colin Powell made his final appeal in his "call to action," I took action. The next morning I drove from Valley Forge to Center City, Philadelphia and went to 1234 Market St. I rode the elevator to the 18th floor, stepped out, turned left and approached the receptionist. "May I help you?" she asked. "I'm here to respond to the call to action," I offered. "Pardon me, who did you come to see?" she queried. "I'm not sure," I responded. "I suppose anyone who could help me to respond to the call to action that Colin Powell gave over the air." Well, it took some doing, but she finally connected me to Dr. Stuart Lord. Lord is the executive director for the Summit, responsible for 90 percent of the Summit's leadership from behind the scenes–one who got no credit for "invisible leadership." Stuart and I hit it off immediately and spent two hours in dialogue. One thing led to another and ultimately he connected me with James Rollings, Summit Editor, who worked with me as a contributing editor for the last month of writing this book. Fortunately, because of Jim's natural perspective as an editor and his astute acumen for rewriting, this book attained its defined level of excellence.

Along with these revised quality controls, something else almost magical or miraculous happened to the book in its final months of composition–it assumed its own unique identity, charisma and personality. You may laugh at me for this, but I will share it with you anyway. Throughout these three glorious weeks of May since my Mother died on May 2, and even as I devote most of my Memorial Day weekend to writing this conclusion, I have sensed the same inspiration that Handel did when he wrote "The Messiah" in 24 days. No, I'm not as capable as he–the book required of me at least 33 years of leadership experience and at least three in writing about it. In the 24 days since my mother's death, I was overwhelmed with the inspiration to rewrite, fine-tune and polish it for publication. Actually, if I was stirred by any more enthusiasm, inspiration and energy, I surely would have had a heart attack.

Of course, I confess–WHAT A WAY TO GO!!! On the other hand, I am committed to keep on helping others to create their own strategies in their little corners of the world. That's what I promised my Master Mind Strategy Group when we met last week–and at which Presidential Summit Executive Director Dr. Stuart Lord, was my honored guest. Clearly, I give him the credit for crystallizing the means and purpose for me. I had been prepared to sacrifice the Leader of Leaders Premier Celebration to be the next "stepping stone" as a follow-up for the Presidential Summit. I was willing to let the Premier promote the application of the administration rather than celebrate this book. He helped me focus on my commitment.

Of course, not everyone agrees with me, not even my own son-in-law, married to my oldest daughter, Debbie! Daron is skeptical of all the government programs for seemingly everything. Hence, he believes that genuine volunteerism will be so impeded and impaired by governmentalism that it will not go very far without disillusionment. People who think as skeptically as he does feel no incentive from the start.

I must admit that my son-in-law has a strong argument as well as a valid objection. At the same time, I prefer to look on the bright side of all this: (1) the Chairman of the Board for the Presidential Summit for America's Future is a conservative Republican, not a liberal Democrat, and I have faith in him as a dependable leader of leaders, *sine qua non*; (2) there are, in fact, models being built in the Philadelphia area right now that are intended to set the pace and inspire other delegations around the country; (3) I, a conservative Republican, will work with Donna Cooper, a liberal Democrat, in a bipartisan manner to fulfill the above-mentioned five purposes of the Summit

Beyond doubt, I believe this book is a significant contribution to this worthy cause. Likewise, the master plan that I have chosen for this book's premier celebration is another contribution towards the cause in terms of:

- A Leadership Prayer Breakfast on the morning (6:45 a.m.) of the Premier at the three-story high statue of George Washington kneeling in prayer;
- Seven inspirational seminars throughout the day to stimulate our thinking;
- Celebration in the evening, but not just about the praises of my book. It will also be dedicated to challenging thousands of leaders to go back to their spheres of influence and encourage volunteers by their example principle of walk the talk, as well as talk the walk.

It is my "core belief" that youths present on this evening as nominees for Leadership Essay Awards and Student Scholarships shall deserve an even greater "prize." Yes, it shall be the "prize" of purpose, direction and enthusiasm for their future to make a positive difference in America's future. To be sure, long before now and still clearly now, I am deliberately planning pointedly a "message" for the youth to receive that evening as they observe:

- The heartfelt honor given to the well-deserving 22 leaders of leaders as thousands of other leaders applaud them with a standing ovation;
- The provocative panel discussion of the relevant issues of "Regionalism, the Necessary Lifeline of the Next Millennium;"
- The uplifting special music;
- The inspiring speech of our distinguished featured speaker.
- Yes, our youth will get a message that will mean more than money. Hopefully, then, the well-received message will diminish some of their disillusionment and skepticism. Hopefully, this message will stop at least to a degree, the "blame game" so many are playing. It is to be hoped that this message will focus each and every one of us on assuming the individual responsibility we have de-emphasized because of our preoccupation with our criticism of others. Then, the message that our youths will receive from today's leaders will inspire them to become the leaders of tomorrow!

As for me, coming to the end of this conclusion, I am excited about how much I've learned in writing it. Equally, I'm excited about how much more I still need to learn–but not in the theory of the classroom, rather in the streets of the city, as I endeavor to create my own strategy and seek to help others to create their own strategy in serving those in need.

"This little light of mine
I'm going to let it shine...
Let it shine,
Let it shine,
Let it shine."

Then one day, because enough other leaders of leaders "go and do likewise," we will together "share all over the universe." And the vision of the thousands of points of light portrayed by leader of leaders President George Bush will be fulfilled.

Of course, this conclusion as "The Power of Commitment" would not be complete without two cautions:

• Do not let the losers of this world get you down. So when you encounter negative thinkers and critical talkers, keep on going to the next one. By all means, memorize and master this formula for the rest of your life.

• **ASK** is an acrostic that stands for:

Ask and you shall receive;
Seek and you shall find;
Knock and the door shall be opened to you

Of all things, this formula is tried and true because it was authored and lived by the One who is called "The Light of the World." Therefore, this sure-fire formula is virtually brilliant in more ways than one. So, use it and apply it to the fullest, especially where it will work best for you–in your little corner of this world where you, too, will shine as a leader of leaders.

The first caution above relates to what you do as a leader, but the second caution refers to what you are to be. Never forget that what you do is not as important as who you are. Results of projects are never to be prized greater than relationships of character. For if a leader gains the whole world but loses his/her own soul, he/she is an unprofitable fool. If a leader gains the whole world but loses his family, he/she is a double whammy fool. And, if a leader gains the whole world but loses his/her friends, he/she is a triple whammy fool.

Therefore, I offer you in the closing of this book, and the commencement of your pathway to become a leader of leaders, the special four-fold check and balance of three prayers. (If you are an atheist, utilize them as inspirational messages.)–and one proclamation.

The first is a very popular, but much-more-needed-to-be-practiced-prayer of Saint Francis of Assisi:

Lord, make me an instrument of Your Peace.
Where there is hatred, let me so Love;
Where there is injury–Pardon;
Where there is doubt–Faith;
Where there is despair–Hope;
Where there is darkness–Light;
And where there is sadness–Joy.

Lord, grant that I may seek rather
to comfort than to be comforted;
to understand rather than to be understood
to love than to be loved.
For it is by Giving that one receives,
by Forgiving that one is forgiven,
and, by Dying that one awakens to Eternal Life.

The second is an anonymous prayer especially for the "movers and shakers" who also want to be leaders of leaders:

God grant me the Serenity to accept the things I cannot change,
Courage to change the things I can,
And Wisdom to know the difference.

The third is a prayer for the goal and project oriented leader who tends to be insensitive to people's feelings and needs:

THE PRAYER OF THE CHOLERIC
by Alexander White

Lord, let me ever be courteous,
and easy to be entreated.
Never let me fall into a peevish or contentious spirit.
Let me follow peace with all men offering forgiveness,
inviting them by courtesies, ready to confess my
own errors and to make amends.
Give me the spirit of a Christian,
charitable, humble, merciful and meek,
useful and liberal, angry at nothing but my own sins,
and grieving for the sins of others, that while my
passion obey my reason, and my reason is religious,

and my religion is pure and undefiled,
managed with humility, and adorned with love
That I may escape thy anger, which I have deserved
and may dwell in thy love, and be thy Son and serve
forever. Amen.

The fourth is a proclamation by the Lord Jesus Christ in answer to the question by the 12 apostles of the first century - Who is the greatest leader? Jesus answered and proclaimed:

"He who is the greatest among you shall be servant of all!"

Now if you have a problem comprehending his awesome truth, by all means, go back to Chapter 10 and digest Demonstration: The Power of Life Messages. Thus, experience the greatest law of learning - review, review, review - as well as the greatest law of leadership - serving, serving, serving.

I recently had the privilege of viewing a new video by Bakker, called "I WILL NEVER LEAVE THEE NOR FORSAKE THEE." At the climax of the awesome message, Jimmie relates how Franklin Graham, son of Billy Graham, visited Jimmie in prison just before he was paroled. But, this was not just a token visit, for Franklin said that he wanted to have Jim be a part of his Foundation and help build another new hospital. Jimmie's response was, "No, Franklin, because I still hurt you and your ministry." Franklin responded, "I was your friend before you went to prison, while you were in prison, and certainly now that you are getting our of prison. And, anyway, I'm all ready for a good fight!!!" WOW!!! The outcome? Jim still didn't accept the offer, but on his first Sunday morning out of prison, guess where Jim went to church? He sat in the front of Billy Graham's home church in North Carolina, surrounded by two rows of the Graham family. And, the last of the Grahams to be seated right next to Jim, was Ruth Graham, Billy's wife! And, guess where Jim's new home and office is located to this day—North Carolina, just down the road from his neighbors, the Grahams.

The rumors you've heard about me from a "Christian" radio station V.P. and others perhaps of his mentality are not true. But, even if they were, if the situation were reversed, I'd stand by your side and fight for you like Franklin Graham did for Jim Bakker. Really, compare or better yet contrast the common definition for our friendship to focus on "the positive and fun" to that of Franklin Graham's emphasis. . .not just of fun but fight to the end, if necessary. Well beyond any notion of "maximum strain," for in "Love which never fails," there is no such thing! You may choose to invent it for or superimpose it upon yourself, but realize it's not of God.

I literally have hundreds and perhaps thousands of "Fairweather friends," because of my extroversion, giving spirit, and sense of humor, if nothing else. But, to have and count on a friend like Franklin Graham is a whole different ballgame. Yes, I know that I can and have proven that kind of friend to you and a few others. But, after everything is said and done, how many or few REALLY SPECIAL FRIENDS do you have like Franklin was to Jimmie? Be honest with yourself like never before in your lifetime. Treat yourself to this "moment of truth." You deserve it. Are you truly satisfied with the friendships you have activated, realizing especially that at least a few of your very best friends are leaders who have mentored you and associates whom you have mentored??? Remember, special friends, not just superficial friends, are common and lead to one another's best. So again I ask you do your friendships measure up to that standard? Well, just in case you are a little lacking like I used to be, here is a final suggestion for you from the very depths of my hear. It is a Proverb: "He/she who wants friends must first commit him/herself to be a friend." You see, just before a leader takes the initiative to lead, he should first take the initiative to be a special friend. Frankly, friendliness should be paramount requirement for leadership. After all, how can a leader fulfill the best interests of a company, city, or country, if he/she is not a genuine kind of friend who is virtually committed to one friend's best interests? On the other hand, if you and I become a special friend to one who needs us, there is no limit how far we shall go.

I just end this book, however, with a challenge once again from Jim Bakker's life message. Someone said to him, "Aren't you sorry for all the friends you lost when you went to prison?" And Jim answered, "No. Because that's when I found out who my real friends were! 'Faithful are the wounds of a friend. . .There is a friend who sticks closer than a brother. A friend loves at all times'." (Proverbs) And, so does a leader of leaders.

Rich in His Lovingkindness,
Donald H. Sautter

RECOMMENDED BOOKS ON LEADERSHIP
With Some Very Relevant Selections Noted by Brief Commentaries Readily Available at Most Book Stores and Libraries

THE ABSOLUTES OF LEADERSHIP by Philip Crosby
Definition - "Deliberately causing people-driven actions in a planned fashion for the purpose of accomplishing the leader's agenda." Four Absolutes:

(1) A clear agenda - personal agenda, organizational agenda, stating the agenda, creating the plan.
(2) Personal philosophy - creating a philosophy, learning, innovating, deciding.
(3) Enduring relationships - Relationships can't be left to chance.
(4) Worldly - being able to utilize new technological advances, having an understanding of one's global marketplace.

THE COMPLETE IDIOT'S GUIDE TO MANAGING PEOPLE by Dr. Arthur R. Pell
Emphasizing LEADERSHIP instead of DRIVERSHIP. Keeping motivational levels soaring.
Encouraging team members to participate in goal and assignment setting.
Coach and counsel to help others meet their goals or address issues.
Understand and comply with equal employment laws.
Use and praise discipline when they're needed.

THE CORPORATE COACH by James D. Miller
Good leadership joins employees and customers in a common cause. He believes in empowering people at every level of the company, in giving them "Playing time" and opportunities to develop, improve and be creative.

THE DISCIPLINE OF MARKET LEADERS by Michael Treacy & Fred Wiersema
Choose your discipline, your real expertise and change your destiny. What unique value do you provide to those you serve? How will you increase that value next year? How do you adapt yourself in an ever more sophisticated and demanding world? NO LEADER CAN SUCCEED TODAY BY TRYING TO BE ALL THINGS TO ALL PEOPLE. SO

he/she must find "THE" UNIQUE VALUE that he/she alone can deliver to a chosen market.

THE EXECUTIVE IN ACTION by Peter F. Drucker
Really 3 books in one:

- MANAGING THE EXISTING BUSINESS
- CHANGING TOMORROW'S BUSINESS
- MANAGING ONESELF

With the publication of his first 2 books: **THE END OF ECONOMIC MAN** (1939) and **CONCEPT OF THE CORPORATION** (1946), Peter F. Drucker established himself as a trenchant and independent thinker of politics, business, economy, and society. But with these three books he is recognized as the founding father of the discipline of management, and is the most influential and widely read thinker and writer on modern organizations (profit and non-profit) and their management.

This compilation of 3 books deals with:

(1) Managing for results
(2) Innovation and Entrepreneurship
(3) The Effective Executive

MANAGING THE NON-PROFIT ORGANIZATION by Peter F. Drucker
Validates that NPO's have had outstanding success in the past 40 years since they allowed management as a consistent reality.

THE EFFECTIVE EXECUTIVE by Peter F. Drucker
Focuses on managing oneself in terms of ongoing learning, time management, knowing your unique values to contribute, making strength productive, first things first, and the elements of effective decision-making.

THE ORGANIZATION OF THE FUTURE
A compilation of many essays, edited by Frances Hesselbein, Marshall Goldsmith, and Richard Beckhard, sponsored by DRUCKER FOUNDATION.

Deals with all the conceivable challenges that both profit and non-profit organizations will face in the ever-changing future.

DON'T FIRE THEM, FIRE THEM UP by Frank Pacetta with Roger

Gittines
The author is the man who turned around sales terms at Xerox. He capitalized on his uniqueness by providing what he believes are his leadership principles in terms of "A maverick's guide to motivating yourself and your team."

Pacetta transformed Xerox's Cleveland district from near bottom of Xerox's national organization to 1st in the region and 4th nationally out of 65 sales districts. His key ingredients were how to develop trust, create loyalty and generate enthusiasm.

THE DRAMA OF LEADERSHIP by Patricia Pitcher
Having witnessed what was a crisis rooted in a misunderstanding of what leadership is all about, she devoted 8 years of research on the rapid collapse of a global giant–ONE WRONG PERSON AT THE HELM TURNED A DREAM INTO A NIGHTMARE. She refutes the notion that good leaders are in short supply; but rather proves that good leaders go unnoticed or are tragically underrated. She exposes the unfortunate trend today that puts leaders into position who lack the very values that our present age demands–Vision, innovation, humanity, and passion. She also clearly points out how these ill-equipped leaders DISTRUCT the real leaders who do possess the much-needed values.

13 FATAL ERRORS MANAGERS MAKE AND HOW YOU CAN AVOID THEM by W. Steven Brown

- **# 1** Refuse to accept personal accountability
- **# 2** Fail to develop people
- **# 3** Try to control results instead of influencing thinking
- **# 4** Join the wrong crowd
- **# 5** Manage everyone the same way
- **# 6** Forget the importance of profit
- **# 7** Concentrate in problems rather than objectives
- **# 8** Be a buddy, not a boss
- **# 9** Fail to set standards
- **#10** Fail to train your people
- **#11** Condone incompetence
- **#12** Recognize only top performers
- **#13** Try to manipulate people

TODAY THE SUCCESSFUL LEADER/MANAGER ACTS AS A FACILITATOR, AS A DEVELOPER OF HUMAN POTENTIAL. Hence, the chal-

lenge for the 90's into 2000's is to RETRAIN THE MANAGER, NOT THE WORKERS.
(John Nesbitt, "Megatrender Newsletter")
Leadership (management) is the art of winning assent to goals and of reaching them through others.

Clearly, it steers the leader away from manipulating by fear or rewards and builds him to motivate by BELIEFS; e.g., the total sales volume of Coca Cola in the first year was $55.00 - like all BIG BUSINESSES of today; they started small. And the strength which got it through the trying times of the depression WAS NOT MONEY because there was no money. That strength or power came from the individual, that man or woman who could face the challenges of the moment. SUCH STRENGTH OF CHARACTER PRODUCES ENOUGH RESILIENCE TO FIGHT BACK, even when the Law of Compensation doesn't work. IT IS HELPING PEOPLE HELP THEMSELVES; HELPING MANAGERS AVOID ERRORS AND BUILD LEADERSHIP QUALITIES. Hence, the greatest management challenge for each of us begins in making sure that on a daily basis our credos become our personal objective and that, by example, in effective management we influence our employees to feel the same way.

THE FUTURE OF LEADERSHIP by Randall P. White, Philip Hodgson & Stuart Crainer
Riding the corporate rapids into the 21st Century.

Forget about safety. Forget about the reassurance of your company's name in neon. Forget about meandering mid-stream, taking it easy. This is the world of white water, and you must change to survive and develop to thrive.

We believe the leader's role is to identify productive areas of uncertainty and confusion and to lead the organization into those areas in order to gain competitive advantage.

"The future of leadership shows that the way to high-performance leadership is not to avoid the corporate rapids, but to seek them out and use them to propel oneself at break-neck speed into the future. Thankfully, the authors also provide the much-needed paddle in a set of practical tools and skills."
Jon Peters, Executive V.P. The Inst. for Management Studies

When moving down the rapids, is it better to look where you are going or to be transfixed by where you have come from?

THE 5 KEY SKILLS ESSENTIAL TO WHITE WATER LEADERSHIP ARE:

#1 Difficult learning - Identifying and learning the things that the average individual or organization find difficult to learn, willing to take risks.
#2 Maximizing energy - To handle being, channel energy of leader and others effectively. A trial-and-error approach to a large proportion of the workload = IDENTIFYING NEW PRODUCTIVE ZONES.
#3 Resonant Simplicity - In the downsizing of companies, KEY MESSAGES FAIL TO GET THROUGH. So the leader who has the ability to "CAPTURE" THE ESSENCE OF AN ISSUE IN A WAY THAT RESONATES WITH THE REST OF THE ORGANIZATION IS GOING TO GET THE MESSAGE THROUGH . . . especially in times of change, chaos, and complexity.
#4 Multiple Focus - "There is no such thing as an interruption. How focused are you on the short-term? How focused are you on the long-term? HOW CAN THE TWO BE BALANCED EFFECTIVELY TO THE BENEFIT OF THE INDIVIDUAL AND THE ORGANIZATION?"
#5 Mastering inner sense - In a data driven culture and society there are 2 problems constantly before us: (1) partial, limited data; (2) data not to be trusted. In these circumstances, the only reliable data to rely on is that of our inner sense. The masterful leader is artful at this and also at encouraging others to do the same.

SO MASTER THESE BECAUSE:

A. The future will be radically different from the past.
B. Leadership will be essential and new forms of leadership even more vital. The leaders of today will be gone tomorrow; we need to discover tomorrow's leaders.
C. The pace of change will continue to increase.
D. The urge to find "ONE"S BEST WAY" solutions will remain instinctive and alluring.

LEADERSHIP IS COMMON SENSE by Herman Cain. Leadership—is the ability to liberate potential.

Detecting the potential for leadership in everyone and helping leaders as well as followers. HARNESS AND FOSTER their God-given abilities in order to achieve the peak of their potential. SHOWS YOU HOW . . . YOU CAN LIVE YOUR DREAMS, IF YOU GO AT SUCCESS AS A JOURNEY.

And as you go against the odds, remember:

(1) Person to person leadership style.

(2) Leadership is dynamic and continuous rather than static and concrete. There's no such thing as a "leadership moment."

3 CRITICAL THINGS A LEADER MUST BE:

(1) D-Factor - Determined, ambitious, self-controlled

(2) E-Factor - Forward-looking, Broad-minded, Imaginative; Independent

(3) F-Factor - Straightforward

3 CRITICAL THINGS A LEADER MUST DO:

(1) Identify Barrier - Competent, intelligent, mature

(2) Lead Actions - Courageous

(3) Inspire People - Honest, inspiring, fair-minded, supportive, dependable, cooperative, caring, loyal

LEADERSHIP AND THE NEW SCIENCE by Margaret J. Wheatley
Learning about organization from an orderly universe. In essence, her concept of organizations is moving away from the mechanical creations that flourished in the age of bureaucracy. She has begun to speak in earnest of more fluid, organic structures, even of boundaryless organizations. We are beginning to see organizations as SYSTEMS, construing them as "Learning organizations" and crediting them with some type of self-renewing capacity. Hence, what some refer to as the "WHITE WATERS OF CHANGE FULL OF RISK" can now be regarded as LIVING SYSTEMS YET TO BE KNOWN AND EXPERIENCE. Hence, we can forego the fear or even despair created by such common organizational events as change, chaos, information overload and cyclical behaviors, if we recognize that organizations are conscious entities, possessing many of the properties of living systems.

LEADERSHIP SECRETS OF THE ROGUE WARRIOR by Richard Marcinko
A translation of leadership in battle to leadership in business. WAR is an

acrostic for We Are Ready. Hence, his leadership principles are primarily based on his own example first, then believing his beliefs; being supportive of his subordinates; patient with mistakes but not with those who don't learn from mistakes.

MANAGERS AS MENTORS by Chip R. Bell
Clarifies the new forms of leadership which are rapidly replacing the old "Boss-subordinate relationship." Leadership now calls for creative ways to foster learning, improvement and everlasting experimentation. It's about power-free facilitation of learning, about teaching through consultation and affection rather than constriction and assessment. It shows how to forge a "Partnership" with learners to help them develop new confidence and competence and to reach continually new levels of mastery.

MANAGING BY VALUES by Ken Blanchard & Michael O'Connor
A strong argument for the classical values of honesty, fairness, etc., STILL relevant in a fast-changing world.

PRINCIPLES CENTERED LEADERSHIP by Stephen R. Covey
Creates more meaningful relationships and successes in the marketplace. This involves a long-term inside-and-out approach to developing people and organizations. His approach to change is to face it with changeless principles.

THE ONE MINUTE MANAGER by Kenneth Blanchard, Ph.D. & Spencer Johnson, M.D.
The runaway #1 National Best Seller, over 2 years on the New York Times Best Seller List! - 7,000,000 copies sold.

Leadership is by 3 secrets:

(1) One minute goals

(2) One minute praisings (catch them doing something right, praise them > help them reach their full potential)

(3) One minute reprimands

THE ART OF WAR by Sun Tzu translated by Samuel B. Griffith
The values of Chinese military strategists adapted to American business. This book is more than 2,400 years old. Perhaps, the chief value of the book is to calm our fears of change. Solomon said, "There's nothing new under the sun." Christ affirmed that the values which count, the most

forever will abide, especially faith, hope and love. Now here is a classic oriental book of military leadership quite adaptable today.

Values like: Careful planning
Commit to a system of communications
Efficient organization
Strict discipline
Persistence to win

THE TIMELESS LEADER by John K. Clemens & Steve Albrecht
Lessons on leadership from Plato, Shakespeare, Antigone, Cleopatra, Martin Luther King, Jr., Gandhi.

THE WILL TO LEAD by Neil H. Snyder & Angela P. Clontz
Managing with courage and conviction in the age of uncertainty; building better teams made up of efficient individual and group talents, and even the entrepreneurial.

WHAT THEY DON'T TEACH YOU AT HARVARD BUSINESS SCHOOL by Mark H. McCormack
#1 National Best Seller - More than 1,000,000 copies
Notes from a street-smart executive
His 3 major areas are:
(1) People
(2) Sales and Negotiations
(3) Running a Business

A good leader is like a golf champion:
(1) Has a dissatisfaction for past accomplishments
(2) Has the ability to peak his past accomplishments
(3) Has the instinct to put his competitors away

LINCOLN ON LEADERSHIP by Donald T. Phillips
- Seize the initiative and never relinquish it
- Encourage "risk-taking" while providing job security
- Avoid issuing orders and instead—request, imply or make suggestions
- Once in a while let things slip, UNBEKNOWNST LIKE

THE AGE OF UNREASON by Charles Handy
Discontinuous change, however uncomfortable, is the only way forward

for society that would prefer to put blinders onto the world around it.

ON BECOMING A LEADER by Warren Bennis
Gets to the heart and essence of integrity, authenticity and vision that can never be pinned down to a manipulation formula. He proceeds to offer a game plan for cultivating the fundamental leadership qualities.

SOURCES AND RESOURCES on LEADER OF LEADERS

Alford, Henry. (Revision by Everett Harrison). The Greek Testament, Vol. II. Chicago, IL: Moody Press, 1958.

Calvin, John. (translated by Jean W. Fraser, Edited by David W. Torrance and Thomas E. Torrance.) Calvin's Commentaries. Grand Rapids, Michigan: Wm. B. Eerdmans Publishing Co., 1960.

Clarke, Adam. Clark's Commentary, Vol. II. Nashville, TN: Abingdon Press, no date.

Drummond, Henry. The Greatest Thing in the World. Phila., PA: Atlemus, 1892.

Gillquist, Peter. Love is Now. Grand Rapids, MI: Zondervan Publishing House, 1970.

Grosheide, F.W. Commentary on the First Epistle to the Corinthians. Grand Rapids, MI: Wm. B. Eerdmans Publishing Co., 1953.

Guder, Eileen. To Live in Love. Grand Rapids, MI: Zonervan Publishing House, 1967.

Henry, Matthew. Matthew Henry's Commentary on the Whole Bible, Vol. VI. New York: Fleming H. Revell Co., no date.

Jamieson, Robert, Fausset, A.R. and Brown, David. A Commentary Critical, Experimental and Practical on the Old and New Testament, Vol. VI. Grand Rapids, MI: Wm. B. Eeermans Publishing Co., 1945.

Kempis, Thomas A. Imitation of Christ. New York: Grosset & Dunlap, no date.

Kittel, Gerhard (ed.). Theological Dictionary of the New Testament, Vol. IV. Grand Rapids, MI: Wm. Eerdmans Publishing Co., 1967.

LaHaye, Tim. How to be Happy Though Married. Wheaton, IL: Tynedale House Publishing, 1968.

LaHaye, Tim. Spirit Controlled Temperament. Wheaton, IL: Tynedale House Publishing, 1966.

LaHaye, Tim. Spirit Controlled Temperament. Wheaton, IL: Tynedale House Publishing, 1971.

Lloyd-Jones, D. Martin. Spiritual Depression: Its Causes and Cure. Grand Rapids, MI: Wm. B. Eerdmans Publishing Co., 1965.

McMillen, S. I. None of These Diseases. Westwood, NJ: Fleming H. Revell Co., 1963.

Miller, Keith. The Taste of New Wine. Waco, TX: Word Books, 1965.

Nicoll, W. Robertson (ed.) The Expositer's Greek Testament, Vol. II. Grand Rapids, MI: Wm. B. Eerdmans Publishing Co., 1967.

Pentecost, J. Dwight. Pattern for Maturity. Chicago, IL: Moody Press, 1966.

Pfieffer, Charles F., and Harrison, Evertee F. (ed.) The Wycliff Bible Commentary. Nashville, TN: The Southwestern Co., 1962.

Robertson, A.T. Word Pictures in the New Testament, Vol. IV. Nashville, TN: Broadman Press, 1931.

Spence, H.D.M., and Excell, Joseph S. The Pulpit Commentary, Vol. 44. Chicago, IL: Wilcox and Follett Co., no date.

Sweeting, George. Love is the Greatest. Chicago, IL: Moody Press, 1974.

Tozer, A.W. The Pursuit of God. Harrisburg, PA: Christian Publications, Inc., 1948.

Trapp, John. Trapp's Commentary on the New Testament. Evansville, IN: The Sovereign Grace Book Club, 1958.

Walker, Granville. The Greatest of These. St. Louis, MO: Bethany Press, 1963.

Wuest, Kenneth S. Acts Through Ephesians, Vol. II. Grand Rapids, MI: Wm. B. Eerdmans Publishing Co., 1958.

Wuest, Kenneth S. Golden Nuggets From the Greek New Testament. Grand Rapids, MI: Wm. B. Eerdmans Publishing Co., 1945.

Dear Reader,
Now that you have gone this far, why not begin all over again and really read, study, memorize, meditate, digest and apply it in your life?